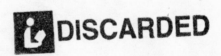

YALE HISTORICAL PUBLICATIONS

ARNO J. MAYER

Political Origins of

the New Diplomacy,

1917-1918

New York · HOWARD FERTIG · 1969

TO MY PARENTS

HOWARD FERTIG, INC. EDITION 1969
Reprinted by permission of Yale University Press

Library of Congress Catalog Card Number: 68-9616

PRINTED IN THE UNITED STATES OF AMERICA
BY NOBLE OFFSET PRINTERS, INC.

PREFACE

DURING the first World War one of the most controversial political issues inside Europe's major belligerent nations was war aims. In the Allied as well as in the Central countries the controversy over this issue of domestic and foreign policy became part of the struggle for power between the "parties of order" (predominantly the Right) and the "parties of movement" (predominantly the Left). The Right tended to favor expansionist war aims and the perpetuation of the Old Diplomacy as part of its determined effort to maintain the internal status quo. The Left pressed for nonannexationist war aims and the adoption of the New Diplomacy in its campaign to change the status quo. In this conflict between the Right and the Left lie some of the important political and ideological roots of the New Diplomacy.

A history and analysis of the politics of war aims from August 1914 to November 1918 in all the major belligerent nations could not be adequately handled in one volume. The chronological scope of the present study has therefore been limited to cover, primarily, only the period from March 1917 to January 1918.

This alternative was preferred to the other choice—concentration on one nation for the full war period—because, first, by focusing on the politics of war aims in more than one nation, it is possible to capitalize on the analytic advantages which can be gained from *comparative* research into history and politics. Second, the particular period covered permits a study of the breakdown of Europe's political and ideological equilibrium under the combined impact of the military stalemate, the Russian Revolution, and the American intervention. This breakdown contributed significantly to the dawning of a new ideological era in international politics, of which Lenin's April Theses and Wilson's Fourteen Points are representative and symbolic.

Except tangentially, this book does not deal with either the doctrine or the ideology of the New Diplomacy. Instead, it seeks to explicate the political dynamics of the emergence of this New Diplomacy in 1917–18. The success or failure of the left-wing campaign for the adoption of liberal war aims depended on domestic as well as international developments. Therefore, the interaction between domestic and international politics will be closely examined in an effort to assess its impact on war aims—that is, on foreign policy.

The introductory chapter presents a historical background as well as an analytic framework for the study of the politics of war aims. All subsequent chapters deal with those political developments, domestic and international, which contributed to the eventual verbal articulation of new aims in the Allied and Associated camp.

Even though this articulation never occurred in the Central camp, there are at least three reasons for including a chapter on Germany. First, the struggle over war aims in this country offers clear evidence of the significance of the interaction between domestic and international politics. Second, it is important to emphasize that in both coalitions the political struggle was engaged in by parties and factions which had not only essentially similar roots of power but also comparable political objectives. Third, once the July 19th coalition had crystallized in the Reichstag, the Allied forces of movement argued, quite realistically, that an official, liberal war-aims pronouncement by the Entente would serve to weaken Germany by further encouraging the forces of movement in the Central camp.

Limitations of space are the main reason for not including a chapter on Italy and one on Austria-Hungary. Also, however, it seems that their role in the diplomacy of the respective alliances in 1917–18 was subsidiary rather than primary. Certainly Italy's influence on Allied diplomacy and ideology in the last year of war was not nearly so crucial as her part in the drafting of the peace treaties. In a projected volume on the Paris Peace Conference, 1919, I plan to give detailed treatment not only to Italian politics and diplomacy but also to the diplomatic legacy of the collapse of the Dual Monarchy.

This book could not have been written without the invaluable scholarly counsel of many of my teachers and senior colleagues. Above all, I must record my profound debt to Hajo Holborn of Yale University. He stimulated my original interest in the diplomacy of World War I and heightened my awareness of the interaction between domestic politics and foreign policy. Throughout all subsequent research and writing stages I had the benefit of Professor Holborn's sound advice.

Charles Seymour, President Emeritus of Yale University and leading historian of America's diplomacy during the war, read two successive drafts of the manuscript and made those critically suggestive comments which have put so many students of the war period in his debt. Carl E. Schorske of Wesleyan University not only gave me the benefit of his expert scholarship on German Social Democracy, but also made incisive suggestions on all parts of the book. Likewise, E. H. Carr of Trinity College, Cambridge, and Robert S. Cohen of Boston University patiently questioned many important points of fact as well as of interpretation. I wish to acknowledge also the equally useful though less extensive help of John Blum, Scott Buchanan, Frank Manuel, Herbert Marcuse, Harry Rudin, and Arnold Wolfers. Needless to say, I alone assume full responsibility not only for all remaining factual errors, but also for my historical judgments and interpretations.

The publication of this book has been greatly assisted by a grant to Yale University by the Southern New England Telephone Company.

Through the Charles P. Howland Fellowship, Yale University made possible my initial research in Europe. To the staff of the following European and American libraries I am grateful for skillful assistance: Sterling Memorial Library at Yale, Widener Library at Harvard, New York Public Library, Library of Congress, Bibliothèque Nationale, and the Bibliothèque de Documentation Internationale Contemporaine. I also wish to thank the curators of the following collections: The House Collection in Yale University Library; the Walter Hines Page Papers in Houghton Library, Harvard; the Wilson and Lansing Papers in the Library of Congress; the E. D. Morel Papers in the London School of Economics; and the Archives of the British Labour party in Transport House, London. Finally, without my wife's careful editorial help and cheerful typing this manuscript would have been delayed many more months. Her unfailing understanding and encouragement have been of essential importance.

A. J. M.

Brookline, Massachusetts
May 1958

CONTENTS

ABBREVIATIONS

CGT: Confédération Générale du Travail (General Confederation of Labor).

Cole: Margaret I. Cole, ed., *Beatrice Webb's Diaries: 1912–1924*, London, Longmans, Green, 1952.

Degras: Jane Degras, ed., *Soviet Documents on Foreign Policy*, Vol. 1 (1917–24), London, Oxford University Press, 1951.

Dickinson: G. Lowes Dickinson, *Documents and Statements Relating to Peace Proposals and War Aims: December 1917 to November 1918*, London, Allen and Unwin, 1919.

DR *Daily Review of the Foreign Press.*

DR, APS *Daily Review of the Foreign Press*, Allied Press Supplement.

DR, EPS: *Daily Review of the Foreign Press*, Enemy Press Supplement.

FR: *Papers Relating to the Foreign Relations of the United States, 1917–19*, Washington, 1931–42.

GFM: "German Foreign Ministry" (microfilm of records, National Archives, Washington, D.C.).

Golder: Frank Alfred Golder, ed., *Documents of Russian History, 1914–1917*, New York, Century, 1927.

Hahlweg: Werner Hahlweg, "Lenins Reise durch Deutschland in April 1917," in *Vierteljahreshefte für Zeitgeschichte*, October 1957.

ILP: Independent Labour party.

JO: Journal Officiel de la République Française, Chambre des Députés, *Débats Parlementaires*, Session Ordinaire, 1917–18.

LP: Labour party.

PD: House of Commons, *Parliamentary Debates*, 5th series, 1914–18.

RAR: C. K. Cumming and Walter W. Pettit, eds., *Russian-American Relations, March 1917–March 1920*, New York, Harcourt, Brace, 1920.

SFIO: Section française de l'Internationale Ouvrière (French Section of the Workers' International, or French Socialist party).

SPD: Sozialdemokratische Partei Deutschlands (German Social Democratic party).

TUC: Trades Union Congress.

UDC: Union of Democratic Control.

USPD: Unabhängige Sozialdemokratische Partei Deutschlands (Independent Social Democratic party of Germany).

VRSB: *Verhandlungen des deutschen Reichstages: Stenographische Berichte.*

Walling: William English Walling, ed., *The Socialists and the War*, New York, Holt, 1915.

HISTORICAL AND POLITICAL FRAMEWORK

1. The Politics of War Aims

THE COMPLEXITY of the causes of World War I is no longer denied. However, the analysis of the prewar chain of fateful events has too often been limited to a study of the collapse of the balance of power. Because domestic determinants of foreign policy are especially consequential in modern times, a study of the causes of the war must not slight those factors of internal politics which affected the foreign policy of the major powers.

The economic and social tensions which left their imprint on the prewar diplomacy remained unresolved by the struggle. Even though the war brought about a new, though precarious, international balance of power, it did not lead to a new and lasting domestic equilibrium inside the belligerent nations of Europe. On the contrary, the intense sociopolitical heat generated by this first total war in history gradually accentuated the domestic disequilibriating tensions.

This is not to deny that initially, in August 1914, the nation states attained a singularly strong social solidarity as a result of the clearly discernible external threat and the shock of foreign aggression. Perhaps the clearest index of this new-found solidarity was the immediate suspension of party rivalry. Whereas Socialists and Conservatives had been engaged in intense political rivalry until the outbreak of war, now they became brothers at arms in the struggle against the barbarous tsarist hordes, the brutal Huns, or the insatiable Anglo-Saxon imperialists. Since all parties saw their foremost enemy abroad rather than at home, they agreed to let the domestic power struggle function within the narrow but rigidly defined limits of the political

1

truce. Yet the stability and permanence of this truce depended upon two factors: the intensity of the political diversities which it was called upon to compromise, and the duration of the conflict. Obviously, a four-year war was likely to strain most seriously the political truce of the countries which had been subject to the strongest pressures against the status quo in 1914.

Perhaps a widely held but narrow view of Clausewitz' dictum that "war is politics continued by other means" accounts for the exaggerated emphasis on the "forcible" aspects of wartime politics. True, the heroic deeds on the battlefields never ceased to overshadow the rather unspectacular feats of the war industries and the foreign offices. Nevertheless, both of these nonmilitary activities remained in the arena of traditional politics. Expanding and critical war industries relied on a fast-growing proletariat which began to participate in politics with a new sense of self-importance; and the political awareness of these workers was being stimulated partly by a relentless exposure to debates on war aims. Meanwhile, in seeking to formulate the nation's war aims, the foreign offices discovered that they were engaged in a highly controversial political assignment which could not be carried out without extensive consultations with the nation's major political factions. Unfortunately for the foreign offices, the rapidly expanding labor force tended to reinforce precisely those political parties and factions which were determined to insist on popular control of foreign policy as a key to a peace based on liberal principles instead of naked power.[1]

1. Though Clausewitz never tired of emphasizing the importance of subordinating "the military point of view to the political," he failed to deal adequately with the internal politics of foreign-policy making. His references to war as "only a part of political intercourse" tended to confine this total intercourse to the external relations between and among nations. Since Clausewitz wrote at a time when party politics had not as yet begun to affect the making of foreign policy, his tangential reference to the internal aspects of external relations is understandable. Meanwhile, he must be given credit for recognizing that "the prodigious effects of the French Revolution abroad were evidently brought about much less through new methods and views introduced by the French in the conduct of War than through the changes which it wrought in state-craft and civil administration, in the character of Governments, in the condition of the people, etc." Clausewitz blamed not the generals but political leaders for having neglected to take into consideration those alterations in policy "produced by the French Revolution, not only in France, but over the rest of Europe as well." The Revolution had called forth "other means and powers" which, once understood, might be used in the conduct of political intercourse. Carl von Clausewitz, *On War* (rev. ed. 3 vols. London, Kegan Paul, 1949), 3, 121–30.

Since, during the war, the issue of war aims inside all the belligerent nations was thoroughly immersed in domestic politics, the Clausewitz formula alone cannot serve as an analytic framework. For not all wartime politics was carried on with the "violent means" which Clausewitz correctly identified as replacing diplomacy in external relations. Certainly internal political relations never registered the violent characteristics of trench warfare; in fact, force continued to be the *ultima ratio*, applied only on those rare occasions when the unity of the home front was seriously threatened. Even in Germany— where Ludendorff and Hindenburg, with the support of the status quo forces, eventually emerged in a preponderant internal power position—the break with peacetime means was far less radical in domestic than in international politics.

 In a study of war aims the focus must be less on the geopolitically conditioned factors of war aims than on their domestic political determinants. In the course of the war it gradually became evident that to a significant degree the formulation of the war aims of the respective belligerent powers would be increasingly affected by the internal struggle for power. The fact of war itself did not autonomously dictate a set of war aims to either Ludendorff or Clemenceau. The roots of political power of the Ludendorff and Clemenceau regimes must be analyzed in order to identify the ultimate origins of their expansionist policies. Just as the political power wielded by Ludendorff and the German Supreme Command was largely a function of the enthusiastic and unwavering support of the conservative forces in Germany, similarly Clemenceau's strength rested on the status quo coalition in France. On the other hand, in both Germany and France the opposition parties and factions, insofar as these were equally unified, pressed for decidedly nonexpansionist and nonannexationist war aims.

Therefore, to the extent that wartime foreign-policy formulations were an outgrowth of the internal power struggle, the focus of a study of war aims must be on domestic politics. Moreover, this political struggle over war aims, both within the major belligerent nations and among the members of the Central and the Allied Coalition, constitutes a necessary prologue to the subsequent peace negotiations in Paris in 1919; war-aims politics and peace-making politics are really two inseparable phases of one and the same historical moment. Perhaps the distinction between immediate and historical causes, so crucial in the analysis of the causes of war, should also be applied to a study of the causes of peace. For it would seem that from the analytic point of view, the political and diplomatic process which leads to the outbreak of war is neither different from nor less complex than the process which leads to the outbreak of peace. Therefore, the politics of war aims should be looked on as part of the *historical,* as opposed to the *immediate,* causes of peace. The peace settlement that was negotiated at the Versailles Peace Conference had its roots not only in a new balance of military power between the Central and the Allied Powers but also in the changed political and economic relations inside the belligerent nations. Thus a peace based largely on President Wilson's Fourteen Points was conceivable only to the extent that Europe's "parties of movement" had improved their power position *vis-à-vis* the "parties of order."

Even though it may be hazardous to force each national political spectrum into a roughly similar bipolar mold, for the purpose of this study the confrontation of the parties of order with the parties of movement is both valid and useful. As employed here, the concepts of order and movement are value-free in that they serve to explain, not to approve or disapprove, the political dynamics inside the national political arenas. This bipolarization becomes both marked and significant whenever politics operates under the influence of the specter of revolution, as it did after March 1917 during the war.[2]

2. John Stuart Mill, in his *Essay on Liberty,* distinguished between "a party of order or stability, and a party of progress or reform." Mill emphasized the utility of the dialectic between these two parties for "a healthy state of political life." In a similar vein, President Lowell of Harvard distinguished between "those who prize most highly liberty or progress on the one hand, and those who care more for order on the other." President Lowell also noted that whereas "under normal conditions such an antithesis does not exist" under conditions of revolt or revolution "the desire for liberty and progress may well be enlisted on one side and the defense of the established order on the other." Abbott Lawrence Lowell, *Public Opinion in War and Peace* (Cambridge, Harvard University Press, 1923), p. 271. While Mill and Lowell based their analysis primarily on the experience of the English two-party system, François Goguel was able to identify two clusters of parties in the multiparty system of the Third French Republic. According to Goguel, during the life of the Third Republic the parties of movement tended to work together in pursuit of certain leftward changes in the status quo; the parties of order coalesced in defense of the prevailing order. Not unlike Lowell, Goguel insists that when crucial, fundamental political issues were at stake, the political spectrum even in a multiparty system tended to be reduced to the bipolarity of order vs. movement. Accordingly, during the major internal crises of the Third Republic, the usual spectrum of left,

In wartime England, until 1917, the political truce was respected almost unanimously by the Conservative, Liberal, and Labour parties, leaving only marginal Labour and Radical elements to express any kind of articulate though politically ineffective dissent. However, after 1917, when war weariness and the Russian Revolution combined to undermine Britain's political truce, the forces of movement gradually became part of a larger Labour-Radical coalition which as of November 1917 drew additional strength from the restive Lansdowne faction in the Conservative camp. Later it will be shown how these disparate political factions crystallized for essentially different motives as a force of movement around a liberal war-aims program. Lord Lansdowne (Conservative), E. D. Morel (Radical), Arthur Henderson (Labourite), and James Ramsay MacDonald (Independent Labourite) eventually united to press for a nonannexationist peace and open diplomacy. That their efforts were not altogether in vain is evident from the war-aims address which Lloyd George delivered before a Labour audience on January 5, 1918.

Likewise in France, the *union sacrée* did not weaken materially until April 1917. Then the French Socialist party (SFIO) took new courage and before long became the nucleus of a united front of all the parties and factions of movement. Henceforth these forces of movement had to contend with the rapidly consolidating forces of order which now gathered in support of Clemenceau. In all essentials the war-aims program of this left coalition coincided with that of its British equivalent. Inside both "progressive" camps, however, there were factions of uneven strength as well as of varying degrees of dissent. The French and British Internationalists were numerically outnumbered inside the forces of movement and were always prepared to give a less rigid interpretation of the national interest than their Social Patriotic colleagues.

Inside Germany the forces of movement did not come together on the specific issue of war aims, or on the broader question of constitutional reform, until July 1917. Whereas heretofore only the few Spartacists and the influential Independent wing of the Social Democratic party (SPD) had clamored for a reformulation of war aims along nonannexationist lines, in mid-1917 the Independents were joined, again

---

left-center, center, right-center, and right eventually disappeared. Goguel, *La Politique des partis sous la IIIe République*, Paris, Editions du Seuil, 1946.

for essentially incompatible political motives, not only by the Social Patriots, but also by the Center party and the Progressive People's party. Eventually, in November 1918, this July 19th coalition took power, only then to constitute the new forces of order against the mounting Spartacist menace.

In Russia the interaction between domestic and foreign policy became especially intense after the March Revolution. Overnight the Cadets, as well as the majority Social Revolutionaries and Mensheviks, were transformed into forces of order; meanwhile the Bolsheviks gradually emerged as the organizing center of the impatient forces of movement which now desperately rallied to the tripartite slogan of peace, bread, and land. In the case of Russia, as also of Germany, the pre-1917 forces of movement often found it easier to agree on a minimum of domestic reforms than on a war-aims program. In Russia after March 1917 the Cadets continued to claim Constantinople, whereas the Mensheviks sought a peace based on self-determination, even though both parties were equally committed to the overthrow of the tsarist autocracy. Similarly in Germany, the forces of movement found it easier to agree on the necessity to liberalize the Prussian franchise than on a common program of war aims. But regardless of these disagreements on foreign-policy aims, the forces for change in both these countries consolidated with the necessary strength and for sufficient time to break the united front of the forces of resistance.

Quite clearly, not only in Russia and Germany but also in the other warring nations of Europe, political and social conditions were markedly altered under the combined impact of war and revolution; but since these developments became apparent almost two years before the Armistice was signed, by 1920 Clemenceau was no longer justified in speaking of peace as "a question of political and social history, to be picked up where the war had interrupted it." [3] An analysis of the same wartime developments had led Lenin to conclude unequivocally that the peace following any war could be "nothing but the accounting and registration of the actual changes in the realities of forces brought about in the course of and in consequence of the war." [4] Domestically, after causing a temporary decline of the parties of movement during the height of the political truce, the war accelerated their growth,

3. In his introduction to André Tardieu, *La Paix* (Paris, Payot, 1921), p. xiv.
4. Vols. *18–21* of Lenin, *Collected Works* (New York, International Publishers, 1929–45), *19*, 68.

until by November 1918 they had surpassed their prewar strength.[5] Internationally, the most striking changes in the relationship of forces were the defeat of Germany as a dissatisfied power, the industrial-military rise of America and Japan, and the military eclipse of Russia. Thus the new picture of power and politics had both an internal and an external dimension. Moreover, this dual aspect of the 1914–18 historic moment was reflected in the inevitability with which—certainly on the verbal level but also on the level of actual policy—the Old Diplomacy gave way to the New.

In this political dialect between the forces of order and the forces of movement it was the former group which supported the methods as well as the aims of the Old Diplomacy. The spokesmen and practitioners of the Old insisted that the purposes of the war should be formulated in secret by the Minister of Foreign Affairs working under the general direction of the Government's chief executive and in intimate consultation with the General Staff. Furthermore, since war aims had to be negotiated among the members of the Central and Allied Powers respectively, their ultimate content should be fixed in secret diplomatic negotiations carried on within a coalition framework. Accordingly, for the exponents of the Old Diplomacy there was an initimate connection between the diplomatic method to be used in the formulation of war aims and the actual content which they were determined to incorporate into these aims. It was not the secret diplomatic method *qua* method which the forces of order advocated, but rather annexations, protectorates, and spheres of influence which, in view of an awakening public opinion, they could not openly claim. Tsarist Russia sought control of Constantinople, Germany of Belgium and Courland, the Dual Monarchy of subject nationalities, France of the Saar, Great Britain of Persia, and Italy of cisalpine Tyrol. Notwithstanding these and other concrete territorial ambitions, the people were told only of war aims like self-defense, and the preservation of national honor and freedom.

In the meantime the parties and factions of movement renewed their prewar attacks on the secret making and execution of foreign

5. In the first postwar election the British Labour party polled 22 per cent of the popular vote, compared to 7 per cent in the last prewar election. From 1914 to 1919 in France the popular vote for the SFIO rose from 1,350,000 to 1,700,000. In the last prewar election the SPD in Germany polled 34.8 per cent of the popular vote; in the first postwar election of January 1919 the German Left (SPD and USPD) increased this total to 45.4 per cent.

policy by insisting that the war cabinets commit themselves publicly
to nonannexationist war aims. In general, they rejected the contention
of the forces of order that the formulation of war aims should not be
subject to political debate in parliament, the press, and on public platforms. Instead, the spokesmen of the forces of movement maintained
that popular control over foreign-policy making should be increased;
they were confident that the mass electorates would be in favor of a
peace without annexations and indemnities on the basis of national
self-determination. In fact, as the war progressed and the forces of
movement increased their political strength, the open diplomacy
formula, coupled with nonannexationist war-aims statements, eventually became the stock-in-trade of all war cabinets and foreign minis-
tries. Especially once the Bolsheviks had published the "infamous" secret treaties in late November 1917 and Woodrow Wilson had stepped
forward as a sponsor of the New Diplomacy, the Old Diplomacy of
the forces of order was on the defensive. In brief, the triumph of the
New Diplomacy during the last year of war must be assessed not only
in the light of Wilson's profound faith in the wisdom of open diplomacy
and popular control over foreign policy, or of the Bolshevik practice
of open diplomacy at Brest-Litovsk and their conversion to self-determination, but also in the light of the decided growth of the forces
of movement in Austria-Hungary, Germany, France, and Great Britain.
As will be shown later, this growth of the forces of movement was considerably advanced by the economic-military exhaustion of all the
major European belligerents, especially during the closing eighteen
months of the war.

2. The Consolidation of the Forces of Order, 1914–16

Since the political forces which reappeared in 1917 and which served
to liberalize these war aims did not spring from a vacuum, their an-
tecedents must be noted.

In March 1916 Lenin rightly observed that "war does not change
the direction in which politics developed prior to the war; it only *accel-
erates* that development." [6] It would seem, however, that this acceleration was not quite so unilinear as Lenin implied. With the outbreak of
war, the leftward movement of prewar politics was interrupted. There
followed a two-year period in which there was considerable consolida-

6. *Works, 19,* 63 (italics mine).

tion of the forces of order, in line with Hegel's contention that successful wars prevent "civil broils" and strengthen the "internal power of the
state." [7] The political acceleration which Lenin anticipated did not
start until the war began to appear less successful and gave rise to the
crisis of 1917–18.

It may be legitimate, therefore, to speak of three separate stages in
the development of the political forces within the major belligerent nations. The first stage was characterized by the precarious equilibrium
in domestic politics immediately preceding the outbreak of war. The
second stage was roughly the years from August 1914 to March 1917,
when the political equilibrium was firmly re-established in favor of
the forces of order. The third stage was the period of acceleration
from March 1917 until the end of (or even after) the war, when the
re-emergence and the actual strengthening of the forces of movement
again introduced instability into domestic politics. This study is
concerned primarily with the third period, particularly with the impact
on war aims of the changing fortunes of the political truce in Russia,
Germany, France, and Great Britain from March 1917 to January
1918.

Much of the precariousness of the domestic political equilibrium
in prewar Europe was due to the decisive growth of Socialist parties
and trade unions. In the last prewar elections three million Socialists,
supported by nine million nonregistered Socialists, had sent 424 Socialist deputies to Europe's parliaments.[8] Moreover, fast-growing trade
unions could be relied upon to help recruit additional members.[9]

In England the Labour movement often enjoyed the political support
of the left wing of the Liberal party (that is, the Radicals), the suffra-
gettes, and the Irish Nationalists. On the Continent the German and
French Socialists led a more lonesome existence, with non-Socialist
support limited to certain fringe elements from the middle class as
well as from the Christian Socialist camp. In the Dual Monarchy
the Socialists sought to capitalize on the aspirations for self-determination of the national minorities that formed the spearhead of the forces

7. See Herbert Marcuse, *Reason and Revolution* (London, Oxford University
Press, 1941), p. 221.

8. For a summary table of the prewar party vote and parliamentary representation of Europe's Socialist and Labor parties, see Merle Fainsod, *International
Socialism and the World War* (Cambridge, Harvard University Press, 1935), p. 40.

9. In 1913 trade union membership stood at 250,000 in Russia, 2,573,718 in
Germany, 3,987,115 in England, and 1,027,059 in France.

against the status quo. Even though the relatively weak Russian Left was torn by serious doctrinal dissensions, a more intimate cooperation of the bourgeoisie, the workers, and the peasants nevertheless was clearly in the offing.

Care must be taken not to exaggerate the extent of these pressures against the status quo during the immediate prewar years. Whereas there were 101 Socialist deputies in the Chamber in Paris, only 6 per cent of France's industrial working class belonged to unions, and of these only a small percentage was affiliated with the General Confederation of Labor (CGT).[10] In England in 1914 the strike wave stood at its lowest ebb since 1910, when the Labour party had gathered 370,802 votes in the general elections.[11] In the Reich, as also in France, strikes appeared to be declining; the parties of order were able to take comfort from the rapid emergence of conservative leaders in the labor movement.[12] Similarly, in Russia the peak trade union membership of 1907 had not been exceeded.[13]

Nevertheless, the political horizon was far from clear, and social harmony was more apparent than real. The British railwaymen, miners, and transport workers were in the process of forging the Triple Industrial Alliance for the purpose of more effectively pressing their wage and hour demands,[14] while in Germany the general strike was again coming into favor in the left-center of the SPD and among the left radicals.[15] In Russia "there was an ominous upsurge in labor unrest which reached a climax during the first seven months of 1914 which was interrupted only by the outbreak of war." [16] Thus in Eng-

10. Roger Picard, *Le Mouvement syndical durant la guerre* (Paris, Presses Universitaires, 1927), p. 21.

11. Elie Halévy, *A History of the English People in the Nineteenth Century* (London, Benn, 1952), 6, Bk. II, p. 527.

12. Picard, *Le Mouvement syndical*, p. 45; Carl E. Schorske, *German Social Democracy 1905–1917: The Development of the Great Schism* (Cambridge, Harvard University Press, 1955), Pt. II; D. W. Brogan, *The Development of Modern France, 1870–1939* (London, Hamilton, 1940), pp. 425–26.

13. Merle Fainsod, *How Russia Is Ruled* (Cambridge, Harvard University Press, 1953), p. 28.

14. George Dangerfield, *The Strange Death of Liberal England* (New York, Harrison Smith, 1935), pp. 389–401; Samuel J. Hurwitz, *State Intervention in Great Britain* (New York, Columbia University Press, 1949), pp. 35–41; Keith Hutchison, *The Decline and Fall of British Capitalism* (New York, Scribner's, 1950), pp. 115–23.

15. Schorske, *German Social Democracy*, pp. 274–84.

16. Fainsod, *How Russia Is Ruled*, p. 30.

land as well as on the Continent the deceptive quiet of the prewar summer was often pierced by the threatening cry of "Wait till autumn."

Elie Halévy has suggested that historians might legitimately query whether the growing sense of discomfort resulting from increasing SPD pressure was one of the reasons why the German Right decided to risk war in July 1914.[17] Similarly, to what extent was Vienna's intransigence *vis-à-vis* South Slav nationalism heightened by official determination to intimidate revolutionary forces in other parts of the Dual Monarchy? [18] Also, could the Russian Tsar have been prepared to repeat the 1904–05 experiment of seeking to ward off pressures for internal reform by engaging in an international venture?

It is impossible to determine accurately the extent to which certain leading European statesmen and politicians may have welcomed, if not actually promoted, the international crisis in the hope of alleviating domestic tensions. Nevertheless, if the three stages in the development of wartime politics are to be seen in a meaningful perspective, this problem should at least be posed. On the strength of his profound knowledge of Britain and France, Elie Halévy concluded that "certainly no responsible statesman would have said, at the beginning of 1914, that he felt safe against the perils of some kind of revolutionary outburst." [19] Likewise, according to a leading historian of modern Germany, "if the war had not broken out in 1914, the conflict between the Imperial Government and the majority of the German nation would have continued to intensify to a point at which a revolutionary situation would have been created." [20]

In his ardent antiwar mood in 1912, Marcel Sembat, one of France's most respected Socialist leaders, had cautioned all French Republicans that in deciding between war and peace they were also choosing between autocracy and democracy. *Faites un roi sinon faites la paix* was the dramatic slogan with which the SFIO sought to awaken all Republicans to the dangers of reactionary domestic politics in war-

17. *The World Crisis of 1914–1918* (London, Oxford University Press, 1930), p. 11.

18. "The rulers of Austria-Hungary believed that there would be revolution if they did not launch a war; the rulers of Germany were confident that there would not be a revolution if they did." A. J. P. Taylor, *The Struggle for Mastery in Europe, 1848–1918* (Oxford, 1954), p. xxiv. See also Otto Bauer, *Die Österreichische Revolution* (Vienna, Volksbuchhandlung, 1923), pp. 11–12, 20, 110.

19. *The World Crisis*, p. 19.

20. Arthur Rosenberg, *The Birth of the German Republic* (New York, Oxford University Press, 1931), p. 58.

time.[21] In a similar vein, on the eve of America's entry into the world struggle, President Wilson was haunted by the thought that war requires "illiberalism at home to reinforce the men at the front." [22] Furthermore, Wilson and many of his pacifist-idealist supporters feared that in time all the reforms of the New Freedom would be lost, since in case of war "the people we have unhorsed will inevitably come into the control of the country, for we shall be dependent upon steel, oil, and financial magnates." [23]

These fears were not altogether unjustified in either Europe or America. The outbreak of war initiated a decided shift to the right in the political equilibrium of all the major belligerents. Free of all Internationalist-pacifist illusions, Conservatives and other Traditionalists had never envisaged a world in which governments pursuing policies of national interest would renounce military force. Hence, at this time most Traditionalists were psychologically as well as doctrinally prepared to shoulder the responsibilities of war leadership; whereas many Socialist and Radical leaders needed time to make their peace with the renewed sanctification of violence as a legitimate instrument of national policy.

The economic foundations of the forces of order consisted of precisely those industries on which the nation would now depend for critical military supplies. Therefore, in order to win the whole-hearted cooperation of industrialists and financiers for war production, the government was likely to free the business community from many restraints. Wilson repeatedly expressed his apprehension that "if war comes, we shall have to get the cooperation of big businessmen and, as a result they will dominate the nation for 20 years after the war comes to an end." [24]

From August 1914 to early 1917 there was a steady and pronounced shift of power to the forces of order. In England the Liberal Asquith-Grey Cabinet eventually was supplanted by the more conservative

21. *Faites un roi sinon faites la paix* (20th ed. Paris, Figuière, 1916), esp. p. xi.

22. Cited in John L. Heaton, ed., *Cobb of the World* (New York, Dutton, 1924), p. 268.

23. Cited in Ray Stannard Baker, *Woodrow Wilson, Life and Letters* (8 vols. New York, Doubleday, Doran, 1927–39), 6, 506.

24. Cited in Eric F. Goldman, *Rendezvous with Destiny* (New York, Knopf, 1952), p. 248. See also Arthur M. Schlesinger, Jr., *The Crisis of the Old Order* (Boston, Houghton Mifflin, 1957), pp. 37–38.

Lloyd George – Bonar Law coalition, whereas in France the Radical Socialist premier Briand was replaced first by Ribot and later by Clemenceau. In Germany the Supreme Command gradually tightened its political bonds with the parties of order to such a degree that an effective challenge of Ludendorff's expansionist plans became impossible. Could Lloyd George have been thinking of this consolidation of the Right when he noted that the "Conservatives entered the war with enthusiasm and the Liberals with reluctant conviction"? [25]

This shift to the right was accentuated still further by the fact that inside the Liberal and Socialist parties the more conservative leaders improved their power position.[26] Gradually Britain's Liberal party became so rigidly committed to an all-out war policy that its Radical wing was forced to search for a new political home. In the meantime Ramsay MacDonald relinquished the leadership of the Parliamentary Labour party to less pacifist colleagues and proceeded to devote all his time and energy to the strengthening of the internationalist Independent Labour party. Similarly, inside the French and German Socialist parties the Social Patriots captured all the important command posts, while trade union leaders dutifully swore not to permit strikes to interfere with war production. Accordingly, in the year 1916 only 152,000 workers were involved in brief token strikes in France, 489,000 in Great Britain, and 517,000 in Germany.[27] Moreover, from August 1914 to the beginning of 1917 the membership of both labor unions and Socialist parties declined markedly, partly because of the steady drain of workers into the armed forces. By 1916 the German trade union membership had fallen from two and a half million to one

25. *War Memoirs* (2 vols. London, Odhams Press, 1938), *1*, 130. Whereas the French parties of order looked upon war as an occasion to reinforce the principle of authority, the parties of movement were concerned primarily by the political consequences of the war emergency. Cf. André Siegfried, *Tableau des partis en France* (Paris, Aimery Somogy, 1930), p. 112.

26. Cf. Robert Michels, "Party Life in War-time," in *Political Parties* (Glencoe, Ill., Free Press, 1949), pp. 393–99.

27. Available statistics on the frequency of and participation in strikes during the war in the various belligerent countries are not very accurate. Nevertheless, a comprehensive picture can be gleaned from Bureau International du Travail, *Enquête sur la production, 4*, Bk. II (Paris, 1924), pp. 225–28, 230–31, 233, 240–43, 247. This study concludes that throughout Europe the number of strikes reached an all-time low in 1915. For a comprehensive and competent study of industrial strikes and unrest in wartime France see William Oualid and Charles Picquenard, *Salaires et tarifs*, Paris, Presses Universitaires, 1929.

million, whereas by March 1917 the SPD membership had dropped to 234,000.[28]

Hence, from August 1914 through 1916, with the forces of movement in full retreat, the old ruling classes of Europe thrived in a temporary yet strong climate of internal political security.[29] The victory of the forces of order seemed even more complete because instead of making their support for the war contingent on certain policy concessions, the Socialist parties agreed to the political truce unconditionally. Thus, domestically, the forces of order achieved a position of power to which they had aspired only in their most daring dreams before the war. Indeed, no peacetime British cabinet of the preceding fifteen years "could have included a Curzon, a Milner, a Carson, a Northcliffe, a Balfour, and a Robert Cecil";[30] nor could the German SPD have suffered such a complete political eclipse. A conservative observer like Guglielmo Ferrero had good cause to predict that nothing would "surprise the historians of the European War more than the general reconciliation of parties and opinions by which its outbreak was followed."[31]

3. War Aims during the Political Truce: the Secret Treaties

While the political truce was firmly secured and the forces of order were in undisputed ascendancy, all major political issues were stricken from the agenda of *public* debate. The issue of war aims was no exception.

The decisive members of the war cabinets never questioned the 19th-century premises "that the foundations of foreign policy were based upon changeless national and imperial necessities and that, as such, they stood outside the arena of party conflict."[32] In the view of these proponents of the Old Diplomacy, policy-making and negotiations in international politics, with a balance of power as the proximate objective, were so complex and unbending that they should be left to specialists and professional diplomats.

28. Rudolf Schlesinger, *Federalism in Central and Eastern Europe* (London, Kegan Paul, 1945), pp. 126, 131.

29. Cf. Paul Louis, *La Crise du socialisme mondiale* (Paris, Alcan, 1921), p. 55.

30. Norman Angell, *The British Revolution and the American Democracy* (New York, Huebsch, 1919), p. 144.

31. *Europe's Fateful Hour* (New York, Dodd, Mead, 1918), p. 193.

32. Harold Nicolson, *Diplomacy* (2d ed. London, Oxford University Press, 1950), p. 10.

It is far from surprising that the Old Diplomacy should have been anxiously embraced as an essential and respected instrument of statecraft, given the two major tasks of early wartime diplomacy. First, the original members of each of the two armed coalitions wanted to reinforce the bonds of alliance among themselves in preparation for a difficult and costly military campaign. Secondly, both coalitions were equally determined to gain additional strength by luring neutral or uncommitted nations to their respective sides. In both undertakings the cabinets had to resort to secret negotiations in which immediate advantages were sought in exchange for promises for the distant postwar future. These promises were kept secret because the governments feared a hostile public reaction to those expansionist provisions in the secret treaties which clashed with official self-defense slogans. Moreover, they had to avoid furnishing the enemy with concrete evidence with which to fortify his "anti-imperialist" propaganda campaign.

The political parties that gained control of the governments after August 1914 were advocates of both the method and the objectives of the Old Diplomacy. Therefore in the war cabinets there was no opposition to entering into secret diplomatic negotiations and agreements, seeking territorial gains, or satisfying the territorial ambitions of potential and actual allies.

It would be incorrect to say, however, that this foreign-policy making was apolitical or nonpolitical.[33] Although the objective imperatives of national survival should not be underestimated, the happy coincidence of the national need for recourse to Old Diplomacy and the supremacy of its political sponsors must also be noted. With the welcome encouragement of the military caste, the political forces which soon consolidated their control over the executive branch of

---

33. The Austrian sociologist Albert Schäffle distinguished between two spheres of politics: those activities which are "routine affairs of state" and those which fall into the sphere of "politics" proper. The former are disposed of in "accordance with existing rules and regulations" and consequently are "in the realm of administration rather than politics." The latter, however, constitute a series of events still in the process of becoming, in which, precisely because new decisions are necessary, there is struggle. Karl Mannheim, *Ideology and Utopia* (New York, Harcourt, Brace, 1940), pp. 100–1. This distinction is clear and helpful, especially insofar as it separates the rational sphere of administration from the irrational sphere of politics. However, in certain situations the parties of order praise the rationality of established administrative and executive procedures, whereas in effect their advocacy of the administrative status quo is merely another phase of their over-all defense of the existing political order.

government were committed to the pursuit of expansionist war aims.

The syndrome of political elements favorable to both the practice and the objectives of the Old Diplomacy was perhaps most apparent in Germany. Hans Gatzke has conclusively shown that a coalition of "industrialists, Pan-Germans, the parties of the Right, and the Supreme Command, was responsible for the stubborn propagation of large war aims." Moreover, Gatzke concludes, "each of these forces had its own particular reasons for wanting to hold out for far-reaching territorial gains; yet one aim most of them had in common—to ensure through a successful peace settlement the continuation of the existing order, to their own advantage, and to the political and economic detriment of the majority of the German people." [34] In pursuit of essentially the same combination of political and economic objectives roughly similar coalitions pressed for expansionist war aims in Russia, Austria-Hungary, France, England, Italy, and Japan.

The forces of order in both coalitions were equally distrustful of "the politics of the street," except when popular emotions could be harnessed for imperial ambitions.[35] Therefore, since they realized that the forces of movement were destined to become the sponsors of compromising war aims, they never relented in their determination to prevent the issue of war aims from becoming embroiled in party politics.

Admittedly, a great national debate on war aims in the midst of war could easily impair a nation's war effort. However, until 1917 the effectiveness of the political truce was so complete that the cabinets and the forces of order did not have to worry about any opposition to official policies. Everywhere an overwhelming wave of nationalism swept the parties of movement into giving their enthusiastic support to the war. In the Entente as well as in the Central nations Liberals and Socialists alike, with few significant exceptions, shelved their antiwar slogans and their "scientific" theories of the causes of war. Henceforth they subscribed to the government-sponsored interpretations of the enemy's unilateral war guilt, and encouraged the war cabinets to pursue an expeditious total, not compromise, victory.

The cabinets' negative attitude toward public war-aims debates and

34. *Germany's Drive to the West* (Baltimore, Johns Hopkins Press, 1950), p. 294.

35. Especially the extreme Right sought to enlist popular passions for the cause of national self-extension and for a war *à outrance*. This populist tactic was pursued with considerable success by the *Action Française* circles in France and the *Alldeutsche Verband* in Germany.

declarations was foreshadowed immediately after the outbreak of hostilities in Paris. Premier Viviani summoned the representatives of the French press to ask them to desist from discussing war aims in order not to create "a very inconvenient state of public opinion." [36] In London, until January 1918, the editors of the semi-official *Times* had no patience with "any request, neutral or otherwise, for a 'restatement', or 'clearer definition' of 'peace terms', 'war aims', or 'peace points', as the objects of both sides were called." [37]

Few detailed monographs of the politics of war aims from August 1914 to March 1917 in any of the major Allied nations have thus far been undertaken.[38] It is perhaps even more surprising that the diplomacy of the secret treaties which registered the expansionist plans of Russia, France, England, and Italy, is only beginning to be studied.[39] However, for the purposes of this study a brief summary of the essential provisions of these treaties is all that is required. Such a summary reveals that the war aims formulated by the Entente *in camera* during the height of the political truce were not very much more modest than those of Germany. But above all, these treaties represent the most vivid incarnation of the spirit, the techniques, and the objectives of the Old Diplomacy against which the forces of movement protested in 1917–18.[40]

36. Pierre Renouvin, *The Forms of War Government in France* (New Haven, Yale University Press, 1927), pp. 46–47.

37. *The History of the Times* (London, 1952), 4, Pt. I, p. 311.

38. Gerda Richards Crosby gives a sketchy account of British war-aims politics from 1914 to early 1917 in *Disarmament and Peace in British Politics, 1914–1919* (Cambridge, Harvard University Press, 1957), pp. 1–37.

39. The "secret diplomacy" of Britain and France has been investigated least thoroughly, largely because the foreign office archives as well as important private papers continue to be closed and inaccessible. In spite of this limitation, an exhaustive study of Entente diplomacy toward both Turkey and Italy from July 1914 to the summer of 1915 has been undertaken in W. W. Gottlieb, *Studies in Secret Diplomacy during the First World War*, London, Allen and Unwin, 1957. For an equally comprehensive monograph on the diplomacy but not on the domestic politics of tsarist war aims see C. Jay Smith, Jr., *The Russian Struggle for Power, 1914–1917,* New York, Philosophical Library, 1956. Both of these studies rely heavily on published Russian documents which, thanks to Bolshevik eagerness to expose the foreign-policy misdeeds of the tsarist regime and the capitalist nations, have become the most important source for the study of Allied wartime diplomacy, 1914–17. Italian war-aims diplomacy has been the subject of two reliable studies by Mario Toscano: *Il Patto di Londra*, Bologna, 1934; and *Gli Accordi di San Giovanni di Moriana*, Milan, 1936.

40. For the protest against the secret treaties by the Allied forces of movement in 1917 see below, pp. 208–14, 279–80.

The original Entente Powers announced publicly on September 5, 1914, that Russia, France, and England had agreed never to desert one another in pursuit of a separate peace. After that, however, all other agreements and treaties among the three Entente Powers not only were negotiated in secret but actually remained closely guarded secrets until the Bolsheviks published official documents from the tsarist archives in November 1917.[41] Also, since all arrangements were cast in the form of executive agreements, Allied parliaments were kept nearly as much in the dark as the public at large.[42]

By March 4, 1915, Russia's Foreign Minister Sazonov had informed Great Britain and France of the territories which Russia desired to acquire "as the result of the present war." Two weeks later the British Government, anxious for Russian support for its impending thrust on the Dardanelles (that is, the Gallipoli campaign) had "given its complete consent in writing to the annexation by Russia of the Straits and Constantinople."[43] In expressing his gratitude for British acquiescence to Russia's claims, Sazonov added that "the Imperial Government expects that in the future its full liberty of action will be recognized in the sphere of influence allotted to it." In return, Russia not only agreed to the incorporation of the "neutral zone" in Persia into the British sphere of influence, but also accorded Britain "security for its economic interests and a similar benevolent attitude on

41. For the fiery ideological statement with which Trotsky announced the publication of the secret treaties on November 22, 1917, see Degras, pp. 8–9. For a French translation of Soviet-published documents see Emile Laloy, ed., *Lès Documents secrets des archives du Ministère des Affaires Etrangères de Russie publiés par les Bolchéviks,* Paris, Bossard, 1920. In 1918 a prominent member of the dissident UDC in London edited, with commentary, an English version of these documents based on the version which had appeared in late 1917 and in early 1918 in the *Manchester Guardian* and the *New Europe:* F. Seymour Cocks, *The Secret Treaties and Understandings: Text of the Available Documents,* London, Union of Democratic Control, 1918. A competent summary of these documents can be found in Ray Stannard Baker, *Woodrow Wilson and World Setilement* (3 vols. New York, Doubleday, Page, 1922), *1,* chaps. 3, 4.

42. Rumors of French and British consent to postwar Russian control of the Straits were quite current by 1916, but repeated attempts by various members of British Parliament to elicit specific information from the Cabinet proved unsuccessful. See the *Labour Leader,* March 2, 1916, and the *Morning Post,* December 16, 1916. In prerevolutionary Russia, however, on December 2, 1916, the tsarist prime minister announced in the Duma that Paris and London had recognized Russia's claim to the Straits and to Constantinople. Cocks, *The Secret Treaties and Understandings,* pp. 16–17.

43. Cocks, pp. 27 ff.

[Russia's] part towards the political aspirations of England in other parts." Specifically, Great Britain acquired Russian sanction for her ambitions in Egypt.[44]

At first France was reluctant to grant Russia's demands, for fear that the Anglo-Russian diplomatic maneuvers might eventually entail military diversions from the Western front to the Ottoman Empire. Also, the Quai d'Orsay was apprehensive that Russia's advance to Constantinople would endanger France's dominant economic and financial position in the Near East. However, by April 10, 1915, France had agreed to Russia's claims in European Turkey "on condition that the war is brought to a victorious conclusion and . . . that France and Britain accomplish their plans in the East as well as elsewhere."[45] Hence, while this Franco-British acquiescence to Russian control of the Straits was primarily calculated to keep the Tsar in the war, it also prepared the ground for further "mutual compensations" to be carved out of the withering Turkish Empire.

The principles and language of the Old Diplomacy continued to leave an unmistakable stamp on other negotiations. In the spring of 1916 the Entente Powers "came to an agreement as regards the future delimitation of their respective zones of influence and territorial acquisitions in Asiatic Turkey." In case of an Allied victory Germany's Turkish ally was destined to lose not only her European lands to the tsarist Empire, but also the greater part of her Asiatic Empire to France, England, and Russia. In the Sykes-Picot agreement of May 1916 the British and French settled their respective spheres of interest in Asia Minor. France secured a sphere of influence over Syria and an extensive hinterland, while Britain acquired similar privileges over Transjordania, Southern Palestine, and Arabia.[46] In turn, Russia was allowed in compensation to push her frontier southwestward into Asia Minor, so as to gain control over Armenia and Kurdistan.[47]

At about this same time the new borders of Germany if defeated also

44. For a careful selection of essential documents as well as for extensive citations of interpretive studies on the "Constantinople Agreement," see J. C. Hurewitz, ed., *Diplomacy in the Near and Middle East* (2 vols. New York, Van Nostrand, 1956), 2, 7–11. See also Smith, *The Russian Struggle for Power*, pp. 217–43; and Gottlieb, *Studies in Secret Diplomacy*, pp. 66–75.

45. Cited in Gottlieb, p. 101.

46. For the essential "Sykes-Picot" documents and for references to the most important secondary sources see Hurewitz, *Diplomacy in the Near and Middle East*, 2, 18–22.

47. Ibid., p. 21.

came under discussion. The Russians stood ready to "allow France and England complete freedom in drawing up the Western frontiers of Germany, in the expectation that the Allies on their part would allow [Russia] equal freedom in drawing up [her] frontiers with Germany and Austria." Moreover, the tsarist Government sought the "elimination of all attempts to place the future of Poland under the guarantee of the Great Powers." On March 11, 1917, three days before the Russian Revolution, these negotiations culminated in a secret agreement between Russia and France (it was kept secret even from the British Government) in which France recognized "Russia's complete liberty in establishing her Western frontiers" in return for Russian support of French plans in Alsace-Lorraine, in the Saar, and on the left bank of the Rhine.[48]

In the meantime, in the middle of June 1916, with Italy a firm partner in the Entente, an Allied economic conference had met in Paris. Although the deliberations of this conference were kept secret, its major resolutions were published.[49] In addition to mapping the strategy for intensified economic warfare against the Central Powers, under the chairmanship of Albert Clémentel the French Minister of Commerce, the Allied representatives also made plans for closing Allied markets to German manufacturers, shipping, and capital, in the postwar period.[50]

So much for the war aims which crystallized in the process of re-ensuring the original Entente coalition. The treaties and agreements which were consummated among the Petrograd, Paris, and London governments give ample evidence of an unhesitating Allied commitment to both the methods and the objectives of the Old Diplomacy. In the meantime the search for new military partners offered further proof along these lines.

To both coalitions Italy at first appeared as the most valuable un-

48. Smith, *The Russian Struggle for Power*, pp. 459–66, and Lloyd George, *War Memoirs, 1*, 947–49. It was only after the return of two French Socialists from Russia in late May 1917 that at a secret session of the *Chambre* France's deputies found out about this secret agreement.

49. G. Lowes Dickinson, *Economic War after the War*, UDC, No. 19a (London, August 1916), pp. 18–20.

50. These plans for continued trade discriminations after the war were immediately subjected to bitter attack in British and French left-dissident circles. See ibid.; Charles Gide, *La Politique commerciale après la guerre*, Paris, 1917; Le Parti Socialiste, *La Guerre et la paix* (Paris, 1918), pp. 129 ff.

committed nation in Europe. Until August 3, 1914, when she declared her "temporary" neutrality, Italy had actually been associated
with the Triple Alliance. By middle October, however, Prime Minister
Salandra made it quite clear that in all future negotiations Italy would
be guided by her own "sacro egoismo." Fortunately for the Allies, the
territories coveted by Italy were primarily in areas where conflicts
of interest with the Dual Monarchy were unavoidable. Consequently,
as Paris and London pressed their campaign to enroll Italy as a belligerent in the Entente, they were able to offer generous inducements
at the cost of enemy (that is, Austro-Hungarian) territory.[51] Gradually Russia's reluctance to see Italy advance into the Eastern Adriatic
was overcome, and on April 26, 1915, the Treaty of London was
signed by Grey, Imperiali, Benckendorff, and Cambon. Italy acquired
Trentino, cisalpine Tyrol to the Brenner frontier, Trieste, Gorizia, all
of Istria as far as Quarnero, North Dalmatia, and part of Albania (that
is, Valona and hinterland). Also the Allies agreed to Italy's continued
ownership of the Dodecanese Islands in the Aegean Sea. In the Treaty
of London the legacy of the Old Diplomacy was twofold. First,
Article 16 unequivocally specified that the Treaty was "to be kept
secret"; second, certain provisions were in clear violation of the nationality principle.[52]

After Italy had entered the war on the side of the Allies, Paris and
London lived in constant fear that on a subsequent occasion Rome
might decide that a separate peace would be in her interest. To
counteract this possibility the Allies thought it wise to offer additional
compensations. Italy was promised her share of Asia Minor with
the justification that her geographic location gave her an interest in
"the maintenance of the balance of power in the Mediterranean."[53]
On April 19, 1917, in the agreement of St. Jean de Maurienne, France
and Britain recognized Italian control over approximately the southern

51. For a balanced analysis of Italy's rigid national-interest diplomacy and of
Allied efforts to satisfy Italy's ambitions see Gottlieb, *Studies in Secret Diplomacy*,
Pt. II.

52. Smith, *The Russian Struggle for Power*, pp. 268–70. Cf. the text of the Treaty
of London in Great Britain, *Parliamentary Papers* (1920), Misc. No. 7, Cmd. 671;
Cocks, *The Secret Treaties and Understandings*, pp. 27–42; Toscano, *Il Patto di
Londra*, pp. 182–89.

53. For the text as well as a careful analysis of Article 9 of the Treaty of London,
dealing with Italy's interest in the maintenance of the balance of power in the Mediterranean, see Toscano, *Gli Accordi di San Giovanni di Moriana*, pp. 18–24.

third of Anatolia, and granted Italy a sphere of influence north of Smyrna.[54]

The Allies followed the same strategy in their efforts to draw Rumania to their side. While the Central Powers held out Russian-controlled Bessarabia as the major inducement, the Allies were in a position to offer extensive and populous Hungarian and Serbian irredentist territories. Thus Rumania joined the Allies after being awarded—in the Treaty of Bucharest on August 18, 1916—Transylvania up to the River Theiss, Bukovania up to the River Pruth, and the Banat.[55] Enemy troops soon overwhelmed Rumania, partly with the help of Bulgaria, which had joined the Central Powers in the secret Treaty of Sofia on July 17, 1915. In this instance the Central Powers won by guaranteeing Albania to Bulgaria, while Allied diplomacy failed largely because it could promise Bulgaria nothing but a southward expansion into Kavalla.[56]

4. War, Revolution, and Crisis, 1917–18

It would seem that Allied war aims, as agreed upon in the secret treaties, were formulated with the expectation that the war would lead to the re-establishment of a European balance of power without markedly disturbing the domestic status quo in any of the major belligerent nations. But what if this conflict (which in the event lasted longer than even the most somber predictions had anticipated) could not be terminated without first generating a profound military, economic, political, and ideological crisis in Europe? Such a crisis was likely to be nourished by a combination of war weariness, economic exhaustion, and rising living costs. Moreover, a war crisis was bound to reinvigorate all the pacifist Internationalist parties and factions which had been divested of effective political influence during the height of the political truce.

54. The decisions taken at Saint Jean de Maurienne are recorded in E. L. Woodward and R. Butler, eds., *Documents on British Foreign Policy, 1919–1939* (London, 1952), 1st ser. 4, 638–39.

55. The complete text of the Treaty of Bucharest is reproduced in Charles Upson Clark, *Greater Roumania* (New York, Dodd, Mead, 1922), pp. 171–77. Article VII of this treaty reads as follows: "The contracting Powers bind themselves to keep the present convention secret until the conclusion of the general peace."

56. Pierre Renouvin, *La Crise européenne et la première guerre mondiale* (3d ed. Paris, Presses Universitaires, 1948), pp. 306–9.

Before the war many of the most articulate spokesmen of the various antiwar groups had repeatedly warned that a major military struggle was likely to ignite civil unrest. The last of these warnings, on the very eve of the war, was sounded by Lord Morley, the leading Radical member of the British Cabinet. In order to dramatize his opposition to the war, Morley resigned his cabinet post with the admonition, addressed to Prime Minister Asquith, that the "atmosphere of war cannot be friendly to order, in a democratic system that is verging on the humour of '48." [57]

While certain left-wing Liberals were genuinely concerned with preventing war-induced civil disorder, the Socialists had a more ambivalent attitude toward the possible contributions which wartime exhaustion might make to the cause of reform or revolution. Perhaps it is not surprising that in spite of their pessimistic expectations about the political fortunes of Socialism immediately after the outbreak of war, the theoreticians of this revolutionary movement should have viewed the war-peace continuum from a broad historical perspective. Consequently, Socialists were likely to be alive to all possible "progressive" consequences of the war they so desperately tried to ward off.

Before the war France's Jean Jaurès had sought to strike fear into the hearts of Europe's ruling classes with the stern warning that any major war would "necessarily, inevitably create a revolutionary situation in Europe." [58] Like so many of his colleagues in the Second International, Jaurès was most skeptical about the political realism of the antiwar appeals which urged the European workers to make war impossible simply by sticking their bayonets into the ground. Moreover, far from welcoming the revolution as an unmixed blessing, Jaurès was deeply troubled by its destructive implications for European culture and civilization.

However, the Second International faced both war and revolution more hopefully. In the Stuttgart manifesto of 1907 it advised the proletariat that if war should break out in spite of Socialism's antiwar campaign, it was the duty of the workers "to intervene in favor of its termination and with all their power to utilize the economic and the

---

57. John Viscount Morley, *Memorandum on Resignation, August 1914* (London, MacMillan, 1928), p. 5.

58. Cited by Pierre Renaudel in *l'Humanité*, November 21, 1918.

political crisis created by the war to rouse the masses and thereby
to hasten the downfall of capitalist class rule." [59] Five years later, in
the Basle manifesto, the Second International reiterated its warning
that "with the present conditions of Europe and the mood of the
working class" the European governments could not "unleash a war
without great danger to themselves." As if to emphasize its resignation to serious political reverses in the early stages of a war, the
Second International reminded friend and foe alike that "the Franco-
German War was followed by the revolutionary outbreak of the
Commune [and] that the Russo-Japanese War set into motion the
revolutionary energies of the peoples of the Russian Empire." [60] Since
the Left never failed to hail both of these events as forward movements
of the revolution, it is somewhat perplexing why the Socialists, who
stood to gain so much from war, were the foremost champions of a
peaceful accommodation of Europe's diplomatic tensions. Or were
these manifestoes meant to convey the Socialist conviction that, with
minor variations in tempo, peace and war alike were predetermined
to promote the political fortunes of the Left? [61]

Especially the most radical elements of the Left were optimistic
about the favorable by-products of the war. Socialist leaders like Lenin
and Rosa Luxemburg, who temperamentally and theoretically were
committed to revolution as opposed to evolution, were extremely
articulate on the dialectics of wartime destruction. Even though they
were full of compassion for the innocent victims of bourgeois-capitalist
wars, the revolutionary Socialists considered all battles, whether political or military, national or international, as necessary stages in the
unfolding world revolution.

Accordingly, in December 1914 Lenin confidently looked upon the
European war not only as "the greatest historical crisis," but also as
"the beginning of a new epoch." [62] The following year he added:

> There have been many wars in history, which, notwithstanding
> all the horrors, cruelties, miseries, and tortures, inevitably con-

59. Cited in Lenin, *Works, 18,* 468.
60. Cited ibid., p. 471.
61. The most detailed and systematic analysis of conflicting doctrinal positions
on problems of war both in the French and in the German Socialist parties is to
be found in Milorad M. Drachkovitch, *Les Socialismes français et allemand et le
problème de la guerre, 1870–1914,* Geneva, 1953.
62. *Works, 18,* 96.

nected with every war, had a progressive character, i.e., they
served the development of mankind, aiding in the destruction of
extremely pernicious and reactionary institutions (as for instance
absolutism and serfdom), or helping to remove the most barbarous
despotism in Europe (that of Turkey and Russia). It is therefore
necessary to examine the historic characteristics of the present
war taken by itself.[63]

The Socialists were not alone in speculating about the impact of
war on traditional Europe. Widely honored but politically uncommitted intellectuals, who did not share Socialist anticipations of beneficial by-products, for some time had been warning of the perilous
consequences of a major European conflagration. Anatole France,
Charles Péguy, Emile Verhaeren, Stefan Zweig, and G. K. Chesterton,
among others, were deeply concerned not only by Germany's economic expansion and military might but also by the inflexibility with
which her demands were being considered by the satisfied powers.
An amorphous group of intellectuals, literati, and political pamphle-
teers, free from involvement in organized political action of the Left,
they argued that instead of allowing the conflicting policies of the
satisfied and dissatisfied powers to lead to armed conflict, enlightened
Europe should explore all avenues of peaceful change—since change
there had to be.[64]

But only a small vanguard of European public figures challenged
the rigid tenets of diplomatic orthodoxy by which government leaders
continued to be guided in the conduct of foreign relations.[65] With
the publication of *The Great Illusion* in 1909 Norman Angell emerged
as one of the best-known and most articulate spokesmen of the non-
Socialist antiwar groups. Angell maintained that given modern war
technology and the primacy of economic objectives in foreign policy,
even though recourse to war was not impossible war had ceased to
be an effective and profitable instrument of national policy. He sought
to alert the attentive public to the dangers of accepting as self-evident

63. Ibid., p. 219.
64. Gilbert K. Chesterton, *What's Wrong with the World* (New York, Dodd,
Mead, 1910), p. 103.
65. Many of the important European public figures who either favored or were
attentive to the New Diplomacy campaign are listed in Norman Angell's article
"War and Peace, 1914," in Julian Bell, ed., *We Did Not Fight* (London, Cobden-
Sanderson, 1935), pp. 43–60.

truths certain axiomatic premises of foreign policy that were either "dangerous half-truths or complete and utter fallacies." [66]

Profoundly skeptical of the widely accepted policy assumption that "the way to be sure of peace is to be so much stronger than your enemy that he dare not attack you," Angell declared that the underlying axioms of international politics—as recently expounded by Admiral Mahan, General Bernhardi, and Winston Churchill—were in need of drastic revision. "We are told by all the political experts that great navies and great armies are necessary to protect our wealth against the aggression of powerful neighbors, whose cupidity and voracity can be controlled by force alone; that treaties avail nothing, and that in international politics might makes right, that military and commercial security are identical, that armaments are justified by the necessity of commercial security; that our navy is an 'insurance', and that a country without military power with which their diplomats can 'bargain' in the Council of Europe is at a hopeless disadvantage economically." Angell argued that this power-based and profit-seeking approach to international politics was sadly inadequate to meet the challenge of Europe's constantly rising diplomatic tensions.[67]

Specifically, in connection with the explosive Anglo-German rivalry, the time had come to raise the basic question of why Germany had turned into a belligerently dissatisfied power. In Angell's view the answer could be found only by examining the combined population and economic growth which was leaving deep imprints on German foreign policy. Neither Europe's diplomats nor Germany's political leaders could afford to ignore these pressures. In vague terms but with profound conviction Angell insisted that largely because the recent intensification of economic and political interdependence among nations had caused a gradual decline in the effectiveness of economic and financial transfers by the victors, such pressures could only be resolved through peaceful accommodation by the leading powers. This vague policy prescription was based on the general proposition "that the world had passed out of that stage of development in which

66. Angell, *After All* (London, Hamilton, 1951), p. 138.
67. Angell, *The Foundations of International Polity* (London, Heinemann, 1914), p. 201, and *The Great Illusion: A Study of the Relation of Military Power to National Advantage* (4th rev. ed. New York, Putnam, 1913), pp. 15–19, 37, 342–49.

it is possible for one civilized group to advance its well-being by the military domination of another." [68]

Would recourse to war, followed by either German or British victory, lead to the indispensable yet difficult integration of Germany's fast-growing economy into the web of international trade? Would the annexation or disannexation of Alsace-Lorraine lead to the liquidation of the parties hostile to the status quo in either Germany or France? For how long could even a successful war enable the Dual Monarchy to delay essential nationality reforms? Only a few troubled minds posed these and similar questions. Angell readily admitted that "a change in the political conduct of Europe [could] only come about as the result of a change of thought," and that however little the Traditionalists "may deem reason to affect the conduct of men, [men nevertheless] go on reasoning." Angell's brief, then, was not primarily for a new morality or ethics in international politics; instead he called for a "hard and systematic intellectual effort" as a vital prerequisite for the amelioration of the threatening crisis. [69]

Moreover, while expressing the earnest hope that domestic and international tensions could be adjusted through rational, peaceful accommodation, a few lonely but articulate voices also warned about the far-reaching moral, economic, and military cost of total war. Perhaps they hoped that such a cost analysis, which was bound to be frightening, might shake some statesmen's trust in war as an effective and legitimate instrument of national policy. They invited Europe's attentive public to consider carefully whether under conditions of modern warfare victory was likely to guarantee political and economic benefits, or whether victor and vanquished alike were destined to share the legacy of large-scale destruction. Also, would a major battle among enemy brothers not endanger Europe's privileged position of world leadership by weakening her vis-à-vis the newly emerging non-European power centers?

68. Angell, *The Great Illusion*, pp. 131-51, 329.

69. Ibid., pp. 341, 356, 374. In addition to Angell, J. A. Hobson and E. D. Morel were influential in shaping the Radical critique of traditional foreign-policy thinking in prewar England. The often conflicting premises of their provocative writings are analyzed in A. J. P. Taylor, *The Trouble Makers: Dissent over Foreign Policy, 1792-1939* (London, Hamilton, 1957), pp. 95-131, and, more briefly, in Laurence W. Martin, *Peace without Victory: Woodrow Wilson and the British Liberals* (New Haven, Yale University Press, 1958), pp. 7-13.

True, once hostilities had broken out, France, Péguy, Wells, Verhaeren, and Zweig—like so many other European intellectuals—were swept along by the war-generated patriotism.[70] Nevertheless a few outstanding European intellectuals, among them leading Radical publicists in England, failed to become completely infected by the nationalist fever and remained unconvinced by slogans hailing the enemy's military defeat as the key to a golden future. For example, André Gide, while nursing tender hopes for a better world, saw that

> Cette guerre n'est pas pareille à une autre guerre;
> Il n'est pas seulement question d'un territoire à protéger,
> D'un patrimoine, d'une tradition . . . Non! c'est un avenir qui
>   veut naître
> Enorme et se dégage en s'ensanglant les pieds . . .
> Pauvre âme incertaine, tu ne peux t'éprendre
> A la fois de l'avenir et du passé.
> Il s'agit de voir si tu veux rester pleurant sur des cendres,
> Si vers la tombe enfin il ne te reste plus qu'à descendre
> Ou si, dans l'inconnu, tu te sens assez jeune encore pour
>   t'élancer.[71]

Sigmund Freud was shocked because he had expected that "the great ruling powers among the white nations upon whom the leadership of the human species has fallen . . . would succeed in discovering another way of settling misunderstandings and conflicts of interest."[72]

70. The changing mood of many of Europe's leading thinkers is clearly reflected in Romain Rolland's published wartime diary and correspondence. After Belgium was overrun by the Germans, Verhaeren turned into an ardent *aboutiste*, while Anatole France and Charles Péguy, even at their advanced age, volunteered their services to the French Ministry of War. Péguy proved his dedication to the French cause by giving up his life on one of the battlefields. Though Zweig never denounced Allied motives publicly, as did Gerhardt Hauptmann, in Rolland's eyes his silence added up to an implicit approval of the Centrist cause. Only Rolland relentlessly voiced his dissent from his self-chosen Geneva refuge. Though he greatly admired Karl Liebknecht and Rosa Luxemburg for their courage in dramatizing their antiwar position inside Germany, Rolland never became a Socialist. He did give his support to the forces of movement, more particularly because he shared the all-European and Internationalist outlook of the Left. Romain Rolland, *Journal des années de guerre, 1914–1919*, Paris, Albin Michel, 1952.

71. *The Journals of André Gide,* trans. Justin O'Brien (3 vols. London, Secker and Warburg, 1948), 2, 96–97 (November 15, 1914).

72. *Collected Papers* (London, Hogarth Press, 1950), 4, 289.

Furthermore, Freud noted that because of the "enormously increased perfection of weapons" the war would be "more sanguinary and more destructive than any war of other days." Like so many of his fellow "civilized cosmopolitans" he stood helpless before a world grown strange, with his "all-embracing patrimony disintegrated." [73]

Romain Rolland, author of the prophetic *Jean Christophe*, and August Rodin, creator of the imposing "Penseur," also trembled for the future of traditional Europe, especially when they heard first of the destruction of Louvain's art treasures and then of the mutilation of the Cathedral at Reims. Rolland courageously stepped *Au-dessus de la mêlée* in order to denounce mercilessly not only German brutality but also the narrow-minded policies of his own Government, which to his mind had contributed to the crisis in July 1914.

> La guerre européenne, cette mêlée sacrilège, qui offre le spectacle d'une Europe démente, montant sur le bûcher et se déchirant de ses mains. . . . Ainsi, les trois plus grands peuples d'Occident, les gardiens de la civilisation, s'acharnent à leur ruine et appellent à la rescousse les Cossaques, les Turcs, les Japonais, les Cinghalais, les Soudanais, les Sénégalais, les Marocains . . . les âmes et les paux de toutes les couleurs.[74]

Even though both Freud's and Rolland's reflections are tinged with racial overtones,[75] they convey the troubled thoughts of great men concerned with the future of their civilization. As the third year of the bitter internecine struggle began, Romain Rolland uttered another pathetic cry of despair: "adieu, Europe, reine de la pensée, guide de l'humanité! Tu as perdu ton chemin, tu piétines dans un cimetière. Ta place est là. Couche-toi! —Et que d'autres conduisent le monde!" [76]

Similar voices were audible in the British isles. In May 1915 Beatrice Webb, momentarily more conscious of her European heritage than of her Socialist convictions, confided to her diary that this furious war seemed "almost like the end of civilization." [77] Likewise, G. B. Shaw considered the war as both a "cataclysm" and "the crash of an

73. Ibid., pp. 292, 294.
74. *Au-dessus de la mêlée* (Paris, Ollendorf, 1915), pp. 24–25. See also Rolland, *Journal*, p. 56.
75. Cf. Rolland, *Au-dessus de la mêlée*, pp. 162–63.
76. *Demain: Pages et Documents*, 11/12 (November/December, 1916), 266.
77. Cole, p. 36.

epoch" whose magnitude and significance were difficult, if not impossible, to describe.[78] By late 1916 D. H. Lawrence, haunted by the danger of spiritual bankruptcy, indirectly asked Lord Asquith "whether England ought not to say 'enough of war' while we are yet alive." [79]

Meanwhile Walter Hines Page, the fervently anglophile American Ambassador in London, confided to President Wilson that if this should prove not to be the last war, "life's not worth living and civilization is a delusion." [80] By the middle of October 1914 the Ambassador, in another dispatch to the President, observed that "it is not the same world it was last July . . . nothing is the same. All one's measures and centers of reference are different; and the people you meet have changed; and all talk somehow seems hollow. You wonder yourself if you mean what you say, for you are all the time readjusting yourself to some great shock of things that has hitherto seemed incredible." [81] Only after having pondered over the many-sided implications of the war for more than a year did Page hesitantly suggest that "this smash of things in Europe may hasten democracy." [82] In a similar vein President Wilson soon concluded that the world would "never be the same after this War is over," and that the change, which might be for weal or for woe, would be "fundamental and tremendous." [83]

Some of Europe's most sensitive minds formulated these premonitions about the deepening of the war into a major crisis before the Russian Revolution had broken out and before the morale-consuming military stalemate had settled over the Continent's battlefields. These prophetic forebodings are important because they were uttered by many of the same men who, once this crisis actually was upon Europe, sought either to formulate or to espouse new ideologies.

The crisis matured in 1917—the year which Raymond Poincaré, the rigidly conservative President of the French Republic, significantly

78. *What I Really Wrote about the War* (New York, Brentano, 1932), pp. 240–41.

79. Correspondence with Lady Asquith, in Aldous Huxley, ed., *The Letters of D. H. Lawrence* (London, Heinemann, 1932), pp. 381–82, 385.

80. Burton J. Hendrick, *The Life and Letters of Walter Hines Page* (3 vols. New York, Doubleday, 1926), 3, 172.

81. Ibid., p. 165.

82. Walter Hines Page, Diary, December 1915, in the Papers of Walter H. Page, Houghton Library, Harvard University.

83. Ray Stannard Baker and William E. Dodd, eds., *The Public Papers of Woodrow Wilson* (6 vols. New York, Harper, 1925–27), 4, 36–37.

chose to christen *l'année trouble*.[84] The year became witness to the
Russian turmoil, to *la guerre des tranchées*, to the turnip winter, to
rising war weariness, to a revival of the Second International, to
serious fissures in Europe's political truce, and to a shift in the center
of world power away from Western Europe.

To many observers the Revolution in Russia seemed to have all
the qualities of the opening act of a revolutionary drama shortly
to be enacted all over Europe. Men of Walther Rathenau's reforming
temperament now expressed the conviction that the war "had been
destined to develop into a world revolution," a conviction soon to be
shared by many Central European statesmen. These statesmen, who
were geographically closest to the Russian upheaval, despaired of
saving the Old Order as the Central European fortress threatened to
collapse. Faced by the irreparable disintegration of the Dual Monarchy, Count Czernin predicted that "the coming generation [would]
not call the drama of the last five years the World War, but the world
revolution which it [would] realize began with the world war."
Similarly, Bethmann-Hollweg declared that the war could be understood only if it were considered in the context of "the total evolution
of humanity and of its spirit." Gustav Stresemann, who also saw the
war as part of a world revolution which would profoundly stir all aspects of life, predicted that this revolution was destined to continue
long after the formal end of hostilities.[85]

Since even representatives of the "establishment" eventually recognized the revolutionary consequences of the protracted military struggle, Europe's Socialists, especially their most radical spokesmen, could
be expected to hail the crisis with enthusiasm. Not even the most
imaginative revolutionaries, however, had looked to Russia for the
initial revolutionary breakthrough. Now many of them hastened to
explain why it was not unnatural that the war should have undermined first the stability of Europe's most politically and economically
retarded belligerent. All along, many revolutionaries had agreed
with Rosa Luxemburg that the war was "ordained to give the cause

84. *Au Service de la France* (10 vols. Paris, Plon, 1932), 9.
85. Walter Rathenau, *Nach der Flut* (Berlin, S. Fischer, 1919), p. 44; Ottokar
Czernin, *Im Weltkriege* (Berlin, Ullstein, 1919), p. 372; T. von Bethmann-Hollweg,
Betrachtungen zum Weltkriege (2 vols. Berlin, Hobbingen, 1922), 2, 32; Gustav
Stresemann, *Von der Revolution bis zum Frieden von Versailles* (Berlin, Staatspoli-
tischer, 1919), pp. 169–70.

of labor a mighty impetus." [86] According to Trotsky, in Russia history presently proceeded to pick up "the end of the revolutionary threads broken by the war." As in the rest of Europe, in the tsarist Empire the war had at first retarded the forces of movement, only to accelerate them "more powerfully in the next period." [87] Especially the most extreme Socialists failed to assess realistically the causes of the Russian Revolution. These Maximalists grossly exaggerated the positive contribution of Russia's Socialist parties at the same time they ignored those adverse economic and military developments which were condemning Russia to both defeat and anarchy.

Guided by their ideological preconceptions, the Maximalists hailed the revolutionary events in Russia as incontrovertible evidence that "there would be no world peace except on the ruins of bourgeois society." [88] Trotsky confidently declared that the war had "transformed the whole of Europe into a powder magazine of social revolution." [89] According to this view, if in semifeudal Russia a relatively weak and ill-organized proletariat had taken such giant strides, the better-organized working classes of Western Europe and Great Britain were bound to make the revolutionary advances which the Basle Manifesto had predicted. The Social Patriots, however, assessed the new situation more soberly, partly because their analyses were colored by the interpretation which the war cabinets placed on the Russian Revolution. On the other hand, although the Independent Socialists were far more optimistic than the majority Socialists, they were more reserved in their enthusiasm than the Maximalists.[90]

86. *The Crisis in the German Social Democracy* (New York, Socialist Publication Society, 1919), p. 12. According to one of the leading students of modern history and politics the war was "destined to serve as the forcing house for the seeds of revolution." See E. H. Carr, *The Bolshevik Revolution, 1917–1923* (3 vols. London, Macmillan, 1950–53), *1*, 65.

87. *The History of the Russian Revolution* (3 vols. London, Gollancz, 1932), *1*, 50, 121.

88. *Spartakusbriefe* (Berlin, 1920), Letter 7 (November 1917), p. 135.

89. Isaac Deutscher, *The Prophet Armed: Trotsky, 1879–1921* (New York and London, Oxford University Press, 1954), p. 246.

90. On March 28, 1917, the *Sozialistische Monatshefte*, p. 20, whose editors at the time were only slightly to the left of the SPD leaders, referred to the war as "an agitated period, bringing the most significant changes in its wake, and which in spite of its horrors will give (*we hope*) humanity a powerful propulsion forwards and upwards." Cf. Karl Kautsky, in *Die Neue Zeit* (March 30, 1917), p. 609; *New Republic* (May 5, 1917), pp. 4–5; *Journal de Genève*, March 18, 1917, and August 2, 1917.

These preliminary reactions to the *année trouble* will have to be supplemented by a detailed analysis of its causes as well as its political and diplomatic consequences. In the meantime, however, Elie Halévy's perceptive conclusion must be noted: "The world crisis was not only a war—the war of 1914—but a revolution—the revolution of 1917." [91] Not since the Napoleonic Wars had the world been thrown into a major crisis in which "millions of bayonets were in search of an idea (ideology)." [92] If the war had lasted but a few months, it undoubtedly "would have been a mere parenthesis in history." [93] However, the conflict dragged on until it not only endangered most of the existing political and economic institutions but also brought about a re-evaluation of many leading conceptions for the solution of long-standing domestic and international problems. This intellectual upheaval was destined to be "the point of departure of that great crisis of modern civilization of which the world war [was] but the prologue—a crisis which promised to be universal, economic, intellectual and moral." [94]

It would seem, then, that in March 1917 the military collision among the major European Powers was being transformed from a war of limited objectives into a worldwide revolutionary and ideological struggle. Even the "wars of Marlborough or Napoleon appear as quiet little affairs when compared to the cataclysm of 1914–1918." [95] No wonder that with "millions of bayonets in search of an idea," efforts to fashion an ideology out of time-tested but emotionally uninspiring formulas like self-defense and security were doomed to failure.

Because the war crisis was instrumental in provoking thought among both leaders and followers, the issues and objectives of the war eventually received more attention than any other subject of public discussion. Especially during the eternal stalemate which taxed the patience and endurance of both soldier and civilian, debates about war aims and peace programs overshadowed all talk of wartime and postwar domestic reforms. Perhaps the clearest index of the priority achieved by war-aims debates in 1917 can be gathered from the Rus-

91. *The World Crisis*, p. 5.
92. Guglielmo Ferrero, *Die Tragödie des Friedens von Versailles* (Jena, Frommanschen, 1923), pp. 6–7.
93. Sir Halford J. Mackinder, *Democratic Ideals and Reality* (New York, Holt, 1942), p. 26.
94. Ferrero, *Europe's Fateful Hour*, p. 197.
95. G. M. Trevelyan, *The War and the European Revolution in Relation to History* (London, University of London Press, 1920), p. 43.

sian situation: the proletariat, the peasants, and the soldiers threw their weight behind the Bolsheviks not so much because Lenin promised an early equalitarian society, but rather because he promised to negotiate peace immediately.[96] To the extent that the Central and Western European governments were less plagued by war weariness and political dissent than Russia, they were in a position to prevent the war-aims debate from leading to a premature, negotiated peace (without victory).

It is interesting to speculate how Europe-at-war would have emerged from this military and political crisis if the United States had not thrown her weight into the scales. Would Germany have been able to make military capital out of Russia's disorganization, only subsequently to bring her full military might to bear on the Western front? In the absence of any promises of help from Washington, could Paris, London, and Rome have resisted internal Socialist pressures for the immediate exploration of a compromise peace based on the Petrograd Soviet's peace formula, especially with Wilson lending his moral authority to a peace without victory? Would a negotiated peace have strengthened the position of the Social Democratic party in Germany? In 1917–18 was there serious danger that Europe's center of political gravity might shift decidedly to the Left as a result of the break-through on the diplomatic front by the parties of movement? Moreover, could a compromise peace in the middle of 1917 have served to stabilize the Provisional Government in Petrograd before the Bolsheviks had a chance to capitalize not only on Russia's rapid military collapse but also on the pathetic peace hunger of the Russian peasantry and proletariat?

Obviously, these questions cannot be answered. They do direct attention, however, to one of the most momentous developments of the war: the simultaneous emergence of Washington and Petrograd as two rival centers of power, both of which momentarily abandoned the Old Diplomacy.

In April 1917 the United States entered the war conveniently free from the fetters of both prewar alliances and wartime secret treaties. Furthermore, her President, who was religiously dedicated to the New Diplomacy, was in a position to assert his diplomatic leadership with the help of crucial reserves of manpower and war materiel. Consequently the Wilson Administration combined its recourse

96. See below, Chap. 5.

to the New Diplomacy with decisive and immediate military and economic strength.

On the other hand, when in March 1917 Russia began to turn into an ardent champion of the New Diplomacy, she was burdened by a legacy of extreme military and economic weakness. Because she was facing imminent military defeat, it is perhaps not surprising that her version of the New Diplomacy, unlike the American version, should gradually have placed increasing emphasis on a negotiated peace. When the foreign-policy platform of the Socialists, who emerged as the political carriers of a compromise peace in Petrograd, was turned into Russian state policy, it necessarily became intertwined with their domestic reform program. And once Russia combined self-abnegation in foreign policy—her renunciation of the Straits—with far-reaching political and economic reforms, she acquired great ideological power which partly, at any rate, compensated for her naked military weakness.

In brief, both Russia and America stepped forward to champion the New Diplomacy; the former from a position of weakness, the latter from a position of strength. Even after Russia's Bolshevik Government left the war, it continued to deny America sole sponsorship of idealistic aims like open diplomacy, self-determination, and popular control of foreign policy. Moreover, as Europe's Socialists and Radicals prepared to agitate for a peace of principles, the Bolshevik synthesis of foreign and domestic reforms was not without attraction.

Hence, during the *année trouble*, when the European forces of movement became politically vocal and impatient, America and Russia —Wilson and Lenin—offered them a similar foreign-policy ideology, though for essentially different purposes. Wilson counseled the Allied Governments to formulate liberal war aims in order to rekindle the fighting spirit of the Allied masses and to strengthen the enemy forces of movement which were undermining the political truce in the Central camp. On the other hand, Lenin sought to advance the proletarian revolution by convincing Europe's war-weary masses that it would be expedient to couple the issues of an immediate compromise peace with those of domestic reform. In the midst of the crisis, however, this ideological rivalry merely served to emphasize further the seriousness of the challenge to the Old Diplomacy. Both Wilson and Lenin rejected secret diplomacy, annexations, and trade discriminations. Therefore it was inevitable that Wilson and the Wilsonians should have ended by fellow-traveling with Socialists of all shades, just as Lenin proceeded to fellow-travel even with pacifist-internationalist Liberals.

It would seem, then, that a study of the emergence of the New Diplomacy must pay careful attention to "various subterranean currents of opinions or events of which the official utterances were often the expression, and which were frequently of more importance in themselves than the formal statements." [97] Indeed, Wilson's war-aims pronouncements, and the subsequently half-hearted Allied endorsement of progressive war aims, can be explicated only by an analysis of the political, economic, and military conditions of their genesis.

5. *The Political Carriers of the New Diplomacy*

This fusion of the war with a revolutionary crisis, which will subsequently be viewed in greater detail, is an essential dimension of the historical background for the study of the evolution of Allied war aims. For the crisis of 1917 fortified those social and political forces which questioned the basic assumption of the struggle and became the carriers of the New Diplomacy.

Undoubtedly "it is curious that the greatest conflict of power in modern times should have been increasingly conducted for the sake of repudiating 'power politics.'" [98] However, the eventual ideological predominance of Wilson's Fourteen Points seems less perplexing once the repudiation of external power politics is viewed against the background of the revival of internal power conflicts. For the very political parties and factions which became the most outspoken and effective critics of power politics were the ones to challenge the power position of the forces of order which had consummated the annexationist secret treaties. Indeed, the fact that the Old Diplomacy was put on the defensive was due "less to any alteration in ethical standards, than to a shift in the center of power." [99]

It follows, therefore, that the destruction in August 1914 of all antiwar and anti-Old-Diplomacy forces, especially of antiwar Socialism,

97. James Brown Scott, ed., in introductory note to *Official Statements of War Aims and Peace Proposals: December 1916 to November 1918*, Washington, Carnegie Endowment for International Peace, 1921.
98. Taylor, *The Struggle for Mastery in Europe*, p. 537.
99. Nicolson, *Diplomacy*, p. 60.

should not be exaggerated.[100] Instead, in view of their reappearance in 1917, it is important to emphasize that these forces were "only submerged for a time, not annihilated." [101] Moreover, the very conditions created by the war were instrumental in resuscitating them from their temporary political eclipse. It should also be noted that the leaders of the major dissenting factions used the years of political submergence from August 1914 to March 1917 to specify and articulate their ideas on foreign policy.

What, then, were the significant components of the forces of movement which gradually reasserted themselves in the course of 1917? Furthermore, what were their foreign-policy platforms? Above all, what were the significant foreign-policy propositions on which these forces of movement, anything but homogeneous, were agreed?

The Socialist parties were by far the largest numerical component of the forces of movement inside each of the major European nations. In spite of bitter disagreements in the prewar years among various Socialist factions on issues like imperialism, military service, and self-determination, on the whole the hatred of war never ceased to be equally pronounced in the Socialist parties of Germany, France, and Great Britain. All Socialists, with the possible exception of the German "social imperialists," shared an ethical revulsion against war which found programmatic expression in pacifist-internationalist resolutions adopted at party and trade union conclaves as well as at international congresses.[102]

But even before August 1914 the theoreticians of pacifist internationalism had found it increasingly difficult to win whole-hearted support for their antiwar stand from the recently crystallized caste of

100. Many students of the collapse of the Second International tend to equate this collapse with the total disintegration of the Socialist parties throughout Europe. They fail to note that both the organizational structure and the ideological pronouncements of Socialism were merely deactivated during the transitional period of the political truce. Cf. Franz Borkenau, *The Communist International* (London, Faber and Faber, 1938), chap. 4; and James Joll, *The Second International, 1889–1914* (London, Weidenfeld and Nicolson, 1955), pp. 158 ff.

101. Halévy, *The World Crisis*, p. 41. In Germany, "the immediate consequence of the war was to bridge over, although not to close" the breach between the Imperial government and the parties of movement. Rosenberg, *The Birth of the German Republic*, p. 58.

102. For a judicious selection of prewar statements and resolutions on various issues of war by individual Socialists or by national and international Socialist congresses see Walling. See also above, n. 61.

party and trade union officials. Especially in Germany centrists like Haase, Kautsky, and Ledebour clashed head on with the leading members of the party and trade union apparatus, even though these centrists' antiwar position instead of being revolutionary was merely "an extension of Social Democratic domestic policy into the sphere of foreign affairs." [103] But all Socialist movements had to sustain this strain of reconciling the ideology of pacifist internationalism propounded by some of their foremost theoreticians with the tenets of loyal patriotism of the party's and trade union's bread-and-butter politicians. In this connection it should be emphasized that in Britain, France, and Germany, much of Socialism's organized numerical strength was in the trade unions: and with the exception of the syndicalist unions in France these tended to cast their lot with the conservative elements of the political Left.

The outbreak of war confirmed the fact that notwithstanding their general intellectual brilliance, the proponents of pacifist internationalism were at the periphery rather than at the center of power in Europes Socialist parties. Immediately the party and trade union leaders stepped forward to proclaim their unswerving loyalty to the national cause, thereby providing the essential basis for the establishment of the *Burgfrieden*. Under the shock of war as well as because of the urgency of declaring their loyalty or disloyalty, the erstwhile opponents of this policy of Social Patriotism either swung over to the majority position or avoided all public pronouncements. Only a very few nationally and internationally recognized leaders had the courage to proclaim that their own country was partly at fault, that a campaign to stop the war should immediately be launched, or that every effort should be made to transform the war into a proletarian revolution.[104]

Once this mass *volte-face* to the national cause had been completed, the spectrum of prewar factions gradually began to reappear.

103. Schorske, *German Social Democracy*, pp. 263–64.
104. Lewis L. Lorwin, *Labor and Internationalism* (New York, MacMillan, 1929), pp. 89–96, 134–46; Edouard Dolléans, *Histoire du mouvement ouvrier* (4th ed. 3 vols. Paris, Armand Colin, 1953), 2, 206–26; Brogan, *The Development of Modern France*, pp. 527–30; David J. Saposs, *The Labor Movement in Post-war France* (New York, Columbia University Press, 1931), pp. 24–32; Sidney and Beatrice Webb, *The History of Trade Unionism* (rev. ed. extended to 1920, London, Longmans, Green, 1920), pp. 636–48, 696–98; Carl F. Brand, *British Labour's Rise to Power* (Stanford, Stanford University Press, 1941), pp. 28 ff.; R. T. McKenzie, *British Political Parties* (New York, St. Martin's Press, 1955), pp. 398–404.

On the extreme right a relatively small ultranationalist faction emerged, led by right-wing revisionists like Paul Lensch, Gustave Hervé, and Havelock Wilson. Obviously this chauvinist sector of the Socialist movement never pressured either the war cabinets or the majority Socialists for a formulation of liberal, nonannexationist war aims. Throughout the war Hervé never faltered in his dedication to peace through unmistakable military victory.

No doubt the war enthusiasm of these right-revisionists compared favorably with that of even the most extreme Conservatives. Nevertheless the war cabinets were interested above all in laying the basis for solid cooperation with the Socialist majority factions whose support would be decisive in the long run, primarily because they commanded the loyalty of millions of workers. These majority Socialists, otherwise also known as Social Patriots, eagerly threw their full weight behind the war effort. This unconditional abandonment of antiwar internationalism by the SFIO and the Labour party immediately brought forth an invitation to participate in coalition cabinets. During the first three years of war, Albert Thomas and Arthur Henderson, in their ministerial capacity, came to symbolize the era of good feeling between the forces of order and the majority of the forces of movement. Meanwhile Léon Jouhaux and J. H. Thomas channeled near-complete trade union support to the war enterprise.

Similarly, in Germany the Social Democratic party and the trade unions enthusiastically embraced the cause of the Central Powers. Even though the SPD never was honored with an invitation to enter the War Cabinet, Philipp Scheidemann and Carl Legien all along discharged their crucial wartime duties with the same diligence and devotion as their confrères in the Allied camp.

Unlike the leaders in the right-revisionist wing, the leaders of the Social Patriots in the Entente as well as in the Central nations never ceased to examine carefully the wartime diplomacy of their respective governments. True, at first they uncritically accepted official interpretations of the causes and issues of the war and rejected all proposals for a negotiated peace. However, especially once the military conflict developed into the crisis of 1917–18, the majority Socialists became increasingly critical of the cabinets' failure to formulate liberal, nonannexationist war aims. With the wartime governments showing signs of severe military and economic strain, the Socialist parties gradually rededicated themselves to the rights of small nations, popular control of foreign policy, control of armaments, and international organization. Official refusal to renounce publicly all projects of national self-extension merely reinforced the pressures in favor of the New Diplomacy.

Undoubtedly the Majoritarians were also driven to this more activist war-aims position by the third faction in the Socialist camp, namely the Independents. During the first year of war this third faction was completely overshadowed by the extreme right and the moderate center, and its influence was negligible. Right from the start, however, it styled itself as the self-appointed custodian of the foreign-policy platform of prewar Socialism. True, this remnant of Socialist Internationalists never came out against the war, and initially joined the majority in voting war credits. Nevertheless, their enthusiasm for the national cause always was dampened by grave reservations about their government's policies. Specifically, the left-revisionists rejected the monolithic interpretation of the causes of the war, demanded an official pronouncement of liberal war aims, and criticized the search for unconditional military victory. It was in this politically marginal but ideologically decisive wing of the various Socialist parties that the most searching discussion of the basic issues of the war was carried out in the light of Socialist doctrine.

In Great Britain the Independent Labour party (ILP) offered a ready-made organizational home for these Labourites who, while supporting the war effort with varying degrees of enthusiasm, immediately decided to press for Britain's commitment both to nonannexationist war aims and to a search for a compromise victory. Though weak politically, both in the Parliamentary Labour party and in Labour's local constituencies, the ILP won considerable stature by virtue of its impressive leadership. Keir Hardie, Ramsay MacDonald, Philip Snowden, and F. W. Jowett, its most noted spokesmen, never wavered in their determination to dissent from the majority's uncritical endorsement of the Cabinet's foreign and domestic policies. Meanwhile, in cooperation with Radical dissidents inside the Union of Democratic Control they proceeded to work out a Radical-Labour war-aims and peace program. Finally, in 1917, the ILP began to influence first Labour's and then Lloyd George's foreign policy.

Unlike their counterparts in England, in France and Germany the Socialist dissidents were not so fortunate as to find a political organization ready to receive them. The French minority Socialists organized a small committee within the SFIO and fashioned an amorphous connection with non-Socialist groups like the Société d'Etudes Documentaires et Critiques sur la Guerre and the Ligue des Droits de l'Homme. As of 1917, under the impact of the stalemate and the Russian Revolution, the war-aims platform of the *minoritaires* was gradually fused with the majority program under the direction and auspices of leading Social Patriots.

Also in Germany the left-wing revisionists at first coexisted uncomfortably with the Social Patriots in the various party and trade union organs, as well as in the SPD Reichstag delegation. They became restless, however, when their SPD leaders acquiesced to what were obviously imperialist objectives. Under the leadership of Haase, Bernstein, Kautsky, and Ledebour, they gradually "urged that the party answer the annexationist threat by taking the national lead in a campaign for a peace of understanding." [105] Since the SPD leaders were not willing to placate their left flank for fear of endangering their privileged relationship with the Government, the dissidents became increasingly rebellious. By the time the Russian Revolution had broken out, Germany's left-wing revisionists had decided to organize the Independent Social Democratic party (USPD). Again, under the pressures of the crisis year, the German Social Patriots also began to assimilate some of the USPD's foreign-policy objectives.

To recapitulate, the major factions of the Socialist spectrum in England, France, and Germany, moving from right to left, were (1) the right-wing revisionists, (2) the Social Patriots, and (3) the Independent Socialists.

Still a fourth Socialist faction must be identified, namely the Revolutionary Socialists, or Maximalists. In all nations except Germany their political importance was altogether marginal, even within the Socialist movement. In Germany, as well as in other belligerent nations, leading revolutionaries like Karl Liebknecht and Rosa Luxemburg were eventually confined to prison. Some of the other Maximalists, and among them many Russian Bolsheviks, were in exile in neutral countries; thus they were able to attend the Zimmerwald and/or the Kienthal Congress.

The war-aims and peace program and strategy of this extreme Left can best be studied in Lenin's writings of the early war years, particularly in those articles which deal critically with the policies of the

105. Schorske, *German Social Democracy*, p. 305.

Independent Socialists. However, only after the Bolsheviks began to preach and practice successfully their revolutionary defeatism in crisis-torn Russia did the Leninist antiwar theses begin to affect the other sectors of the Socialist movement.

Throughout Europe, with the significant exception of Russia, the effective influence and power of the Left never ceased to be vested in the Social Patriotic center. However, this uninterrupted monopoly of effective political power was not paralleled by a constancy in ideological commitments. After the crisis of 1917 had matured, the Majoritarians began to challenge the Independents' monopoly on Socialist war-aims and peace programs. Eventually the Social Patriots almost completely supplanted the left-revisionists as the effective political carriers of the New Diplomacy.

Before the end of the war a double movement had occurred. First, by becoming the carriers of the central tenets of the New Diplomacy, the Social Patriots denied their Independent rivals the platform with which to compete for the allegiance of the proletariat and of other sectors of the forces of movement. Second, by incorporating, even if only on the verbal level, certain liberal foreign-policy ideas into official war-aims pronouncements, the war cabinets avoided a deepening of the rift between the forces of order and the forces of movement. In Russia, however, effective power shifted toward first the Independents and then the Maximalists, no doubt partly because the domestic crisis became so serious that verbal concessions ceased to be adequate. Only the Bolsheviks were prepared to transform the slogan of peace without victory into immediate state policy.

No less important than the diverse Socialist components of the forces of movement were the non-Socialists. They consisted of the Radical wing of the Liberal parties, and of politically unorganized but far from uninfluential intellectuals. It should immediately be noted that disagreements among Socialists, Radicals, and intellectuals on domestic reforms did not hinder their cooperation on questions of war and peace, on which their ideas were remarkably similar.

Just as the Independents deserted from the Socialist establishment, taking the Internationalist ideology with them, so the Radicals prepared to separate from the Liberal majority, claiming the heritage of Gladstone and Bright for themselves.

In September 1914 certain Liberals like H. G. Wells enthusiastically supported the British War Cabinet after prematurely convincing themselves that this struggle was the War That Will End War. Likewise, across the Channel Anatole France summoned his compatriots to be *debout pour la dernière guerre*. Gladstonian Liberals on both sides of the Channel and the Atlantic further rationalized their war ardor with the belief that this terminal war would lead to the destruction of the last remnants of autocracy.[106] Though neither the first Asquith Coalition nor the left-of-center Radical Socialist cabinets in Paris officially identified themselves with such crusading slogans and beliefs, they tactfully refrained from interfering with this self-deception. Meanwhile, without flinching in their championing of the national cause, many Radicals joined with other progressives in a common effort to convert first the forces of movement and then the war cabinets to a liberal war-aims position.

In England such Radicals joined forces with Independent Labourites in the Union of Democratic Control. Though this united front was slower to develop in France, one or two similar pressure groups were organized in Paris. In Central Europe cooperation between left-wing Liberals and Socialists eventually also increased—without, however, taking the form of political organization.

The disillusionment that contributed to, and was an early manifestation of, the 1917–18 crisis led many intellectuals and literati to take an interest in political questions, above all in problems of war and peace. According to Karl Mannheim, because the class position of intellectuals tends to be less clearly defined than that of other classes which participate more directly in the economic process, they tend to have a less rigidly fixed political viewpoint. Especially that portion of the intelligentsia which is "socially unattached" is particularly prone to develop an acute alertness toward contemporary historical reality. When confronted with a crisis, many intellectuals tend to become the carriers of a "total orientation and synthesis . . . which will retain much of the accumulated cultural acquisitions and social energies of the previous epoch." [107] In 1917–18 many intellectuals developed a decided affinity for the foreign-policy ideology of the nascent united front, largely because this minority view now seemed to them useful in their search

106. H. G. Wells, *The War That Will End War* (London, Palmer, 1914), and *Experiment in Autobiography* (New York, Macmillan, 1934), p. 570.

107. See Mannheim, *Ideology and Utopia*, pp. 136–46.

for a total perspective. Especially in Europe, where intellectual élites are held in such high esteem, the importance of their conversion to left-sponsored internationalism should not be underestimated.

This synopsis of the major constituents of the forces of movement would be incomplete without a reference to Woodrow Wilson. When shortly before declaring war on Germany he spoke of the desirability of a "peace without victory," it became apparent that the American President's universe of discourse was similar to that of Europe's forces of movement. Once America had become a belligerent, Wilson abandoned all talk of mediation; instead he favored war-aims and peace formulas that were widely known and warmly espoused in progressive circles abroad.

It is generally acknowledged that Wilson's idealistic pronouncements about his war objectives successfully rallied most American pacifist-idealist, liberal, and Socialist reformers. Among the notable recruits to the crusade to make the world safe for democracy were Herbert Croly, Charles Beard, George Creel, Walter Weyl, Ray Stannard Baker, Frank Cobb, Upton Sinclair, Waldo Frank, and William Jennings Bryan. However, what is significant in the context of the political origins of the New Diplomacy is that Wilson was no less successful in winning the support of Europe's forces of movement. Although in England and France his war and peace aims helped to renew their allegiance to the Allied cause, in the enemy camp they served to undermine the political truce. Hence, before the war was over, the bourgeois-liberal President enjoyed the support not only of Radical Liberals and intellectuals like Norman Angell, Gilbert Murray, Joseph Paul-Boncour, Romain Rolland, Walther Rathenau, and Stefan Zweig, but also of Social Patriots and Independent Socialists like Arthur Henderson and Ramsay MacDonald, Albert Thomas and Jean Longuet, Philipp Scheidemann and Karl Kautsky.

6. Labour, UDC, and Lenin

How was this political fusion of Liberals and Socialists, particularly of Radical Liberals and of Independent Socialists, consummated in practice during the first two years of war? There are three reasons for viewing this fusion in England rather than on the Continent: first, because the political and ideological cooperation of Radicals and Independents was both most evident and most influential in Britain;

second, because in his polemic against the Morel-MacDonald axis in England, Lenin articulated the Maximalist critique of the nonrevolutionary war-aims position of the forces of movement; third, because the ideological position of the dissident Left in Britain has a close affinity to the final war-aims platform of President Wilson.

No sooner had the British Government declared war than certain leading Labour and Liberal dissidents began to explore ways of preparing public opinion for a "progressive" peace, which would prevent the sowing of seeds for future wars. Understandably they were concerned lest the inevitable war psychosis—the by-product of full-scale war mobilization—would interfere with the propagation of those war aims which alone, in their view, might justify the impending slaughter and destruction. Moreover, Britain's loyal dissidents hoped that they might counteract the patriotic fever more effectively by keeping a clear slate of liberal war aims before the public than by bemoaning the inevitable impairment of freedom of speech and assembly.[108]

As early as August 5, 1914, Ramsay MacDonald and Norman Angell conferred about the advisability of uniting all like-minded dissidents in a new nonpartisan pressure group. That same day Charles Trevelyan informed E. D. Morel that he and three other Radical MP's—Arthur Ponsonby, Philip Morrell, and Arnold Rowntree—were trying to establish a "connection with the Labour party" and that they might want Morel to become secretary of their group.[109]

Even before the war the left fringe of both the Liberal and the Labour parties had realized that in spite of their lack of agreement on domestic reforms, their views about international affairs had evolved in the same general direction. They were equally convinced of the dangers of secret diplomacy, competitive armaments, colonial rivalries, and trade restrictions. Nevertheless, for the time being Labourites and Radicals carried on separate antiwar campaigns in an effort to awaken the British public to the seriousness of mounting diplomatic tensions.

108. F. W. Hirst to E. D. Morel, August 19, 1914, in the E. D. Morel Papers, Library of the London School of Economics.

109. Angell, *After All*, p. 189; Charles Trevelyan to Morel, August 5, 1914, Morel Papers; Charles Trevelyan, *The Union of Democratic Control: History of Its Policy* (London, 1919), p. 1. The basic secondary sources for the history of UDC are H. M. Swanwick, *Builders of Peace*, London, Swarthmore Press, 1924; F. Seymour Cocks, *E. D. Morel: the Man and His Work*, London, Allen and Unwin, 1920; and Hermann Lutz, *E. D. Morel, der Man und sein Werk*, Berlin, Verlagsgesellschaft für Politik und Geschichte, 1925.

Actually, on the eve of the war there were sound tactical reasons for not fusing these two antiwar agitations. Especially the Labourites appreciated the tactical advantage of arousing non-Labour antiwar opinion through an independent Radical group untainted by overt leftist connections. Hence when Norman Angell approached Keir Hardie about the expediency of publishing a penny "Labour" edition of *The Great Illusion,* the dean of British Labour felt that it would be best not to "associate it too much with men like me." [110] Incidentally, even without official Labour endorsement Angell's thesis left a permanent mark not only on the British Left but also on Jean Jaurès and Marcel Sembat.[111]

In late July 1914 C. P. Scott, the forceful editor of the *Manchester Guardian,* forewarned that Britain's Liberal Government would be forced to turn conservative in case of war and predicted that "the next advance would have to be based on Radicalism and Labour." [112] Early in the war both Liberal and Labour parties rallied to the support of the War Government, while the radical wing of the Whigs and the Independent Labour party proceeded to fashion a common basis for loyal dissent. The war emergency served merely to crystallize further the dissidents' agreement on questions of foreign policy. Moreover, by striking questions of economic reform, on which the dissidents were least agreed, from the political agenda the war crisis actually helped to facilitate political cooperation between the Radicals and the Independent Labourites in the field of foreign affairs—more particularly in war aims. Furthermore, the gradual but persistent conservative reorientation of two successive Asquith cabinets, coupled with their inability or refusal to publicly spell out nonannexationist war aims, also cemented this union.

Presently the Union of Democratic Control was organized. Within a short time the UDC became the institutional medium for the interpenetration of the foreign-policy doctrines and ideologies of Britain's Radicals and Independent Socialists. Since domestic issues were not their primary concern, and since the UDC was a limited-purpose pres-

110. Angell, *After All,* p. 170. In France, "the question of peace and war, of foreign policy and militarism, linked Jaurès and an important section of the Radicals." Brogan, *The Development of Modern France,* p. 428.

111. Max Bonnafous, ed., *Oeuvres de Jean Jaurès* (9 vols. Paris, Editions Rieder, 1931–39), 4, 237; and Sembat, *Faites un roi sinon faites la paix,* pp. 256–58.

112. Cited in J. L. Hammond, *C. P. Scott of the Manchester Guardian* (London, Bell, 1934), p. 178.

sure group, each faction maintained its regular party affiliations. For the moment Radicals like Trevelyan, Ponsonby, Morel, Angell, Noel Buxton, and Charles Buxton stayed with the Liberal party, hopeful that after the first flush of nationalist intoxication Lord Asquith and Sir Edward Grey would espouse the UDC platform. The Socialist contingent in UDC, consisting of Ramsay MacDonald, Philip Snowden, George Lansbury, and H. N. Brailsford, was perhaps no less confident that before long the Labour party and the Trades Union Congress would return to an internationalist position. [113]

In Parliament a small group of UDC backbenchers spearheaded by MacDonald, Snowden, Ponsonby, and Trevelyan repeatedly questioned the unqualified prowar position of both the Labour and the Liberal parties. In view of the dominant Liberal role in two successive Asquith cabinets which failed to formulate progressive war aims, it is not surprising that the Radicals became increasingly estranged from their parent party. Furthermore, their intimate contact with the dynamic and confident leaders of the ILP—Ramsay MacDonald, Fenner Brockway, Bruce Glasier, F. W. Jowett, George Lansbury—made them doubtful of the Liberal party's future ability to count on worker votes to maintain its position in the House of Commons.

For the time being, Morel, as secretary of the nonpartisan UDC, did not declare himself a Socialist. Nevertheless, he agreed that if "Socialism means, as I take it to mean, the betterment and increased happiness of humanity," how could he be taken for anything else? Furthermore, Morel recognized that "it may well be that the time will come when I shall have to 'classify' myself so far as internal politics are concerned." [114] Especially after the overthrow of the Tsar both Morel and Trevelyan became ever more "sceptical as to whether the Liberal Party could be brought to act as the principal instrument of the inevitable social revolution." [115] Attracted by the enthusiasm with which the Left approached world problems, and impatient with the hesitancy of the disintegrating Liberal party's domestic reform policy, Angell, Morel, Trevelyan, and the Buxtons seemed to move instinctively into the Labour camp.

113. Cf. Cole, pp. 33–34.
114. Morel to E. H. Driffill, August 10, 1916, Morel Papers.
115. Charles Trevelyan, *From Liberalism to Labour* (London, Allen and Unwin, 1921), p. 21. See also the foreword by G. P. Gooch, in Mosa Anderson, *Noel Buxton, a Life* (London, Allen and Unwin, 1952), esp. p. 7.

Consequently MacDonald did not need to convince his Radical partners in the UDC that the rapidly expanding Labour movement was more receptive to progressive foreign-policy ideas than were the middle-class constituencies of the gradually waning Liberal party. Therefore "the appeal of U.D.C. was from the first directed to the workers."[116] In May 1915 the UDC Executive Committee appointed a special commissioner for the specific purpose of proselytizing the Labour world.[117] Two months later this committee resolved to concentrate the UDC's propaganda and organizational efforts "on Brotherhoods and meetings where a large attendance of Labour might be anticipated." In August 1916, at the request of the Executive Committee, Ramsay MacDonald undertook to circularize the Trades Union Councils with a letter "describing the policy of the U.D.C."[118]

The UDC's publication program indicated that its leaders were striving to reach two quite distinct audiences. On the one hand, in an effort to reach Britain's educated public, the UDC published some forty pamphlets by such respected authors as Angell, Ponsonby, Tawney, MacDonald, Russell, Brailsford, Dickinson, Gooch, and Hobson. On the other hand, the UDC also issued a series of leaflets which were addressed to the working masses directly.[119] In turn, once the *Nation* had deserted the Radicals in favor of Asquith and Grey, the *Labour Leader*, under the able editorship of Fenner Brockway, became the UDC's most effective channel of communication to the Labour world.[120]

Soon it was apparent that the Radicals actually performed a dual function. They provided Labour with a coherent body of ideas on foreign affairs and they became a communication channel to the middle class both for the UDC – Labour foreign-policy plank and for the domestic reform program of British Socialism. They were the "middle-class brains" which Beatrice Webb was so anxious to enlist in the British Labour movement.[121] It may be fair to conclude, therefore,

116. Swanwick, *Builders of Peace,* p. 57.
117. Ibid., p. 51.
118. UDC, *Minutes of the Executive Committee,* July 27, 1915, and August 1, 1916, in the London office of the UDC.
119. For a listing of UDC publications see the appendix in Swanwick, *Builders of Peace,* pp. 189–91.
120. Ibid., p. 52; Morel to Emily Hobhouse, October 23, 1914, Morel Papers; Brand, *British Labour's Rise to Power,* p. 82.
121. Cole, p. 45.

that "as a pathway from Liberalism to Labour" the significance of the UDC cannot be overestimated.[122]

However, this movement of the Radicals from their parent party to the British Left was gradual. In 1918 only five of the eleven members of the UDC's Executive Committee were Labourites, though the remaining six joined the Labour movement subsequently.[123] Both Trevelyan and Morel realized that there was something "inevitable" about their gravitation "toward the Socialist position." And when Morel finally joined the ILP, he felt confident that he had taken the plunge with "intellectual honesty." [124]

Meanwhile these new Liberal recruits were not likely to strengthen the "extremist" elements in the Labour movement. On the contrary, instead of permeating Liberalism with Socialism the intellectual vanguard of the bourgeoisie seemed to be infiltrating the British proletariat. Morel realized only too well that there was "Socialism and Socialism," and therefore reassured himself and some of his followers [125] that his own brand of Socialism was "of the reasonable and moderate kind." But in their spirited crusade for a new international order both Morel and Angell decided to work with political forces which were really far too radical for their liking.[126]

Clearly, these Radicals were carried leftward primarily by a quasi-religious dedication to a New World and a New Diplomacy. The Liberal party offered little if any satisfaction to those intellectuals and politicians who were convinced that the World War was ushering in a new age which could not be denied major ideological and institutional adaptations except at immense cost. Consequently, many Radicals who were not Socialists before the war but who were determined "to keep the revolutionary impulse in touch with the peace-making movement," turned "to some form of Socialism as the best hope of saving the world from that madness which threatens to send whole nations down the steep places to destruction." [127]

---

122. William P. Maddox, *Foreign Relations in British Labour Politics* (Cambridge, Harvard University Press, 1934), pp. 95–96.

123. Swanwick, *Builders of Peace*, p. 52.

124. Angell, *After All*, p. 227; Trevelyan, *From Liberalism to Labour*, p. 19; Morel, in a memorandum (n.d., early 1918?), Morel Papers.

125. In a memorandum (n.d., early 1918?), Morel Papers.

126. Angell, *After All*, p. 219.

127. Wells, *Experiment in Autobiography*, p. 594; and Angell, *The British Revolution and the American Democracy*, p. 148.

Undoubtedly British Labour considerably bolstered its strength and stature by enthusiastically welcoming this "deserting" élite. By actually joining either the Labour party or the ILP, this middle-class élite helped to broaden the appeal of the Left to certain nonproletarian sectors of the British electorate. On the other hand, this merger also threatened to bring in its wake a certain dilution of Labour's "domestic" Socialism. British Liberals, no matter how extreme in their foreign-policy views, could hardly be expected to encourage schemes of drastic economic reform like the nationalization of basic industries. The middle-class "brain-workers" did not dispossess Labour brains, however, even though they did begin to occupy many of the vacant chairs around the Socialist policy-making table. Henceforth, just as the Left was resolved not to tolerate dominance by the Radical intellectuals, especially in domestic affairs, the new converts to Labour were no less determined to escape the bondage of "a stereotyped and perhaps doctrinaire program." [128]

From 1914 to 1917 the UDC never ceased to be under attack from right-wing quarters. While some publicists sought to discredit it by labeling it German-inspired, chauvinist papers like the *Morning Post* attacked it for acting as a foil for the "antiwar" ILP.[129] The Government also was anxious to have the UDC silenced, primarily because its propaganda clashed head-on with official pronouncements on Germany's unilateral war guilt. In addition, the Right feared that the UDC might constitute a fertile nucleus for an expanding popular-front movement. Before the war, Traditionalists had been tolerant of the *Great Illusion* type of thinking. However, now that Norman Angell and Ramsay MacDonald had joined forces, the *Times* and the *Morning Post* detected the Labour threat in what had formerly been considered a distinctly British middle-class, antiwar idealism.[130]

The revolutionary Left was no less concerned than the Right by this deliberate fusion of the forces of movement. Although the dismal

128. *New Republic* (December 1, 1917), p. 119. Bertrand Russell, who eventually joined the Labour party, and J. A. Hobson, both active members of UDC, were most typical of these intellectuals.

129. June 22, 1915.

130. When Morel sought to transmit two of his own published pamphlets by messenger to Romain Rolland, he was charged with a technical violation of a Defense of the Realm regulation. Printed matter could be sent to neutral countries only through the mails. Morel seems not to have known that Rolland, a French citizen, was residing in neutral Switzerland. Hence, Morel spent six months in jail. Swanwick, *Builders of Peace,* pp. 89–106.

collapse of the Second International in July–August 1914 foreshadowed for many observers an indefinite postponement of the proletarian revolution, Lenin soon declared that the Left had been forced into a merely temporary eclipse. In his view the war itself was bound to contribute decisively to Socialism's political recovery. According to Lenin the impending Socialist revolution "must not be looked upon as one single act, but must be considered as an epoch, a number of stormy political and economic upheavals, a most sharpened class struggle, civil war, revolutions and counter-revolutions." [131] Lenin emphasized that the "change from imperialist war to civil war [could not] be 'made' as it [was] impossible to make a revolution—it grows out of a multiplicity of diverse phenomena, phases, traits, characteristics, consequences of the imperialist war." [132]

While the war continued to strain the constitutional and socioeconomic fabric of Europe's war-engulfed nations, Lenin engaged in a systematic analysis of the causes for eventual dissent and of the available political channels for its expression. By July 1915 he had concluded that only two major roads of political action were open to the Socialists: "Either aid the growth and development of revolutionary actions against one's own bourgeoisie and one's own government, or hamper, calm, extinguish the revolutionary sentiment." He proclaimed that it was the duty of all true Social Democrats to take advantage of the gradually developing "mass sentiment of peace" by ardently participating in "every movement and in every demonstration made on this basis." However, the Maximalists should "not deceive the people by assuming that in the absence of a revolutionary movement it [was] possible to have peace without annexations, without the oppression of nations, without robberies." Evidently Lenin was apprehensive lest the "liberal bourgeoisie and opportunists," obsessed by the rising specter of revolution and intent on avoiding a rupture with the masses, would agree to make verbal consessions to the Left. Accordingly, he anticipated that the war cabinets and their Social Patriotic supporters eventually would make "promises concerning disarmament, peace, repudiation of annexations, reforms of every kind." [133]

In Lenin's view, then, the growing privations of the war were bound to force the governments to have recourse to peace slogans in order to

131. Lenin, *Works, 18,* 269.
132. Ibid., pp. 199–200.
133. Ibid., pp. 207, 235.

prevent the peace-hungry workers and peasants from deserting to the revolutionary cause. Lenin attacked both the non-Marxist Fabians and the Marxist Kautsky because, without denouncing the war and without espousing the revolutionary cause, they combined their defense of "social chauvinism . . . with a readiness to utter sugary, humane and near-Left phrases about peace, disarmament, etc." He had nothing but scorn for most exponents of the "neither victory nor defeat" slogan (forerunner of Wilson's peace without victory formula) whom he accused of "unconscious" chauvinism or of "petty bourgeois" pacifism.[134]

Lenin was clear in his own mind that the Socialists never could succeed in taking over the war governments peacefully on the basis of their war-aims program. At best, under mounting dissident pressures, the war cabinets might be compelled to pay lip service to progressive war-aims slogans without, however, making substantive political concessions. As a result, the Left might become dispossessed of its potentially powerful internationalist ideology. Lenin warned Europe's Socialists that the war cabinets would promise to fulfill the dreams of peace which "without the propaganda of revolutionary action only represent the horror of war and have nothing to do with socialism." [135] In Lenin's view the two and the two-and-a-half Internationalists, influenced by the Radicals, were allowing themselves to be used as political carriers for nonrevolutionary ideas and interests.

No wonder that in April–May 1915 the UDC attracted Lenin's attention; for here, in microcosm, was the ideal type of Radical-Socialist fusion. In a perceptive article entitled "English Pacifism and Dislike of Theory" he readily conceded that the UDC's program stood "for peace, disarmament, the right of every nation to decide its own fate by plebiscite, and democratic control over foreign policy." Moreover, he praised Morel "for turning from chauvinist bourgeoisie to pacifist bourgeoisie." Lenin maintained, however, that Morel and the UDC were bourgeois nevertheless, "since without revolutionary actions on the part of the proletariat" the UDC platform could never hope to be effectively enacted and implemented. Furthermore, Lenin noted that even though Morel "parted ways with the liberals on the question of the present war [he remained] a liberal as far as all the other economic and political questions [were] concerned." [136]

Once Lenin had underscored the almost complete identity of the

134. Ibid., pp. 163, 201.
135. Ibid., p. 180.
136. Ibid., pp. 162–67.

war aims sponsored by both Radicals and Independent Socialists, as symbolized in the UDC's platform, he queried how men like Mac-Donald and Kautsky could continue to commend themselves to the proletariat as *revolutionary* Socialists. After all, their daring internationalism had become tied to domestic reformism, in the Allied countries as well as in Germany.

As one of Europe's most respected and best-known Marxist theoreticians, Kautsky was likely to carry great weight in left-wing circles by propagating the thesis that Socialists ought to pressure their Government into adopting progressive war aims. In an effort to forestall the successful dissemination of this advice, Lenin proceeded to attack virulently Kautsky's essentially nonrevolutionary foreign-policy platform. He asserted that if "undeveloped political relations and the absence of political freedom" had not prevented the establishment in Germany of a UDC–type "bourgeois league for peace and disarmament," Kautsky's reformism would stand out as distinctly as Morel's.[137]

Hereafter two currents of dissident Socialism were in irreconcilable conflict: the loyal Kautsky-MacDonald revisionist war-aims Socialism, and the disloyal Leninist revolutionary antiwar Socialism. In the first two years of war Lenin saw clearly that in case of a deepening crisis, the Internationalists would become more serious competitors for the Maximalists than the Majoritarians. For they had a potent ideology with which to intercept disgruntled workers and peasants before they could reach the revolutionary columns. Nevertheless, even though Lenin criticized MacDonald and Kautsky mercilessly, he reminded his supporters that their "attitude towards the vacillating elements in the International" was terribly important. He maintained that these "Socialists of a *pacifist* shade," such as Britain's Independent Labour party, could "be our fellow travellers" in the struggle against the social chauvinists. However, since Kautsky and MacDonald would eventually side with "Scheidemann, Vandervelde, and Sembat," against the Third International, Lenin kept stressing the importance of remembering that "they [were] *only* fellow travellers." [138]

7. Methods and Objectives of the New Diplomacy

Thus far neither the methods nor the objectives of the New Diplomacy have been defined. This exposition has assumed an inner

137. Ibid., pp. 164–65.
138. Ibid., pp. 247–48.

harmony not only among the various practices and objectives of this New Diplomacy but also among its political sponsors. However, since the different unequal factions of the forces of movement tended to emphasize different aspects of the same syndrome of war aims, the doctrinal and political factors of inconsistency and variability should not be overshadowed by the elements of coherence and uniformity. In subsequent chapters it will be shown that from the same or closely related principles of methods and objectives in foreign policy, different factions often derived conflicting policy demands. Provided these variant elements and conditions are duly emphasized, certain assumptions of uniformity are justified, especially since the ultimate concern of this study is the total impact of the composite New Diplomacy movement on the policies of the war cabinets.

Broadly speaking, what was the content of the New Diplomacy that was being advocated by the forces of movement? This doctrine of the New Diplomacy actually was formulated as a criticism of the practice, theory, and objectives of the Old Diplomacy. Therefore the positive features of the New Diplomacy will stand out more clearly after a reference to those features of the Old Diplomacy which constitute its antithesis and which the progressives condemned.

The spokesmen of the New Diplomacy indignantly charged that secret diplomacy had been one of the decisive causes of the prewar tensions which had led to the outbreak of hostilities. Moreover, in the progressive camp it was widely held that economic pressures resulting from a combination of overproduction and restrictive foreign-trade practices had contributed heavily to the waning of peace. For example, the colonial rivalries among the satisfied and the dissatisfied powers were traced back to those economic roots. Also, there was considerable concern about increasing armaments as a cause of war. Whereas some progressives emphasized the dangers resulting from security-motivated armaments races, others underlined the pernicious influence on foreign policy of profit-seeking armaments manufacturers.

All along, the advocacy of domestic reforms and the opposition to aggressive policies abroad were closely related. The forces of movement contended that although in the democracies in the 19th century public opinion had come to count for much in the making of domestic laws, the people were not being consulted in foreign affairs. Progressives held that just as increased democratization of domestic politics had produced important economic and social reforms, the foreign policies of democratic states could also improve as a result of popular participation and control. In effect the forces of movement believed that unlike the permanent officials of the foreign offices, democratic electorates would not be tempted to sanction expansionist politics. Also, they insisted that forcible annexations should be avoided in order not to inflame the nationalist feelings of subject peoples.

Implicit in this critique of the old system—which reads like a partial catalogue of the causes of war—is the program of the New Diplomacy which became the core of the war-aims demands of the forces of movement. Possibly the most succinct, representative, and symbolic summary of this reform program is to be found in the UDC platform, four of whose five cardinal points were formulated in November 1914.

1. No Province shall be transferred from one Government to another without the consent by plebiscite or otherwise of the population of such Province.

2. No Treaty, Arrangement or Undertaking shall be entered into in the name of Great Britain without the sanction of Parliament. Adequate machinery for ensuring democratic control of foreign policy shall be created.

3. The Foreign Policy of Great Britain shall not be aimed at creating alliances for the purpose of maintaining the "Balance of Power," but shall be directed to concerted action between the Powers and the setting up of an International Council whose deliberations and decisions shall be public, with such machinery for securing international agreement as shall be the guarantee of an abiding peace.

4. Great Britain shall propose as part of the Peace Settlement a plan for the drastic reduction by consent of the armaments of all the belligerent Powers, and to facilitate that policy shall attempt to secure the general nationalization of the manufacture of armaments and the control of the export of armaments by one country to another.

5. The European conflict shall not be continued by economic war after the military operations have ceased. British policy shall be directed toward promoting free commercial intercourse between all nations and the preservation and extension of the principle of the Open Door.[139]

139. These five "cardinal points" are reproduced in Swanwick, *Builders of Peace*, pp. 39–40. The fifth point, which was added in May 1916, was drafted by J. A. Hobson, author of the classic study *Imperialism*. UDC, *Minutes of the Executive Committee*, January 4 and May 25, 1916.

This UDC program enunciates principles of diplomatic methods as well as of foreign-policy objectives. In relying so heavily on popular control (not negotiations) in connection with both territorial transfers and treaty ratification, the Left expressed its trust in the infallibility of public opinion. Like Woodrow Wilson, Europe's progressives also assumed that the politically emerging masses of workers and peasants were equipped with sufficient reason and rationality to enable them to judge and support an enlightened foreign policy for their nation. Clearly, political parties would be an essential part of an "adequate machinery for ensuring democratic control." The progressives expected that at the polls the parties of movement would win overwhelming majorities with their democratic foreign-policy platform. As a result a rapidly growing number of representatives in the national legislatures would be sworn to support a foreign policy based on principles like self-determination and the reduction of armaments, and would oppose external commitments inspired by balance-of-power calculations.

Indeed, in the tradition of John Bright, the spokesmen of the forces of movement considered the balance of power as a "ghastly phantom" and a "foul idol." Accordingly, the elusive pursuit of the balance of power was accused of inevitably engendering distrust and insecurity among nations, rival alliances, impairment of trade, and increasing military expenditures.[140]

The forces of movement insisted that in order to break out of this vicious balance-of-power cycle, foreign-policy makers would have to cease being guided primarily by selfish calculations of national power and interest. Instead, a rational analysis of the causes of war should lead them to avoid taking those external measures which tend to increase international tensions. For example, armaments should not be increased, in order not to exacerbate the sense of insecurity of other nations. In making these proposals on the limitation of armaments, on the open door, and on self-determination, progressives always assumed that *all* major states would soon be governed by democratic constitutions; in turn, their foreign offices would follow an identical set

140. Especially England has had a long-standing tradition of Radical dissent in foreign policy. The genesis of this tradition, its doctrinal content, and its concrete historical manifestations from the French Revolution to World War I are reviewed in Taylor, *The Trouble Makers* (above, n. 69), chaps. 1–4. Professor Taylor's assertion that "dissent is a quality peculiar to English-speaking peoples" is too sweeping.

of liberal principles and would be equally committed to the search for peace.

Henceforth the foreign-policy demands of all nations would cease to be a function of national power. Instead, they would rest on national self-limiting objectives which would be articulated publicly in national parliaments as well as in the deliberative chamber of a League of Nations. In the event that two national policies would nevertheless come in serious conflict, this League would provide compulsory mediation and arbitration services which would make all recourse to unilateral military violence illegitimate and unnecessary.

Depending on the degree of their Socialism and on their national heritage, different factions of the forces of movement emphasized different aspects of the New Diplomacy program. The further they were to the left on the spectrum of dissent, the more prominent was the emphasis on the need for eliminating capitalism and on the importance of nationalizing munitions industries. On the other hand, the closer they were to the Radical position, the more pronounced was the demand for the limitation of armaments and for supranational arbitration. As for the "national" variables, British progressives were immensely concerned with free trade, while their American and German counterparts respectively emphasized freedom of navigation and colonial liberation.

It is important to distinguish between the rational formulation of assumptions and objectives by world reformers and the essentially irrational espousal of war aims and peace programs by the inarticulate masses. Many of the criticisms of the Old Diplomacy were rationally founded and had implicit within them reforms which were calculated to remove certain causes of war. However, the full meaning of the proposed New Diplomacy was clear only to those who were immediately involved in the formulation of this system. For countless millions what counted were abstract catch phrases which soon became transformed into emotionally charged symbols. It was only with the deepening of the crisis, when formulas of "national survival" ceased to have sufficient emotional appeal, that these symbols became politically operational and relevant.

"Power politics," "secret diplomacy," "armaments races," "trade wars," "colonial rivalries," and "annexations" were phrases which singly or in varying combinations were used ever more widely to explain the causes of World War I. On the other hand phrases like "community of power," "open diplomacy," "disarmament," "free trade," and "self-determination" came to represent an articulate but vague program which, if adopted, would guarantee a future perpetual peace. In 1917 the forces of movement were in the enviable position of being the custodians of an ideology that was sufficiently universal to help effect social and political consolidation.

In *The German Ideology* Marx and Engels asserted that in modern times "increasingly abstract ideas hold sway, i.e. ideas which increasingly take on the form of universality." Moreover, they maintained that in the class struggle a new class invariably is compelled to "represent its interest as the common interest of all the members of society, put in an ideal form; it will give its ideas the form of universality, and represent them as the only rational, universally valid ones." This same class will make every effort to appear "not as a class but as the representative of the whole society" since it can achieve "hegemony only on a broader basis than that of the ruling class." [141]

Regardless of whether the 1917 crisis and the accompanying political conflicts fit into the pattern of the Marxist class struggle, this analysis of the function of *ideology* in the struggle for national and international political power is relevant here. The European forces of movement and Woodrow Wilson claimed both rationality and universality for their foreign-policy program. In so doing, far from compromising the vital national interest of any particular belligerent, they merely sought to draw additional strength to the state while at the same time improving their own power position.

141. *The German Ideology* (New York, International Publishers, 1947), pp. 40–41.

FIRST PHASE: STRAINS IN THE POLITICAL TRUCE

1. THE MARCH REVOLUTION AND
THE PETROGRAD FORMULA

WITH THE OUTBREAK of war the overwhelming majority of the Russian forces of movement hastened to make their offerings on the altar of Russian nationalism. The Liberals assured the Tsar that further political reforms like the extension of the franchise and guaranteed civil liberties could safely be postponed until such time as Holy Russia had reasserted her great power position in the struggle against Germany and the Dual Monarchy. In the Duma, Paul N. Miliukov, in the name of the Faction of Popular Freedom, proclaimed that Russia's Liberals, without presenting "any conditions or demands," were fully determined to defend their homeland against foreign aggression.[1] Likewise, the entire Left, with the notable exception of the politically minuscular Bolshevik faction, agreed to enter into the political truce unconditionally.[2] Even Plekhanov, who at the time of the Russo-Japanese War had taken an unusually valiant internationalist position, stepped forward to embrace the Entente cause. Indeed, it would seem that Tsar Nicholas II had little, if any, difficulty in convincing the forces of movement that in "this hour of threatening danger" domestic strife should be forgotten.[3] According to the Tsar and his advisors, Russia was fighting a war of self-defense; before long, however, they injected a Messianic element into most official war-aims pronouncements by insisting that Russia was also fighting for "the

1. The complete text of Miliukov's Duma address is cited in Golder, pp. 35–36.
2. In the name of the Duma Labor Group, Alexander F. Kerensky read a declaration summoning all citizens to the defense of Russia. Cited ibid., pp. 33–35.
3. Quoted from the Tsar's Imperial Manifesto of August 2, 1914, cited ibid., pp. 29–30.

honor and dignity . . . [of] Our Slav brothers, who are one with US in blood and faith." [4]

The various major nationalities within the Empire also enrolled in the war of self-defense, while the "Austrian" and "Russian" Poles were urged to "reunite under the scepter of the Russian Tsar" in order to become free in "faith, language, and self-government." [5] Foreign Minister Serge Sazonov, who with the support of the bourgeois elements in the Duma had been the main architect of Russia's pro-Entente and anti-German foreign policy, now prepared to exploit the war as an instrument for the expansion of Russian influence into the Balkans and European Turkey. France and Great Britain were only too anxious to enter into secret negotiations for the purpose of agreeing on a division of spoils among the Entente Powers, partly because such agreements would also serve to bolster the wartime alliance. Throughout the prewar years Sazonov had often fought an up-hill battle against many of the Tsar's extreme right-wing associates who had never ceased to press for a Russo-German accommodation. Even now, during the war, these pro-German elements continued their machinations, until at last they succeeded in dislodging Sazonov and in having B. V. Sturmer appointed to head the Foreign Ministry. In the meantime, however, in an effort to tighten the anti-German alliance Paris and London had agreed to secret treaties which assured Russia (1) control of the Straits and European Turkey, (2) extensive freedom in fixing her frontiers with Germany, and (3) a share of Turkey's Asiatic Empire.[6]

Insofar as the politics of Russian war aims is concerned, it cannot be emphasized sufficiently that whereas Russia's Liberals never made a secret of their imperial ambitions, most of the Russian Left was opposed to all projects of imperialist expansion. Even though the Russian Left supported the war effort, neither the Mensheviks nor the Social Revolutionaries supported Sazonov's diplomacy. Notable prowar Menshevik émigrés like Plekhanov and Martov never wavered in their commitment to a nonannexationist war-aims program; the war-aims platform of the exiled Social Revolutionaries was equally hostile to territorial acquisitions.

4. Quoted from the Tsar's address to the members of the Duma on August 8, 1914, cited ibid., p. 31.

5. See Proclamation of the Supreme Commander-in-Chief to the Poles, dated August 14, 1914, cited ibid., pp. 37–38.

6. See above, pp. 18–20.

Particularly in the Internationalist wings of both parties—those Internationalist factions which in 1917 were to move closer to the Bolsheviks—restrictive war aims were passionately advocated. V. M. Chernov, the widely respected leader of the left Social Revolutionaries, "was invincibly determined that Russia should not have the Straits." Like the Bolsheviks, "the Internationalists sought to counter the argument that the Allied coalition merited Socialist support because the virtues of Western liberalism outweighed the sins of Russian absolutism. They took up the cudgels on behalf of oppressed colonial peoples; they talked of Morocco and Egypt, of Persia and India, and they did not overlook symptoms of imperialism in Europe itself. They spoke of the hypocrisy involved in claims that a 'war of liberation' was being conducted by such powers, and of the futility of thinking that these powers could exert, or would care to exert, a liberalizing influence. . . . The Internationalists addressed themselves to the task of overthrowing the 'legend of liberation' which served the 'defensists' as the basis for their 'idealization' of the war." As opposed to Lenin, however, Chernov and his Internationalist followers sanctioned defense, though they did not sanction a peace of victory.[7]

In sum, like the majority and Independent Socialists in the other belligerent countries, Russia's non-Bolshevik Socialists were defensist, except that even the most ardent Russian defensists were little inclined to condone their Government's hard war aims. Nevertheless, because so many Mensheviks and Social Revolutionaries—not to speak of Bolsheviks—were either in exile or in prison, before the March Revolution their protests against Sazonov's war-aims diplomacy were politically ineffective.

On the other hand, the Cadets were much more successful in attacking the Government. Since they shared most of Sazonov's foreign-policy goals, they attacked the Government not for its territorial aspirations in themselves but rather for compromising these aspirations under the pressure of pro-German, reactionary elements. After a trip

7. Oliver H. Radkey, *The Agrarian Foes of Bolshevism: Promise and Default of the Russian Socialist Revolutionaries, February to October 1917* (New York, Columbia University Press, 1958), chap. 4, esp., pp. 101–6. For a comprehensive survey of written opinions and attitudes of the various factions of the Russian Left during the first two years of war see the two articles by G. Tschudnowsky, "Schriften russischer Sozialisten über den Krieg," and "Russische Sozialisten über den Krieg, II," in *Archiv für die Geschichte des Sozialismus und der Arbeiterbewegung*, 7 (1916), 60–94; and 9 (1921), 356–412.

to Paris and London, Miliukov actually mounted the rostrum of the
Duma on November 14, 1916, in order to declare defiantly that the
Government had "neither the knowledge nor the ability which were
indispensable" to win the complete victory to which he and his followers continued to be dedicated. In particular he protested the re-
placement of Sazonov by Sturmer because this cabinet change had
weakened the mutual confidence between Russia and her Allies which
was so crucial for the "agreement on Constantinople and the Straits." [8]

It would seem, then, that as the Russian war effort continued to
show signs of serious deterioration, the extreme Right was out to
salvage the autocratic regime by preparing the ground for a separate
peace with Germany, while the Liberals now schemed to take power
in order to carry on the war with renewed vigor. In this Liberal enterprise the entire Left could be counted upon to do more than its
share, not because it was anxious to gain control over the Straits but
rather because of its determination to use any means to precipitate
liberal-bourgeois constitutional reforms. Hence, in late 1916 and early
1917 the ardently prowar Russian forces of movement and the antiwar Bolsheviks were ranged against the forces of order, which became increasingly dedicated to an antiwar position.[9] Strangely enough,
unlike the various wings of the French and British forces of movement which were more widely agreed on issues of foreign policy than
of domestic reform, the composite Russian forces of movement found
their largest common denominator immediately prior to the Revolution in the area of domestic reform.[10] Subsequently, once the March
Revolution had been consummated, Miliukov's expansionist foreign
policy became one of the major, if not the major, obstacle to a stable
relationship between the First Provisional Government and the Petrograd Soviet.

8. Golder, p. 160.

9. At this time two revolutionary streams merged: "from below came the movement of peasants, soldiers, and workers yearning for peace and for bread; from
above that of the liberal middle class seeking victory and conquests." Arthur Rosenberg, A History of Bolshevism (London, Oxford University Press, 1934), p. 82.

10. A similar situation obtained in Germany. There the forces of movement also
tended to find more common ground on issues of domestic reform, primarily because
even according to the Marxist revolutionary timetable, the first phase of the revolution initially would entail primarily political, not economic and social, reforms. However, on the war-aims issue, not only were the Liberal and Socialist parties and
factions in disagreement, but even within the Left there was a great deal of dis-
sension, particularly about Germany's eastern borders. See below, Chap. 2.

This is not the place either to discuss the causes of the March Revolution, or to analyze which components of the forces of movement made the heaviest contribution to the overthrow of the tsarist autocracy.[11] Suffice it to stress that the First Provisional Government was overwhelmingly composed of Liberals who, though prepared to make certain limited concessions to the Finns, as well as the Poles, had no intention of abandoning the core of Sazonov's foreign policy. Moreover, as Miliukov proceeded to demonstrate the essential continuity in Russian war aims, he did so in full awareness that he could count on the support of the British Foreign Office and the Quai d'Orsay.

It is interesting that the very first statement issued by the new Provisional Government, dated March 16, 1917, and addressed to Russia's citizens, should have made no reference whatever to the war-aims issue.[12] After announcing that the Executive Committee of the Duma had "succeeded in triumphing over the obnoxious forces of the old regime in such a manner that we are now able to proceed to a more stable organization of the executive power," the new Cabinet outlined eight principles on which its policies would henceforth be based. These principles dealt with political amnesties, civil liberties, a Constituent Assembly to be elected by universal suffrage, and soldiers' rights and privileges; but nothing was said about the purposes for which the New Russia would continue to fight the war.

Perhaps the fact that enemy troops were occupying substantial areas of Russia's sovereign land made any reference to the most immediate war aims quite superfluous. The Provisional Government took it for granted that the war against Russia's enemies would continue, though in the March 16th statement it went out of its way to assure the people that it had "no intention to profit by the circumstances of the war to delay the realization of the measures of reform above mentioned." Evidently the Government, unlike the other belligerent nations, planned to structure the new political truce so that it would not preclude domestic reforms during wartime. However, since freedom of speech, press, and organization were licensed, not only issues of domestic reform but, above all, problems of foreign policy were foreordained to become subject to heated political controversy. In brief,

11. See, e.g., Trotsky, *The History of the Russian Revolution, 1,* chaps. 8 ("Who Led the February Insurrection?") and 9 ("The Paradox of the February Revolution").

12. For the complete text of the Provisional Government's March 16th statement see *RAR*, pp. 1–2.

the crucial question confronting revolutionary Russia was where the
new political truce would or could be consolidated.

Clearly, both Russia's enemies and allies had a vital stake in the
future course of her internal developments. Whereas it was in the
immediate interest of the Central Powers that the Russian political
truce should continue to go from bad to worse, the Entente was
desperately interested in a new political consolidation which alone
might enable Russia to regain a solid military posture. Hence, it would
seem that since both war coalitions were equally determined to take
all measures within their power to influence the course of events in
Russia, the Russian Revolution was internationalized at its very birth.
Russia continued to be a vital military and economic factor in "stale-
mated" Europe, more particularly because America did not take
Russia's place in the wartime military balance of power until early in
1918.

Indeed, as at the time of the French Revolution, all the major governments at first regarded the Russian Revolution "as only a local
problem, and judged it according to their interests. They stimulated
or calmed the revolution according to whether it was advantageous
to support . . . or else to weaken it." [13] What the cabinets were struck
by primarily was the impending eclipse of Russian power. Depending
on whether they were friends or enemies of Russia, depending on
whether they needed her or feared her, they either rejoiced at or condemned the Revolution.[14] Consequently the immediate national interest became the sole guide of politicodiplomatic judgments and
policy decisions; national-interest motives inspired both those states
which were seriously inconvenienced by the Revolution and those
states which stood to gain from it.

However, unlike the time of the French Revolution, in 1917 the
definition of the national interest was no longer the exclusive province
of the foreign chancelleries. In the course of the 19th century political
parties had become increasingly involved in the making of foreign
policy. True, the executive branch of government continued to be in a
strategic initiative-taking and policy-making position. But the issue of

13. Albert Sorel, *Europe under the Old Regime* (Los Angeles, Ritchie Press,
1947), p. 44. This is a translation by Francis H. Herrick of the first chapter of Bk. I
of Sorel's classic *L'Europe et la révolution française*, 8 vols. Paris, Plon.

14. Cf. Sorel, *L'Europe et la révolution française*, 2, 31.

popular or parliamentary control of foreign policy had become terribly real throughout Europe, more particularly because the restless forces of movement were taking such an excited interest in diplomacy. Ever since August 1914 every demand for a public formulation of liberal war aims was another index that the dissident Left, especially, persisted in denying the foreign offices the prerogative of defining the national interest without consulting the major parties which represented the electorate.

So now, in March 1917, as the Russian Revolution symbolized and accelerated the weakening of the political truce throughout Europe, the official interpretations of foreign policies and war aims were being challenged. The most decisive challenge came in Russia where the vocal Petrograd Soviet, in the name of the Russian Left, refused to recognize Russian control of the Dardanelles as essential to the Russian national interest. In their efforts to influence the course of Russian events, the major belligerents presently sought ways of strengthening the hand of those political parties or factions inside Russia which promised to sponsor an interpretation of the Russian national interest favorable to them. Thus the Germans were anxious for Lenin to get to Petrograd so that under his guidance the Bolsheviks should help to undermine Russia's precarious political truce. On the other hand, the Allies encouraged the return of exiled Russian Social Patriots and dispatched Allied Social Patriots to Petrograd in the hope of influencing the Soviet to continue being favorably disposed toward the Entente. Meanwhile, the French and British, as well as the German forces of movement exerted incessant pressure on their respective governments in order to gain a voice in the formulation of war aims. Once the Stockholm project was launched, it became apparent that party politics had become internationalized, much more so than it had ever been at the time of the French Revolution.

Before examining the impact of the March Revolution on Russian as well as on inter-Allied politics of war aims, it may be helpful to record the initial reactions in the camp of Russia's enemies. Even though in Germany there was a wide range of views on how the Central Powers could exploit the Russian Revolution most effectively, there was almost complete consensus on the extent of Russia's disintegration. The editorial writers of all major newspapers were agreed that economically Russia had reached such an "advanced state of exhaustion" that it would be "impossible for her to carry out a victorious campaign, or even to continue the struggle much longer." [15] Accordingly, the semi-official *Kölnische Zeitung,* after emphasizing the widely held belief that England had engineered the March Revolution, asserted that "the English may revolutionize Russia, they may even succeed in dethroning the Tsar, but they cannot feed the hungry people, they who are themselves day by day more deeply in the throes of a severe economic crisis." [16] Similarly, the Russian expert of the Liberal *Berliner Tageblatt* insisted that war weariness was "universal" among the Russian masses.[17]

Especially the right-wing press recognized that the political "tendency that inspired the Revolution was anything rather than friendly to Germany." [18] The Liberal *Frankfurter Zeitung* suggested that even though the Revolution had gone further than the British had hoped, nevertheless it had been inspired by a resolve to make the Russian Government more efficient in her war enterprise.[19] Likewise, the Socialist *Vorwärts* refused to see anything but "a change of ministers" in the Revolution which according to the Independent Socialist *Leipziger Volksstimme,* gave the bourgeois opposition political supremacy.[20]

In view of the fact that the Lvov-Miliukov Government seemed determined to pursue the war with renewed enthusiasm, Germany's semi-official press called for an all-out military offensive which would swiftly knock Russia out of the war. The editor of the moderate right-wing *Vossische Zeitung* thought that in case prompt and pronounced military pressure should lead to civil war in Russia, no harm would be done, since the "party that means to conquer" would have to make peace "whether it is friendly or hostile to Germany." [21] In Vienna also the dynastic and imperialist *Reichspost* proclaimed that even though "it might be all right for England if there were no Extremists," the worse the revolutionary situation for Russia, "the better for us." [22]

Those German Conservatives who opposed expansion into Eastern

15. *DR,* EPS (March 29, 1917), p. 279.
16. Cited ibid., p. 280.
17. Cited ibid.
18. *Norddeutsche Allgemeine Zeitung* (March 16, 1917), cited ibid., p. 279.
19. Cited ibid., p. 280.
20. Cited ibid., p. 281.
21. Cited ibid. (April 5, 1917), p. 300.
22. Cited ibid. (March 29, 1917), p. 285.

Europe and favored conquests in the West and in Africa joined the Liberals and Socialists in urging the Government to seek a rapprochement with Russia. Especially the Liberals and the Socialists, who predicted a rapid increase in the influence of the "pacifist" Soviet, wanted their Government to encourage the Russian peace movement by formulating a slate of nonannexationist war aims.[23] At any rate, it seems that all German political parties to the right of the dissident Left in March–April made proposals primarily calculated to lead to a speedy liquidation of Germany's Eastern front.

Just as Germany was anxious to withdraw her eighty divisions which continued to be tied down in the East in spite of the fact that the Russian armies were continually deteriorating, so the Allies were determined to do everything in their power to improve Russia's failing military health in order to perpetuate Germany's involvement in a major second front. Immediately, and almost without exception, the Allied press hailed the Revolution as a decidedly anti-German development.[24] Also, people of such diverse political commitments as Lenin and Lansing assumed that the Allies had had a hand in the Petrograd events. Analyzing the political forces which had converged to make the Revolution succeed so quickly, Lenin maintained that the "conspiracy of the Anglo-French imperialists had encouraged Miliukov, Guchkov, and Co. to seize power, with the object of prolonging the imperialist war," while from below had come a "profound proletarian and popular mass movement . . . of a revolutionary character, for bread, peace, for real freedom." [25] Thus Lenin "accused" England and France for their part in the March Revolution, just as later in 1917 the Entente Powers were going to charge that Germany, through Lenin and his party, was actively promoting the November Revolution.

Across the Atlantic, Secretary of State Lansing told President Wilson on March 15 that he presumed that the Allies were "favorable to the revolutionists since the Court party [had] been, throughout the War, secretly pro-German." [26] Similarly, one of America's leading specialists on Russia, Samuel N. Harper, advised the State Department that

23. *Berliner Tageblatt* and *Leipziger Tageblatt* (March 24, 1917), cited ibid. (April 12, 1917), p. 309.

24. See ibid. (March 29, 1917), p. 279.

25. Lenin, *Works, 20,* Pt. I, p. 31.

26. Lansing to Wilson, in the Woodrow Wilson Papers, Library of Congress, Washington, D.C.

same day that the aim of the Revolution, as also of the Duma and other public organizations, was "to create conditions that would make it possible for Russia to bring into force all her strength."[27]

As of March 18 there was no need for further speculation: the Government of the New Russia was firmly in the hands of pro-Allied political forces. Paul Miliukov, as Minister of Foreign Affairs in the Cabinet, hastened to reassure the Allies that the First Provisional Government would "remain mindful of the international engagements entered into by the fallen regime and [would] honor Russia's word." Not only would Russia continue to fight without cessation "against the common enemy until the end," but her war effort would be improved because the Government proposed to "repair as quickly as possible the errors of the past which hitherto [had] paralyzed the aspirations and self-sacrifice" of the people. Miliukov was quite confident that the revolutionary enthusiasm would soon multiply the strength of Russia and her valiant Allies.[28] Two days later, in a manifesto addressed to the citizens of Russia, the Provisional Government proclaimed, for domestic consumption, that it would "observe all alliances uniting us to other powers and all agreements made in the past."[29]

Indeed, the Allies had good reason to expedite their recognition of the new regime. Russia had shed its tsarist garb to make a long-delayed entrance into the ranks of representative democracy, thereby enabling the Entente coalition to commend itself as the camp of progress not only to Europe's forces of movement but also to President Wilson.[30] Moreover, the Government of Russia now promised to use every last resource in the struggle against the common enemy without asking for a redefinition or renegotiation of any of the inter-Allied agreements. Hence, since revolutionary Russia showed great promise of once again becoming a most desirable war partner, Paris and London continued to be quite willing to admit Russia to the Straits. It was certainly clear to the Allies that Miliukov had no intention of renouncing Constantinople. Once he was advised that the

27. Paul V. Harper, ed., *The Russia I Believe in: The Memoirs of Samuel N. Harper, 1902–1941* (Chicago, University of Chicago Press, 1945), p. 97.

28. For the complete text of Miliukov's address to the Allied chancelleries, see *RAR*, pp. 2–4.

29. Cited in *RAR*, p. 5.

30. See below, Chap. 3.

Allies might have gathered a contrary impression from some of his April statements which were drafted under the anti-annexationist pressure of the Soviet, Miliukov hastened to assert that the "main thread" of his policy had always been to "get the Straits for Russia." [31] Justifiably the *New Republic* predicted that the Russian liberal state might "well prove more pertinacious in its attempts to win Constantinople than autocratic Russia ever was." [32]

The Government which thus proclaimed the basic continuity in Russian war aims was a national coalition similar to the one which ruled in Paris and London. With Premier G. E. Lvov, head of the Union of Zemstvos, assisted by Miliukov (Constitutional Democrat) in the Foreign Ministry, and by A. I. Guchkov (Octobrist) as Minister of War, it was apparent that the Cabinet was not of unduly "left" composition. But since in the still smoldering revolutionary situation the pressure of the Left was more pronounced than it had been in England or France at any time since August 1914, the leaders of Russia's *new* forces of order were under greater pressure to win the support and confidence of the Left than were either Lloyd George or Ribot.

As early as March 12, 1917, after the soldiers and workers had rioted in the streets of Petrograd without waiting for orders from either Duma or Socialist leaders, the Temporary Committee of the Duma had sought to broaden its range of influence by electing Alexander F. Kerensky (Social Revolutionary) and Nicholas Chkheidze (Menshevik) to its ranks. However, the Petrograd Soviet which was then being formed was in no mood to share the responsibilities of power with the "bourgeois" factions before the Revolution had been pushed further along the Socialist path. After unhesitatingly declining the offer to join Russia's newly emerging Executive organ, Chkheidze became, significantly, the President of the Petrograd Soviet. Subsequently, as Vice-President of the Soviet, Kerensky obtained Chkheidze's sanction to join the First Provisional Government in the capacity of Minister of Justice. It would seem, however, that with Kerensky, as with Arthur Henderson in Britain and Albert Thomas in France,

31. Golder, p. 334. See also Bernard Pares, *My Russian Memoirs* (London, Cape, 1931), pp. 434–35; and Michael Smilg-Benario, *Von Kerenski zu Lenin: die Geschichte der zweiten Revolution* (Zurich, Leipzig, and Vienna, Amalthea, 1929), p. 34.

32. *New Republic* (March 24, 1917), p. 214.

his specific portfolio was not nearly so important as his more en-
compassing assignment of trying to gain for the Government the
support of the unsettled Left.

This, then, was the beginning of the eight months of strained dual-
power relationship between the successive Provisional governments
and the highly restive Soviet. The latter's first major act, which might
well be taken as its declaration of political independence, was the
issuance without prior consultation with the Minister of War of Army
Order No. 1 abolishing the military salute and providing for the
"popular" election of new officers.[33] This Order was symptomatic of
the intimate connection between the further course of the Revolution
at home and the war at the front. In the absence of well-established
legislative chambers and their attendant experienced political parties
in Russia, the war weariness and discontent which had given the
Revolution its populist stamp henceforth was going to be expressed
through the Soviet. The anarchy which was spreading through the
army was not a function of Order No. 1, Bolshevik agitation, or German intrigue. Kerensky himself admitted that "the anarchy in the
army was already a fact when the Provisional Government assumed
power" and that the same "was true of the entire country." [34] This
retrospective judgment coincides with contemporary assessments of
Russia's turmoil by the German Supreme Command as well as by the
German press, though it conflicts sharply with the initially overly optimistic estimates in the Allied countries.

The crucial point to note, however, is that in Russia "the entire
process of the inner struggle . . . was inseparably bound up" with
the conduct of the war. Kerensky rightly emphasized that whereas the
French Revolution came *before* the revolutionary and Napoleonic
wars, and the German monarchy fell after the Great War, "in Russia
the Revolution came IN THE MIDST OF WAR." [35] It became impossible
to disengage the internal struggle for power between the Provisional
Government and the Petrograd Soviet from the war, just as the war
could not be divorced from the Revolution. Moreover, it soon appeared that the forces of order would seek to use the war for their
political purposes, since appeals to patriotism and self-defense could

33. For the text of Order No. 1 see Golder, pp. 386–87.
34. Alexander F. Kerensky, *The Catastrophe* (New York, Appleton, 1927), p. 159.
35. Ibid., p. vii. See also Karl Kautsky, *Sozialisten und Krieg* (Prague, Orbis,
1937), pp. 604–5.

serve as an instrument of political consolidation. Even from a great distance Max Weber, who was extremely well versed in Russian affairs, suggested that "those in power needed the war to support their power position." [36] On the other hand, taking their cue from the rapidly spreading war weariness and exhaustion, the Russian forces of movement proposed to drive the Revolution forward by calling for peace, bread, and land.[37]

It is not surprising, then, that the first Proclamation by the Petrograd Soviet to the Peoples of the World, dated March 27, 1917, should have dealt primarily with the war and peace issue. This proclamation declared that the Russian people, who had just gained full political liberty, would now assert its "mighty power" in internal affairs as well as in foreign policy. Whereas little if anything was said of the next step in domestic reforms, the manifesto declared that the Russian people had initiated "a decisive struggle against the intentions of conquest on the part of the Governments of all countries; the time [had] come for the peoples to take into their own hands the decision of the question of war and peace." [38] And, as if in direct reply to Miliukov's assurance to Russia's Allies, the manifesto publicly announced that the Petrograd Soviet would "by every means, resist the policy of conquest" of Russia's ruling classes, though it also committed itself not to retreat "before the bayonets of conquerors." This conditional acceptance of defensism placed the Provisional Government on notice that the Petrograd Soviet was styling itself as a loyal opposition which would seek to bargain its support of the political truce for concessions in the field of war aims.

At this time even most Bolsheviks still were pressing for a similar bargaining policy both within the Soviet and outside. In the absence of Lenin, who had not as yet returned from Switzerland, L. B. Kamenev declared in the name of Russia's Bolsheviks, that even though the war

36. Max Weber, *Gesammelte politische Schriften* (Munich, Drei Masken, 1921), pp. 120, 124.

37. "But the first and most important slogan of the revolution was *peace*. If the revolution didn't finish the war, the war would strangle the revolution. We knew beforehand that a dragging on of the war would deprive people of bread, land, and the whole revolution; it would mean the destruction of the national economy, hunger, shortage of goods, reaction among the peasants, and the triumph of the counter-revolution." N. N. Sukhanov, *The Russian Revolution 1917*, edited, abridged, and translated by Joel Carmichael (London, Oxford University Press, 1955), p. 264.

38. For the complete text of the Petrograd Soviet's First Proclamation see *RAR*, pp. 7-9.

should not be ended by "submitting to the will of the neighboring imperialist conquerer . . . a people that [had] liberated itself [had] the right to know what it [was] fighting for." [39] Consequently, according to Kamenev, the Russian Left should exercise maximum pressure on the Provisional Government "with the aim of forcing it openly, before world democracy . . . immediately to come forth with an attempt to induce all the belligerent countries forthwith to start negotiations concerning the means of stopping the World War." [40] Notwithstanding Kamenev's war-aims position, it must be noted that the March 27th Manifesto was drafted in full awareness that in order to be accepted by the Soviet it would have to satisfy both the right wing of the Left, which "inclined to open defensism and social-patriotism," as well as the left wing, which "was mortally afraid of 'chauvinism', of 'defense' in general, and of everything that might sanction international armed struggle." [41]

Henceforth those forces in the Soviet which were committed to urging the Provisional Government to revise Russia's war aims never let up their pressure, more particularly because their ranks kept swelling. Shortly after this first Soviet Manifesto had been issued, the "question of 'regulating our war slogans'" was placed on the agenda of the Soviet's Executive Committee by some non-Bolshevik Internationalists.[42] But the majority of the Mensheviks and Social Revolutionaries on that Committee presently took a defensist position, and therefore sought not only to tame the sloganizers but also to take the peace issue out of revolutionary politics. Nevertheless, there was enough agreement on the Executive Committee to empower the Soviet's Liaison Commission to approach the Provisional Government on the urgency of bringing about a greater degree of harmony between Miliukov's foreign-policy pronouncements and the Soviet Manifesto. Whereas in a conference on April 6 the Foreign Minister at first refused even to debate the issue, a majority of the Cabinet, sensi-

39. L. Kamenev writing in the March 28, 1917, issue of *Pravda* under the title "Without Secret Diplomacy," cited in Lenin, *Works, 20*, Pt. II, pp. 379–80.

40. Ibid., p. 380. Prior to Lenin's return to Russia, Stalin shared Kamenev's position. See W. H. Chamberlin, *The Russian Revolution, 1917–1921* (2 vols. New York, Macmillan, 1935), *1*, 115–16; and Trotsky, *The History of the Russian Revolution, 1*, 336.

41. Sukhanov, *The Russian Revolution 1917*, pp. 206, 216–17.

42. For a report on these discussions by an extreme left-wing, non-Bolshevik, internationalist participant see ibid., pp. 239 ff.

tive to the importance of not alienating the left "loyal opposition," apparently agreed to prepare a public statement. Moreover, Kerensky and one of his Cabinet colleagues publicly went on record against Miliukov's Sazonov-type foreign policy. Between April 6 and 9 negotiations between the Liaison Commission and the Cabinet continued in a search for phrases which would satisfy all parties concerned. The Cabinet was particularly reluctant to come out against annexations and to emasculate its defensist appeals, whereas the Liaison Commission placed its main emphasis on the need for anti-annexationist guarantees.[43]

The statement which the Provisional Government issued on April 9, 1917, resulted directly from Soviet pressures; consequently, even though it was destined to have a wide circulation in both official and unofficial quarters abroad, its primary audience was the people of Russia. The concessions to the forces of movement at home came in the crucial paragraph which declared "that the purpose of free Russia [was] not domination over other peoples, nor spoliation of their national possessions, nor the violent occupation of foreign territories, but the establishment of a permanent peace on the basis of the self-determination of peoples. The Russian people [were] not aiming to increase their power abroad at the expense of other people, they [had] no aim to enslave or oppress anybody." [44]

From the over-all perspective of the politics of Allied war aims, the decisive import of this declaration is that it represented the first official public pronouncement on the vital issue of self-determination. The Government of the nation which hitherto had harbored the most ambitious annexationist plans in Europe went on record with a self-denying ordinance which was buttressed by concrete concessions to the Polish peoples.[45] From Russia's domestic point of view it must

43. Ibid., pp. 246–53, and Smilg-Benario, Von Kerenski zu Lenin, pp. 28–29. For the most recent judicious analysis of the struggle between Miliukov and the restive Left over foreign policy see Robert D. Warth, The Allies and the Russian Revolution: From the Fall of the Monarchy to the Peace of Brest-Litovsk (Durham, Duke University Press, 1954), pp. 47–65.

44. For the complete text of the April 9th statement see RAR, pp. 11–12.

45. After the Petrograd Soviet had called for Poland's right to independence, on March 30 the Provisional Government issued a proclamation to the Poles. Accordingly, the Polish state, "united with Russia in a free military alliance," could look forward toward eventual independence. Even though this was only a promise of limited independence, the proclamation marked a decisive departure from tsarist policy toward Poland. Individually Buchanan, Balfour, Paléologue, and

be noted that not only was defensism reaffirmed but also the Government undertook to observe fully "all obligations made in regard to our Allies." It is clear that the latter clause was more than just an afterthought, because Miliukov (who stayed in office for another five weeks) as well as all the other members of the Cabinet rebelled at any suggestion that the secret treaties should be denounced or that Russia should set out in search of a separate peace.[46]

Yet in the Central camp certain calculated efforts were being made to lure the Provisional Government into a peace dialogue. Whereas in Berlin Chancellor Bethmann-Hollweg made two relatively conciliatory speeches on March 29 and May 15,[47] in Vienna Foreign Minister Czernin publicly intimated that the Dual Monarchy would welcome negotiations with Russia.[48] Many newspapers in the Central camp suggested that in case a relatively direct diplomatic approach should fail, the Berlin and Vienna Governments should seek to strengthen the

---

Thomas expressed satisfaction about this new turn in Russian policy; moreover, collectively the Allied governments sent a joint note of approval to Miliukov. See Joseph Blociszewski, La Restauration de la Pologne et la diplomatie européenne (Paris, 1927), pp. 50–66; Roman Dyboski, Poland (London, 1933), pp. 76–78; Robert Machray, Poland 1914–1918 (London, 1932), pp. 77–79; Casimir Smogorzewski, La Pologne et la guerre (Paris, 1929), pp. 74–77. Subsequently, on April 4, Miliukov called for a "reorganization of Austria-Hungary and the liberation of her subject nationalities" which would necessitate "the creation of an independent Czecho-Slovak state . . . the restoration of the Italians to Italy, of the Rumanians to Rumania, and the natural union of the Serbian people, as well as the union of the Ukrainian population of the Austrian regions with the population of our Ukrainian lands." Regardless of any hopes Miliukov may have nursed about extending Russia's sphere of influence into some of these areas, his "statement in favor of the dissolution of Austria-Hungary and the liberation of her subject peoples . . . was the first such declaration by a responsible Russian statesman." Victor S. Mamatey, The United States and East Central Europe, 1914–1918: A Study in Wilsonian Diplomacy and Propaganda (Princeton, Princeton University Press, 1957), p. 95.

46. RAR, p. 10. One might argue that even though Russia had an obligation toward the Allies not to make a separate peace, she was not obligated to take advantage of all the territorial and sphere-of-influence concessions which the Allies had made to her in the secret treaties. This argument was advanced by Lord Robert Cecil in PD, 93 (May 16, 1917), col. 1668, and by Briand and Ribot in the Comité Secret (June 1, 1917), pp. 514, 535.

47. For excerpts from the Chancellor's March 29th speech as well as for German press comments see DR, EPS (April 12, 1917), pp. 308–9. Most of Bethmann-Hollweg's May 15th Reichstag address is cited in Scott, Official Statements of War Aims and Peace Proposals, pp. 98–102, esp. p. 101.

48. Bertrand Auerbach, L'Autriche et la Hongrie pendant la guerre (Paris, Alcan, 1925), pp. 265 ff., esp. p. 298.

peace forces inside Russia by appealing to them with a slate of liberally reformulated war aims. After the April 9th statement of the Russian Government had been hailed by the German press for being softer than the earlier Miliukov line,[49] the *Frankfurter Volksstimme* held that now it was "the turn of Germany to declare her own war aims in plain language and to proclaim that she does not desire any conquests." [50] Naturally most Germans and Austro-Hungarians rejoiced at those very omissions in the April 9th statement which caused such deep grief to Alexandre Ribot: there was no mention of Russia's resolve to fight for total victory, "Germany was not even mentioned," and there was no reference whatever to French war aims.[51]

As if to add insult to injury, the All-Russian Conference of the Soviet of Workers' and Soldiers' Deputies was equally restrained in its enthusiasm for the Allied cause. On April 25 this Conference called not only on enemy peoples but also on Allied peoples "to bring pressure on *their* Governments to give up their plans of conquest . . . [and] to make a general renunciation of annexation and indemnity." Moreover, the Conference emphasized "the necessity for the Provisional Government to enter into discussion with the Allies for the purpose of working out a general agreement along the line indicated." [52]

All these indices of the Provisional Government's inability to impose an effective political truce in Russia began to cause deep concern in official Allied quarters. Sporadic rumors of a possible Russo-German rapprochement made matters still worse, as did the apparent affinity between the Soviet pronouncements and the project of the emerging Stockholm movement. In order to reassure the Allies, but also in the hope of placating Kerensky and the Soviet, Premier Lvov instructed Miliukov to prepare a covering note with which to dispatch the April 9th statement as a "state paper" to the Allied chancelleries. Whereas Miliukov considered such a step catastrophic,[53] Lvov hoped that a

49. *DR*, EPS (May 3, 1917), pp. 6–11.
50. *Frankfurter Volksstimme* (April 12, 1917), cited ibid. (May 3, 1917), p. 6.
51. Ribot, *Lettres à un ami: Souvenirs de ma vie politique* (Paris, Bossard, 1924), p. 228.
52. Golder, p. 332.
53. A most striking and accurate report of Miliukov's hostile war-aims position *vis-à-vis* the Soviet is recorded in the diary of the ardently pro-Miliukov French Ambassador. See Maurice Paléologue, *An Ambassador's Memoirs* (3 vols. London, Hutchinson, 1923–25), *3*, 310 ff.

careful study of the statement by Ribot and Lloyd George would give them confidence in Russia's loyalty and might possibly serve to elicit a moderate war-aims pronouncement from the Allies.

Along these same lines, Ambassador Francis urged Washington to send a message which might help to calm the peace faction in the Soviet which was "using 'peace without victory' and other expressions in the President's address to Senate of January 22 to justify their advocacy of peace." [54] On the strength of Francis' dispatches, Lansing advised Wilson that some of his slogans were being "used by radical Socialists (probably under German influence) to force the Provisional Government to declare a policy which [would] remove the chief incentive to Russian offensive operations, namely, control of the Dardanelles and possession of Constantinople." In order to stop this "insidious" plan, the Secretary of State thought that the President should try composing a message in which "some interpretation of the language which [was] being used" would "remove" these treacherous ideas.[55]

In the meantime, having drafted the accompanying note, Miliukov transmitted it to the Allied governments on May 1, 1917, without prior clearance with the Executive Committee of the Petrograd Soviet.[56] According to this note "the general principles enunciated by the Provisional Government [were] in entire agreement with those lofty ideals which [had] been constantly expressed" by many Allied statesmen and "which were given especially vivid expression" in Wilson's war message.[57]

What "lofty ideals," beyond the "ideal" of self-defense and the defeat of Germany, had been formulated in Paris or London? Since Russia's Allies in late April were still a long way from embracing a liberal, nonannexationist, self-determination war-aims program, Miliukov's message was merely a reaffirmation of Russia's allegiance to her earlier commitments. True, on April 2 President Wilson had enrolled America in a war to make the world safe for democracy. But in his Congressional message Wilson had given a strictly unilateral interpretation of the purposes of the war, a declaration which in spite of its ideological verve could not have invalidated the Allied secret treaties. In his frantic efforts to deny the Petrograd Soviet a monopoly on the

54. FR, Russia, 1918, 1, 52.
55. Cited in Baker, Woodrow Wilson, Life and Letters, 7, 76.
56. See Sukhanov, The Russian Revolution 1917, p. 314.
57. For the complete text of Miliukov's explanatory note see RAR, pp. 11–12.

liberating ideology around which the Russian forces of movement threatened to build a mass movement, Miliukov now sought to capitalize on Wilson's message. Consequently, in this note he proclaimed that since "emancipated Russia" could now "use language" which would be understood by modern democracies, she was hastening "to add her voice to that of her Allies."

It would seem that even though neither his personality nor his political commitments permitted the Russian Foreign Minister to practice the politics of the street, he did make an attempt to heed Kerensky's warning on the urgency of changing "entirely the language of all our diplomatic notes and declarations." Although the Minister of Justice felt that Miliukov never went far enough in accommodating himself to the new Petrograd spirit, it must be noted that Kerensky himself, far from prepared to make substantive concessions to the Internationalists, was willing to yield only "in form to the new national psychology." [58] Meanwhile Miliukov and Kerensky were equally determined to observe strictly all the engagements which Russia had assumed toward her Allies, and to fight on to a "decisive victory."

It is difficult to disagree with the verdict that the "new Note annulled everything the revolution had accomplished on behalf of peace up to then." [59] The French Ambassador himself admitted that by couching his explanatory note "in intentionally vague and diffuse terms," Miliukov had done his best "to counteract the arguments of the manifesto." [60] In his determination to perpetuate Sazonov-type foreign-policy objectives, Miliukov tended to ignore the peculiarities of the relationship between domestic and foreign policy under modern revolutionary conditions.

Instantaneously a storm of protest broke loose both inside the Petrograd Soviet and in the streets of the Russian capital.[61] The Soviet leadership could not help being provoked, since the Miliukov note seemed to negate the April 9th Manifesto which had been issued under its pressure after laborious negotiations. Furthermore, in addition to the spontaneous outrage in many sectors of the population, anti-Government demonstrations were inspired and led by the Bolsheviks, who could hardly have asked for more perfect proof for their

58. Kerensky, The Catastrophe, pp. 130–31.
59. Sukhanov, The Russian Revolution 1917, p. 314.
60. Paléologue, An Ambassador's Memoirs, 3, 328.
61. Trotsky, The History of the Russian Revolution, 1, 332 ff.; and Smilg-Benario, Von Kerenski zu Lenin, pp. 39–46.

anti-Government accusations. Now that the "cards were on the table," it was clear to Lenin that the Government continued (1) to practice an antirevolutionary, tsarist foreign policy, (2) to subscribe to the secret treaties, and (3) to be subservient to Paris and London.[62]

These anti-Government pressures seriously endangered the all too precarious political truce between the Lvov Cabinet and the Soviet of Workers' and Soldiers' Deputies. On May 4 the Provisional Government set out to calm the highly agitated Soviet by presenting it with an official "explanation" of Miliukov's note. Accordingly, after taking full responsibility for the Foreign Minister's action, the Government sought to convey the impression that the note was in essence a rededication to the April 9th communication; and that by speaking of "penalties and guarantees" necessary for a durable peace it had in view "the reduction of armaments, the establishment of international tribunals, etc." [63] Whereas this explanation enabled the pro-Government forces to win a slim majority in the Petrograd Soviet, Miliukov's position gradually became even less tenable. For even though the relationship between the Provisional Government and the shadow government was momentarily improved, the Internationalists inside the Soviet with good reason interpreted the explanatory note as a victory for the forces of movement.

The Soviet looked upon this explanation as evidence that the revolutionary democracy of Russia would "never agree to a return of the tsarist foreign policy," and announced its intention to continue to work for international peace.[64] By May 9 the Petrograd Soviet issued a preliminary call for the meeting of an International Socialist Conference to be held in a neutral country for the purpose of exploring all avenues to an early peace.[65] Less than a week later, on May 15, it launched the much more aggressive and revolutionary Appeal to the Socialists of All Countries inviting "all the Socialist parties and factions in every country" to participate in this Conference. Evidently the explanatory note had encouraged the left-wing dissenting factions in the Soviet to articulate their peace offensive with a new history-making formula which they insisted had also become the platform of

62. Lenin, Works, 20, Pt. I, p. 234.
63. The text of the Provisional Government's explanation is cited in RAR, pp. 12–13.
64. Golder, p. 337.
65. Ibid., p. 339.

the Provisional Government: "Peace without annexations or indemnities on the basis of the self-determination of peoples." [66] Incidentally, at no time did the Government have sufficient strength to compel the Soviet to give Miliukov an explanation for any of its own questionable, if not treasonable, utterances.

Meanwhile, the All-Russian Conference of Bolsheviks had been meeting in Petrograd May 7–12 in order to consolidate its ideological as well as organizational position, and in order to increase left-wing pressures on the more moderate and loyal leaders of the Soviet. It accused the Government of deceiving the Russian people about the true character of the war by concealing the secret treaties from them. The Bolsheviks insisted that the "plundering treaties" should be published forthwith and that "all the nationalities should at once be given the opportunity to vote freely whether they wish to be independent States, or part of some other State." Should they get control of the Government, the Bolsheviks promised "immediately and openly" to offer all peoples "a democratic peace, on the basis of the complete renunciation of every kind of annexation and indemnity." [67] Lenin had made it clear, however, that this renunciation of annexations and indemnities was a "remedy" which by its very nature was revolutionary.[68] Even though the Leninist position was held by only a small though highly articulate and dangerously well-organized minority, it had the crucial effect of keeping the Social Revolutionaries and the Mensheviks from moving closer to the Cadets and the Octobrists, and of frightening the bourgeoisie into a more conciliatory mood.

In the face of these pressures, the Provisional Government could not help recognizing that the effective locus of power was in the process of shifting to the Soviet. According to N. N. Sukhanov, the Government was "completely powerless" and even though it reigned, it could not rule.[69] The intensifying demand for peace, bread, and land among the masses continued to spread further into the army. Guchkov, the Minister of War, was the first minister to resign from the Cabinet; he resigned because the Soviet was not effectively enjoined from encouraging the soldiers to question the authority of their officers.[70]

66. For the complete text of this appeal see RAR, pp. 16–19.
67. Cited in Golder, pp. 337–38.
68. Lenin, Works, 20, Pt. I, p. 277.
69. Sukhanov, The Russian Revolution 1917, p. 326.
70. Guchkov's reasons for resigning stand out clearly from his letter to Premier Lvov and a subsequent interview in Rech, both cited in Golder, pp. 396–97.

Presently negotiations between the Cabinet and the Executive Committee of the Petrograd Soviet were initiated for the purpose of broadening the coalition toward the Left. Above all, the Government sought to draw a number of leading Socialists into the Cabinet in order to have them act as a damper on the restless peace forces in the Soviet.

Before the Executive Committee gave its consent to a more extensive Cabinet participation by the Left, it debated the war-aims question at length with Lvov and some of his colleagues. Because of the left-revisionists' stubborn insistence that the Government accept the "no annexations, no indemnities" formula, Miliukov was fated to become the victim of a leftward cabinet reorganization. At last he resigned under protest on May 16, thereby facilitating a new accommodation with the forces of movement.

When the new center-left coalition was formed on May 18, the Socialists held a total of six ministerial positions. More significant, still, was their willingness to shoulder the responsibility for the two most crucial policy positions: Kerensky emerged as Minister of War and Marine, and his Radical-Liberal friend, M. I. Tereshchenko, a (Cadet) sugar magnate, as Foreign Minister.[71] Henceforth the second Lvov Cabinet would make every effort to convert the peace enthusiasm of the Soviet into a new fighting patriotism by having the aims of the war interpreted to Russia's masses by leftists instead of by spokesmen of the bourgeoisie. The French press, which naturally deplored Miliukov's resignation, expressed the hope that Kerensky would talk some sense and patriotism into the restive Soviet.[72] However, by becoming ardent Social Patriots in the new Liberal-Socialist Cabinet, the majority Mensheviks and the majority Social Revolutionaries began to share the responsibility for all government decisions in a country where the domestic and military situation was condemned to steady deterioration. Furthermore, as the new backbone of the War Cabinet—without which a political truce with the Soviet would have been impossible—the Social Patriots were in imminent danger of los-

71. For the negotiations between the Provisional Government and the Executive Committee of the Soviet see Golder, pp. 349–53. A vivid eye-witness account of these crucial negotiations is given by Sukhanov, *The Russian Revolution 1917*, pp. 335 ff. The full slate of the new coalition Cabinet is given in Golder, p. 353.

72. See *DR*, APS (May 30, 1917), p. 83. In the Central camp it was generally held that in spite of his belligerent tone, Kerensky was a big improvement over Miliukov.

ing the leadership of the war-aims and peace campaign to the dissident left-wing, more particularly to the Bolsheviks.

That the reorganized Provisional Government had no thought of abandoning the Triple Entente was publicly announced in an inaugural policy statement. The new Cabinet repudiated any suggestion of a separate peace, though it placed on record its intention of "effecting an agreement with the Allies on the basis of the declaration of April 9." Unlike Miliukov, the new ministers admitted that thus far no lofty aims had been formulated in Paris and London. Furthermore, they stated that if it was truly their intention to strive for a "peace without annexation or indemnity and based on the right of nations to decide their own affairs," they would have to bring the Allied war cabinets around to accepting the Soviet image of the future peace. In the meantime, however, the Provisional Government would not "suffer the German troops to destroy [their] western Allies and then throw themselves upon [Russia] with the full force of their arms." [73] Thus, although Foreign Minister Tereshchenko energetically opposed the immediate publication of the secret treaties because this would be "equivalent to rupture with the Allies and [would] result in the isolation of Russia," he did become the first Allied (and belligerent) Foreign Minister to stand up for new war aims.[74] Within two months the Revolution had succeeded in transforming the most autocratic and expansionist of all the belligerent states into at least an open, verbal exponent of a reasonable and democratic peace.

Naturally, the Allied governments had a vital interest in Russia's internal developments; it was evident that these developments would determine the war-making capacity of the Russian armies. As early as March 15 Sir George Buchanan, the British Ambassador in Petrograd, advised London that whereas the Duma was for a strengthening of the war effort, the "Social Revolution" was in favor of "peace at any price." [75] Similar dispatches were sent from the French and American embassies.[76] Moreover, before long the Allied and Associated ambassadors were forced to conclude that the Cadets and the Octobrists would have to compromise with the moderate Left in order to get an effective national union Government. The three ambassadors

73. The full text of the new Provisional Government's public declaration dated May 18, 1917, is cited in RAR, pp. 19–21.
74. FR, Russia, 1918, 1, 76.
75. Lloyd George, War Memoirs, 2, 1117–18.
76. See, e.g., FR, Russia, 1918, 1, 35.

may have disagreed in their estimates of the importance of moderate
left-wing support for the Provisional Government, but they were
fundamentally agreed that their foremost diplomatic assignment was
to marshal the type of Allied assistance which would best help to
keep Russia fighting actively and efficiently on the Entente side. Even
though the embassies were far from enthusiastic about the popular
agitation either for peace or for a formulation of war aims, they
nevertheless set out to investigate how they could assist in laying
the basis for an effective political truce in which most of the Left
would cooperate willingly and energetically. All along, however,
Buchanan, Paléologue, and Francis continued to be equally hostile
to the "Socialist" revolution. They differed only in the extent to which
they allowed this hostility to interfere with their respective appraisals
of the prevailing situation in Russia. While Sir George was perhaps
the most realistic and objective reporter, the French Ambassador ran
a close second. If Ambassador Francis' reports were not always as accurate as those of his colleagues, his failings were in large part due to
lack of diplomatic experience.

Since Allied Socialists and syndicalists were staunch supporters of
the war effort, the ambassadors decided that perhaps spokesmen of
the Allied Left could help to consolidate the Russian political truce.
The Embassies, therefore, undertook to counsel Paris, London, and
Washington to enlist prominent Social Patriots to carry the defensist
message to Russia in writing as well as in person.

Sir George inquired whether British Labour leaders could be prevailed upon to send a telegram to Kerensky, Chkheidze, and their comrades expressing their confidence that they would continue to support
the "free peoples fighting German despotism" because victory for
Germany would spell disaster "to all classes of the Allies." The British
Ambassador suggested, furthermore, that this telegram also "refer to
the unity of all classes in Britain, and especially to what the working
classes are doing." [77] Likewise, on March 23, even prior to America's
entry into the war, Ambassador Francis cabled Washington that because the danger from the Socialist elements had not entirely been
dissipated, a cable from "Gompers and other well known labor leaders
. . . would be opportunely helpful." [78]

77. Lloyd George, *War Memoirs*, 2, 1117–18.
78. *FR, Russia, 1918, 1,* 15–16. In his dispatch Francis indicated that leaders of
French and British Socialist and labor organizations had sent such cables to their
Russian comrades.

At the request of the War Cabinet, Arthur Henderson drafted a message which was sent to the Socialists in the Duma in the name of organized Labour in Great Britain. Henderson suggested that just as English and French labor were making "unprecedented efforts and sacrifices," the Allied Left confidently looked forward "to assistance of Russian labour in achieving the objects to which we have devoted ourselves." [79] From the United States Samuel Gompers reminded the Russian Left that since freedom was the product of evolution and hence could not "be established by revolution only," Russia's workers and masses should maintain what they had "already achieved." [80] In Paris the Social Patriotic Cabinet ministers Jules Guesde, Marcel Sembat, and Albert Thomas immediately sent a joint cable to Kerensky in order to encourage him and the new Russia to step up their efforts at defeating Prussian militarism. Likewise Pierre Renaudel, editor of the French Socialist l'Humanité, emphasized in a separate cable the importance of defeating the common enemy,[81] while his paper reminded Russia's Socialists that "an immediate and separate peace by Russia would be a peace against the French Republic." [82] Moreover, the SFIO parliamentary delegation issued a manifesto declaring that through the Revolution "Russia had tightened her alliance with the Western Democracies." [83]

Soon it was felt, however, that these long-distance messages could not plead the cause of defensism so effectively as small delegations of well-known Allied Socialists who stood firmly within the majoritarian camp. To be sure, even though not all Social Patriotic actions toward Russia were taken at the direct and explicit request of the war cabinets, they invariably received enthusiastic support from high Government circles. Thus in Paris the SFIO parliamentary faction, in agreement with the Foreign Affairs Commission of the Lower House, decided to send three of its members on a good-will mission to Petrograd. Even le Temps and l'Action Française considered the dispatch of Marcel Cachin, Marius Moutet, and Ernest Lafont a "wise

79. Cited in Lloyd George, War Memoirs, 2, 1118.
80. A first cable by Gompers dated March 21 seems to have been lost; hence he dispatched a second cable on April 2. See FR, Russia, 1918, 1, 16–18. Subsequently the American Federation of Labor sent two more messages, one on April 25 and another on September 18. Ibid., pp. 32, 194.
81. Georges Michon, The Franco-Russian Alliance, 1891–1917 (London, Allen and Unwin, 1929), pp. 276–78; and L. Marcellin, Politique et politiciens pendant la guerre (2 vols. Paris, Renaissance du Livre, 192–?), 2, 96.
82. L'Humanité, March 24, 1917.
83. Cited ibid., March 17, 1917.

move." [84] On the suggestion of the SFIO and at the request of the British Government, the Labour party charged William Sanders, Will Thorne, and James O'Grady with a similar assignment. According to Bonar Law, these gentlemen were "going with the one object of encouraging, so far as they can, the present Russian Government in the prosecution of the War." [85]

It was the declining military strength of a major ally which forced the Paris and London Cabinets into the unorthodox position of seeking political advantage from Socialist internationalism. However, both Governments saw to it that only highly loyal Majoritarians would be commissioned to bolster the patriotism of the Russian Left. Initially all dissidents were kept from such diplomatic missions for fear that they might encourage those Socialist elements in Russia which set stringent war-aims conditions for their acceptance of the political truce. In these efforts the cabinets could count on the Social Patriots, who were equally anxious to keep their Independent rivals in political isolation.

The organization of the Cachin mission gave rise to considerable controversy within the French Left. In addition to being leading Majoritarians, Cachin and Lafont were members of the important Foreign Affairs Commission of the Lower House, which encouraged their expedition. Hence both they and the no less loyal Moutet had the unhesitating support of the Cabinet as well as of the SFIO leadership. This very support, however, immediately raised the suspicions of the minority Socialists, who complained both about the arbitrary way in which the mission had originally been appointed and about the absence of minority representation. When this protest eventually caused Pierre Renaudel to suggest the inclusion of Jean Longuet in the mission, Longuet refused because in his view the mission had "a quasi-official and governmental character." Likewise in England, Philip Snowden criticized the composition of the delegation "sent by the Government to carry out the Government's policy." [86]

In addition to dispatching Allied Social Patriots to Petrograd, Paris and London did everything in their power to facilitate the return to Russia of those left-wing Russian exiles who, once back in their home-

84. *Le Temps*, March 27, 1917, and *l'Action Française*, April 6, 1917.

85. *PD*, 92 (April 14, 1917), col. 1277.

86. *Deuxième Circulaire de la minorité du Parti socialiste* (Paris, May 1917), pp. 28–31; and *PD*, 92 (April 23, 1917), col. 2035.

land, could be counted upon to reinforce the defensist cause. Even though the return of Lenin through Germany eventually caused an indignant stir in Paris and London, it must be noted that of the approximately 500 Russian émigrés who returned from Switzerland via Germany, 400 were Social Patriots. With much justification the Russian Bolsheviks complained in *Pravda* that whereas the British were delaying the return of Trotsky and other Zimmerwaldites, the trip of Plekhanov and Cachin received full Allied sanction and cooperation.[87] While the Bolsheviks did their best to cast suspicion on the political independence of the Allied Socialist delegations about to arrive in Russia, the Independent Labour party sent a cable to Petrograd accusing Thorne and his colleagues of being paid government agents who were not representative of British Socialism or Labour. The French *minoritaires* sent a similar message to the Petrograd Soviet.[88]

But the highly restive Petrograd Soviet needed none of these caveats in order to be on guard against the defensist arguments of the Cachin-Thorne delegations which arrived in Petrograd on April 13.[89] Not only was the composition of these delegations too blatantly Social Patriotic—at a time when the USPD invaded the political scene in Germany and the Independent factions were making headway in the Allied Left—but they came equipped with arguments and exhortations which failed to take account of the ideological and power realities in revolutionary Russia. Cachin, Thorne, and their colleagues appealed to their Russian comrades for continued enthusiastic support of the war in much the same terms in which Scheidemann, Sembat, and Henderson had drawn their followers into the political truce on August 4, 1914. But since then, the Petrograd Soviet not only had issued its March 27th Memorandum but also had forced the Provisional Government to subscribe to its peace formula in the April 9th statement. The Soviet did not expect Cachin and Thorne to step forward as flaming spokesmen of Zimmerwaldism; however, it did

87. See Deutscher, *The Prophet Armed*, p. 274, n. 1; and *DR*, APS (May 23, 1917), pp. 70–71. Axelrod, Martov, and Martynov, in addition to Trotsky, were temporarily detained by the British.

88. Rosalind Travers Hyndman, *The Last Years of H. M. Hyndman* (London, Grant Richards, 1923), p. 143; and Hubert Bourgin, *Le Parti contre la patrie* (Paris, Plon, 1924), p. 210.

89. Olga Hess Gankin and H. H. Fisher, eds., *The Bolsheviks and the World War: The Origin of the Third International* (Stanford, Stanford University Press, 1940), p. 588.

look for evidence that the Allied Left, while supporting the war
cabinets, was also pressing for the same reformulation of war aims
which the Revolution had placed at the top of Russia's political
agenda.

Consequently, though the Allied delegations were very much in
favor with the Provisional Government as well as with the Allied and
Associated Ambassadors, the Petrograd Soviet received them with a
mixture of tolerant indifference and sharp distrust.[90] The first encounters with the Soviet were far from easy, primarily because the Socialist delegates were confronted with embarrassing questions, like
"What will you do to bring the war to an early end?" and "What
pressures are you exercising on your governments?" According to
Moutet, he and his colleagues felt as if they had been summoned before a tribunal.[91]

After a few days in the Russian capital the Allied delegates began
to inject into their speeches revolutionary phrases which they had not
used since the war began. The excited atmosphere in Petrograd led
Cachin to address the Soviet on April 15 with a flaming speech which,
even according to one of his severest critics, was like a "hymn to the
great revolution" that revived "the romance of its first days." Likewise
O'Grady fired the enthusiasm of the assembly with the assertion that
the working class of the whole world was indebted to "the present
Russian generation and its great work." [92]

Notwithstanding such passing oratorical triumphs, the encounters
with the Executive Committee of the Petrograd Soviet were far from
encouraging. What did France and England propose to do to strike
imperialist objectives from their war aims? What political action,
if any, were the French and British Social Patriots taking in order
to help bring about the "purification" of Entente diplomacy? Since
the minority Socialists in France and Great Britain seemed to be
speaking the Soviet language so much more courageously and convincingly than Cachin and Thorne, why were they not represented
in these delegations? In brief, in Petrograd the Allied Social Patriots
were being cheered primarily by the extreme right wing of the Rus-

90. See FR, 1917, Supplement 2, 1, 35.
91. Comité Secret, pp. 497–98. For a good summary of the cool reception accorded to the visiting Social Patriots see Fainsod, International Socialism and the
World War, pp. 128–30.
92. Sukhanov, The Russian Revolution, 1917, pp. 261–63.

sian Left and by the middle class. Gompers' message did not fare much better,[93] and "the ovations and demonstrations" for the American entrance into the war were all being made "by the people of the middle classes." [94] No wonder that before long even Sir George Buchanan urged his Government to make it possible for Ramsay MacDonald to come to Petrograd in the hope that an officially sanctioned presentation of the Allied ILP position might exert a calming influence on the restless Soviet.[95]

Undoubtedly there were compelling reasons which prejudiced Russia's Socialists against agreeing unconditionally to a political truce. On the other hand, the terribly real peril of further German advances into Russia served to remind many Menshevik and Social Revolutionary leaders of the hazards of pressing a political offensive against the Provisional Government while the Russian armies were trying to mount a military offensive against the Central Powers. Whenever Cachin and Thorne spoke of the manner in which continued domestic instability was likely to aggravate the dangers not only of long-term German domination of Russia but also of immediate military pressure on the French and British democracies, their listeners became solemn and attentive. For in Petrograd it was no secret that, unlike the Entente Powers, the Central Powers had every interest in undermining the political, economic, and military strength of Russia.

Germany could hardly send her Socialists into enemy Russia for the purpose of preaching sedition, insubordination, peace, and anti-Allied as well as pro-Central propaganda. She was nevertheless determined to participate in every possible way in Russia's internal political struggle, which she knew to be extremely decisive for the future course of the war. The most straightforward way for Germany to affect this struggle was to maintain a steady military pressure which would help to undermine further the military morale of Russia and would nourish the peace hunger of a dispirited, war-weary, and impatient population. In the field of diplomacy the Central Powers could explore ways of making a separate peace attractive to an enemy who gradually would have to recognize that his military establishment was no match for that of the well-disciplined and adequately equipped

93. *FR, Russia, 1918,* 1, 55.
94. Ibid.
95. Sir George Buchanan, *My Mission to Russia and Other Diplomatic Memories* (2 vols. London, Cassell, 1923), 2, 142–43, 147.

German armies. Moreover, Berlin and Vienna could participate in the international civil war by encouraging, helping, and publicizing the efforts of the antiwar forces in Russia.

Just as the Allies realized that the Cadets and the right-wing Socialists were their champions in Russia, so the Germans could not help noticing that in pressing their anti-Government campaign the Russian Zimmerwaldites, more particularly the Bolsheviks, were in a position to help promote the German national interest. In pursuit of her primary objective, which was the defeat of the Russian armies, Germany was certainly justified in exploiting every political means at her disposal. And nothing was more natural than to undermine the strength of an enemy on his military as well as his domestic front.

Thus Germany's Eastern Command "tried, by means of propaganda, to increase the disintegration that the Russian Revolution had introduced into the Army." General von Hoffmann candidly reports that just as he sent shells into enemy trenches or discharged poison gas at them, as an enemy he had "the right to employ the expedient of propaganda against [enemy] garrisons." [96] Since in modern warfare the home front is as much a part of military garrisons as front-line infantry regiments, it should not come as a surprise that German propaganda tried to reach as deeply as possible into the Russian political turmoil.[97] As the peace hunger in Russia kept growing, the Eastern Command declared that one of Germany's primary jobs was to watch internal Russian developments carefully in order to encourage the "process of disintegration." Also, the Government should handle all proposals for a separate peace in such a way as to channel them toward actual peace negotiations.[98]

Certainly, if the Central Powers could contribute to Russia's difficulties by merely allowing the Russian Bolshevik émigrés in Switzerland to travel through Germany on their way home, they were obliged to take advantage of such a safe and inexpensive opportunity.[99] Even as early as 1915—hence, long before the Revolution—not only Gisbert Freiherr von Romberg, the German Ambassador in Bern, but also the

---

96. Gen. Max von Hoffmann, *The War of Lost Opportunities* (New York, International Publishers, 1925), p. 180.

97. See Erich Ludendorff, *Meine Kriegserinnerungen, 1914–1918* (Berlin, Mittler, 1919), p. 327.

98. Ibid., p. 353.

99. This discussion of the politics of Lenin's return to Russia follows the comprehensive and probably definitive study, primarily based on German Foreign Ministry documents, of Hahlweg, pp. 307–33.

German ambassadors in Copenhagen and Stockholm had been reporting to Berlin about the antitsarist activities of Russian antiwar Socialists in the neutral countries.[100] But until March 1917 the ambassadors
and the Government had merely gathered information about these potentially useful rebels; presently, however, such information became
the first step to action. On April 2 Graf Brockdorff-Rantzau, Ambassador in Copenhagen, suggested that in secrecy Germany should seek
to strengthen the extremists in Russia because these were committed
to spread chaos there. Almost simultaneously Bethmann-Hollweg advised von Romberg to be in contact with the Russian exiles in Switzerland with a view to offering them a safe return through Germany.[101]

Meanwhile, immediately after the Revolution, 560 émigrés in
Switzerland had formed a "Central Committee for the Return of the
Swiss-domiciled Russian Political Refugees." When it became apparent
that the Allies were not likely to expedite their homeward journey,
by March 19 even the non-Bolshevik members of this Committee decided to favor an approach to von Romberg about the possibilities
and conditions for transit rights through Germany. The Committee
chose the pacifist-oriented Robert Grimm, Secretary of the Swiss Social Democratic party, to be its spokesman both with the Political
Department of the Swiss Government and with the German authorities.[102]

Immediately upon finding out about Grimm's representations with
the Swiss Government, on March 27 von Romberg advised the German Foreign Ministry about the "outstanding Russian revolutionaries"
who had expressed a "desire to return to Russia through Germany." In
turn, that same day, the Foreign Ministry advised the Supreme Command of this impending request for transit. Furthermore, after stating that it was in Germany's interest "that the influence of the extremist
wing should gain the upper hand in Russia," Secretary of State Zimmermann requested the military's approval for the Government's unorthodox project.[103] The Supreme Command seems to have been as
enthusiastic as the Ambassador and the Foreign Ministry. By Ludendorff's own admission he had no objections, since Berlin had assured

100. Ibid., pp. 309–11.
101. Ibid., pp. 312–14.
102. Ibid., p. 315; and Fritz Platten, *Die Reise Lenins durch Deutschland im
plombierten Wagen* (Berlin, Neuer Deutscher, 1924), pp. 22 ff. Both Hahlweg and
Platten rightly emphasize that the émigrés took the initiative themselves, and did
not wait to be approached by the German Embassy.
103. Cited in Hahlweg, pp. 315–16.

him that this diplomatic maneuver promised to "improve peace possibilities through the internal weakening of Russia." [104]

While the German Government's policy was taking shape, serious tensions developed within the émigré Committee in Zurich. Whereas the majority of the exiles were opposed to accepting German patronage without prior approval from the Provisional Government, Lenin and some thirty supporters were determined to pursue the negotiations regardless of such approval. Anxious to avoid all further delays, Lenin struck out on his own. He made Fritz Platten, a respected member of the left wing of the Swiss Social Democratic party, his intermediary with the competent authorities. By now Lenin was sensitive to the danger of being labeled a German agent for accepting the transit privileges. Therefore, on April 4 Platten informed the German Embassy of the conditions on which Lenin would agree to travel through Germany. Even though von Romberg thought it most unusual that an "individual" should set conditions to a "government," he nevertheless advised the Chancellor to accept them.[105]

Finally, on April 9, a convoy of thirty-three exiles left Zurich; among the nineteen Bolsheviks Lenin, Zinoviev, and Radek were the most prominent. But before leaving, on April 5, Lenin and his supporters had to counter the violent censure of the remaining exiles; also, they were anxious to articulate their own awareness of the expediency which guided not so much their own action, as that of the Berlin Government. In a revolutionary farewell address Lenin defiantly proclaimed, much to the discomfort of von Romberg, that he was "fully aware of the fact that the German Government allows the passage of the Russian Internationalists only in order thus to strengthen the antiwar movement in Russia." [106] Needless to say, as opposed to the Central Powers the Allies helped the return of only those émigrés who could be counted upon to be loyal both to the Provisional Government and to the Allied cause.[107]

Lenin and his party arrived with German blessings in Petrograd on

104. Cited in Richard Fester, *Die politischen Kämpfe um den Frieden, 1916–1918 und das Deutschtum* (Munich and Berlin, Lehmanns, 1938), p. 166.

105. Hahlweg, pp. 318–21. See also Platten, *Die Reise Lenins*, pp. 62–66.

106. Lenin, *Works, 20*, Pt. II, p. 385. Von Romberg wired the complete text of Lenin's address to Bethmann-Hollweg. See GFM, Container 2090. This "Lenin" convoy was the first of a series of convoys of "pacifist Socialists" which the Germans either sent or prepared to send into Russia. See GFM, Container 2160 and 2161.

107. Hahlweg, p. 329.

April 16, three days after Plekhanov and the Cachin-Thorne delegation had pulled into the Finland Station under Allied auspices. While the arrival of the latter delegations had been preceded by cables from Allied dissidents and by German propaganda charging them with being agents of the Allied governments, Lenin's arrival was the subject of extensive Allied propaganda to the effect that the Bolsheviks had entered into a nefarious pact with the Central Powers. Regardless of the truth of these charges and countercharges, the political field in Russia was so structured that by advancing the Revolution Lenin was serving the German cause, while by seeking to consolidate the political truce Plenkhanov was in effect advancing the interests of the Allies.

It is difficult to determine what contribution, if any, these Allied Socialist delegations made to the strengthening of defensism in the Russian Left. However, the impact on their home countries is less difficult to measure: once back in Paris and London they became relentless and effective disseminators of the Petrograd peace formula and of a profound concern for the fortunes of the Russian Revolution.[108]

In the meantime, however, the Allied governments took an additional step calculated to help channel Russian left-wing support to the Provisional Government. Instead of cabling a slate of liberal war aims to their Petrograd embassies, they sought to strengthen pro-Allied sentiments by another "personnel" maneuver: the war cabinets appointed their two most prominent Social Patriotic ministers to replace the French and British ambassadors in the Russian capital. On April 22 Albert Thomas arrived in Petrograd with instructions to take the place of Paléologue.[109] Five weeks later the British Cabinet commissioned Arthur Henderson to proceed to Petrograd in order to study the Russian situation at first hand; also, should he conclude that Sir George either was reporting unsatisfactorily or had become a political liability, Henderson was to stay on as ambassador.[110] On both these assignments the Allied Socialist leaders ceased to make any pretense of acting in a party capacity. When they descended on the Russian capital as official representatives of the war cabinets they must have known that

108. See below, Chap. 4.
109. Albert Thomas and his party arrived at the Finland Station on April 22, 1917, where they were met by Paléologue, Miliukov, Tereshchenko, and Konovalov. Paléologue, *An Ambassador's Memoirs, 3*, 309.
110. Mary Agnes Hamilton, *Arthur Henderson* (London, Heinemann, 1938), p. 125.

the Entente cabinets were primarily interested in exploiting their party affiliations in the interest of Allied diplomacy.

Whereas Henderson and Buchanan agreed both on the diagnosis of the Russian situation and on future policies,[111] Thomas and Paléologue had contrasting views about the nature of Russia's problems. Paléologue was so concerned with the war against the Central Powers that he looked at developments in Russia exclusively in the light of war imperatives. Devoid of any faith in the ability of Kerensky and his Soviet supporters to reorganize the army effectively, he seemed prepared to encourage those anti- and non-Socialist political forces which promised to set about restoring rigid order on the home front as well as in the army. On the other hand, Thomas decided that the only chance of salvaging the Eastern front was to support the Kerensky elements, which alone might enlist the revolutionary enthusiasm of the worker and peasant proletariat into the Entente cause. In pursuit of this objective, in agreement with Kerensky, Albert Thomas and Arthur Henderson sought to convince their governments that a revised war-aims statement was essential to a revival of popular enthusiasm for the war. However, Paléologue lost no opportunity to convince the French Cabinet that in making such war-aims recommendations both Thomas and Cachin had "illusions" about chances of a Russian revival.[112] No wonder that in Kerensky's view Albert Thomas and Paléologue held such opposing views and attitudes toward the March

111. No sooner had he arrived in Petrograd than Henderson realized that Buchanan's reports had been unusually realistic and perceptive. Henderson immediately advised the Cabinet that Sir George should stay on as ambassador. See ibid., pp. 126–28. Bernard Pares, who worked with Buchanan in Russia during this period, concluded that Sir George "was the only foreigner who understood Kerensky's difficulties from the start, and who did not want to push him unduly." Pares, *My Russian Memoirs*, p. 425. For the text of some of the public speeches that Henderson as well as Thomas delivered in the course of their visit to Russia, see A. J. Sack, *The Birth of the Russian Democracy* (New York, 1918), pp. 364–76.

112. According to Paléologue, two days after his arrival in Petrograd, Albert Thomas was convinced that the "whole strength of the Russian democracy lies in its revolutionary fervor [and that] Kerensky alone is capable of establishing, with the aid of the Soviet, a government worthy of our confidence." On April 25, in a long conversation with Thomas, Kerensky insisted that a revision of war aims in conformity with the Soviet's resolutions would soon have to be undertaken if the Allied Governments were not to "lose all their credit with the Russian democracy." From Petrograd, Paléologue and Thomas sent conflicting policy recommendations to Ribot, with Paléologue insisting that if France would give in to the Soviet's war-aims pressure, she would help to undermine confidence in the Lvov-Miliukov Government. Paléologue, *An Ambassador's Memoirs*, 3, 310–17; Ribot, *Lettres à un ami: Souvenirs de ma vie politique*, pp. 233–34; Poincaré, *Au Service de la France*, 9, 152.

Revolution that they would forever remain two symbolic figures in the unfolding Russian catastrophe.[113]

The American Government was equally concerned about the mounting tension between the Soviet and the Provisional Government, and sought ways of reinforcing the Russian war elements. On April 9 and 11 Secretary Lansing suggested to President Wilson that something be done "to prevent the socialistic element in Russia from carrying out any plan which would destroy the efficiency of the Allied Powers." [114] From various sources the White House was being urged to send a goodwill mission to Russia. It was generally agreed that the members of such a mission should be not only "men of large view" with "a sympathetic appreciation of just what it is they have been sent over for," but also "genuinely enthusiastic for the success of the Russian revolution." President Wilson even queried whether the members of the proposed mission should "look the part." [115]

With the President's well-attuned sensitivity to the movements of reform and his great sympathy "with the things that had recently been happening in Russia" [116] it seems surprising that he should have chosen Elihu Root to head the Mission. Quite apart from the former Secretary of State's eminent professional qualifications for so delicate a task, he neither "looked the part" nor sympathized with the revolutionary stirrings in Petrograd. American Liberals actually felt that Mr. Root might "have served his country better by refusing than by accepting." [117] James Bryce feared that because of the intoxicated "atmosphere of dreams and vague phrases" Root's wisdom would be wasted

113. Kerensky, *La Révolution russe, 1917* (Paris, Payot, 1928), chap. 18 ("Albert Thomas et Maurice Paléologue"), pp. 335–45, esp. p. 342. Significantly, Sazonov came to the Finland Station on May 16, 1917, in order to bid farewell to Paléologue, who was returning to Paris. On that occasion Sazonov remarked that the resignation of Miliukov which had just been announced was "the end of a political era." Moreover, it was Sazonov's belief that Miliukov's presence in the Provisional Government had been "the last guarantee of fidelity to our diplomatic tradition." Paléologue, *An Ambassador's Memoirs*, 3, 342.

114. Cited in Baker, *Woodrow Wilson, Life and Letters*, 7, 16.

115. Ibid., pp. 16–17.

116. Ibid., pp. 56–57.

117. *New Republic* (May 5, 1917), p. 2. See also Josephus Daniels, *The Wilson Era* (Chapel Hill, University of North Carolina Press, 1946), pp. 57–58. By November 25, 1918, Wilson refused to consider Root for an appointment to the Peace Commission because he had had opportunity "of knowing just how hopeless a reactionary he is" and because Root's appointment "would discourage every liberal element in the world." Cited in Donald Day, ed., *Woodrow Wilson's Own Story* (Boston, Little, Brown, 1952), p. 302.

and that a "practical, sturdy labor leader" might have a better chance.[118] However, not even the appointment of James Duncan, first vice-president of the American Federation of Labor, and Charles Russell, a right-wing Socialist, imparted to the Root Mission the kind of political color likely to impress the Soviet.[119]

On May 26, in explaining the purposes of the Root Mission to the Provisional Government, President Wilson actually embraced the war-aims principles of the Petrograd Soviet; he insisted, however, that the Russian people should pay no attention either to the internal or international peace agitation because both were German-inspired.[120] On the same occasion Secretary of State Lansing issued a similar appeal. However, even though Root and his colleagues were not vulnerable on the explosive secret-treaty issue, the American Mission, for obvious reasons, did not fare any better in Petrograd than its French or British counterpart.[121]

Since the Allied and Associated ambassadors, delegations, and missions were primarily concerned with drawing wider sections of the Russian Left to the Provisional Government, they were destined to be in intimate contact with Kerensky. For, first as Minister of Justice and then as a Minister of War, he was the most authoritative spokesman for the majority Social Revolutionaries and majority Mensheviks in Government circles. Moreover, he was the natural and least compromising line of communication with the Petrograd Soviet. Unfortunately, however, this intensive partnership with the Allied emissaries contributed to reducing Kerensky's sensitivity to local conditions by causing him to direct too much of his attention and energy to the prosecution of the war.[122] Hence, much like the Cadets and the Octobrists he now looked upon the Revolution as the most important and effective

118. Cited in H. A. L. Fisher, *James Bryce* (2 vols. New York, Macmillan, 1927), 2, 164.

119. For a full listing of all members of the Mission see *FR, Russia, 1918, 1,* 109. A critical discussion of the Mission's membership is given in William Appleman Williams, *American-Russian Relations, 1781–1947* (New York, Rinehart, 1952), pp. 87–90, 93–95.

120. The full text of Wilson's message is cited in Baker and Dodd, *The Public Papers of Woodrow Wilson, 5,* 49–53.

121. Cf. *America's Message to the Russian People* ("Addresses by the Members of the Special Diplomatic Mission of the United States to Russia in the Year 1917") Boston, 1918. For a comprehensive discussion of the Root Mission see Philip C. Jessup, *Elihu Root* (2 vols. New York, Dodd, Mead, 1938), 2, 353–71.

122. R. H. Bruce Lockhart, *British Agent* (New York, Putnam's, 1933), p. 181.

stimulant to the Russian war effort. He pressed the Western emissaries for a revision of Allied war aims with the conviction that an ideological primer from Paris and London was all that was needed to swing the skeptical Soviet over to an enthusiastic prowar position. In the meantime, however, Kerensky also had to compromise with the bourgeoisie, because for the time being he considered its support and leadership crucial for the conduct of the war. As the great compromiser dedicated to safeguarding the gains of the first Revolution and the confidence of the Allied Powers, Kerensky gradually lost much of the ideological attraction which had belonged to the Social Revolutionaries and Mensheviks in March 1917. For fear of straining relations with the Cadets still further and thereby endangering the war enterprise, many of the Social Revolutionary and Menshevik leaders, under Kerensky's guidance, ceased to press for further economic and social reforms.

Step by step the extremists were left free to capture the ideological fortress of the Revolution. The Bolsheviks were prepared to make political capital out of Russia's desperate economic situation, since they did not hesitate to blame all calamities and privations on the Provisional Government. According to them, it was only with Kerensky's support that the Lvov Cabinet was able to continue the war; and as long as the war lasted there could be no hope of any serious economic improvement or reform. Thus the Bolshevik formula called for revolution as the key to peace, and peace as the key to basic reconstruction and reform. Eventually the Bolsheviks emerged as the self-styled spokesmen of the soldiers, peasants, workers, and subject nationalities. For as more of the latter fell prey to war weariness they began to listen to the magical diagnosis according to which the secret treaties were all that stood in the way of a peace of no annexations and no indemnities, on the basis of self-determination.

But before the fact and the ideas of the Russian Revolution went on to their next stage, they had left a profound imprint on politics in Germany, France, and Great Britain.

2. TOWARD THE REICHSTAG RESOLUTION

IN LATE JULY and early August 1914 Allied Conservatives and progressives, including all shades of Socialists, anxiously followed the deliberations of the German Social Democratic party. Because "Bebel's" party was widely respected for its large membership, its efficient internal organization, and its competent leadership, the SPD's decision for or against war was bound to have momentous repercussions, both national and international. Nationally an effective *Burgfrieden* depended on the SPD's continuing loyalty to the German state and nation; internationally, precisely because it had long been Europe's most powerful and influential Socialist party, German Social Democracy's course of action was expected to affect decisions inside Europe's major Socialist parties.

Having polled four and a half million popular votes in the parliamentary elections of 1912, the SPD had a delegation of 110 deputies in the Reichstag.[1] This imposing political strength, combined with equally decisive syndical power, caused many of Europe's leading Socialists, including revolutionaries like Lenin, to anchor their revolutionary hopes in the German proletariat. Great was their disappointment when Germany's Socialist leaders, in the name of one million SPD members and of two and a half million trade unionists, came out in support of the war. Unlike Robert Michels, many if not actually most European Socialists had failed to realize that this mass membership of the German Left had become the basis for a rigidly stratified organ-

1. Joseph A. Berlau, *The German Social Democratic Party, 1914–1921* (New York, Columbia University Press, 1949), p. 348. See also Edwyn Bevan, *German Social Democracy during the War*, New York, Dutton, 1919; and Eugen Prager, *Geschichte der U.S.P.D.*, Berlin, Verlagsgenossenschaft Freiheit, 1922.

izational structure in which a conservative bureaucracy planned as well as executed a power-compromising strategy.[2] By the time the Archduke was assassinated at Sarajevo, the triple impact of economic forces, organizational developments, and ideological reformulations had caused German Socialism to abandon its revolutionary ambitions. Like Germany's other major political parties, the SPD fought for political, economic, and social reforms by legitimate, not by revolutionary, means.[3]

Needless to say, the prewar ideological debates which had accompanied this shift to political gradualism and respectability were at all times as heated as they were exalted. Especially on speakers' platforms and in editorial columns revisionist, left-center, and maximalist theoreticians seemed to rout their intellectually colorless but politically astute majoritarian opponents. But these theoreticians' triumphs were oratorical rather than political. True, under their influence German Social Democracy had signed the revolutionary antiwar manifestoes of the Stuttgart and Basle congresses of the Second International. However, like the SFIO and the Labour party, the SPD voted these and similar antiwar resolutions only after acrimonious internal debates in which the precariously allied Internationalists scored essentially empty ideological triumphs. The July–August 1914 crisis proved that the nationalist faction had deliberately retreated from the verbal battle over antiwar resolutions in order to fortify its position inside the apparatus of the party and the trade unions. Futhermore, the revolutionary and/or Internationalist convictions of many if not actually most left-Socialists were so fragile that they snapped the moment they were put to the first serious test.

Of the 110 Socialist Reichstag deputies, only fourteen were genuinely hesitant about approving the war credits.[4] On August 3, 1914, at Karl Kautsky's suggestion, these recalcitrants urged their majority colleagues that they should make their support of the war conditional on the Government's acceptance of war aims which would be com-

2. Michels, *Political Parties*, esp. Pt. VI.
3. The two most searching studies of the advance of conservative tendencies inside the German Socialist movement are Rudolf Schlesinger, *Central European Democracy and Its Background* (London, Routledge, 1953), esp. pp. 115–18; and Schorske, *German Social Democracy*.
4. Friedrich Stampfer, *Sozialdemokratie und Kriegskredite*, Berlin, Paul Singer, 1915. See also Schorske, *German Social Democracy*, pp. 285–91; and Bevan, *German Social Democracy during the War*, chap. 2.

patible with the principles of international Socialism, instead of giving the Government *carte blanche*.[5] This suggestion never got beyond the caucus stage, primarily because the fury of the nationalist wave which swept over Germany in those fateful August days spared neither the mass of German workers nor their political and syndical leaders.[6]

In this emergency, partly in the hope of surmounting lingering suspicions of their loyalty in official circles, all Socialists were equally anxious to give immediate evidence of their allegiance to the fatherland. When the Reichstag convened on August 4 to authorize the war credits, even the fourteen factious Social Democrats had abandoned their momentary faithfulness to the International; by dutifully abiding by the long-standing rules of party discipline they enabled the SPD parliamentary delegation to cast a unanimous prowar vote. The Kaiser instantly responded by solemnly assuring the Socialist leaders as well as the public at large that henceforth political labels would cease to be of import: regardless of political affiliations, all citizens would be considered equally loyal Germans. Since in Germany, unlike France and England, the Socialists were virtually the exclusive carriers of the whole tradition of "movement," the net effect of this unanimous vote was the establishment of a solid political *Burgfrieden*. Within the framework of this political truce most SPD and trade union leaders now eagerly helped the Government mobilize the military, economic, and ideological resources of the German nation.

In the light of the enormous gains which both the Government and the parties of order derived from the political truce, the unconditional vote by the SPD seems like a major political surrender. In appreciation for this crucial support, the Government at first did no more than abandon its plan of arresting certain prominent yet basically harmless Socialist leaders whose loyalty until recently had been suspect.[7] The Left gained few additional advantages in exchange for its instantaneous acceptance of the party truce which soon advanced the political fortunes of the parties of order. During the first two and a half years of war this truce enabled the Conservative, National Liberal, and Center parties to move further to the right.

5. Kautsky, *Sozialisten und Krieg*, pp. 446–50, 458–60. Though himself not a member of the Reichstag, Kautsky wielded great influence as the foremost theoretician of the left center and as editor of the weekly *Die Neue Zeit*.

6. William Maehl, "The Triumph of Nationalism in the German Socialist Party on the Eve of the First World War," *Journal of Modern History, 24* (1952), 40.

7. Friedrich Meinecke, *Staat und Persönlichkeit* (Berlin, Mittler, 1933), p. 207.

Presently a right-wing political coalition crystallized which saw "in a German victory the last hope of salvation for the old Germany," [8] and which often was allied with smaller groups of die-hard reactionaries. Especially the latter, which were a "numerically unimportant but politically, financially, and intellectually powerful minority . . . took the lead in the evolution of a German program of war aims. Among these radical annexationists the great industrialists played a particularly important role. . . . It was a combination of elements, then, industrialists, Pan-Germans, the parties of the Right, and the Supreme Command, that was responsible for the stubborn propagation of extreme war-aims." [9]

By May 20, 1915, the five leading economic associations, in a detailed memorandum to Chancellor Bethmann-Hollweg, specified extensive territorial and economic concessions in both Europe and the colonies which, in their view, should be acquired as a result of the war. Five months later, on the advice of Matthias Erzberger, a prominent Centrist leader, the *Gewerkschaft Deutscher Kaiser* sent two memoranda to the Foreign Ministry, one of them dealing with "The Interests of the Thyssen Enterprise in France and her Colonies," the other outlining "The Importance of the Briey Basin for the German Steel Industry." Meanwhile, by late October 1914, a high official in the Foreign Ministry had prepared independently a lengthy policy paper entitled "Reflections about the Coming Peace" proposing equally concrete and ambitious war aims in Belgium, Alsace-Lorraine, Courland, Lithuania, and Africa.[10]

The salvation of the Old Germany and the success of expansionist plans were dependent not only on the ultimate outcome of the military conflict but also on its duration. A swift victory promised to secure a long-term consolidation of the status-quo forces which in the prewar years had retreated slowly but steadily under the sustained pressure of the SPD and the trade unions. On the other hand, a protracted military struggle, by straining Germany's limited military and economic resources, was likely not only to rekindle but actually to sharpen prewar party struggles and class differences.[11]

8. Rosenberg, *The Birth of the German Republic*, p. 103.
9. Gatzke, *Germany's Drive to the West*, p. 294. See also Alfred Kruck, *Geschichte des Alldeutschen Verbandes 1890–1939* (Wiesbaden, Steiner, 1954), pp. 71–90; and Karl Helfferich, *Der Weltkrieg* (2 vols. Berlin, Ullstein, 1919), 2, 80–81.
10. All four papers are in GFM, Container 1498.
11. Rosenberg, *The Birth of the German Republic*, p. 87.

In full awareness of the long-range countervailing military power of the Entente and the precariousness of the emergency-inspired *Burgfrieden*, Bethmann-Hollweg resisted the formulation of war objectives which could at best be secured after a long, drawn-out military effort.[12] Whereas the Imperial Chancellor hoped that, externally, modest aims in the East might eventually lead to a separate peace with Russia, thus cutting sharply into the enemy's military power, internally he eventually took certain timid steps calculated to secure labor's continuing support of the war effort.

After deciding against the arrest of the SPD and trade union leaders who had been listed as security risks, Bethmann-Hollweg sought to reinforce the *Burgfrieden* by informing the Reichstag through Clemens Delbrück, State Secretary for the Interior, that the wartime political truce would be followed by a *Neuorientierung* immediately after victory. This vague promise of a new constitutional order after the war seemed a small price to pay for the concerted support of the progressive forces. However, the extreme Right considered even this amorphous pledge altogether superfluous; henceforth the intransigent defendants of the old order opposed Bethmann-Hollweg's repeated efforts to solidify his connections with the forces of movement by granting them wartime concessions or postwar promises.[13]

Incidentally, this vague pledge for reforms had been neither formulated nor delivered by August 4, 1914, when the SPD had unanimously decided to support the Government. How, then, did the Socialist leaders justify to themselves and to their followers their sudden shift to a prowar position?

Even though the Cabinet, the Supreme Command, and the non-Socialist press propagated the idea that the Central Powers had been the innocent victims of foreign aggression, they themselves never believed, nor sought to convince the public, that Germany's war aims should be confined to a straightforward restoration of the status quo. Unlike the Right, the Social Democrats tended to take these pious self-defense slogans at face value and read into them essentially modest

12. On June 8, 1915, Graf Tisza and Bethmann-Hollweg agreed that "if possible" the Central Powers should not "excessively prolong the war"; therefore, modest war aims should be stipulated, particularly *vis-à-vis* Russia. GFM, Container 1498.

13. Philipp Scheidemann, *Memoiren eines Sozialdemokraten* (2 vols. Dresden, Reissner, 1928), *1*, 310–11; and Graf Westarp, *Konservative Politik im letzten Jahrzehnt des Kaiserreiches* (2 vols. Berlin, Deutsche Verlagsgesellschaft, 1935), *2*, 25.

war-aims implications. The SPD enrolled in what it labeled a war of legitimate self-defense, the only kind of war which, under certain circumstances, was sanctioned even by Socialist doctrine.

It must have been convenient for the SPD high command that tsarist Russia was one of the three leading members of the enemy coalition. No lesser Socialist theoretician than Engels had suggested in the late nineteenth century that since a tsarist military victory in a future Russo-German conflict might spell not only the defeat of the politically and industrially advanced German state but also the destruction of the world's strongest Socialist party, German Socialism might have to support a war of self-defense.[14] In other words, there was a ready-made doctrinal and ideological justification on which the SPD leaders were able to base their endorsement of the war. In 1914 it was not a question of defending the capitalist fatherland from aggression by equally advanced and rapacious capitalist nations; instead, it was a case of foreign aggression sponsored by Europe's most backward and authoritarian regime. In the party ideology, hatred for the class enemy within Germany was promptly replaced by fiery denunciation of the many-sided evils of the reactionary tsarist regime which was threatening from abroad.

In justifying the unanimous war-credit vote Hugo Haase, political leader of the left center, in the name of the entire SPD parliamentary group, declared in the Reichstag that "much, if not all, [was] at stake for our people . . . in case victory should be on the side of Russian despotism."[15] The entire Social Democratic press hastened to belabor this theme. Having become Social Democracy's foremost enemy overnight, Russian tsarism was labeled simultaneously as "the bloody horde of European reaction," "the enemy of all progress and culture (*Kultur*)," and "the mortal enemy of democracy and freedom."[16] According to the *Bielefelder Volkswacht* of August 4, Social Democrats of all shades were uniting behind the slogan "Against Russian Despotism and Treachery." A week later the Hamburger *Echo* assured its readers that the SPD would fight with unbounding enthusiasm because this was "a war for civilization." By August 28 *Die Neue Zeit*, the

14. See Kautsky, *Sozialisten und Krieg*, pp. 251–54, 441.

15. Cited in R. H. Lutz, ed., *Fall of the German Empire, 1914–1918* (2 vols. Stanford, Stanford University Press, 1932), *1*, 15–16.

16. *Frankfurter Volksstimme*, July 31, 1914; *Hallesches Volksblatt*, August 5, 1914; *Lübecker Parteiorgan*, September 4, 1914.

party's major theoretical weekly of decidedly left-center orientation, proclaimed that the German working class would "defend itself from the Western allies of Russian barbarism in order to bring about an honorable peace," and that in this process it would "give to the task of destroying tsarism the last breath of man and beast." [17]

Hence, long before Woodrow Wilson proclaimed World War I a crusade for democracy, German Social Democracy had elevated the war of the Central Powers to a crusade against Russian despotism.[18] On the other hand, the German Government not only carefully abstained from embracing this proseletizing objective, but also refrained from criticizing this "propagation of the destruction of tsarism" because it helped Social Democracy to justify a decision which "under the pressure of events inevitably had to be taken." [19]

In the Socialist ideology, then, both anticapitalism and internationalism were promptly discarded with the convenient help of the "tsarist excuse." Lenin protested in vain that instead of destroying tsarism, the war would merely prolong its life by placing "the purse" of the English, French, and Russian bourgeoisie at its disposal.[20] However, Lenin also anticipated that, in case of a protracted war, class antagonisms would eventually produce a revolutionary situation first in Germany, and subsequently in Russia and the other belligerent nations.

But even before the Second Empire's political and military leaders

17. For a highly critical but thorough analysis of the SPD press position on the tsarist menace in August 1914, with extensive quotations, see Luxemburg, *The Crisis in the German Social Democracy*, pp. 52–53, 66–69.

18. This is not to imply that German Social Democracy stood ready to apply self-determination to the subject nationalities in the Russian or Austro-Hungarian Empires. As Arthur Rosenberg points out, "the German working class pursued with special hatred anyone who proclaimed himself to be in favor of the annexation of Belgium, and especially of the Flanders coast, while they made no opposition to proposals for annexations in the east." Rosenberg, *The Birth of the German Republic*, p. 105. Especially the right wing of the SPD which during the war crystallized around Lensch, David, Cunow, and eventually Noske took a geopolitical and economic view of the eastern nationalities problem. Since power considerations were never absent from Scheidemann's eastern policy, only the Independents seemed prepared to stand up for an integral application of self-determination, both West and East.

19. See "Reflections about the Coming Peace" dated October 29, 1914, by the Prussian Minister of Interior von Löbell, in GFM, Container 1498.

20. Lenin, *Works, 18*, 78–79.

woke up to the prospect of a drawn-out war, which would seriously strain the *Burgfrieden,* there were isolated but unmistakable indications that not all dissident Socialist voices had been stifled. On December 2, 1914, Karl Liebknecht, who four months earlier had reluctantly submitted to party discipline, delivered a stirring threefold indictment of Germany's prewar diplomacy, of capitalism as the decisive cause of the war, and of the betrayal of internationalism by the SPD. With the subsequent support of Rosa Luxemburg's brilliant *Junius* pamphlet,[21] Liebknecht renewed his allegiance to the Basle Manifesto and having expressed unqualified opposition to the war as well as to defensism urged the German proletariat to transform the internation conflict into civil war.[22] Both Liebknecht and Luxemburg were destined to spend most of the later war years behind prison bars, but before going to jail they formulated the platform which became the rallying point for the small faction of German Maximalists. True, the followers of Liebknecht, Luxemburg, Mehring, and Zetkin were few in number. Nevertheless, largely because of the ideological clarity and terseness of their propaganda organ, the *Spartakusbriefe,* whose first issue was circulated clandestinely on January 27, 1916, these revolutionaries acquired a disproportionately powerful voice and influence.[23]

Throughout 1915 the number of Socialist deputies who opposed the unconditional defensist position in the party caucus gradually rose from fourteen to forty-three. But by December 21, 1915, only twenty representatives openly voted against war credits in the Reichstag, though another twenty-two indicated their dissent by abstaining. With few exceptions these parliamentary dissidents and their followers in the party and the trade unions opposed the revolutionary stand of the Spartacist faction which before long was completely dissociated from the SPD. Instead, they constituted a rapidly growing minority inside the defensist ranks before they emerged, in April 1917, as the Independent Social Democratic party. Many left-centrists and revisionists who had violently fought each other before the war now joined forces,

---

21. The author of *The Crisis of the German Social Democracy* remained anonymous throughout the war. In Germany the pamphlet was known as the *Junius Broschüre.*

22. The evolution of Liebknecht's opposition thought and action emerges clearly from his *Klassenkampf gegen den Krieg,* Berlin, 1919.

23. For a collection of Spartacist Letters, including Letter 1, see Karl Liebknecht, *Reden und Aufsätze,* Hamburg, 1921.

primarily because they were equally hostile to the war aims not only of the Government but also of their majoritarian colleagues.[24]

Even though these future Independents still endorsed the Social Patriotic emphasis on the dangers of tsarist penetration into Central Europe, they criticized Scheidemann and Ebert for endorsing the Government's boisterous denial of war responsibility and its apparent pursuit of expansionist war aims. Like the Spartacists, the Independents denounced the imperialist pressures of the capitalist economic system as the most compelling determinant in the diagram of forces which had plunged Europe into war in August 1914. In their view, these capitalist pressures were equally strong inside both the Central and the Allied nations. Furthermore, they argued that even assuming that initially Germany had acted in legitimate self-defense, by late 1915 it was evident that the Government had abandoned its self-defense protestations in favor of the annexationist war aims of both the parties of order and the Supreme Command. Under the leadership of Bernstein, Haase, Kautsky, and Ledebour, the non-Spartacist dissidents not only violently denounced these imperialist designs but also espoused a different set of war aims.

In an idiom similar to that of the British and French minority Socialists and Radicals, the German Independents called for a peace without victory on the basis of the national self-determination of peoples. Moreover, while pushing their constructive campaign for a compromise peace they simultaneously stepped up their assault on the war aims of the Social Patriots. Even though Scheidemann made liberal use of New Diplomacy language, he could not conceal his approval of the Government's political and economic ambitions in Belgium, Alsace-Lorraine, and particularly in Eastern Europe. Haase repeatedly charged Scheidemann with putting up a verbal smoke screen behind which the Bethmann Administration practiced the Old Diplomacy.

The relations between the Independents and the majority Socialists became increasingly tense, until finally the latter voted to bar Haase from placing his views before the Reichstag. Haase, however, refused to be silenced, and on March 24, 1916, after defiantly addressing the Reichstag, the Independents seceded from the SPD parliamentary group in order to be free from the rigid party discipline. Together with seventeen left-center and revisionist supporters, Haase formed the

24. Scheidemann, *Memoiren eines Sozialdemokraten, 1,* 352; and Kautsky, *Sozialisten und Krieg,* p. 473–76.

Sozialdemokratische Arbeitsgemeinschaft. This minority faction hereafter opposed the Scheidemann-led majority both inside and outside the Reichstag; it dramatized its opposition by stubbornly refusing to vote new war credits.[25]

As Germany entered the third year of war and the U-boat champions began to receive a serious hearing in military as well as in political circles, Bethmann-Hollweg became seriously concerned over the gulf separating the right-wing parties from both major Socialist groups. This mounting political tension looked even more ominous in the light of the intensifying food and raw materials shortages. In spite of these shortages and of the Reichswehr's failure to exploit successfully the resources of the German-occupied borderlands of Russia, the Dual Monarchy became increasingly dependent on German supplies. The eventual recourse to unrestricted submarine warfare was dictated by very serious supply problems, which threatened to impair not only the military effort of the Central Powers but also their precarious *Burgfrieden.*

The Chancellor decided that even though he was powerless to bring about a balanced discussion of war aims, he might at least fortify the allegiance of the forces of movement for the impending trials by giving them a clearer picture of postwar reforms. But the parties of order immediately accused him of riding Scheidemann's coat tails. In turn he warned them, in a Reichstag speech on February 27, 1917, that the adoption of a postwar *Neuorientierung* was no longer a question of personal preference. "No, gentlemen! The new era and the new nation are here! The war has created them!" Simultaneously, the SPD, encouraged by the Liberal *Berliner Tageblatt* and *Frankfurter Zeitung,* criticized the Chancellor for being too vague in his reform program.[26]

Under left-wing pressures on March 14, 1917, Bethmann-Hollweg again warned the German right-wing leaders in the Prussian Landtag of the danger of "failing to recognize the signs of the times." He maintained that "after a crisis the like of which the world had never

25. Hugo Haase and seventeen other Independents were excluded from the SPD parliamentary caucus by a vote of 58 to 33, with four abstentions. Prager, *Geschichte der U.S.P.D.,* pp. 93–96; and Bevan, *German Social Democracy during the War,* pp. 94–96.

26. For the text of this speech and German press reactions see *DR,* EPS (March 15, 1917), pp. 227–29. See also Friedrich Meinecke, *Strassburg, Freiburg, Berlin, 1901–1919: Erinnerungen* (Stuttgart, Koehler, 1949), pp. 214–17.

seen" they could not hope to pick up life where they had left off in August 1914.[27] This speech was discussed extensively in the press, more particularly in Socialist papers which encouraged the Chancellor to continue broadening his popular support. The pro-Chancellor press suggested that "the whole proceedings of yesterday produced the impression that an epoch [had] begun in which two ideas of life [would] fight out their final battle in the Fatherland." [28]

Bethmann-Hollweg's pleadings with the Right must be seen against the background of Liebknecht's unrelenting attacks on both the Government and the Social Patriots. In the summer of 1916 Liebknecht's trial and conviction had provoked some labor unrest and had also aggravated the tensions between Scheidemann and Haase. By January 1917 a more significant, though still comparatively unimportant, strike wave had broken out in Leipzig and Braunschweig.[29] Furthermore, a meeting of all left-wing dissidents had been summoned by the Sozialdemokratische Arbeitsgemeinschaft in order to lay the foundations for a conference at which the USPD was to be chartered.[30]

Throughout 1916 the growing minority faction had come ever closer to endorsing the criticism of the *Burgfrieden* which Rosa Luxemburg had formulated as early as 1915. Accordingly, many Independents now admitted that "the cessation of the class struggle was a deplorably one-sided affair"; the rigid political truce denied all Socialists the opportunity to make their "influence effectively felt in determining the extent of the war and the terms of the peace." [31] There can be little

27. For friendly and hostile views of this speech see respectively Gustav Noske, *Aufstieg und Niedergang der Deutschen Sozialdemokratie* (Zurich, Aeroverlag, 1947), p. 32; and Westarp, *Konservative Politik im Letzten Jahrzehnt des Kaiserreiches*, 2, 218.

28. For these and other press comments see *DR*, EPS (March 29, 1917), pp. 275–78.

29. Ossip K. Flechtheim, *Die Kommunistische Partei Deutschlands in der Weimarer Republik* (Offenbach a.M., Bollwerk-Verlag Karl Drott, 1948), pp. 24–25; and Heinrich Scheel, "Der Aprilstreik 1917 in Berlin," in Albert Schreiner, ed., *Revolutionäre Ereignisse und Probleme in Deutschland während der Periode der grossen sozialistischen Oktoberrevolution, 1917–1918* (Berlin, Akademie Verlag, 1957), pp. 3–7.

30. See the appendix in Emil Eichhorn, ed., *Protokoll über die Verhandlungen des Gründungsparteitages der U.S.P.D., vom 6. bis 8. April 1917 in Gotha*, Berlin, 1921.

31. Luxemburg, *The Crisis in the German Social Democracy*, pp. 82, 87. For the most telling Spartacist criticism of the unconditional acceptance of the political truce by the SPD see ibid., chap. 6, pp. 78–90.

doubt that during the first two and a half years of war the official SPD increasingly became the captive of the Government; nor can it "be denied that the general orientation since August 4 was essentially along conservative lines." [32] Both the Spartacists and the Independents sought to reassert the political power of the German proletariat against the hardening parties of order which confidently relied on the SPD to protect their left flank.[33] Without substantial political compensations, the loyal SPD and trade union leaders respectfully accommodated the Government by forestalling strikes and by defending Bethmann's war-aims policy against the allegations of the Socialist minority; furthermore, through their contacts with many of their comrades abroad, German Social Democrats provided the Foreign Ministry with a useful link to neutral countries.

In the months immediately preceding and following the Russian Revolution, the Independents, though relentless in their criticism of the manifestly conservative implications of the political truce,[34] issued increasingly fearless appeals for the renunciation of all annexationist designs and for the formulation of liberal war aims. Deteriorating food stocks and rising prices caused many workers and peasants to listen to this dissident war-aims campaign. Even though in the short run Germany seemed to be in a favorable strategic position, her long-run economic and political condition was seriously impaired. At the same

32. D. Dr. Bredt, *Der deutsche Reichstag im Weltkrieg* (Berlin, Verlagsgesellschaft für Politik und Geschichte, 1926), p. 69.

33. In January 1917, by forming a coalition for the purpose of defeating the Spartacist Mehring in a by-election, the Government and the majority Socialists gave evidence of their political intimacy. Shortly before the election they published a manifesto declaring that the non-Socialist parties of Potsdam had decided to uphold the *Burgfrieden* by refraining from nominating their own candidate. Consequently a Social Patriot was left to run against Mehring. Even the *Volkspartei* and the *Reichsverband für die Bekämpfung der Sozialdemokratie* urged their followers to vote for Stahl, "the representative of the Scheidemann-oriented SPD which did not abandon the fatherland in the hour of need." Obviously, Mehring was beaten decisively. See Prager, *Geschichte der U.S.P.D.*, p. 137; and *Protokoll über die Verhandlungen des Parteitages der Sozialdemokratischen Partei Deutschlands* (October 1917), pp. 19–20.

34. In early February 1917 the Independents opened their public campaign against the official leaders of the SPD with the following appeal: "Party Comrades! The hour of decision is at hand for all of us! Since the outbreak of war the Party Executive and the majority of the Reichstag delegation have engaged themselves in an anti-Socialist direction which by becoming progressively worse, is transforming the official SPD into a National-Socialist, government party." Cited in Prager, *Geschichte der U.S.P.D.*, p. 135.

time that the Spartacists issued their revolutionary summons, the Independents argued that the moment to propose a liberal and honorable peace was now, while German troops still held the enemy at bay on foreign soil.[35] The momentum of this dissident war-aims campaign was such that even the Pan-German propaganda could no longer ignore it.

At this juncture the Russian Revolution affected the political scales in Germany. Once the tsarist villain against whom the SPD had mounted such a powerful crusade had been slain by a combination of German military power and Russian backwardness, the Social Patriots were obviously confronted with a serious ideological crisis. Suddenly and unexpectedly the chief war aim of German Social Democracy had been attained: Russia's reactionary autocracy had been destroyed and seemed destined to be superseded by a Liberal, possibly even a Socialist, republic. Because of the antiquated suffrage system in Prussia and the all-powerful German imperial throne, the constitution of the Second Empire now had the dubious distinction of standing out as Europe's most backward constitution. Simultaneously the world's most advanced proletariat and Socialist movement now found itself listening intently, even enviously, to the debates of the first workers' councils which had been established by Europe's least developed working-class movement.

On March 27, 1917, the Proclamation of the Petrograd Soviet reminded the German proletariat that "from the first days of the war you were assured that by raising arms against autocratic Russia, you were defending the culture of Europe from Asiatic despotism. . . . Now even this justification is gone." [36] Each subsequent proclamation and manifesto by the Petrograd Soviet carried the further implication that, by not following the example of the Russian workers and peasants, the German proletariat was shirking its duties. The Russian Revolution served to strengthen the Chancellor's recent admonitions to the forces of order by causing the three wings of the Socialist move-

35. The German peace offer of December 12, 1916—just prior to, yet made in knowledge of, Wilson's impending mediation offer of December 18—tended to capitalize in a rather aggressive tone on the Reich's favorable strategic position. Cf. Matthias Erzberger, *Erlebnisse im Weltkrieg* (Stuttgart and Berlin, Deutsche Verlagsanstalt, 1920), p. 229.

36. *RAR*, p. 8. Cf. the article by Norman Angell in the *New Republic*, July 21, 1917.

ment, as well as important sections of the bourgeois parties, to intensify their pressure in favor of long-overdue constitutional reforms.[37] The official organ of the Social Patriots rightly argued that the question of internal reforms had at that time become "the main question of foreign policy," primarily because Germany could not "appear to all her enemies as politically the most backward state in Europe." [38]

Evidently the Russian Revolution was the *immediate* cause for the momentous debate on domestic reforms and war aims which now broke out in the Reichstag as well as in the country at large. Karl Helfferich flatly asserts that Germany's "domestic problems only came to the fore with the Russian Revolution in March 1917." [39] Bethmann-Hollweg specifically points to the new Reichstag debates as ample evidence of the changing politicopsychological dispositions in the ruling groups. The Revolution "threw its sparks" into the "reactionary dogmas of an antiquated era" which had been uttered so fervently even as recently as March 14. Now even the National Liberals "thought it wise, in direct contradiction to their policy thus far, to embrace decidedly democratic demands." [40] Among the intellectuals the repercussions of Russian developments on Germany also called forth an intensified concern with political questions. With great historical acumen, though still opposed to parliamentary government, Friedrich Meinecke concluded that events in Petrograd suggested the need for immediate reforms because "only a state which is tied closely to its people and the masses of its people can wage this stupendous war of self-defense." [41] Max Weber also joined the forces of movement by

37. Erich Otto Volkmann, *Die Annexionsfragen des Weltkrieges* (Berlin, Deutsche Verlagsgesellschaft für Politik und Geschichte, 1929), pp. 128–33. A thorough analysis of the German press from March 14 to 19 recorded a "dramatic change . . . in the attitude . . . to the war aims controversy. . . . Certain indications point to a phase of depression. Secondly, the Chancellor's dramatic speech, in favor of domestic reform in Prussia, has concentrated attention on internal rather than external controversy. Thirdly, and most important, the Russian Revolution absorbs all minds, and seems likely to produce important reactions in regard to war aims and peace moves." *DR*, EPS (March 29, 1917), p. 272.

38. *Vorwärts*, March 30, 1917. See also *Die Neue Zeit* (March 30, 1917), p. 612.

39. Helfferich, *Der Weltkrieg*, 2, 92.

40. Bethmann-Hollweg, *Betrachtungen zum Weltkriege*, 2, 181. Cf. Helfferich, *Der Weltkrieg*, 2, 93.

41. Meinecke, *Preussen und Deutschland im 19. und 20. Jahrhundert* (Munich, Oldenburg, 1918), p. 548.

advocating franchise reforms as well as the eventual adoption of a republican form of government.[42]

Thus a growing dissident coalition, which eventually culminated in the July Reichstag majority, began to subject the *Burgfrieden* to a double-pronged assault by combining the two major forms of anti-status-quo pressure: (1) the unceasing demand for a clear definition of, and an unqualified commitment to, the ill-defined *Neuorientierung,* and (2) an unrelenting insistence on the need for an unequivocal statement of nonannexationist war aims.

If the Russian Revolution was the immediate cause for this great debate, both the war weariness resulting from the continuing military stalemate and the repercussions of the Allied blockade created the socioeconomic conditions for this slackening of the political truce. These socioeconomic developments weighed on Emperor Karl's mind when he wrote to the German Kaiser that the Central Powers were now "fighting against a new enemy which [was] more dangerous than the Entente—the international revolution, which [was] finding its most powerful ally in the universal semi-starvation." [43] This type of reflection was bound to originate in the Austro-Hungarian Empire, where Vienna seemed threatened by serious food shortages and where the subject nationalities were aroused by the self-determination gospel which the Petrograd Soviet was preaching. Possibly because he had experienced the stirring impact of the Russian Revolution on Poland, Friedrich Naumann, who in 1915 had published an ambitious blueprint for a German-controlled *Mitteleuropa,* was convinced that "the introduction of universal suffrage in Prussia must be undertaken now." Naumann insisted that he was guided by his "historical" sense, rather than by a fit of passing impatience, in suggesting that the Russian Revolution and the inevitable curtailment of the bread ration made the postponement of reforms until after the war impossible.[44]

It soon was apparent that, as in the case of the increasing war-aims pressures, some leaders demanded internal reforms because these promised to serve the Central cause in this moment of crisis; on the other hand, there were those political groups which, without neglect-

42. See Meinecke, *Staat und Persönlichkeit,* pp. 157 ff.; and Weber, *Gesammelte politische Schriften,* pp. 126 ff.

43. Cited in Erich Ludendorff, *The General Staff and Its Problems* (2 vols. London, Hutchinson, 1920), 2, 420.

44. Theodor Heuss, *Friedrich Naumann* (Stuttgart and Berlin, Deutsche Verlagsanstalt, 1937), pp. 469–70.

ing the needs of the moment, were more strongly motivated by a less expedient and opportunistic commitment to democratic principles. But above all, the military, diplomatic, and political implications of Russian developments now became the subject of extensive secret and public controversy.

In March 1917 there were four major German interpretations of the causes of the Russian Revolution and of its probable impact on the military situation. The Supreme Command initially labeled the Revolution British-inspired, and predicted that Miliukov was likely to fight more obstinately than Sazonov for traditional Russian goals. Another wing of the Right renewed its call for a separate peace with Russia, at this time as part of a policy which would seek to restore the Tsar to his throne. Whereas Bethmann-Hollweg also suspected a British conspiracy, his estimate of Russian liberalism was more charitable than Ludendorff's; like certain sectors of the bourgeois press he anticipated that the Russian Socialists would eventually temper Miliukov's foreign policy. With still greater confidence the German Socialists, while considering the Revolution bourgeois in origin, maintained that Russian Socialists were in the process of gaining control. But regardless of political orientation, by early April the entire German press was encouraging the Russian Socialists (including the Bolsheviks), because by calling for a restatement of Allied war aims through the Petrograd Soviet, the Russian Left was accentuating the diplomatic strains in the enemy camp. Likewise, much praise was heaped on those Russian Socialists who undermined the effectiveness of the Russian army. In sum, there was endless speculation about the future course of the Revolution in Russia and its impact on the military balance between the Central and the Allied Powers.

The new political and military situation created by the Russian Revolution came under detailed scrutiny in Berlin on March 26–27, 1917, at a meeting between Count Czernin and Bethmann-Hollweg, and their respective advisors. Notwithstanding the many signs of continuing Russian disintegration, both statesmen were far from optimistic. Especially Czernin, whose primary ambition now was to bring the Dual Monarchy out of the war in a *status quo ante bellum* position, expressed his concern about the precariousness of the political equilibrium inside his Empire. After painting a pessimistic picture of food, manpower, and raw materials shortages, he indicated that he was not certain whether Austria-Hungary could hold out until

August or September; certainly, the Empire "could not possibly continue the war beyond next fall" without risking serious internal dis-
turbances. Thereupon Bethmann-Hollweg, after insisting that the
Central coalition would have to hold through the summer, confessed
that "a fourth winter would also be difficult" for Germany. Czernin
hastened to interject that for Austria-Hungary a fourth winter was
out of the question. The Austrian Foreign Minister stated furthermore that because "our weeks and months are numbered" every effort
should be made to engage in separate negotiations with one of the
Allies; in pursuit of this policy he had sent Count Mensdorff to Switzerland.[45]

Hereafter Count Czernin was the foremost champion for a peace
by conciliation in the official councils of the Central Powers. At his
insistence Berlin and Vienna agreed at this Berlin conference on a
minimum war-aims program according to which both Powers were
prepared to withdraw their armies from the occupied territories in
Russia (including Poland), Montenegro, Serbia, Albania, and Rumania, provided the *status quo ante bellum* was restored in the West
as well as in the East. But the conferees also envisaged a happier turn
of events. In case "the war should terminate favorably for our coalition," the Central Powers agreed on a maximum program which went
beyond the reestablishment of their territorial integrity to "the lasting
incorporation of enemy territories." Whereas the Dual Monarchy would
seek concessions in Rumania, Germany would expand "primarily"
(*hauptsächlich*) in the "East." [46]

Since Czernin was convinced that the major obstacle to an accommodation with France was the Reich's ambitious designs in Alsace-
Lorraine, he sought to convince Berlin to relinquish the greater part
of these two provinces in exchange for the Briey basin. Whereas
Bethmann-Hollweg apparently was prepared to cede a minor sector
of Alsace to France, he knew that he had to contend with the Supreme
Command, which in addition to economic control over Belgium and
Alsace-Lorraine also insisted on political and military domination of
these areas. Meanwhile Czernin proved his conciliatory disposition by
declaring Austria-Hungary's readiness to grant Serbia an access to the

---

45. See the minutes of the March 26th conversations in GFM, Container 1498.

46. These minimum and maximum aims were incorporated in a one-page résumé,
dated March 27, 1917, and signed by Czernin and Bethmann-Hollweg. For the
text of this résumé see GFM, Container 1498.

sea and to relinquish Austrian-controlled Galicia in favor of a future German-controlled Polish Kingdom.[47]

Before parting, Czernin and Bethmann-Hollweg agreed to focus their diplomatic probings sharply on Russia, the weakest political and military link in the Entente Coalition. In their view the essential preliminary step in the search for a basis of negotiations with Petrograd was the publication of a liberal war-aims program which would encourage the Socialists within Russia to intensify their demand for a separate peace. Since the drafting of such a program was bound to raise a political storm, especially in Germany, every effort was to be made to keep this domestic war-aims debate in check. According to the German Chancellor all extreme formulations, whether rightist or leftist, should be avoided. Hence he sought to influence "the Social Democratic and the bourgeois-pacifist press" to minimize domestic conflict in order to facilitate diplomatic overtures to the Russians; simultaneously, Bethmann-Hollweg sought to convince the Right, "and above all the *Alldeutschen,*" that given Germany's situation, the Reich could not ask for the impossible and therefore should seek negotiations before America's power could be brought to bear against the Central Powers.[48]

However, by now the debate between the German forces of movement and the forces of order was so heated that verbal counsels of moderation were altogether ineffective. Moreover, even though the Supreme Command would have welcomed the liquidation of the Eastern front, Ludendorff was not prepared to settle on "modest conditions." Likewise, the Kaiser, who supported the Supreme Command in its ambitious schemes, advised his Chancellor that Germany could not accept a "Socialist-sponsored peace without territorial annexations and without monetary reparations." [49] At best Ludendorff was prepared to substitute for the unequivocal but ideologically harmful word "annexations" the purposely ambiguous phrase "frontier readjustments." However, in Bethmann-Hollweg's view this new phrase, as applied to territorial rearrangements with Russia, was equally damag-

47. Ibid. On April 2, 1917, the German Ambassador in Vienna reported that Czernin had indicated his readiness also to sacrifice South Tyrol.

48. See the letter dated April 18, 1917, by Bethmann-Hollweg to von Grünau, Foreign Ministry liaison officer with the Kaiser, GFM, Container 1498.

49. Telegram from Ludendorff to the Chancellor, May 10, 1917, ibid., Container 1499; telegram from von Grünau to the Chancellor, April 20, 1917, ibid., Container 1498.

ing. Instead, the Foreign Ministry suggested that the "renunciation of Courland and Lithuania might be made palatable to the Russians by dressing both of them up (*zu frisieren*) as independent states." [50]

In the meantime, on April 5, 1917, von Hindenburg concluded that the war would "probably be decided in the current year" and that peace negotiations "might begin in the foreseeable future," precipitated by "Russian developments." Hindenburg advised the Chancellor that without further delay Germany should decide on her minimum peace conditions before consulting about these conditions with her own allies.[51] Then, about two weeks later, the Kaiser telegraphed Bethmann-Hollweg from Supreme Headquarters that Germany must prepare herself for impending negotiations with Russia. In preparation for these negotiations William II summoned the Chancellor to Kreuznach for April 23, 1917, for discussions with the Supreme Command; in his summons the Kaiser indicated his readiness to mediate any possible disagreements between the civilian and military authorities.[52]

That neither the Kaiser nor the Supreme Command ever contemplated anything but an expansionist peace was soon confirmed during the Kreuznach consultations. On this occasion Ludendorff not only insisted on Courland and Lithuania, but also asked for continuing military control over Belgium, pending its eventual political and economic integration into the Reich. At the very minimum Liège and the Flanders coast, including Bruges, would have to be kept under permanent military control; furthermore, Arlon-Luxembourg and Longwy-Briey would have to be under German sovereignty.[53]

This war-aims program now became Government policy. Whereas it represented the maximum demands to which the Chancellor and the Foreign Office agreed, apparently this was the minimum program which the Supreme Command was reluctantly prepared to settle for.[54] Unlike Czernin and Bethmann-Hollweg, Ludendorff was confident that militarily time was on Germany's side. Furthermore, he insisted that

50. Telegrams between Ludendorff and Bethmann-Hollweg, May 7, 1917, ibid., Container 1499.

51. Telegram dated April 5, 1917, ibid., Container 1498.

52. Telegram dated April 20, 1917, ibid.

53. Notes on the April 23d meeting at Supreme Headquarters, ibid.

54. See the letter of January 26, 1918, by Bethmann-Hollweg to Chancellor Count von Hertling, ibid., Container 1500.

politically, in the interest of both ruling families, Germany and Austria-Hungary needed a favorable peace: "respect for the monarchy will suffer if the peace does not secure Courland-Lithuania for Germany." [55] In addition to the support of the Kaiser, Ludendorff was assured of solid backing by the Pan-German parties and factions which were not in the least inclined to woo Russia's favor by offering reasonable peace talk, let alone reasonable peace terms. The military and their political associates were deaf to the oft-repeated admonition that "the danger threatens that the war agitators in Russia may get the upper hand if the peace cry is not answered, if it does not find an unmistakable echo." [56]

However, because Bethmann-Hollweg lacked the necessary parliamentary support for diplomatic and domestic moderation, which eventually crystallized in early July 1917, he was forced to yield to Ludendorff. Nevertheless, in late April he sent Graf Hertling to Vienna to reassure Czernin that the *Alldeutschen* were not in control in Berlin and that Germany still sought a separate peace with Russia. As soon as he heard about this Hertling mission, Ludendorff hastened to register a protest with the Chancellor in the hope of stopping any further consideration of a Czernin peace.[57] Also, in order to cancel out the impact of Viennese and Social Democratic peace pressures, the right-wing parties sought to extract both anti-Czernin and anti-Scheidemann assurances from the Chancellor.

Thus far the war-aims debate had been carried on either officially in secret or unofficially in the press and on the political platform. Now this debate moved to the formal but public hall of the Reichstag. On May 3, 1917, the SPD, hard-pressed by the Independents, countered the political offensive of the Right by formulating the following questions in the Lower House: "Is the Chancellor aware that the Provisional Government of Russia and the allied Austro-Hungarian Government have alike declared themselves ready to conclude peace without annexations? What does the Chancellor intend to do to bring about an agreement among all those concerned [so that it should be] possible to conclude the coming peace on the basis of mutual recon-

55. Telegram from Supreme Command to Foreign Ministry, April 29, 1917, ibid., Container 1498.

56. *Frankfurter Volksstimme*, April 15, 1917, cited in *DR*, EPS (May 17, 1917), p. 68.

57. See the telegram from Ludendorff to Bethmann-Hollweg, May 10, 1917, GFM, Container 1499.

ciliation without annexations and war indemnities?" [58] Then, on May 15, there followed a major war-aims debate.

In this debate Scheidemann formally proclaimed Social Democracy's recent conversion to a reasonable, negotiated peace. Without mentioning specifics, he insisted that the SPD was opposed to all forceful annexations, a position which he and his colleagues also proposed to defend at the coming Stockholm Conference. After asking Scheidemann how he could guarantee Germany's future military and economic security without certain territorial acquisitions, Dr. Roesicke, the spokesman for the extreme Right, called on the Chancellor to define Germany's war aims. However, since Bethmann-Hollweg was not prepared to break with the military authorities, he simply declared that at this time a programmatic war-aims pronouncement would not be in the national interest. By implication the Chancellor adopted a middle position between Roesicke and Scheidemann, a position which Peter Spahn endorsed in the name not only of his own *Zentrum* party but also of the Progressive Peoples' party, the National Liberals, and the majority of the *Deutsche Fraktion*. After supporting the view that an accommodation with Russia should be sought, Spahn went on to deny the Allies the right to interfere in Germany's internal affairs.[59]

Finally it was Ledebour's turn to speak in the name of the Independent Socialists. Unlike Spahn he accused Bethmann-Hollweg of not liberating himself from the Supreme Command; also, he prophetically proclaimed, "beware the Chancellor who is incapable of reading the signs of the times." [60] In a positive vein Ledebour urged the Government to accept the Petrograd formula, which could lead to a Russo-German accommodation as well as to increased Russian pressure on Paris and London in favor of moderation. Ledebour then concluded his remarks on a well-justified partisan note: "What Herr Scheidemann declared from this Reichstag tribune today is essentially in agreement with the program with which we Independents have opposed Herr Scheidemann for nearly two years. . . . Now the Social Democrats should break with the Government." [61]

Ledebour's partisan remarks in the Reichstag were a carry-over

58. Cited in *DR*, EPS (May 17, 1917), p. 66.
59. *VRSB*, *Legislaturperiode* 13, Session 2, Vol. *310* (May 15, 1917), pp. 3384–98.
60. Ibid., p. 3401.
61. Ibid., pp. 3399–401.

from factional disputes within the Left which the Russian Revolution had so greatly intensified. As in the rest of Europe, in Germany the three major Socialist factions now emerged in sharp outline. Liebknecht, Luxemburg and their supporters stepped up their campaign in favor of immediate peace and civil war which would usher in the Socialist millennium first in Germany and then in the other Western European countries. Needless to say, inspired by recent Russian developments the Spartacists now became hardened in their assault on those compromising centrists and revisionists who were united in the USPD. In turn, Bernstein, Haase, Kautsky, and Ledebour pressed their attack against the Social Patriots with excited vigor. These ideological and political spokesmen of the Independents attacked the Majoritarians for their failure to insist that "the clarification of war aims by the Reich Government was now more urgent than ever." [62] Scheidemann and Ebert watched this radicalization on their left with great concern, particularly because of the strong impact of the war-aims slogans of the Independents on the rank and file.

Obviously, the mutually recriminating charges which the three major Socialist factions leveled at each other seriously impaired the power of the German Left. However, the very sharpness of this internecine struggle was concrete evidence for the accelerating impact of the Russian Revolution on Germany's domestic front.[63] Most directly relevant for the Government's policy was the gradual radicalization of the Social Patriots. Particularly in the light of rising defections to the Independents, who on April 7 had organized the USPD as a distinct political party, the SPD high command was compelled to reappraise its position. By April 20, 1917, the Social Democratic Central Committee adopted a resolution welcoming the Russian Revolution and calling for an official statement of nonannexationist war aims. The SPD's increasingly critical attitude toward the Government became public when, in spite of official protests, the text of this resolution was published in the *Vorwärts*.[64]

But the SPD did not limit its criticism to the diplomatic realm.

62. Ibid., *308* (April 24, 1917), pp. 2940–41; and *Die Neue Zeit* (March 30, 1917), p. 612.

63. Cf. Klaus Mammach, *Der Einfluss der russischen Februarrevolution und der grossen sozialistischen Oktoberrevolution auf die deutsche Arbeiterklasse, Februar 1917 – Oktober 1918*, Berlin, Dietz, 1955.

64. Cf. Westarp, *Konservative Politik im letzten Jahrzehnt des Kaiserreiches, 2*, 84–85.

Like the Independents it now also warned that with the democratization of the Entente coalition, Germany's autocratic political system was bound to become a key target of Allied propaganda. On March 29, 1917, in a major Reichstag debate, the right-Majoritarian Gustav Noske bolstered the SPD's plea for the immediate consideration of suffrage reform and the equalization of power among the German states with the contention that the Russian Revolution was being used in France and in England "as a thrust against reactionary Prussianism." Moreover, he asserted that in the Entente "they compare German conditions and the defunct tsarist regime on the same basis. . . . It will become increasingly difficult for reactionaries to maintain the present system if Germany is to be surrounded by democracies not only in the West, North, and South, but also in the East." [65] In this same debate Scheidemann held that heretofore Germany may have appeared as fulfilling a liberating mission against reactionary Russia, but that now this role had vanished into history.[66] A variation of the slogan which had been used to rally the German proletariat in August 1914 was about to be turned against the Reich. The Reich had begun by leading a campaign against Eastern despotism; now, in 1917, Germany was about to become the victim of a crusade for democracy.

The forces of movement seemed to focus their attack on Prussia's archaic election laws, which were most symbolic of the *ancien régime* which the war had done so much to reinforce. Even the Independents did not call for the immediate establishment of a Socialist commonwealth; as faithful Marxists, convinced of the impossibility of skipping stages in history, they formulated suffrage reform as their minimum program. That they did so also testifies to the fact that, except for the Spartacists, all German Socialists were equally concerned with safeguarding the national interest, and never transgressed the bounds of legitimate political action.

The SPD now won the support of the left wing of both the National Liberal and the Center parties, as well as of all the Progressives, for the establishment of a parliamentary committee to study constitutional reforms. On March 30, in concluding the two-day Reichstag debate, this committee was charted by a resounding vote of 238 to 33.

65. Cited in Lutz, *Fall of the German Empire, 1,* 248.
66. Bredt, *Der deutsche Reichstag im Weltkrieg,* p. 118. See also article by Max Cohen, entitled "Russische Revolution und deutsche Politik," in *Sozialistische Monatshefte* (April 11, 1917), pp. 353–56.

When four weeks later Scheidemann was elected chairman of this constitutional committee, it was evident that the SPD was spearheading a broadening coalition intent on liberalizing the German constitution in the interest of a more effective pursuit of the war.[67]

The parties and factions which were in the process of reluctantly moving leftward never failed to bestow honors on the SPD leaders, in the hope that by drawing them into closer cooperation with themselves the reforming zeal of the Left might be tamed. Also, they correctly calculated that once this constitutional committee was charted, the intensifying political debate would be removed from the highly publicized platform of the Reichstag. Bitterly but unsuccessfully the *Vorwärts* soon complained [68] of "middling work at a great time." Even certain Liberals began to suggest that if the committee were to continue to "confine itself to empty window dressing," it might as well be dissolved.[69] The apparent unwillingness of the Conservatives to explore the constitutional problem provoked the *Berliner Tageblatt*, the *Leipziger Tageblatt*, and the *Frankfurter Zeitung* into urging "Bethmann-Hollweg to be a man, to stand up for his beliefs, and to say NO to the Right." [70]

Many Liberals and most Socialists had agreed to the establishment of this committee primarily because they had been intimidated by right-wing admonitions that political deliberations should not be allowed to undermine the war effort. As early as March 26, 1917, the Ministry of War had advised the Chancellor of dissident Liberal and Socialist papers whose editorials linked German domestic developments with the Russian Revolution in order to dramatize their own political demands. Especially the left-wing parties were accused of accentuating domestic tensions by exploiting the Russian Revolution for their own selfish political purposes. Since reports from various military theaters testified that the effects of this political unrest were already being felt in the army, the Chancellor was asked to take action "in order to counteract effectively the nefarious repercussions of the Russian Revolution." [71]

67. Bevan, *German Social Democracy during the War*, p. 160. Cf. Westarp, *Konservative Politik im letzten Jahrzehnt des Kaiserreiches, 2,* 235.
68. May 6, 1917.
69. *Berliner Tageblatt,* May 5, 1917.
70. Cited in *DR,* EPS (May 24, 1917), p. 99.
71. Erich Otto Volkmann, *Der Marxismus und das deutsche Heer im Weltkrieg* (Berlin, Sobbing, 1925), pp. 286–87.

Meanwhile, on the advice of his ministers, the Kaiser joined the great public debate by issuing a special Easter proclamation on April 7, 1917, whose conciliatory tone was calculated to help cushion the shock of a further curtailment of the bread ration. By promising post-war suffrage reform the Kaiser hoped to assure a postponement of all phases of the *Neuorientierung* until after the war.[72]

The right-Conservatives considered this Easter proclamation as "cause for intensified opposition," and set about marshaling their forces in a determined effort to stem the rising *Neuorientierung* tide.[73] Still intent on using the war as a means for preserving the Old Germany, the press of the extreme Right vigorously denounced all proponents of war-aims or franchise concessions, insisting that without a complete German victory an "effective German monarchy" could not survive. Especially the reactionaries were opposed to any discussion of war aims, since they preached that only "victory and its exploitation" could secure "the future of the German Empire and of the monarchial idea." [74]

At this time the political front was agitated further by the first mass strikes which threatened to curtail war production. Notwithstanding the Easter proclamation, on April 16 in Berlin as well as in other key industrial cities workers protested the new cut in bread and flour rations which went into effect that day. In Berlin alone between 200,000 and 300,000 workers laid down their tools. In the capital the strike movement was most extensive in the metals and munitions industries, though other war industries were also affected. In Leipzig the strikes took a radical turn when under the influence of the distant Russian Revolution and of local Spartacists the strikers set up a local workers' council. Simultaneously the workers in Berlin began to couple their bread-and-butter demands with political claims, in spite of determined efforts by SPD leaders to dampen the entire movement. Especially the Independent and Spartacist leaders took this occasion to point to the similarity of Russian and German developments. They led the two-day strike movement with the slogan "Down with the War! Down with the Government! Peace! Freedom! Bread!" [75]

72. Bethmann-Hollweg, *Betrachtungen zum Weltkriege*, 2, 186–87. Cf. Carl W. Ackermann, *Germany, the Next Republic?* (New York, Doran, 1917), p. 261.
73. Westarp, *Konservative Politik im letzten Jahrzehnt des Kaiserreiches*, 2, 267.
74. *Deutsche Tageszeitung*, April 16 and 20, 1917.
75. Prager, *Geschichte der U.S.P.D.*, pp. 160–61; Bethmann-Hollweg, *Betrachtungen zum Weltkriege*, 2, 183; Westarp, *Konservative Politik im letzten Jahrzehnt*

Certain leading members of the bourgeois intelligentsia also felt called upon to revise their earlier interpretation of the world struggle in the light of recent developments. The general nature of this reassessment is clearly evident in a remarkable series of addresses delivered in the Prussian Landtag on May 18, 22, and 25. A searching analysis of President Wilson's war message led Adolf von Harnack to warn of the serious political consequences which might result from the President's ideological offensive. With Friedrich Meinecke he prophesied that Germany's enemies would now try to expand the conflict into a battle of constitutions in an attempt to *impose* democratic freedoms on Germany. Meinecke saw quite clearly that because of the recent destruction of Russian autocracy the Allies were gathering "redoubled hope of effecting a great victory of the Western spirit" over Germany.[76] Then, after Max Sering had given a comparative analysis of "Constitutional and Social Organization in the Western World and in Germany," Ernst Troeltsch rounded out the picture by speaking on the dynamics of "The Assault by Western Democracy." [77]

Not only the Socialists but also considerable sections of the bourgeoisie and intelligentsia foretold that the Entente would increasingly direct its psychological warfare at "Germany—the last bastion of autocratic government." Meinecke aptly suggested a possible meeting ground for the opposing internal forces with the query whether some terrain in Germany's constitutional landscape might not be cleared in order to permit a more efficient political as well as military conduct of the war.[78]

However, the Supreme Command and its political partners failed or refused to recognize the deep-rooted causes for this mounting unrest. According to Bethmann-Hollweg, Ludendorff considered the April strikes the proletariat's "provocative rejoinder" to the Kaiser's

---

des Kaiserreiches, 2, 299; Mammach, *Der Einfluss der russischen Februarrevolution*, pp. 22–45; Scheel, "Der Aprilstreik 1917 in Berlin," in Schreiner, ed., *Revolutionäre Ereignisse und Probleme*, pp. 22 ff.

76. Meinecke, *Preussen und Deutschland*, pp. 544–45. For the complete text of Meinecke's address see ibid., pp. 532–52. Meinecke's most important political articles of the year 1917 are conveniently accessible in Friedrich Meinecke, *Politische Schriften und Reden* (Darmstadt, Toeche-Mittler, 1958), pp. 146–221; these articles clearly reveal his growing impatience with the Right's refusal to make essential reform and war-aims concessions in the national interest.

77. The entire speech series was published in book form: Adolf von Harnack et al., *Die deutsche Freiheit*, Gotha, 1917.

78. Meinecke, *Preussen und Deutschland*, p. 545.

compromising Easter message. Furthermore, after condemning all political reforms of a democratic and parliamentary nature as "weak-minded concessions to the so-called *Zeitgeist*," [79] the Quartermaster General cautioned William II against allowing himself to be influenced by his irresolute Chancellor. Until the Russian Revolution the Supreme Command and the Right had been spoiled because their rigidly conservative version of the *Burgfrieden* had prevailed. At this time, however, with the Socialists pressing for a less one-sided political truce, the forces of order indignantly accused the forces of movement of taking undue advantage of those patriotic Germans who reluctantly yielded to certain reforms only because they hesitated to agitate the home front any further.

Scheidemann probably never seriously considered breaking with the Government; instead, he set himself the assignment of exacting the most extensive war-aims and reform concessions for the SPD's continuing support. He capitalized on the menacing pronouncements of the Independents in order to frighten both Cabinet and Emperor into a conciliatory mood. However, since Bethmann-Hollweg was at least certain of Scheidemann's incontrovertible loyalty, he sought at a marginal cost to fashion the SPD into his most effective weapon against the unruly dissidents on the Left. In turn, this strategy unwittingly gave the SPD "a new sense of power upon the Government machine." [80]

In April–May 1917 the Government also began to rely on the SPD to help fight its diplomatic battles. Now that the initiative for the Stockholm Conference was passing to the Petrograd Soviet, it looked as if the renascent International might become a useful instrument in the search for a separate peace with Russia. Furthermore, by issuing passports to both majority and minority Socialists for Internationalist consultations in Stockholm, the Central Powers hoped to lessen the profound psychological and ideological victory which the Allies had scored with Wilson's war message.

As early as March 30, 1917, in reporting the Dutch Socialist Troelstra's intention of proceeding to Petrograd for consultations with the Soviet, the German Embassy in Holland advised Bethmann-Hollweg that Germany "ought to facilitate this trip." [81] Apparently the German

---

79. Bethmann-Hollweg, *Betrachtungen zum Weltkriege, 2,* 191.
80. Bevan, *German Social Democracy during the War,* p. 159.
81. Telegram from Ambassador Rosen to Bethmann-Hollweg, in GFM, Container 2090.

Government advised Ambassador Rosen at the Hague to encourage Troelstra's initiative, for on May 14, 1917, the Hague Embassy reported that "through the promotion of the idea of the Dutch Socialist leader Troelstra we contributed to bringing close to realization a great international Socialist Conference in Stockholm." [82] Once in Stockholm, Troelstra, who was pro-German, enjoyed the cooperation of the German Embassy there. With its help he succeeded in a week's time in securing transit facilities through Germany for his Dutch comrade Willem Vliegen. Throughout May the German Embassies in Bern, the Hague, and Stockholm kept in continual touch with Berlin about the revival of the Second International. From the Stockholm Embassy came an urgent request for German Socialist literature, with the reminder that the "literature destined for the Conference should be labeled 'printed in Berlin.'" The Bern Embassy, on the strength of its perusal of the Allied press, recommended that German Socialists of all shades be allowed to attend in order to embarrass the French Cabinet; therefore, the decision to issue these passports should be widely publicized in France. [83]

First, the passports were authorized for the majority Socialists whose delegation to the preliminary consultations with the Organizing Committee in Stockholm was composed of leading figures like Ebert, Scheidemann, and Legien. Then, at the request of Ebert, the Government issued traveling papers to the pro-German Belgian Socialist Edouart Anseele, who was to counteract Vandervelde's pro-Allied influence. [84]

In support of the diplomatic goals which Bethmann-Hollweg pursued just then, passports were also issued to the Independents. Thus a USPD delegation composed, among others, of Bernstein, Haase, Kautsky, and Ledebour, arrived in Stockholm on June 21, 1917, intent on overshadowing the majority group. [85] Also, since Czernin was anx-

82. Ambassador Rosen to Bethmann-Hollweg, ibid., Container 2160.
83. The Stockholm Embassy to the Foreign Ministry on May 21 and 23, 1917, and the Bern Embassy to the Foreign Ministry on May 18, 1917, ibid.
84. Ebert made this request on official SPD stationary on May 23, 1917. On May 29 the request was granted in a letter signed by Zimmermann and addressed to the Executive Committee of the SPD, ibid.
85. For a complete roster of both the SPD and the Independent delegates see Comité Organisateur de la Conférence Socialiste Internationale de Stockholm, *Stockholm* (Stockholm, Tidens, 1918), p. xiv. About May 20 Troelstra wrote to the German Ambassador in Stockholm thanking him for the decision of the Reichsregierung to issue passports to the minority faction. Stockholm Embassy to Foreign Ministry on May 21, 1917, GFM, Container 2160.

iously in quest of a peace by accommodation, he gladly assisted Victor Adler, Seitz, Ellenbogen, and Renner, in getting to the Swedish capital.[86]

In Stockholm the policy disagreements between the two German delegations crystallized very clearly. Whereas the Independents admitted Germany's share in the responsibility for the war, the majority Socialists persisted in their contention that Germany had drawn the sword only in self-defense against unprovoked foreign aggression. Furthermore, even though Scheidemann did not question Belgium's right to independence, he refused sternly to discuss Alsace-Lorraine. This position was in accordance with his interpretation of the Petrograd peace formula as a status-quo formula in which the emphasis was not on the principle of self-determination but rather on a peace "without annexations and indemnities." In Stockholm the majority Socialists also became the forerunners of the Bolshevik Government in asking for the Allied liberation of Ireland, Egypt, and India. On the other hand, the Independents, by calling for a plebiscite in Alsace-Lorraine, attested to their acceptance of both the spirit and the letter of the Petrograd formula.[87]

By bringing both delegations together with many of their former comrades from the Second International, this excursion to the Swedish capital served to rekindle the Socialist fire in the heart and mind of many Socialists. Having heretofore uttered their dissent in the face of heavy political opposition, the Independents in Stockholm gathered courage from the growing internationalism which was expressed in many of the answers to the Stockholm questionnaire.[88] The Soviets were consolidating their hold throughout Russia, the ILP was reasserting its influence in the British Labour movement, the SFIO was moving toward a less chauvinist position, and President Wilson had

86. *Fremdenblatt* (Vienna), April 28, 1917. See also Czernin, *Im Weltkriege,* p. 228.

87. See the text of the USPD manifesto on the Stockholm Conference which Hugo Haase read in the Reichstag, in Prager, *Geschichte der U.S.P.D.,* pp. 157–60. The complete text of the SPD declaration submitted in Stockholm on June 2, 1917, is cited in *Protokoll über die Verhandlungen des Parteitages der Sozialdemokratischen Partei Deutschlands* (Würzburg, October 14–20, 1917), pp. 39–44. The Scheidemann and Haase positions are compared in Bevan, *German Social Democracy during the War,* pp. 161–80.

88. For the complete text of the answers to the questionnaire by Allied, Central, and neutral Socialists see Comité Organisateur de la Conférence Socialiste Internationale de Stockholm, *Stockholm.* See also below, Chap. 4.

launched his crusade for democracy. Convinced that its own program was only one tributary of a swelling democratic current, the USPD delegation returned to Germany determined to intensify its offensive against the SPD, Bethmann-Hollweg, and the Conservatives.

Even though Scheidemann had taken a rigid nationalist stand at Stockholm, it was not surprising that he, too, returned in a more progressive mood. Apparently the debates with various members of the Second International reminded him of some of his prewar Socialist convictions. Furthermore, he also sensed that a powerful wave of democracy was sweeping over Europe, supported by the momentum of the Russian Revolution and the American intervention. Indeed, Stockholm convinced him that the SPD would have to continue its critical self-examination on war aims as well as on domestic reforms. Nowhere else than at Stockholm could he have compiled more telling evidence for his campaign against both the suffrage system in Prussia and the imperialist ambitions of the right-wing parties. On June 24, in the *Vorwärts*, Scheidemann publicly proclaimed his "unalterable conviction" that preliminary to any peace Germany would have to be democratized:

> We say extensive and radical reforms are imperative at once. . . . Let it not be supposed that our people will remain ignorant of the constitutional differences between Germany and other countries. . . . We Social Democrats took up this cry very long before there was any thought of war. . . . Only much later, when the enemy observed that Germany in this matter of the *Neuorientierung* had come to a deadlock, when Russia achieved her gigantic revolution and America entered the war, were we faced with the humiliation *of having our own demand imposed on us as a war formula.*[89]

Meanwhile, the USPD was preparing to vote against the new war credits on July 3. Therefore it became particularly difficult for the SPD leaders to continue as the servile prisoners of the Government. When the SPD Executive finally decided to seek immediate franchise and war-aims concessions, the middle and the right-wing parties were

89. Cited in Bevan, *German Social Democracy during the War*, pp. 175–77 (italics mine). In late April, Eduard Bernstein had suggested to a non-Socialist member of the Reichstag that he pay attention to Scheidemann's speeches because they were "a good barometer." See Hans Peter Hanssen, *Diary of a Dying Empire* (Bloomington, Indiana University Press, 1955), p. 182.

put on notice that a concerted assault was about to be launched on the *Burgfrieden*.

The Scheidemann thesis, as put forth in the *Vorwärts*, won editorial support in diverse political quarters. Papers like the *Berliner Tageblatt* expressed agreement because they were concerned by persistent rumors that unless the Petrograd formula were officially accepted, not only the Independents but even the Social Patriots would refuse the next war credits.[90]

In view of the constitutional committee's continuing stalemate, some of Germany's outstanding intellectual leaders of conservative convictions—among them Hans Delbrück, Emil Fischer, A. von Harnack, Friedrich Meinecke, Friedrich Thimme, and Ernst Troeltsch —also urged immediate concessions to the reform elements. In a public manifesto they declared that

> In order to maintain the German people in that confidence to which it has a right, it is necessary to set to work without delay. We do not, therefore, hesitate to raise publicly the demand of the day, viz., that the Government without delay shall lay before the Landtag a franchise reform which shall include a suffrage which is not only universal, direct, and secret, but also equal, and that in other respects the Government shall give effective and valuable expression to the confidence which the German people deserves.[91]

The pleas of this influential sector of the intelligentsia were of great moral importance; but meanwhile infinitely more decisive political support had matured inside Germany's second largest political party. The Center party, under Matthias Erzberger's erratic leadership, now also proceeded to a re-evaluation of the political, military, and diplomatic situation. As leader of Central Europe's most powerful Catholic party, Erzberger was in continual contact with the Austro-Hungarian leaders who were ardent champions of Catholicism. Presently Erzberger, as a result of one of his frequent visits to Vienna, was advised of Czernin's pessimism regarding the chances of bringing Europe's only major Catholic Empire out of this war unscathed.

90. *Berliner Tageblatt*, June 25, 1917.
91. The complete text of this manifesto appeared in the *Vossische Zeitung* on July 3, 1917, and is cited in *DR*, EPS (July 12, 1917), p. 304.

In a recent memorandum, addressed to Emperor Karl but actually intended for Bethmann-Hollweg and William II, Czernin had predicted that another winter campaign would unleash "revolutionary movements" within the Empire which he, "as the responsible defender of the dynastic principle, should regard infinitely more dangerous than a bad peace concluded among sovereigns." [92] This Czernin memorandum, which had found its way into Erzberger's hands, implied that peace negotiations should be attempted before the Allies were aware of the growing exhaustion of the Central Powers.[93] Increasingly convinced that "peace with Russia [was] the key to the situation," [94] Czernin and Emperor Charles now renewed their pressure for diplomatic accommodation. Moreover, the Vienna Government needed the cooperation of the Austrian Social Democrats in order both "to influence the masses" and to explore the possibilities of peace with the Russians; in exchange for their cooperation the Social Democrats exacted "the proclamation of the principle of peace without annexations." [95]

Though Erzberger was deeply concerned about the fortunes of the Dual Monarchy, he was no less sensitive to the battle which was looming on Germany's political horizon. The battlecry "Down with the Pan-Germans and Annexationists" was reawakening the class spirit of the German proletariat; the bonds of the *Burgfrieden* were in danger of being irretrievably and fatally broken as the proletariat "began once more the fight for political power." [96] Consequently, Erzberger decided that the moment had come to tame the Supreme Command in order to prevent a decisive leftward dislocation of Germany's political equilibrium. "There existed the danger that Social Democracy would make its vote for the war credits dependent on the acceptance of a program which is roughly described as the Scheidemann peace. This would have been, from the point of view

92. Cited in Ludendorff, *The General Staff and Its Problems*, 2, 421–25.
93. Ibid., p. 476. Erzberger returned to Berlin "steeped in Viennese pessimism." Prince Max of Baden, *The Memoirs* (2 vols. New York, Scribner's, 1928), *1*, 117.
94. Emperor Charles to Kaiser Wilhelm, June 7, 1917, in GFM, Container 2160.
95. Edouard Beneš, *Souvenirs de guerre et de révolution, 1914–1918: La Lutte pour l'indépendance des peuples* (2 vols. Paris, Ernest Leroux, 1928), *1*, 460–61. The Austro-Hungarian Foreign Minister gives an account of his own search for a negotiated peace in Czernin, *Im Weltkriege*, pp. 183–252.
96. Rosenberg, *The Birth of the German Republic*, pp. 96, 104, 109.

of our party, detrimental to German interests, harmful at home as abroad. Therefore a positive formula had to be found." [97] At home the war-aims offensive of the SPD and the USPD had to be forestalled, whereas abroad the notion that Germany was fighting for territorial annexations had to be counteracted. Furthermore, since Erzberger now came to the conclusion that "whoever would help Russia to consolidate her internal position now would gain the great trump for the future," [98] he also prepared to exploit diplomatically the Russian chaos.

Hence, Bethmann-Hollweg, Erzberger, and Scheidemann were in agreement on *one* point: Germany should make every diplomatic effort which might help to separate Russia from her Allies. One step in this direction would be to issue a liberal war-aims pronouncement which would have the additional merit of getting "the French and British Governments into the greatest difficulties." [99] Even though neither Erzberger nor the Chancellor was as optimistic as Scheidemann about the peace potential of the Russian Socialists, they both were prepared to encourage the Petrograd Soviet.[100]

The speech which Erzberger read in the Steering Committee of the Reichstag on July 6 coincided essentially with the official SPD thesis. However, for all non-Socialists this analysis sounded immeasurably more convincing now that it was appropriated by one of the Reichstag's most respected Traditionalists. Furthermore, whereas Erzberger until recently had placed great hope in the submarine weapon, he now strengthened his case for war-aims revision by proving conclusively that all hopes of a "submarine victory" were illusory.[101] Presently the Center party, whose executive committee rather reluctantly endorsed Erzberger's analysis, came to the help of the SPD, and "the Reichstag was forced to do what the Chancellor did not dare do for fear of the

97. This explanation for Erzberger's reversal was published in the *Zentrum* paper *Germania* on July 16, 1917, and is cited in *DR*, EPS (July 26, 1917), p. 268. See also Erzberger, *Erlebnisse im Weltkrieg*, pp. 252–53, 255, 260. Erzberger tended to exaggerate the danger of massive left-wing dissent in order to make the shift from his erstwhile expansionist position more palatable to some of his reluctant followers.

98. Erzberger, pp. 234–35, 266–68. For a thoroughly documented analysis of Erzberger's politics and diplomacy in mid-1917 see Klaus Epstein's forthcoming *Erzberger and the Dilemma of German Democracy* (Princeton, Princeton University Press, 1959), chaps. 7 and 8.

99. Bredt, *Der deutsche Reichstag im Weltkrieg*, p. 118.

100. Cf. ibid., p. 122.

101. Erzberger, *Erlebnisse im Weltkrieg*, pp. 214–16, 222–25.

Right." [102] The Progressives also joined Erzberger and Scheidemann in their struggle for a liberal war-aims resolution.[103]

Because of his continuing refusal to issue or sanction an official war-aims pronouncement, Bethmann-Hollweg became an obstacle to this emerging war-aims coalition, which now had a majority in the Reichstag. The Chancellor's inflexible position, however, was due to constant pressures from Ludendorff, who not only opposed any war-aims compromise but also undertook military actions which were calculated to interfere with a diplomatic approach to Petrograd. On July 8, 1917, upon hearing of the preliminary text of the majority-sponsored Reichstag resolution, Ludendorff informed Bethmann-Hollweg that "from the military point of view he would most deeply regret such a resolution"; in this same telegram Ludendorff "advised his Excellency in strictest confidence that by decision of His Majesty the Kaiser the Russians would be attacked around the middle of July." [104] Thus, whereas the Supreme Command and its political allies suspected the Chancellor of fellow-traveling with the new Reichstag majority, this majority was suspicious in turn of his continuing subservience to Ludendorff. It was Bethmann-Hollweg's undeserved fate to find himself caught between these opposing coalitions.

Even though in pursuit of conflicting long-range objectives, these two coalitions temporarily combined to bring about the downfall of the Chancellor. The Conservatives and the National Liberals voted

102. Scheidemann, *Memoiren eines Sozialdemokraten*, 2, 30.

103. In a letter dated July 7 another influential Traditionalist, Prince Max of Baden, expressed his concern about the "growing war weariness among all classes, a strong ferment in the poorer classes of the population, especially in the working classes, fostered by the suggestion of the Western and American democracies and their agents, and strongly influenced by events in Russia. . . . In the big towns and industrial areas scarcity of food plays its own part. A more extensive part is played by the submarine war, for the population had placed great hopes in a rapid and decisive result from this weapon. . . . On all sides our enemies are saying to our people: 'you can have peace, when you have democratized yourselves, but no sooner.' This infamous suggestion is believed, and is being made use of, at least by the Social Democrats. It is falling on fruitful soil." Thus Prince Max, even though he agreed with the substance of the war-aims resolution which was in the making, thought that "its form and occasion had been very badly chosen," and instead tended to favor internal reforms. He queried whether Germany could "continue the war without the risk that serious internal unrest will damage our unity and jeopardize the manufacture of munitions unless we immediately meet the desire of the people for 'democratization.' " Prince Max of Baden, *The Memoirs*, 1, 113, 121–22.

104. Telegram from Lersner, Foreign Ministry liaison officer at General Headquarters, to Bethmann-Hollweg, July 8, 1917, GFM, Container 1499.

against Bethmann-Hollweg because in addition to rejecting his further rapprochement with the war-aims forces, they opposed his *Neuorientierung* inclinations. Though Erzberger may have been motivated partly by personal ambition, he marshaled the *Zentrum* party against Bethmann-Hollweg primarily in the hope of getting a more effective "peace Chancellor." However, since politically the anti-Bethmann coalition had nothing in common with the new Reichstag majority except that the Center party belonged to both, this search for a peace Chancellor promised to be difficult, if not impossible.[105]

Even though the Reichstag majority might have looked upon the projected Peace Resolution as a program with which to introduce parliamentary control of cabinet formation, it was unable to overcome the following obstacles: disagreement within the new Reichstag majority over a candidate, the autocratic tradition of cabinet formation of the Second Empire, and effective opposition by the Supreme Command and its political associates. Therefore the advice of Ludendorff and Hindenburg was decisive in the Kaiser's choice of a new Chancellor. Neither Erzberger, nor his candidate, Prince von Bülow, was even considered for the vacant post. Instead, by July 14 the little-known but politically safe Georg Michaelis was sworn in as Bethmann-Hollweg's successor.[106]

The Peace Resolution which had been drafted in the Steering Committee was brought before the full Reichstag on July 19, 1917. This happened in spite of Hindenburg's warning that the Resolution "would intensify the existing unrest in the army and would be regarded as a sign of internal weakness." [107] When the Resolution was put to a test it passed by a vote of 212 to 126, with 17 abstentions.[108] In the legislative branch the SPD, the *Zentrum*,[109] and the Progressives [110] de-

105. See Bethmann-Hollweg, *Betrachtungen zum Weltkrieg*, 2, 226.

106. Ibid., pp. 226–27; Erzberger, *Erlebnisse im Weltkrieg*, pp. 261, 288; Georg Michaelis, *Für Staat und Volk* (Berlin, Furche, 1922), p. 324.

107. Cited in Ludendorff, *The General Staff and Its Problems*, 2, 462.

108. For the stenographic record of the July 19th session of the Reichstag, see GFM, Container 1396.

109. The shifting positions of the Center party on the war-aims issue are traced in F. Wacker, *Die Haltung der Deutschen Zentrumspartei zur Frage der Kriegsziele im Weltkriege 1914–1918*, Würzburg, 1937.

110. Under the leadership of Friedrich von Payer, all the members of the Progressive People's party except one voted for the Resolution. See Hermann Ostfeld, *Die Haltung der Reichstagsfraktion der Fortschrittlichen Volkspartei zu den Annexions-und Friedensfragen in den Jahren 1914–1918* (Würzburg, 1934), p. 25.

fiantly as well as publicly challenged and defeated the Supreme Command and the forces of order; however, in the executive branch the influence of the forces of movement remained altogether negligible.

Most of the *Zentrum* deputies no doubt agreed with Friedrich Naumann, a prominent Progressive, that the Resolution "was no more moral than the position of the *Vaterlandspartei*," but that "it was politically more realistic." [111] After insisting that Germany was fighting merely a war of self-defense, the controversial Peace Resolution stated:

> The Reichstag strives for a peace of understanding and the permanent reconciliation of the peoples. With such a peace forced acquisitions of territory and political, economic, or financial oppressions are inconsistent. The Reichstag also rejects all schemes which aim at economic barriers and hostility between the peoples after the war. The freedom of the seas must be made secure. Only economic peace will prepare the ground for a friendly intercourse between the nations. The Reichstag will actively promote the creation of International Law Organizations.[112]

This Resolution deviates most conspicuously from the Petrograd formula by its failure even to mention self-determination.

Since the Resolution could easily serve as a basis for a status-quo peace, Ludendorff must have objected as much to its spirit as to its wording. Undoubtedly the Quartermaster General agreed with Count Westarp, spokesman for the Conservative party in the July 19th debate, that Germany could "not come one step nearer to peace through speeches and resolutions of peace or through moral admonitions to the conscience of our enemies." [113] Likewise, the new Chancellor seems to have shared this view, since Michaelis qualified his agreement to the Resolution with the reservation, which was subsequently widely commented upon, that it was subject to his own interpretations (*wie ich sie auffasse*). In a report to the Crown Prince on July 26, Michaelis asserted that with this reservation he had "deprived the Resolution of its greatest danger" and that, in fact, one could "make any peace one likes, and still be in accord with the Resolution." [114] Consequently

111. Heuss, *Friedrich Naumann*, p. 511.
112. For the complete text, in translation, of the July 19th Peace Resolution see Dickinson, pp. 44–45.
113. Cited in *DR*, EPS (August 2, 1917), p. 393.
114. *VRSB, Legislaturperiode* 13, Session 2, Vol. *312* (July 19, 1917), pp. 3570–72. Letter from Michaelis to the German Crown Prince dated July 26, 1917, cited

the Reichstag majority, which had come together for the purpose of effecting a check on the extreme Right, was canceled out by the new "War Chancellor" who by his own admission had a decided affinity with the *Vaterlandspartei*.[115]

Still, Michaelis was not so confident as Ludendorff that time was on Germany's side. Like his predecessor, he was not sure whether Germany could survive a fourth year of war. Michaelis recognized that with the Russian Revolution the domestic situation had become worse, particularly because of the growing unrest among the workers and because of the stepped-up parliamentary campaign of the forces of movement. Even though the Chancellor believed that success on the battlefields could eventually solidify the home front, in the meantime he also pursued the search for a prewinter peace. In Vienna Count Czernin, after reminding Michaelis that Germany's internal situation had become comparable to Austria-Hungary's, again pressed the urgency of an early peace. Convinced that a general peace could not possibly be secured before the onset of winter, the Austrian Foreign Minister renewed his plea for a separate peace with one of the Allies, particularly with France. Consequently he urged Michaelis to compromise on Alsace-Lorraine as well as on Belgium. Czernin added that France was advised of the Vatican's plan to offer mediation on some such basis. Eventually, in September, Michaelis did ask the Supreme Command for clarification on the Belgian issue.[116]

Meanwhile Ludendorff had readily acknowledged the serious worsening of Germany's, as well as of Austria-Hungary's and Bulgaria's, political, economic, and financial difficulties. He insisted, however, that "these internal difficulties had to be and could be overcome by the resolute leadership of the present Government." Like Clemenceau, Ludendorff concluded that the war had now become primarily a test of endurance. In his view, the situation inside the Allied countries was worse than that inside the Central camp. France and Italy were suffering serious coal shortages; as a result of the German blockade, peace pressures were mounting in England; and the Allies could

in Rosenberg, *The Birth of the German Republic*, p. 176. For a self-justifying interpretation of the new Chancellor's reaction to the Resolution see Michaelis, *Für Staat und Volk*, p. 329.

115. Michaelis, *Für Staat und Volk*, p. 332.

116. Minutes of the Michaelis-Czernin conversations in Vienna on August 1, 1917, and "Notes on the Political Situation" by von Kühlmann, September 3, 1917, GFM, Container 1499.

no longer count on Russia. America had become the Entente's only hope, but in Ludendorff's view the American potential should neither be overestimated nor underestimated. In brief, compared to the enemy, Germany's over-all military position was better, her alliance system more solid, and her internal difficulties less intense. Nevertheless, Ludendorff also advocated a prewinter peace; however, he wanted such a negotiated peace only provided it guaranteed "basic essentials which we need to secure our economic development, and provided it leaves us in a military and economic position which will enable us to contemplate confidently some future defensive war." In Ludendorff's view Germany could not achieve this safe position without control over Courland, Lithuania, Poland, Alsace-Lorraine, and Belgium.[117]

In the midst of the July crisis the *Vorwärts* suggested that "anyone who [had] watched the last few days with open eyes [could] no longer doubt the fact that the Reich is on its way to a peaceful revolution"; though the process was not yet completed, it could no longer be stopped.[118] Erzberger saw in the Resolution "the starting point and the firm basis for a solid majority in the Reichstag and thus the beginning of the parliamentary regime." [119] A different interpretation was offered by Spengler, who considered it "the first act of the German revolution" which was a rebellion not "against the authority of an incapable ruler, but against authority as such." [120]

The *Burgfrieden* had failed to reinforce the archaic political institutions which had become increasingly dependent on an expansionist peace. The spectacular Peace Resolution tended to overshadow all promises for electoral reform. Yet, especially for a hard core of Traditionalists the Reichstag majority's demand, in October 1917, for suffrage reform in Prussia symbolized the breakdown of the existing order, as well as the end of an era. According to Hindenburg "the atmosphere of parliamentary faction inclined more and more to the left, and as far as deeds were concerned, and in spite of many fine

117. Ludendorff Memorandum, September 14, 1917, ibid., Container 1499.

118. Cited in Lutz, *Fall of the German Empire*, 2, 277. A summary report of the SPD Executive Committee for the years 1914–17 made the exaggerated claim that "the terrible world events which exact such gigantic sacrifices with irresistible force have accomplished the Social Democratic demand for the democratization of the Empire and of the State." *Protokoll des Parteitages* (October 1917), p. 6.

119. Erzberger, *Erlebnisse im Weltkrieg*, p. 269.

120. Oswald Spengler, *Preussentum und Sozialismus* (Munich, Beck, 1922), p. 8.

words, began to represent the elements which were intent on the destruction of the ancient political order in the State." [121] The Conservatives and their allies bitterly complained that henceforth political life would proceed on the assumption that the "democratic movement was insurmountable and that consequently all concessions would have to be made in good time because resistance would be of no avail." [122]

Similarly, Ludendorff complained that the connection between the war-aims and the suffrage debate on the one hand and the Russian Revolution on the other had been too obvious. Whereas he agreed that the Prussian franchise needed to be liberalized, he insisted that this reform should have come as the gracious gift of a strong Government before the war.[123] During wartime, however, even though the extreme Right was apprehensive of the expansion of revolutionary agitation into Germany, it proposed to meet the rising reform pressures by outright repression and censorship. Unlike Bethmann-Hollweg, Czernin, and the Reichstag majority, Ludendorff was not haunted by the specter of revolution. He decried the apparent abdication of leadership to Parliament because in his view only a strong executive was capable of inspiring people with great "aims and missions" (*Ziele und grosse Aufgaben*).[124]

In retrospect Ludendorff flatly declared that Germany's "decline began obviously with the outbreak of the Revolution in Russia." [125] Because in the middle of 1917 he could not have foreseen that it would "undermine our strength at a later date," [126] he rejoiced when the Revolution relieved the pressure on Germany's Eastern front. As early as July 25, however, he was disturbed by the dangerous and seditious

121. Marshal Paul von Hindenburg, *Out of My Life* (2 vols. New York, Harper, 1921), 2, 116.

122. Westarp, *Konservative Politik im letzten Jahrzehnt des Kaiserreiches*, 2, 218.

123. Ludendorff, *Meine Kriegserinnerungen*, p. 355. Obviously, others before him, both non-German and German, had reached this conclusion long ago. "It is the Russians who are smoking out the Chancellor and the Kaiser. They have infected the diplomacy of the Allies with the leaven which it has so sorely needed. They have succeeded in beginning the disintegration of the cast-iron patriotic morale of the German nation." *New Republic* (July 14, 1917), p. 287. A contemporary student of German politics concluded that "the formation of the new Reichstag bloc was due to the Russian Revolution and its consequences, which had led some annexationists to change their views." Bevan, *German Social Democracy during the War*, p. 189.

124. Ludendorff, *Meine Kriegserinnerungen*, p. 349; and Westarp, *Konservative Politik im letzten Jahrzehnt des Kaiserreiches*, 2, 232.

125. Ludendorff, *Meine Kriegserinnerungen*, p. 355.

126. Ibid., p. 327.

propaganda which the Independents were carrying into the ranks of the Reichswehr. To combat this war-aims propaganda of the USPD as well as of all other leftists, Hindenburg and Ludendorff set up the *Vaterländische Unterricht*, a new army unit designed to prepare and disseminate orientation lectures.[127] A few weeks later the Supreme Command asked Michaelis to establish a civilian *Aufklärungszentrale*.[128]

The Independent Socialists voted against the July 19th Resolution which they criticized as vigorously and in much the same terms as the Allies. They attacked this document for its failure to clarify Germany's policy toward Belgium and Alsace-Lorraine, as well as for its failure to define the basis for a settlement in Eastern Europe. In the Reichstag, Haase scornfully indicted Michaelis for his self-made escape clause and bluntly accused the non-Socialist supporters of the Resolution of pure and simple opportunism; to Haase their recent advocacy of expansionism was an even more serious weakness than the absence of a clear commitment to self-determination in the Resolution. Moreover, Haase supported his claim that the Resolution was ineffective by pointing to the arbitrary, nonparliamentary manner in which the new Chancellor had been appointed.[129]

In the Allied and Associated nations Germany's internal developments were carefully watched. Whereas Allied progressives looked upon the weakening of the political truce in Germany as an additional index of the expanding all-European peace movement, official quarters publicly disregarded the Resolution. Instead, they pointed to Michaelis' interpretation as well as to his appointment as conclusive evidence that no effective policy change had taken place.[130] Henceforth the Entente Governments closely observed the right-wing anti-

127. Ibid., pp. 365, 369. See also Ludendorff, *The General Staff and Its Problems*, 2, 385–400.

128. Notes on Michaelis-Ludendorff consultation held in Kreuznach on August 9, 1917, GFM, Container 1499.

129. *VRSB, Legislaturperiode* 13, Session 2, Vol. *312* (July 19, 1917), pp. 3583–96.

130. See, e.g., the reports of the U.S. ministers in Sweden and Switzerland in *FR*, 1917, Supplement 2, *1*, 128–29, 139–40. On July 26, 1917, on a motion by Ramsay MacDonald, the British House of Commons centered a war-aims debate around the Reichstag Resolution. *PD*, *96* (July 26, 1917), col. 1481. At about this same time Michaelis made political capital out of the Doumergue conventions, whose provisions had leaked to the press after they had been disclosed in a secret session of the French Lower House.

Resolution forces which by early September had chartered the *Vater-landspartei*,[131] while simultaneously stepping up their propaganda campaign calculated to sharpen political and social conflicts inside Germany.

Paris and London, and particularly Wilson and House, never hesitated to capitalize on their enemies' domestic difficulties. Wilson would not listen to officially inspired editorials in the German press which called on him "to stop concerning himself with the internal conditions in Germany," and which suggested that "the battle against the plutocracy in his own country" should really keep the President fully occupied. Moreover, Wilson refused to heed Berlin's advice that he compare his own war-aims pronouncements with the secret treaties of the Allies in which "France and England promise Constantinople to Russia, and in exchange Russia promises France not only Alsace-Lorraine, but also the left bank of the Rhine." [132] On the contrary, Wilson stepped up his ideological offensive until it caused concern even within the Supreme Command.[133]

On the other hand, the Social Patriots and the Independents eagerly

131. *FR*, 1917, Supplement 2, *1*, 199; and Bevan, *German Social Democracy during the War*, p. 206. The following was the composition of the antiresolution forces: the Conservatives, the Supreme Command, a great part of the officer corps, the All-German Union, the Independent Committee for a German peace, the *Vaterlandspartei*, and the great economic associations (e.g. Central Association of German Industries). Earlier in the war this same coalition had taken the lead in advocating unrestricted submarine warfare. See Westarp, *Konservative Politik im letzten Jahrzehnt des Kaiserreiches*, 2, 669. For the initial statement of purpose of the *Vaterlandspartei*, apparently drafted by Wolfgang Kapp, see Karl Wortmann, *Geschichte der Deutschen Vaterlands-Partei (1917–1918)* (Halle, Otto Hendel, 1926), pp. 29–32.

132. After Wilson's May 26th message to Russia the Foreign Ministry and the Supreme Command agreed to plant a rebuttal in the *Norddeutsche Allgemeine Zeitung*. For the text of the article, which was published in the June 15th issue of this paper, as well as telegrams about it among the Foreign Ministry, the Supreme Command, and the Embassy in Vienna, see GFM, Container 1499.

133. Carl Ackermann, who conferred with Colonel House upon his return from Germany, insisted on the title page of his book that "the title *Germany, the Next Republic?* is chosen because the author believes this must be the goal, the battlecry of the United States and her Allies. . . . Permanent peace will follow the establishment of a Republic. But the German people will not overthrow the present government until the leaders are defeated and discredited. . . . The world cannot afford to consider peace with Germany until the people rule. The sooner the United States and her Allies tell this to the German people officially the sooner we shall have peace." For the House-Ackermann meeting see Charles Seymour, *The Intimate Papers of Colonel House* (4 vols. Boston, Houghton Mifflin, 1926–28), *3*, 129.

sought to justify their pressures on the Government by emphasizing the dangers of this external propaganda onslaught. In their view only immediate internal reforms could destroy the effectiveness of Wilson's interference. Kautsky incessantly argued that "the question of world peace continues to grow more intimately interwoven with the democratization of Germany"; [134] in turn, democratization would bring a compromise diplomacy in its wake.

Likewise, Friedrich Meinecke predicted that in their efforts to disorganize Germany the Allies would relentlessly press their democratization campaign. He insisted that the enemy would continue to disseminate propaganda slogans because the Allies knew that the German people were in conflict about whether and to what degree they "were in need of democracy." [135]

Meinecke's analysis of Allied propaganda strategy, if set in the context of the rapid extension of carefully calculated psychological warfare, conflicts with the interpretation according to which Wilson's pronouncements about the democratization of Germany and about nonannexationist war aims were merely symptomatic of a moralistic-legalistic tradition or proclivity in the making of American foreign policy.[136] Quite apart from President Wilson's evangelic and proselytizing predilections, there were objective conditions in Germany which dictated this ideological emphasis to the Allies as they were about to launch a full-scale propaganda offensive. Though the Allied forces of movement were more sensitive than the forces of order to the opportunities which the political tensions in the Reich offered to Allied propaganda, even official sources began to hold up Liebknecht and Haase to the German people as their only trustworthy spokesmen. Since the Supreme Command continued to dominate the German Government, the Allies were bound to focus their propaganda onslaughts on the *Vaterlandspartei*, which emerged as the most perfect symbol of Prussian imperialism.

As of mid-1917 the German political truce never regained its former firmness, even though the parliamentary opposition did not seriously weaken the Right's effective control over the civilian and military

134. *Die Neue Zeit* (August 31, 1917), p. 512.
135. Meinecke, *Preussen und Deutschland*, p. 505.
136. Cf. George F. Kennan, *American Diplomacy, 1900–1950* (Chicago, University of Chicago Press, 1951), esp. pp. 71–72; and John Morton Blum, *Woodrow Wilson and the Politics of Morality* (Boston, Little, Brown, 1956), esp. pp. 145–46, 158.

authorities. The very gradually but nevertheless constantly shrinking forces of order successfully defended their annexationist objectives against the clamor for war-aims moderation of the expanding forces of movement. Only the Spartacists and the Independents called for the open diplomacy which was especially dear to the British Left. Within the Reichstag majority the emphasis tended to be on a more or less restrictive interpretation of the Petrograd formula, together with a growing demand for universal suffrage and genuine parliamentarism. It seems hardly surprising that the spokesmen of the German forces of movement should have agitated for general parliamentary control of the executive before focusing on the narrower question of parliamentary control of foreign policy which agitated the Left in the established democracies of the West.

3. ALLIED WAR AIMS IN TRANSITION

In July–August 1914 the Russian and German governments had little difficulty in fashioning national unity in the face of threatening external dangers. The constitution of both governments was sufficiently autocratic to permit recourse to martial law without legislative sanction. However, since neither a general strike nor a social revolution broke out, the state's executive agencies did not have to use any emergency measures. Likewise, in France and England the consolidation of national unity was achieved even before the Paris Chamber invested the Cabinet with exceptional powers (August 4) and before Commons voted the first Defense of the Realm Act (August 8).

This emergency legislation temporarily suspended many time-honored constitutional guarantees and safeguards. However, since neither parliament was dissolved nor were any parties proscribed, political life in Paris and London continued on the assumption that in the last analysis the legislature would exercise effective control over the executive. Meanwhile, as long as the military and economic machines worked smoothly, successfully, and with fairness, there was little disposition on the part of individual legislators and organized parties to challenge the Government.

In the French and British capitals more than in the provinces, antiwar manifestations and leaders had to be tamed in the Socialist movement before the latter would instruct its parliamentary delegations to support the Government. At heated mass meetings in Trafalgar Square and at the Salle Wagram, the Allied Left gave last-minute populist demonstrations of its opposition to war.[1] Moreover, certain that war

1. ILP, *Report of the Annual Conference* (Norwich, 1915), p. 7; and Dolléans, *Histoire du mouvement ouvrier*, 2, 211 ff.

could no longer be forestalled, Socialist leaders in the intimacy of political and trade union caucuses faced the grim prospect of being forced to choose between the Nation and the International. In the competition for the allegiance of the working class and its leaders the democratic Nation presently scored as easy a triumph as its autocratic German and Russian counterpart.

> But on both sides of the Channel this triumph was preceded by a struggle in the Socialist ranks between the prowar majority and the pacifist minority. Before the British Labour party declared its support of the war effort on August 5, Ramsay MacDonald resigned in protest from the chairmanship of the Parliamentary Labour party. In his dissent, MacDonald was joined by Snowden, Hardie, Jowett, and Richardson; henceforth all five sat in Commons under ILP auspices, and waged a consistent battle for an early negotiated peace and for a formulation of moderate war aims.[2] Gradually the antagonism between the Parliamentary Labour party and this minuscular ILP faction developed to a breaking point, "the latter being now in close communion with the sentimental Whigs of the Arthur Ponsonby, C. P. Trevelyan, Courtney type."[3] However, regardless of their view on the origin and the likely outcome of the war, even these dissidents insisted that England had to go through with it.

Meanwhile, having replaced MacDonald as chairman of the Parliamentary Labour party, Arthur Henderson guided the Labour MP's in manning their Social Patriotic stations. Together with the Parliamentary Committee of the Trades Union Congress the Labour MP's secured an electoral and an industrial truce. In view of England's voluntary military recruiting system, it is not surprising that by August 28 Prime Minister Asquith should have asked, through Henderson, for Labour's help in an "all-party" recruiting campaign; the National Executive immediately endorsed the Parliamentary party's decision to take a prominent part in this vital defense task.[4] Since British Labour's participation in the first Asquith coalition Government was still more than half a year away, its support of the war effort followed the same pattern as the SPD's support of the German war enterprise. However, whereas the German Social Patriots fought simply to forestall the

2. LP, *Report of the Fifteenth Annual Conference* (Bristol, 1916), p. 51; and J. R. Clynes, *Memoirs* (2 vols. London, Hutchinson, 1937), *1*, 172–73.
3. Cole, pp. 33–34.
4. LP, *Report of the Fifteenth Annual Conference* (Bristol, 1916), pp. 4–5.

triumph of Russian despotism, the British Labourites immediately formulated their war purposes in loftier terms. In addition to protecting England and Europe "from the evils that would follow the triumph of military despotism," the British Left came out for the protection of small nations, as well as for international arbitration and conciliation.[5] The fact that England did not declare war on Germany until after Belgium's neutrality had been violated explains this emphasis made in official, as well as in Labour, statements on the cause of small nations and the sanctity of treaties.

In France the antiwar militants were more numerous in the CGT than in the upper echelons of political Socialism. Deeply steeped in the doctrine of the general strike, syndicalist leaders like Léon Jouhaux and Alphonse Merrheim sought to stop the drift toward war by raising the specter of noncooperation. The CGT joined with the SFIO in announcing further antiwar demonstrations for the first days of August. However, Russia decreed partial mobilization, the alert was sounded in Germany, and Berlin issued an ultimatum asking Russia to demobilize within twelve hours.[6]

At the insistence of General Joffre the French Government proceeded formally to order general mobilization a few hours before Germany independently took a similar step. Meanwhile, however, the Minister of War, Messimy, had urged the application of "Carnet B" in order to forestall left-wing interference with the impending mobilization. He recommended the arrest or the dispatch into the front lines of some 1770 syndicalists, anarchists, and left-wing Socialists—all of whom the Ministry of the Interior had listed in Carnet B as *dangereux au point de vue social*. Among the security risks listed figured the names of Hervé, Jouhaux, Merrheim, and Laval.[7]

But when the Council of Ministers discussed Messimy's proposal on July 29, it was decided, on the strong urging of L.-J. Malvy, Minister of the Interior, not to apply Carnet B. Malvy was a protégé of Joseph Caillaux and, like him, a left-oriented Radical. At the outbreak of war,

---

5. For the key passages from a declaration dated October 14, 1914, and signed by an overwhelming majority of the best-known Labour leaders see Walling, pp. 164–66.

6. Dolléans, *Histoire du mouvement ouvrier*, 2, 217 ff.; and Paul Louis, *Histoire du socialisme en France* (5th ed. Paris, Rivière, 1950), pp. 321–26.

7. L.-J. Malvy, *Mon Crime* (Paris, Flammarion, 1921), pp. 35–37; Paul Allard, *Les Enigmes de la guerre* (Paris, Portiques, 1933), pp. 35–38; Dolléans, *Histoire du mouvement ouvrier*, 2, 215–16.

and until September 1917, he was the spokesman of the forces of movement in the Cabinet, where he controlled the all-important Ministry of Interior. Apparently Malvy, not unlike Bethmann-Hollweg in Germany, was instrumental in striking a bargain according to which no arrests would be made provided the antimilitarists promised not to interfere with mobilization. On July 31, in a wire ordering all prefects to forego arrests, Malvy insisted that "the present attitude of the syndicalists inspires confidence"; therefore, the prefects were asked merely to "exercise an attentive but discrete surveillance over them." [8] Indeed these events proved that as in Germany fears of massive left-wing dissent were largely groundless.

That same evening Jean Jaurès was assassinated by a mentally disturbed superpatriot. Even though a few of his colleagues pronounced moving Internationalist orations at his funeral,[9] the tragic death of Jaurès symbolized the collapse of Socialist internationalism in France. Once the important syndicalist leaders had pledged their loyalty, the political arm of the Socialist movement could hardly have been expected to refuse its support for the war. Even though the SFIO had been militantly antimilitarist, for many years reformism had been advancing at the cost of revolutionary Socialism.

By August 4, then, the French Government was assured of the domestic order which it needed to fight the German enemy effectively; the mobilization could proceed unhampered, and industrial peace was secured. On the morning of the 4th Jaurès was buried; in the afternoon President Poincaré, in his message to Parliament, claimed with considerable justification that France "would be heroically defended by all her sons whose *union sacrée* in the face of the enemy could never be broken." [10] The French Socialist party jointly with the Belgian Labor party promptly issued a manifesto declaring that by accepting the dire necessity of war they were not only defending their countries against German imperialism, but also "supporting the prin-

8. For the text of Malvy's telegram see Picard, *Le Mouvement syndical*, p. 52. The Maximalists in the CGT and SFIO subsequently censured Malvy for his part in securing the loyalty of the workers in exchange for the freedom of their leaders. Cf. Alfred Rosmer, *Le Mouvement ouvrier pendant la guerre: De l'union sacrée à Zimmerwald* (Paris, Librairie du Travail, 1936), pp. 152 ff.

9. Alexandre Zévaès, ed., *Le Parti Socialiste de 1904 à 1923* (Paris, Rivière, 1923), pp. 142–43. Cf. Dolléans, *Histoire du mouvement ouvrier*, 2, 223.

10. The text of Poincaré's message is cited in Georges Bonnefous, *Histoire politique de la Troisième République* (2 vols. Paris, Presses Universitaires, 1956–57), 2, 29–30.

ciple of liberty" and "the right of the people to dispose of themselves." [11]

Like France, England was ruled by a left-center Liberal government in July–August 1914. In London, even though the Conservatives constituted the largest single party in Commons, they could not muster sufficient support to endanger Asquith, whose working majority consisted of "Liberal, (Irish) Nationalist and Labour groups." [12] Nevertheless, beset by security, munitions, and supply problems, Asquith was forced to make an opening to the right in May 1915; he now headed a center-*right* coalition Cabinet.

In France the first crisis matured much more rapidly than in England. The frontier defeats immediately resulted in concerted pressures for strong government and leadership, in spite of the fact that after having adjourned on August 5 Parliament did not reconvene until December 22. Without parliamentary consultation or approval, René Viviani sought to translate the recently born *union sacrée* into political terms. He formed a Ministry of National Defense in which Delcassé took over Foreign Affairs, Ribot became Minister of Finance, and Millerand headed the Ministry of War. Within half a year the concessions to the Right were punctuated still further by the inclusion of the right-wing Catholic leader Denys Cochin in the Briand Government. [13]

Three years of morale-consuming stalemate had to pass before the pronounced right-wing Clemenceau Cabinet came into power. In the intervening years, however, the forces of movement willingly pledged their support to the *union sacrée* Government. Not only did Viviani continue as Premier, and Malvy as Minister of Interior, but two leading Socialists actually were invited into the Cabinet. Even though Jules Guesde had been, until recently, a most resolute opponent of Socialist participation in bourgeois-dominated governments, he now was eager to serve as minister without portfolio. Marcel Sembat, author of the widely circulated antiwar tract *Faites un roi sinon faites la paix*, agreed without hesitation to serve as Minister of Public Works. [14]

Since this participation in a bourgeois government was contrary to

11. The text of this manifesto is cited in Walling, pp. 175–77. Cf. Louis, *Histoire du socialisme en France*, p. 332.

12. Lloyd George, *War Memoirs*, 1, 130. The Asquith Cabinet was composed of twenty Liberals and one Labourite (John Burns, who resigned at the outbreak of war).

13. Goguel, *La Politique des partis sous la IIIe République*, p. 157.

14. Alexandre Zévaès, *Le Socialisme en France* (Paris, Fasquelle, 1934), p. 88.

the doctrine and charter of the SFIO, some explanation to the rank-and-file was no doubt called for. Accordingly, in a manifesto of August 28, 1914, the party declared that it had designated Guesde and Sembat as "its delegates for the national defense" in a nonparty government (not a bourgeois government) whose primary task was the defense of France.[15] It is noteworthy that this drastic reversal of long-standing Socialist policy was approved unanimously by the 102 members of the SFIO parliamentary delegation, by the party's Permanent Administrative Commission, and by the Administrative Council of *l'Humanité*.

Five months later, when unquestioned Social Patriotism was still at its height, this same group reasserted its faith in the cause of the Entente. In a New Year's manifesto the party claimed that French Socialists were fighting *against* foreign aggression, Prussian imperialism, and savage militarism; at the same time they were fighting *for* a "free" return of Alsace-Lorraine, "fighting so that this war, this atrocious war, be the last war," and fighting in order to reduce "the immense burden of armaments." [16]

Certainly during the first year of war the overwhelming majority of the British Labour and the French Socialist movement accepted the political truce enthusiastically. Except for the few Russian Bolsheviks no militant Allied Socialists of stature emerged to proclaim the unqualified opposition to war which Liebknecht, Luxemburg, Mehring, and Zetkin had expressed in Germany by the end of 1914. Whenever dissent was formulated in the Allied nations it took the form of pronouncements of noble war aims.

At Vandervelde's suggestion, the British Section of the International Socialist Bureau called an inter-Allied Socialist Conference in London for February 14, 1915. Some forty delegates from England, France, Belgium, and Russia convened under the chairmanship of Keir Hardie. Though heavily outnumbered by militant Social Patriots, Hardie, MacDonald, Merrheim, and their Internationalist colleagues succeeded in leaving their imprint on the resolutions which the Majoritarians were determined to adopt unanimously.

In the first resolution, instead of merely denouncing Germany for her militarist imperialism, the Allied Socialists insisted that they were not pursuing "the political and economic crushing of Germany" and

15. For the complete text of this manifesto see Le Parti socialiste, *La Guerre et la paix*, pp. 110–11. The principal paragraphs are translated in Walling, pp. 178–79.
16. Walling, pp. 348–50.

were not "at war with the peoples of Germany and Austria, but only with the governments of these countries by which they are oppressed." This distinction between the people and their governments subsequently became prominent in Allied war-aims diplomacy and propaganda, especially under the influence of Wilson. The first London resolution also demanded that "those populations that have been annexed by force shall receive the right freely to dispose of themselves." While the assembled delegates recorded their inflexible determination "to fight until victory is achieved," they decided concurrently to firmly "resist any attempt to transform this defensive war into a war of conquest." After condemning secret diplomacy and armaments races, they also called for compulsory arbitration and for the creation of an international authority.[17]

The adoption of these and similar new war aims served to some extent to appease the scruples of the Radical and Socialist conscience. However, the war cabinets neither acknowledged nor challenged this enlightened formulation of war purposes. Instead they were engaged in the exacting task of negotiating secretly with Russia about Constantinople and the Near East, and with Italy about the conditions of her entrance into the war on the side of the Allies. Now that the war threatened to be prolonged indefinitely, the cabinets sought to draft every possible resource which might help the war effort. Whereas the secret treaties were calculated to bolster the over-all military position of the Entente *vis-à-vis* the Central Powers, all further political openings to the Right and/or Left were made as part of the same search for additional national power.

The Constantinople agreements were concluded by April 10, 1915; the Treaty of London was signed on April 26, 1915. The United States remained the last *major* uncommitted nation; obviously, her adhesion to either bloc could not be secured by the same diplomatic methods employed in negotiations with Italy, Bulgaria, and Rumania. Mean-

---

17. For the complete text of this resolution see ILP, *Report of the Annual Conference* (Norwich, 1915), p. 121. MacDonald was forced to explain to the left wing of the ILP why he and his Internationalist colleagues had signed this resolution calling for a fight until victory. Ibid., pp. 53–54. Parenthetically, it might be noted that in the name of the Russian Bolsheviks, who were not formally seated at the Conference, Maxim Litvinov presented a declaration both calling for the immediate resignation of Guesde, Sembat, and Vandervelde from their ministerial posts, and condemning the repeated war-credit votes by Socialists. Lenin, *Works, 18,* 140–43.

while, "diplomatic" negotiations inside these nations between the cabinets and the forces of movement were bound to intensify. The longer the duration of the war, the higher the consumer price index, the greater the food shortage, the more numerous the military reverses —the more crucial was the power of trade union and Socialist leaders who had access to that sector of the population in which there were great reserves of energy.

Hence, when in May 1915 the "shell shortage" crisis led Asquith to seek a Coalition Cabinet to replace his Liberal Government, he followed the Viviani pattern. Asquith not only invited nine Tories [18] to reinforce the executive, thereby creating a center-right Cabinet, but on May 19 also invited Labour, through Henderson, to participate in this wartime Coalition. Now it was the Labour party's turn to decide whether to enter into a predominantly non-Labour cabinet, a step which would be in clear violation of clause III of the party constitution. Though a negative decision was hardly likely, it should nevertheless be noted that, unlike the events in France, in late August 1914 the issue now provoked extensive debate in the Parliamentary Labour party and in the National Executive Committee. Curiously enough, whereas the Executive Committee gave its assent to Asquith's request by a 9 to 3 vote, there was considerable opposition in the parliamentary delegation, even among such ardent prowar Labourites as J. R. Clynes.[19] "A joint meeting of the NEC with the PLP was then held and after a full discussion the joint meeting decided to accept the Prime Minister's invitation by a vote of 17 to 11." [20] This decision was endorsed first by the Trades Union Congress in September 1915 [21] and then, in the middle of January 1916, by the annual conference of the Labour party. At this party conference a favorable vote of 1,674,000 to 269,000 was recorded after the Executive Committee had declared that the circumstances prevailing at the time of the invitation, "and the results accruing from the presence of working class opinion in the Government, have justified the Party in its action." [22]

18. Balfour, Curzon, Bonar Law, Lansdowne, A. Chamberlain, Walter Long, Robert Cecil, Selborne, and Carson.

19. Clynes, *Memoirs, 1*, 188.

20. McKenzie, *British Political Parties*, p. 400.

21. Ibid. At this TUC congress there was a "display of ardent patriotism." Subsequent TUC congresses kept endorsing ministerialism in spite of basic opposition to the Cabinet's conscription policies. Cole, pp. 42–45, 53–54; and Clynes, *Memoirs, 1*, 199.

22. LP, *Report of the Fifteenth Annual Conference* (Bristol, 1916), pp. 124–25, 55.

In the coalition which was formed in June, Labour was assigned one major and two minor ministerial posts. As President of the Board of Education, Arthur Henderson was the major Labour appointee.[23] Evidently, his formal position was nominal; Henderson's ability, energy, and influence were spent in advising an essentially conservative Cabinet on important labor questions and in consolidating the truce between the forces of movement and the forces of order.

Likewise in France on May 22, 1915, Albert Thomas, a leading Socialist, joined the Government with a political assignment similar to Henderson's. Thomas' appointment as Under-Secretary of State for Munitions, and his advancement in December 1916 to full-fledged Minister of Munitions, aroused considerable protest in the SFIO federation of the Seine and at the party congress in late 1916.[24] In England, also, in 1916 a certain restlessness began to be evident—primarily, however, over the peculiarly British conscription issue. But on the whole, the French as well as the British Left gave their respective governments "very little to worry about for the first two and a half years of war." [25]

Nevertheless, Lloyd George had recently concluded that "Labour must have a more substantial and effective representation in the new Government and that one of its most prominent and respected leaders should be a member of the small body which had the supreme direction of the War." [26] Therefore when he was called upon to form the second Coalition Government on December 7, 1916, he offered Labour still larger representation than it had enjoyed under Asquith. Once again the invitation to Labour was conveyed through Henderson, who at a joint meeting of the Parliamentary Labour party and the National Executive Committee led the majority which favored continued participation. "The meeting was unable to reach a decision, but it was decided to hear Lloyd George in order that he might outline the policies which his new Government would pursue." [27] This meeting took place at the War Office at noon that same day. There, "the pro-war Labour members drank in his sweet words: [and] the pacifists

23. W. Brace became Under-Secretary for Home Affairs; G. H. Roberts became Junior Lord of the Treasury.

24. Louis, *Histoire du socialisme en France*, pp. 335–36; and Zévaès, *Le Parti Socialiste de 1904 à 1923*, p. 168.

25. Brogan, *The Development of Modern France*, p. 531.

26. Lloyd George, *War Memoirs*, 1, 624. Cf. Hamilton Fyfe, *The British Liberal Party* (London, 1928), pp. 206–20.

27. McKenzie, *British Political Parties*, p. 401.

maintained a stony silence while Sidney [Webb] and one or two of
the waverers asked questions to which Lloyd George gave noncommittal answers." [28] After extensive debate, a resolution to turn down the
invitation was defeated 18 to 12 with the help of MP's like Clynes and
Thomas, who, though they had voted against the first Coalition, felt
that England's "position was now so grave that . . . it was not the
time . . . to register aesthetic doubts." [29] At Manchester on January
23, 1917, the party conference endorsed this second Coalition decision
even more decisively than it had endorsed the Asquith Coalition a
year earlier.[30]

The Lloyd George Coalition, in which the Conservatives and Liberal-
Imperialists were granted extensive influence, included six Labourites.[31] Of these two were of general Cabinet rank,[32] while Henderson,
as spokesman of the forces of movement, was admitted to the newly
constituted War Cabinet of Five. Perhaps it should be noted, too, that
four of the six Labour office holders had a solid trade union background
(Barnes, Hodge, Brace, Roberts). Indeed, Labour had gained "a larger
share in the Government of the country than anybody would have
anticipated five years ago." [33] But the question remains whether Labour
representatives had an effective voice in molding Government policy,
or whether they served merely in an administrative capacity while
performing the political function of guaranteeing the loyalty of the
proletariat.[34]

28. Cole, p. 72. Cf. LP, *Report of the Sixteenth Annual Conference* (Manchester,
1917), pp. 3–4.
29. Clynes, *Memoirs, 1,* 203–4.
30. LP, *Report of the Sixteenth Annual Conference* (Manchester, 1917), p. 98.
31. The party distribution of ministerial posts reveals the predominant influence
of the forces of order in the Lloyd George Coalition: 19 Conservatives, 6 Liberals,
and 3 Labourites. For a convenient comparison of the composition of the Asquith
and Lloyd George coalitions see the *Liberal Magazine, 24,* (1917), 631–36. Bonar
Law and Curzon were the leading Conservatives in this Lloyd George Coalition,
while Milner was the spokesman for the Liberal-Imperialists. All three now became
members of the Cabinet of Five, with Bonar Law and Milner particularly close to
the Prime Minister.
32. John Hodge became Britain's first Minister of Labour, while G. N. Barnes
was appointed to the newly created Ministry of Pensions. Brace continued in his
former position, Roberts was promoted to Parliamentary Secretary of the Board of
Trade, and James Parker became Junior Lord of the Treasury.
33. The Fabian Society, *34th Annual Report for Year Ended 31 March 1917,*
pp. 3–4.
34. LP, *Report of the Sixteenth Annual Conference* (Manchester, 1917), pp. 43,
86 ff.

According to one of the leading students of French Socialism, although the bourgeoisie offered the Left a part of public power, it "had no intention to make concessions to Socialism nor to espouse its ideas; rather, it hoped that by associating the leaders of the labor organizations with the government the masses could be controlled, their faith harnessed and all whims of opposition could be counteracted." [35] Surveying the British wartime labor picture, the Webbs concluded that "this enormous draft on the patriotism of the rank and file could only be secured by enlisting the support of official representatives of the Trade Union World—by according to them a unique and unprecedented place as the diplomatic representatives of the wage-earning class." [36] Similarly, when the Lloyd George Coalition was formed, Britain's leading Liberal daily observed that "in the last resort it is labour which in one way or another is the decisive factor in modern war, and for that reason above all we rejoice that the representatives of Labour have in a great majority thrown in their lot with the new Government and are to be well represented in important offices." [37]

Undoubtedly the French Socialists and British Labourites who sat in official councils influenced government policy to some extent in industrial relations, rationing, etc. However, until March 1917 they had no part whatever in formulating war-aims policy or in controlling the diplomatic conduct of the war. No doubt this absence of influence in the foreign-policy area was due in some measure to the unconditional acceptance of the political truce by the Franco-British Social Patriots. Like their Majoritarian comrades in Germany, they became so totally committed to the pursuit of military victory that by default the gradually growing Independent minority was left free to protest against the governments' war-aims policies as well as against their own support of these policies.

The militant Majoritarians tended to participate in the denunciation of those Socialists who insisted that the Left should press the cabinets for a formulation of nonannexationist war aims on the basis of which a peace without victory might be sought. Before going to the Inter-Allied Socialist Conference in London in February 1915, Jules Guesde declared that "there could be no talk of peace until German imperialism

---

35. Louis, *Histoire du socialisme en France*, p. 329.
36. Sidney and Beatrice Webb, *The History of Trade Unionism*, p. 637.
37. *Manchester Guardian*, December 9, 1916; cited in Brand, *British Labour's Rise to Power*, p. 41.

was crushed." [38] In a similar vein John Hodge, the leader of the steel workers who became Minister of Labour in the first Lloyd George Coalition, proclaimed at the Trades Union Congress in September 1915: "There can be no talk of peace with us until German Prussianism or militarism . . . has been laid in the dust. The men who talk about peace today are traitors to their country." [39]

At successive trade union and political congresses, resolutions calling for a more concrete formulation of Socialist as well as official war aims were defeated decisively. As long as the political truce was unimpaired, two factors contributed heavily to the lack of support for a clear-cut war-aims platform. First, the vast majority of workers continued to be under such a strong patriotic and anti-German spell that they were completely oblivious to war-aims debates. Second, the intensified contact with non-Socialist Government leaders heightened the susceptibility of Arthur Henderson and Albert Thomas to the national-interest perspective on problems of war and peace. It should also be remembered that the coalitions in which the British and French Social Patriots participated were further to the Right politically than were the Radical cabinets of July 1914. Henderson and Barnes, Thomas and Guesde were no match for Bonar Law and Milner, Millerand and Poincaré.

In the meantime, the nonrevolutionary left-wing minorities had stepped up their doctrinal attacks on unqualified defensism. Before long even some leading Social Patriots like Henderson and Thomas were going to abandon their blind adherence to the sacred union.

In France the *minoritaires* were active within both the CGT and the SFIO. As of 1915 Albert Bourderon, Alphonse Merrheim, Jean Longuet, Fernand Loriot, Pierre Monatte, Alfred Rosmer, and Boris Souvarine organized a caucus of dissidents which agitated within the SFIO for a clarification of official war aims and for a resurrection of the International. Especially under the guidance of Alphonse Merrheim, the influential leader of the fast-growing Metal Workers Union, this caucus voiced an essentially loyal criticism of their Majoritarian colleagues' blind Social Patriotism. [40] In November 1915 Merrheim and Bourderon

38. Cited in Walling, pp. 422–23.
39. Cited in Brand, *British Labour's Rise to Power*, p. 59.
40. A. Ferrat, *Histoire du parti communiste français* (Paris, Bureau d'Editions, 1931), pp. 49–50; and J. Rocher, *Lénine et le mouvement zimmerwaldien en France* (Paris, Bureau d'Editions, 1934), pp. 12–26.

courageously attended the Zimmerald Conference, where they found themselves in sharp disagreement with Lenin. Whereas Lenin went there to propound his civil-war thesis, Merrheim and Bourderon, together with the Zimmerwald majority, sought to precipitate a Europewide movement of left-wing opposition to the war cabinets' stubborn *aboutisme*.[41]

Once the two French labor leaders were back in France they organized the Comité International d'Action which dispatched to all syndical organizations a circular propounding the theses of the Zimmerwald majority. By late December 1915 the *minoritaires* of the CGT and the SFIO began to consider the advisability of constituting one common organization for all left-wing dissenters.[42]

In January 1916 the minority caucus of the SFIO and the Comité International d'Action of the CGT were transformed into the unified Comité pour la Reprise des Relations Internationales. This new committee became the rallying center for all French Zimmerwaldians, whether of the minority or the majority variety. As secretaries of the committee Merrheim and Bourderon gathered around themselves centrist colleagues like Pressemane, Mistral, Brisleux, Hubert, and Barry, as well as Maximalists like Loriot, Saumoneau, Rappoport, Rosmer, and Trotsky.[43] Because of the dominant influence of its two secretaries, the committee followed an essentially left-revisionist course. The committee assured the Social Patriots as well as the Government that it did not intend to become a rival to either the CGT or the SFIO; nor did it seek a division or a scission. Instead, the committee proposed to "supplement the party and the CGT in France in the same manner and under the same conditions that the International Zimmerwald Commission supplements the failing Bureau of the Socialist International." [44]

Throughout 1916 these *minoritaires* increased their strength and influence. In September the committee aroused widespread attention in the entire Left when it violently protested the banning of the Paris-

41. For a Zimmerwald majority and minority account of the Merrheim-Lenín clash see respectively Dolléans, *Histoire du mouvement ouvrier*, 2, 235–38; and Rocher, *Lénine et le mouvement zimmerwaldien en France*, pp. 29–32.
42. Rocher, pp. 38–41.
43. Ibid., p. 45.
44. See the first tract published by the Comité pour la Reprise des Relations Internationales, under the title *Aux Organisations socialistes et syndicales: A leurs militants*, Paris, 1916?.

published Russian daily *Nache Slovo,* and the expulsion from France of Leon Trotsky, one of this paper's editors. The *minoritaires* were especially indignant because neither Guesde nor Sembat nor Thomas nor any of their republican allies had questioned this repressive police measure.[45]

Meanwhile the tensions between the two major factions of the minority began to mount. The extreme Left now published a widely discussed pamphlet in which it distinguished between the two major dissident factions: the true Zimmerwaldians who believed that "national defense [had] nothing to do with Socialism," and the bulk of the *minoritaires* who, while calling for a public war-aims pronouncement, simultaneously continued to support the national war effort.[46] Especially Loriot became increasingly critical of his revisionist comrades who gained an ever larger following. A letter which the Majoritarian-controlled SFIO parliamentary delegation addressed to Prime Minister Briand on November 15, 1916, shows that the Social Patriots were not altogether immune to minority pressures. In this letter the Socialist deputies insisted that in view of the unexpected duration of the struggle and an oncoming lassitude in the nation the Government "must convince everybody that it has no bad designs" and that "we do not ask our soldiers to spend their efforts in pursuit of territorial conquests." [47]

In Britain the ILP never abandoned its attitude of splendid but loyal opposition. MacDonald and Snowden correctly maintained that Labour could only function as an independent critic provided it remained free of Coalition responsibilities and advantages. Accordingly, right from the beginning the ILP insisted that if Labour officials were to participate in the recruiting drive they should do so from Labour, and not from "all party," platforms.[48] Subsequently, the majority of the ILP never gave its approval to Labour's coalition policy.

45. Comité pour la Reprise des Relations Internationales, *Aux Groupements socialistes, aux organisations syndicales,* Paris, September 25, 1916. See also Leon Trotsky, *My Life* (New York, Scribner's, 1930), chap. 20.

46. Comité pour la Reprise des Relations Internationales, *Les Socialistes de Zimmerwald et la guerre* (Paris, 1916?), esp. pp. 9–11. The author's identity does not appear on this pamphlet and is still in dispute. Rocher, *Lénine et le mouvement zimmerwaldien en France,* p. 71, claims that the pamphlet was written by Loriot. Rosmer, *Le Mouvement ouvrier pendant la guerre,* p. 464, insists that it was written jointly by Trotsky and Loriot, with Trotsky making the greatest contribution.

47. The text of this letter is cited in Le Parti Socialiste, *La Guerre et la paix,* pp. 92–93.

48. ILP, *Report of the Annual Conference* (Norwich, 1915), pp. 10–11, 50–51.

The Independents were no less persistent in their demand for an early negotiated peace. In their view all the nations were equally responsible for the war, and in order to prevent the recurrence of similar tragedies a reasonable, not a vindictive, peace would have to be concluded. Therefore, the ILP program, parallel with the UDC theses, called for self-determination, the nationalization of armaments, the abolition of secret diplomacy, legislative control of foreign policy, international arbitration, free trade, and a federation of nations.[49] In cooperation with Radical dissentients, the ILP championed this program until in late 1917 much, if not actually most, of it was incorporated into the official Labour party platform. In an earlier section of this study it has been shown that the doctrinal as well as the political cooperation of the ILP and the UDC were extremely important for the over-all evolution of Labour war aims.[50]

The war-aims emphasis was also characteristic of the Fabian Society. However, most of the Society's members enthusiastically supported the Labour party's prowar position partly because they considered the struggle a war for democracy. Nevertheless, many Fabians shared Beatrice Webb's view that if the terms of peace were oppressive, they would lead "to a war of revenge"; however, if they were conciliatory, they could lead "to supernational law."[51] Hence by early 1915 the Fabian Society commissioned Leonard S. Woolf to undertake "an enquiry into possible developments of supernational law."[52] This inquiry resulted in the famous two reports on *International Government* which in 1916 were published in book form by the Fabian Research Department. The publication also included a Fabian project for a "Supernational Authority That Will Prevent War."[53]

In his Introduction to this rightly famous Fabian tract, G. B. Shaw maintained that even though many people agreed that "This Must Never Occur Again," war would certainly return "if nothing is done to prevent it." He then suggested that this Fabian report was calculated

49. F. W. Jowett insisted that now was "the time to speak and ensure that never again will the witch's cauldron of secret diplomacy brew the war broth of hell for mankind." At its Norwich convention in April 1915 the ILP called on the Government to "immediately disclose the terms upon which they are prepared to negotiate peace." Ibid., pp. 88–89.

50. See above, pp. 44–50.

51. Cole, p. 31.

52. Ibid., p. 32.

53. L. S. Woolf, *International Government: Two Reports Prepared for the Fabian Research Department*, New York, Brentano, 1916.

"to help explain what is needed as an alternative to war." [54] In the Fabian view the world had desperate need for an international organization to help mediate conflicting interests between and among nations compelled to carry on complex and intensive relations. The emphasis in the Fabian proposals was on compulsory adjudication of justiciable disputes and, in all other cases, on a compulsory cooling-off period before recourse to violence.

By late 1916 the unofficial formulation and articulation of new war aims might well have gone further in the two Western Allied nations than in Germany, but the groups which were their political carriers were still at a considerable distance from the locus of power. In introducing Leonard Woolf's report Shaw felt obliged to forewarn "that . . . nobody with any executive authority will take the smallest notice of it." He predicted that in all likelihood the future Peace Conference

> will be a repetition of the Congress of Vienna: that is, a crowd of diplomats will gather round the booty, and try to secure as much as they can as best they can for their respective States. Few if any of them will have ulterior views; and most of them will regard those who look for an end of war as an institution as vulgar ideologues. Nevertheless, the reaction against the monstrous slaughter and destruction of the war, and the heavy financial burden it will leave, may be too much for diplomatic routine: and it may also happen that the only acceptable terms of peace may be impracticable without new supernational machinery of a much more permanent kind than the old Concert of Europe . . . which was so dismal a failure as regards the prevention of war.[55]

The fact is that though statesmen and politicians eventually, in 1917–19, took notice of reform proposals in the area of international politics, for the time being the war cabinets were inattentive. In the Central as well as in the Entente Coalition "the same state of mind prevailed: the idea of a 'white peace' was nowhere officially accepted in government circles; the program in both camps was annexationist." [56] Whereas in

54. Ibid., pp. xi, xvii.
55. Ibid., pp. xxi–xxiii. For a more detailed analysis of the development of the Fabian Society's war-aims position see Austin Van Der Slice, *International Labor, Diplomacy, and Peace, 1914–1919* (Philadelphia, 1941), pp. 123–28; and Henry R. Winkler, *The League of Nations Movement in Great Britain, 1914–1919* (New Brunswick, Rutgers University Press, 1952), pp. 7–16.
56. Renouvin, *La Crise européenne*, p. 410.

secret treaties the governments spelled out their concrete ambitions, in public pronouncements they continued to speak of self-defense, the need to defeat the enemy decisively, and the search for security and peace. Only occasionally were there tangential references to the principle of self-determination, compulsory arbitration, and the like. Incidentally, the American President presently called attention "to the fact that the objects, which the statesmen of the belligerents on both sides have in mind in this war, are virtually the same, as stated in general terms to their own people and to the world." [57]

On December 18, 1916, when Woodrow Wilson offered to mediate between the belligerents, he correctly observed that "never yet have the authoritative spokesmen of either side avowed the precise objects which would, if attained, satisfy them and their people that the war had been fought out." Consequently, Wilson invited all governments to make "an avowal of their respective views as to the terms upon which the war might be concluded and the arrangements which would be deemed satisfactory as a guarantee against its renewal or the kindling of any similar conflict in the future . . ." [58]

declare aims!!

The Paris and London governments were unable and unwilling to send Wilson an honest, satisfactory answer; instead, they scornfully insisted that "if a peace were signed which left German military power unimpaired in the midst of a weakened and exhausted Europe, it would be even less secure than the peace existing before the War." [59] This reply was a further elaboration of Lloyd George's recent interview with a United Press correspondent in which he declared that the "squealing" Germans would get no peace until they had been dealt "a knockout blow." [60] And on December 19, 1916, in an effort to forestall Wilson's mediation effort, the British Prime Minister had called in Commons for "complete restitution, full reparation, effectual guarantees." [61]

57. Baker and Dodd, *The Public Papers of Woodrow Wilson, 4*, 404.

58. For the entire text see ibid., pp. 402–6. See also Edward H. Buehrig, *Woodrow Wilson and the Balance of Power* (Bloomington, Indiana University Press, 1955), pp. 250–53. While preparing his mediation move in the fall of 1916 Wilson learned about the war-aims position of the British dissidents from Colonel House, who, through W. H. Buckler, was beginning to receive letters and printed materials from Lord Loreburn, Noel Buxton, and Charles Trevelyan. Martin, *Peace without Victory*, pp. 115–20.

59. Cited in Lloyd George, *War Memoirs, 1*, 658.

60. Clynes, *Memoirs, 1*, 203.

61. Cited in the *Liberal Magazine, 24* (1917), 606.

But apparently Wilson never really expected a meaningful reply from either the Allied or the Central governments. He himself admitted that he was speaking to "neither the Senate nor foreign governments . . . but to the *people* of the countries now at war." [62] Even though there was no spontaneous outburst of popular enthusiasm, the militant dissident minority of the Allied forces of movement jubilantly cheered the President's attempt to elicit war aims, and severely criticized their Governments' evasive response.

In England the ILP rightly claimed that Wilson's request for war-aims clarification echoed its own policy. The Secretary of the ILP's Administrative Council sent the President a letter expressing the "fervent hope that negotiations may be begun now which will lead to a settlement on such terms as will be just and honourable to all the countries involved." [63] The UDC Executive Committee passed a resolution along these same lines.[64] Meanwhile, a Christmas Congress of the CGT, at which the dissentients were in the ascendancy, unanimously adopted a resolution urging the French Government "to send a favorable reply" to Wilson's note. Moreover, this conference pledged "to support and spread" Wilsonian ideas among the workers "in order to put an end to the present indefinite and ambiguous situation, which can only benefit secret diplomacy." [65] Almost simultaneously, on December 27, the National Congress of the SFIO by 2838 to 109 votes asked the

---

62. In a letter dated January 29, 1917: Wilson, writing to J. P. Gavit, cited in Arthur S. Link, *Woodrow Wilson and the Progressive Era, 1910–1917* (New York, Harper, 1954), p. 264. European progressives earlier in the war had tried to win Wilson's backing for their war-aims campaign. As early as May 1915 E. D. Morel addressed "An Appeal to President Wilson" which was published in the New York *Tribune* July 4, 1915, and is printed in Morel, *Truth and the War* (London, 1916), chap. 13. On October 1, 1914, Romain Rolland sent a copy of his article "Au-dessus de la mêlée" to President Wilson with the following accompanying lines: "Dans cette guerre néfaste, dont le résultat, quel qu'il soit, sera la ruine de l'Europe, les yeux de ceux qui ont le triste privilège d'échapper aux passions de la mêlée, se tournent souvent vers vous et vers votre pays. Puissiez-vous bientôt faire entendre votre voix juste et ferme, au milieu de ces frères ennemis! Il n'y va pas seulement de l'intérêt des peuples qui sont aux prises, mais de la civilisation toute entière, menacée par ces luttes sacrilèges. Que les Etats-Unis d'Amérique rappellent à l'Europe démente qu'aucun peuple n'a le droit, pour satisfaire son orgueil et ses haines, d'ébranler l'édifice du progrès humain qu'il a fallu tant de siècles de génie et de peines pour élever!" Rolland, *Journal*, pp. 65–67.

63. ILP, *Report of the Annual Conference* (Leeds, 1917), pp. 8–9.

64. UDC, *Minutes of the Executive Committee*, January 9, 1917.

65. Cited in Dolléans, *Histoire du mouvement ouvrier*, 2, 240. Cf. Lenin, *Works*, 19, 415.

Allied governments to inform Wilson that they were prepared to make their war aims known.[66]

On January 22, 1917, President Wilson reacted to the reply of the Central and Allied Powers. In his address to the Senate he explained why the peace "must be a peace without victory . . . Victory would mean peace forced upon the loser, a victor's terms imposed upon the vanquished. It would be accepted in humiliation . . . and would leave . . . a bitter memory upon which terms of peace would rest not permanently, but only as upon quicksand." Also, he insisted that "there must be, not a balance of power, but a community of power"; he proposed "government by the consent of the governed"; he spoke of "a peace to be made secure by the organized major force of mankind"; he called for "freedom of the seas"; he advocated a "moderation of armaments." It is not surprising that this pronouncement, which had so much in common with the Socialist-Radical platform, should have caused even more excitement in the European Left than his preceding note. Curiously enough, Wilson himself underlined his kinship with the European "people," not governments, in the following terms: "May I not add that I hope that I am in effect speaking for liberals and friends of humanity in every nation and of every programme of liberty?" [67]

The reaction of the French forces of movement was instantaneous. On January 24, at a meeting of the SFIO parliamentary group, Vincent Auriol declared that the group should greet Wilson's message with a manifesto and should seek to keep contact and agreement with the President. Bedouce seconded this proposal and a committee consisting of Auriol, Bedouce, Cachin, and Mistral was charged with drafting a text. The actual drafting was done by Cachin who at this time was still an ardent Social Patriot. His draft, which the parliamentary group endorsed on January 26, "registered with joy the admirable message of President Wilson . . . and asked that the French Government in-

66. The text of the declaration voted by this congress is cited in l'Humanité, December 28, 1916. For a right-wing Social Patriotic report of the proceedings at this congress see Bourgin, Le Parti contre la patrie, pp. 176–78; for a maximalist report see Henri Guilbeaux, Le Mouvement socialiste et syndicaliste français pendant la guerre (Petrograd, 1919), pp. 21–24.

67. For the complete text see Baker and Dodd, The Public Papers of Woodrow Wilson, 4, 407–14. The phrase "Peace without Victory" had served as the title of an editorial in the New Republic (December 23, 1916), pp. 201–2. On February 3, 1917, pp. 5–7, the New Republic approvingly commented on Wilson's speech under the heading "The Facts behind the Phrase."

stantly and clearly declare its agreement with Wilson's noble words of reason." [68]

Neither the Government nor the majority of Parliament had any intention of following this Socialist request. Meanwhile, away from the halls of government, le Temps vigorously criticized the SFIO message to Wilson.[69] Also, the pro-Wilson movement within the Socialist party and the CGT precipitated serious disagreements not among the Social Patriots but in the ranks of the minority.

Whereas Merrheim and Bourderon eagerly endorsed Wilson's appeal for a peace without victory, Loriot refused to associate himself with the message to the President whom he scornfully referred to as a bourgeois-pacifist. In their efforts to prevent Wilson's "poisonous ideology" from penetrating any deeper into the French Left, the Maximalists accused Merrheim and Bourderon of engaging "in platonic internationalism" and of "placing themselves in tow of Wilsonianism." [70] This rift in the French minority is one of the earliest concrete examples of the manner in which Wilson's war-aims policy eventually served to weaken the revolutionary Left by drawing the Independents further away from the Maximalists.

Henceforth Merrheim, Bourderon, Pressemane, and Mistral carried on their activities outside the framework of the Comité pour la Reprise des Relations Internationales. Instead, they started a slow uphill battle for revised war aims within the party itself. On March 4, at the next meeting of the National Council, they unsuccessfully sponsored a resolution which while reiterating their defensist position also criticized "the ideological formulas in whose name all belligerents . . . want to assure an eternal peace and the liberation of people through a military victory." In their view Wilson "was right to say that a peace without victory was an essential condition for a lasting peace to be supported by the institution of international arbitration." [71] At this time the Social Patriots and the Ligue des Droits de l'Homme [72] also

68. Bourgin, Le Parti contre la patrie, pp. 190–93. For the text of the message to Wilson see l'Humanité, January 27, 1917.

69. Le Temps, January 28 and 29, 1917.

70. Merrheim and Bourderon were expelled from the Comité pour la Reprise des Relations Internationales. Ferrat, Histoire du parti communiste français, pp. 55–56.

71. Deuxième Circulaire de la minorité du Parti socialiste (Paris, May 6, 1917), pp. 5–8.

72. Henri Sée, Histoire de la Ligue des Droits de l'Homme, 1898–1926 (Paris, 1927), p. 153.

declared themselves converted to Wilsonianism; however, neither was prepared to contemplate anything less than a decisive military victory over the Central Powers.

Across the Channel the UDC Executive circularized all its branches with a letter expressing enthusiastic agreement with the President's views. Furthermore, it disseminated a leaflet under the following title: "British Working Men, Observe! French Workers Support Wilson." Philip Snowden declared that the ILP and the UDC were "entitled to feel and express special gratification with the fact that the head of the greatest neutral Power in the world has come to the support of the same ideas and proposals which they have long advocated." [73] Further to the right, the Annual Conference of the Labour party unanimously passed on January 23 a resolution calling for "the formation of an international League to enforce the Maintenance of Peace on the plan advocated by the President of the United States." [74]

This resounding response on the European Left, but chiefly in the ranks of the Independents and Radicals, did not go unnoticed by Lenin. Under the title "A Turn in World Politics" he pointed to a shift "from *imperialist war*, which brought the people utter misery and the great betrayal of Socialism by Messrs. Plekhanov, Albert Thomas, Legien, Scheidemann, etc., toward an *imperialist peace*, which will bring the people the greatest deception in the form of nice phrases, semi-reforms, semi-concessions, etc." [75] According to Lenin, because the political truce was weakening it now was "necessary, by throwing out a few sops, to *pacify* the masses, whose anger is rising against the war and the high cost of living: why not promise . . . 'reduction of armaments'?" Lenin violently denounced the "imminent *amalgamation* of the social-patriots with the social-pacifists against the international Socialists"; this amalgamation threatened to transform all non-Leninists into "ordinary bourgeois reformists." [76] In Lenin's view, all that Wilson had done was to paraphrase the social-pacifist phrases of Turati and Kautsky, thereby assisting in the diversion of the masses from the revolutionary struggle. Could it be that Lenin feared that as the War of 1914–16 merged into the crisis of 1917–18 the European cabinets would expediently subscribe to social-pacifist formulas in

73. Cited in Brand, *British Labour's Rise to Power*, p. 133.
74. LP, *Report of the Sixteenth Annual Conference* (Manchester, 1917), pp. 134–35.
75. Lenin, *Works*, *19*, 423.
76. Ibid., pp. 428, 435.

their determination to keep the allegiance of the restless masses? How would such an "ideological" turn affect the revolutionary fortunes?

The news about the revolutionary developments in Russia reached Central and Western Europe at a time when the forces of movement were becoming impatient with the rigidity of the political truce. The fall of the Tsar and the victory of the combined bourgeois-Socialist forces stimulated a strong emotional response among the tired yet not disheartened people; among the Social Patriotic leaders these events intensified a mounting susceptibility to criticism by the minority factions. Above all, the inevitability of a further consolidation of the forces of order was challenged.

Allied Radicals and Socialists hailed the destruction of Russian despotism as the greatest victory the Entente had thus far scored in the war. Heretofore, whereas the threat of tsarist expansion had served to rally the German Left in defense of European *Kultur*, the alliance with tsarism had dampened the enthusiasm with which the Allied Left enrolled in the war of self-defense. When John Morley had resigned from the British Cabinet on August 5, 1914, he had urged Asquith to consider what "would happen if Russia wins," and whether a Russian victory would be "good for Western civilization." Once war had broken out, British Radicals like Norman Angell queried whether they should "fight for a Russian Europe." Even though H. G. Wells was so overcome with enthusiasm for the Entente cause that he labeled it *The War That Will End War*, he nevertheless placed his "Liberal Fear of Russia" on record.[77]

In his idealistic insensitivity to balance-of-power considerations, Ramsay MacDonald summarized a sentiment which was widespread among British and French Socialists: "Russia in arms with us to free Europe from an autocracy whether political or military, is a grim joke."[78] The ILP went even further and warned that "if Russia [were] permitted to gratify her territorial ambitions and extend her Cossack rule, civilization and democracy [would] be gravely imperiled." However, these and similar slurs on a desperately needed military ally were immediately countered by faithful Social Patriots. In early 1915 Sembat accurately noted that without Russia France "would have been overwhelmed"; he invited all Socialists to "think of this every time the in-

77. Morley, *Memorandum on Resignation*, p. 6; Angell, *After All*, p. 183; Wells, *The War That Will End War*, pp. 63–72.
78. Cited in Fainsod, *International Socialism and the World War*, p. 34.

ner conditions of that great country strike you." For those who required more than self-defense assurances, Guesde predicted that
"Russian politics, because of the war, [would] automatically be made
accessible to modern influences." Moreover, it was suggested that by
liberating Russia from German economic servitude "the road to bourgeois development would be opened and the bourgeoisie would enforce liberal forms of government." [79]

Even though Russia's current democratization was a function of
military defeat rather than of victory, it served to purge the Entente
of its major political and ideological handicap. Whereas the transformation of Russia now denied the SPD its major ideological justification for continued loyalty to the Central cause, the Allied forces of
movement could at long last claim that this was *their* war. Yesterday
Russia's corrupt Government vitiated the nobility of the Allied cause;
today her reformation gave this cause a new baptism.[80]

In the middle of 1918 H. G. Wells aptly portrayed the ideological
transformation which was set off by the Russian Revolution, and which
then was abetted by the military stalemate and war weariness:

> In the latter half of 1914 a few of us were writing that this war
> was a "War of Ideas." A phrase, "The War to end War," got into
> circulation, amidst much skeptical comment. . . . It was a phrase
> whose chief content was its aspiration. . . . While we talked of
> this "war to end war," the diplomatists of the Powers allied against
> Germany were busily spinning a disastrous web of greedy secret
> treaties. . . . That was three years and a half ago, and since
> then this "war of ideas" has gone on to a phase few of us dared
> hope for in those opening days. The Russian revolution put a
> match to that pile of secret treaties and indeed to all the im-
> perialist plans of the Allies; in the end it will burn them all.[81]

Almost nine months had to go by before the Bolsheviks published the
secret treaties. In the meantime, however, the March Revolution left
a deep imprint on all sectors of the Allied public. The editor of the

79. Cited in Walling, pp. 155, 423, 344.
80. See the *New Republic* (March 24, 1917), p. 212. "For the first time the
Entente presents the morally united front of a combination of Liberal Powers." The
(London) *Nation* (March 24, 1917), p. 816.
81. H. G. Wells, *In the Fourth Year: Anticipations of a World Peace* (London,
Chatto and Windus, 1918), pp. v–vi. See also Irene Cooper Willis, *England's Holy
War* (New York, Knopf, 1928), pp. 238 ff.

Manchester Guardian felt the "wonderful and glorious event . . . stirring in his bones." [82] Even the Liberal party, which recently had moved considerably to the right, hastened to send enthusiastic congratulations to the "Russian parties of movement." [83] UDC distributed the Petrograd Soviet's March 27th Manifesto in leaflet form; also, UDC's Executive Committee urged all branches to hold "meetings of sympathy" for the Russian Revolution.[84] A huge rally was held at Royal Albert Hall for the purpose of congratulating "the Russian people on their freedom." At this rally a dozen "speakers represented all that [was] most advanced in Trade Union, Labour, Socialist and Radical movements." [85]

Obviously, the enthusiasm in the different factions of the forces of movement increased the further they were to the left on the political spectrum. The three major Socialist factions were equally excited, except that they tended to emphasize different aspects of the Russian revival. On the extreme Left, in the ranks of the British Socialist party, the events in Petrograd were hailed as the forerunner of a Europe-wide civil war. It was the Independents who were most impressed by the Petrograd peace formula which further stimulated their war-aims campaign. Though the official Labour party also soon championed a peace without annexations and indemnities on the basis of self-determination, its chief concern was with the way in which Russian events would bolster the Allied war effort.

The reactions of the French parties and factions of movement were roughly the same as those of the British. The Ligue des Droits de l'Homme invited the people of Paris to a special meeting on April 1 in order to "celebrate the Russian Revolution." On this occasion its Vice-President, Professor Victor Basch, declared that this celebration had to be initiated by the Ligue because by "the imminent logic of events as well as of words, the Ligue des Droits de l'Homme et du Citoyen now had also become the Ligue du Droit des Peuples." These remarks

82. Hammond, *C. P. Scott of the Manchester Guardian,* p. 212.

83. *Liberal Magazine, 24* (1917), 152.

84. UDC, Leaflet 34b; and *Minutes of the Executive Committee,* April 3, 1917.

85. *Russia Free!* London, 1917. This pamphlet contains the speeches which were delivered at this rally on March 31, 1917, among others by George Lansbury, Robert Smillie, Israel Zangwill, Josiah Wedgwood, and W. C. Anderson. For the reaction of the British Left to the March Revolution see Stephen Richards Graubard, *British Labour and the Russian Revolution, 1917–1924* (Cambridge, Harvard University Press, 1956), pp. 18–20.

were symbolic of the connection which the Allied forces of movement established between 1789 and 1917, between individual liberty and national self-determination, between the consummated emancipation of the bourgeoisie and the impending emancipation of the proletariat. In a decidedly more revolutionary vein on May Day the Comité Pour la Reprise des Relations Internationales sponsored a mass meeting at which ten thousand Parisians cheered the Russian Revolution as "the signal for the world revolution." [86]

Of course, the exiled leaders of the restive Eastern and Southeastern European nationalities movements had special reason to rejoice. Thus far the grudging and heavily qualified endorsement of self-determination by the Allied Powers had thrown them into despair; but now the Russian Revolution promised to turn into a powerful "solvent of imperialism for the benefit of nationality." [87] Heretofore Russia's imperial ambitions had prevented the Allies from paying more than lip service to the principles of self-determination, but in "liberating herself" Russia now took the lead in placing "the seal upon the liberty of Europe." Eduard Beneš suggests that once self-determination had become a keystone of New Russia's diplomacy, the Allied governments failed to win effective control over the onrushing nationalities currents. Under the exuberant title "From Theocracy to Democracy" Thomas Masaryk heralded the political tidings from Petrograd; he also expressed the hope that these revolutionary developments would not frighten the Allied governments which during the political truce had become so conservative. Similarly, as of March 1917, the New Europe's pages reflected a marked sense of confidence and inevitability about the impending liberation of the suppressed nationalities.[88] Even the British, French, and American supporters of the committees-in-exile, many of whom were staunch Conservatives, were fired with new zeal. Among many others, Wickham Steed, the influential foreign editor of the London Times, added his powerful voice to the clamor for war-aims revision.

Though the Conservative press displayed a more reserved en-

86. *Bulletin officiel de la Ligue des Droits de l'Homme,* Nos. 13–14 (July 1–15, 1917), pp. 476, 478; and Guilbeaux, *Le Mouvement socialiste et syndicaliste français pendant la guerre,* p. 28.

87. Halévy, *The World Crisis,* p. 55.

88. *New Europe* (April 26, 1917), p. 40; Beneš, *Souvenirs de guerre, 1,* 341, 348–49; *New Europe* (March 22, 1917), p. 303. See also Bauer, *Die Österreichische Revolution,* pp. 16–17, 45, 57, 109–12.

thusiasm, the facts of war nevertheless caused it to react favorably to the Revolution. The *Times* gave its blessings to the Provisional Government primarily because this Government promised to pursue the war more vigorously than its predecessors.[89] Even *le Temps* proclaimed that by "infusing the cause of the Entente with new enthusiasm," the Russian Revolution was reaffirming the "popular character" of the war.[90] In the Allied camp there was a universal tendency to pass rather lightly over the economic and military disintegration which had ignited the Russian Revolution and which was unlikely to disappear before the courageous pronouncements of either the Provisional Government or the Petrograd Soviet. It is not surprising, therefore, that from the overthrow of the Romanovs until July 1917 the dominant tendency of the captions and the over-all emphasis in, for example, the New York *Times* were so optimistic as to be misleading.[91]

The British and French governments lost no time in publicly welcoming the Revolution. In so doing they hoped to spur the recovery of the Russian war effort and to gain maximum ideological advantage. On March 24 in a cable to Premier Lvov, Lloyd George declared that since the "great Ally Russia now [stood] with the nations which base their institutions upon responsible Government," the Revolution was not only Russia's greatest contribution to the Allied cause but also revealed "the fundamental truth that this war [was] at bottom a struggle for popular government as well as for liberty."[92] Two days earlier, in the House of Commons, Bonar Law, the Conservative leader in the center-right War Cabinet, moved a resolution sending fraternal greetings to the Duma upon the establishment of free institutions in Russia; he claimed that these institutions would contribute to a steadfast and vigorous prosecution of the war.[93] Likewise, in the French Lower House there was unanimous applause when its President, Paul Deschanel, read a similar message on March 21.[94]

89. *The History of the Times, 4,* Pt. I, p. 241.

90. *Le Temps,* March 16, 1917.

91. Walter Lippmann and Charles Merz, "A Test of the News," *New Republic* (Special Supplement, August 4, 1920), p. 2.

92. Cited in Lloyd George, *War Memoirs, 1,* 970.

93. *PD,* 91 (March 22, 1917), col. 2085. In August 1917 Gilbert Murray noted that even Bonar Law had broken "into poetry over the Russian Revolution." Gilbert Murray, *The Way Forward* (London, Allen and Unwin, 1917), p. 17.

94. *JO* (March 21, 1917), p. 183.

On the eve of Wilson's momentous decision about the future course of American diplomacy, nothing harmonized better with his conviction "that war, if it were accepted, must be based upon constructive ideals" than the news from Russia.[95] The American Ambassador in Petrograd, David R. Francis, had advised Washington that since the Revolution was "the practical realization of the principles of government which we have championed and advocated," America should immediately recognize the new Government in order to have a "stupendous moral effect" on the Russian situation. While Ambassador Francis recommended that the United States should be the first country to extend diplomatic recognition, Colonel House counseled Wilson to coordinate American policy with French and British diplomacy.[96] On March 20, 1917, barely two weeks before President Wilson went before Congress with his War Message, instructions for the recognition of the Provisional Government were cabled to Petrograd.[97]

By this time the American Government had undoubtedly reached a point at which its decision to declare war on Germany had become irreversible. Nevertheless, it is worth noting that even though the French and the British Governments had experienced no particular qualms about their alliance with tsarist Russia, the Wilson Administration would have felt uncomfortable in such a partnership. The Russian Revolution facilitated Wilson's task of justifying morally and ideologically America's declaration of war. Russia's conversion to democracy gave a progressive stamp to the entire Entente cause, thereby providing Wilson with great ideological leverage. Certainly to go to war to save democracy was more appealing than to draw the sword in defense of neutral rights on the high seas. Even Robert Lansing, the rather traditionalist Secretary of State, "felt strongly that to go to war solely because American ships had been sunk and Americans killed would cause debate, and that the sounder basis was the duty of this and every other democratic nation to suppress autocratic governments like the German."[98] Lansing now suggested that a declaration of war by America would not only encourage and strengthen the

95. Baker, *Woodrow Wilson, Life and Letters*, 6, 501.

96. David R. Francis, *Russia from the American Embassy* (New York, Scribner's, 1921), p. 91; and House to Wilson, March 17, 1917, Wilson Papers.

97. *FR*, 1917, p. 1208.

98. "Memorandum of the Cabinet Meeting Held from 2:30 to 5:00 P.M. on March 20, 1917," Lansing Diary (Blue Boxes, Box 2, Confidential Memoranda and Notes, p. 83), in the Robert Lansing Papers, Library of Congress.

new democratic Government of Russia, but would also assist the democratic elements in Germany "who [were] beginning to speak boldly
and to show their teeth to their rulers." [99] In a similar vein President
Wilson told his Cabinet that "if our entering the War would hasten
and fix movements in Russia and Germany it would be a marked
gain to the world and would tend to give additional justification for
the whole struggle." [100] By making it evident that democracy was involved, the Russian Revolution appeared to have "removed one
stumbling block to Americans." [101]

The March Revolution unquestionably influenced the mood as well
as the tone of the Presidential War Message. Wilson made a direct
reference to Russian events in order to dramatize the crusading spirit
with which the enlarged Allied Coalition was about to enter a new
phase of the war:

> Does not every American feel that assurance has been added to
> our hope for the future peace of the world by the wonderful and
> heartening things that have been happening within the last few
> weeks in Russia? . . . The great, generous Russian people have
> been added in all their naive majesty and might to the forces
> that are fighting for freedom in the world, for justice, and for
> peace. Here is a fit partner for a League of Honor.[102]

As for Wilson's discussion of democracy, the Russian Revolution "was
simply confirmation for his belief that democracy was sweeping the
world; it probably permitted him to go further in his remarks than
he would have if Russia had still been autocratic." [103] Because the Tsar
was their ally, in August 1914 it would have been difficult for Asquith

99. *FR, Lansing Papers, 1,* 627. After the war Raymond Robins, the American
agent in Russia at the time of the revolutionary turmoil, testified that in urging the
Russians to keep fighting he insisted "that America did not go into the war until
after they [the Russians] had overthrown their Czar." U. S. Senate, Committee on
the Judiciary, *Bolshevik Propaganda* (Washington, 1919), p. 771.

100. David F. Houston, *Eight Years with Wilson's Cabinet* (2 vols. New York,
Doubleday, Page, 1926), *1,* 244.

101. Walter H. Page, writing in his Diary on April 2, 1917, after a conversation
with Herbert Hoover, who had recently arrived in London from the U.S. According
to the (London) *Nation* (April 5, 1917), p. 2, the Russian Revolution "may well
have been the decisive factor which induced Wilson to make common cause with
the Allies."

102. Baker and Dodd, *The Public Papers of Woodrow Wilson, 5,* 6–16, esp. 12.

103. Harley Notter, *The Origins of the Foreign Policy of Woodrow Wilson*
(Baltimore, Johns Hopkins Press, 1937), pp. 648–49.

or Viviani to proclaim that "the world must be made safe for democracy" and that "peace must be planted upon the tested foundations of political liberty."

Evidently Elie Halévy rightly concluded that World War I should be divided "into two parts, before and after the Russian Revolution of 1917."[104] Because no sooner had the Petrograd peace formula penetrated into the Allied political arena, than official dispatches, newspaper columns, and private diaries testified to a new hopefulness about the future benefits of this destructive war. Everyone who was in the least bit susceptible to Liberal and Socialist ideas took new courage. In America the *New Republic* urged that it was time for radicals, reformers, revolutionists, and progressives to recover from their war shock. The *New Europe* insisted that now that Russia had given democracy a new opportunity "it should be the deliberate task of all Liberals—in the broadest sense of the word—to create an unofficial alliance of their forces in all the Allied countries for the purpose of achieving a democratic peace."[105]

President Wilson's War Message seemed to assure Europe's forces of movement that for ideological inspiration they could look not only to Petrograd but also to Washington. Even Georges Clemenceau, while aspiring to the French premiership in a center-right Cabinet, commended Wilson for suggesting that "the Russian Revolution and the American Revolution complete each other marvelously to mark definitely the whole idealistic range of the conflict."[106] Likewise, the "unselfish intervention of the U.S. and the Russian Revolution" led the SFIO to count "upon a more perfect realization of a really durable and just peace than it formerly dared to hope."[107] In England the Liberal *Westminster Gazette* speculated whether the Russian Revolution and America's entry into the World War might "constitute between them the most momentous change in the history of mankind that [had] been witnessed for centuries."[108]

104. *The World Crisis,* pp. 41–42.
105. *New Republic* (March 24, 1917), p. 221; and *New Europe* (March 31, 1917), p. 201. "The intransigeant pacifists came in contact with the dissatisfied workers, thus leading to the formation and expansion of a revolutionary movement directed against both capitalism and the war." Halévy, *Histoire du socialisme européen,* p. 253.
106. *L'Homme Enchaîné,* April 4, 1917.
107. Cited in *The French Socialist Party and War Aims* (New York, 1918), p. 2.
108. Cited in Page, Diary, April 2, 1917.

Nevertheless, it must be strongly emphasized that in the Allied camp the sudden emergence of this new "ideological" optimism coincided with a wave of despair and defeatism. The Russian Revolution itself, though ideologically so inspiring and promising, was an unmistakable symptom of military and economic weakness. Though on a much smaller scale, the military and political disintegration which beset Russia also became manifest inside Europe's other war-infested nations. In both France and Great Britain the military stalemate, accompanied by staggering casualties and severe privations, generated war weariness on the homefront and, to a lesser degree, in the armed forces. Hence, the Entente's military campaign was in danger of suffering setbacks not only on the Russian, but also on the Western, front.

In the Chamber in Paris Victor Augagneur, a prominent Republican Socialist who until now had been a staunch supporter of Briand and Ribot, queried whether and by what means, in view of Russia's disintegration and the spreading fatigue in France, the Allies "could hope to continue until victory." Significantly he also asked the Government "whether it was not obliged, because of certain military developments, to be satisfied with more modest war aims than heretofore." Augagneur was skeptical whether further British and especially American help could arrive with the necessary dispatch.[109]

It is difficult to assess how seriously the Entente crisis would have been aggravated if the United States, with her giant military, economic, and moral potential had not joined the Allies at this critical juncture. In May W. H. Buckler, the liberal-minded Counselor at the American Embassy in London, thought that gradually "the role to be played by the U.S. [was] that of a deliverer, in other words, of helping the Entente out of a serious hole." Similarly, James Bryce confided to Colonel House that "prospects would be dark but for [America's] entrance into the War." Le Temps simply urged that "while looking toward Petrograd one should not forget to also look toward the United States. An immense aid for us is being prepared on the other shore of the Atlantic, perhaps more rapidly than we tend to assume." [110] Meanwhile, however, there continued to be elements of weakness and

109. Comité Secret, pp. 519–20.
110. W. H. Buckler to Colonel House, May 11, 1917, Wilson Papers; James Bryce to Colonel House, July 28, 1917, Wilson Papers; le Temps, June 6, 1917.

crisis in the Allied camp which caused the war-aims debate to gain momentum in the late spring and throughout the summer of 1917.

The military stalemate precipitated serious consequences in the French Army, especially as a result of the failure of the Nivelle offensive. By May 20 the aftermath of this defeat developed into a wave of mutinies which in turn were affected by the revolutionary tidings from Petrograd. According to the best yet still incomplete accounts, it appears that more than half the French Army experienced varying degrees of unrest. A total of fifty-four divisions were affected to a greater or lesser degree, including seventy-five infantry regiments, two colonial infantry regiments, one Senegalese infantry regiment, thirty-one alpine batallions, eight artillery regiments, and numerous rear-line service units. Between May 25 and June 10 there were seven or eight cases of group indiscipline daily.[111]

The French Cabinet and High Command were seriously concerned by these unmistakable symptoms of declining morale.[112] Would the enemy manage to get intelligence on this general state of unrest? Moreover, would the German General Staff find out which sectors of the front were most seriously affected, and then hasten to apply military pressure at the weakest point of the Allied lines? In order to forestall such a move, the British units launched the Paeschendale offensive as a diversionary maneuver. Even though this offensive was a costly failure, it nevertheless served two vital purposes. The French Army was given time to convalesce from the Nivelle setback, and

111. Lt. Colonel Henri Carré, *Les Grandes Heures du Général Pétain: 1917 et la crise du moral* (Paris, Editions du Conquistador, 1952), p. 102. In the 97th infantry regiment, e.g., 110 men mutinied, in the 159th an entire company; in the 57th alpine batallion 145 men mutinied and 98 deserted. The total number of desertions rose from 509 in 1914 to 21,171 in 1917. Paul Allard, *Les Dessous de la guerre révélés par les Comités Secrets* (Paris, Editions de France, 1932), pp. 170, 189–90, 212. See also T. C. King, *Generals and Politicians: Conflict between France's High Command, Parliament, and Government, 1914–1918* (Berkeley, University of California Press, 1951), pp. 172–73; Malvy, *Mon Crime,* pp. 115–21; Marcellin, *Politique et politiciens,* 2, 143–51.

112. According to General Douglas Haig the failure of the Nivelle offensive caused "extreme restlessness and mutiny broke out here and there which developed so rapidly as to cause considerable uneasiness both at G.H.Q. and in the French Government." Quoted from "Memorandum on Operations on the Western Front, 1917–1918," in Robert Blake, ed., *The Private Papers of Douglas Haig, 1914–1918* (London, Eyre and Spottiswoode, 1952), pp. 368–69. See also Alfred Vagts, *A History of Militarism* (New York, Norton, 1937), p. 300.

Germany was kept from using western units for a "final" assault on Russia's highly vulnerable fighting forces.[113] Meanwhile, however, Allied military and civilian leaders began to realize that they would have to postpone any major offensive on the Western front either until later that year, or until some time in 1918.

In brief, the Allied military effort was threatened with a precarious stalemate in the West—and with no less ominous reverses in the East. The uncertainties of the Eastern front were so great that they presented Allied generals with extremely elusive strategic variables. Not only did the politicians differ sharply from the generals on the recovery potential of the Russian war effort, but even the generals were unable to reach a unanimous verdict among themselves. And now, while anxiously watching the Provisional Government's determined efforts to restore discipline in the Russian armies, French and British leaders suddenly were faced with a similar though less difficult task on the Western front.

In an effort to meet the crisis, General Nivelle was relieved of his command and the hero of Verdun, General Pétain, was promoted to be *Général en Chef* of the French Army. Obviously, Pétain's first major task was to quarantine the mutinies as well as to restore discipline in the affected units. Upon searching into the underlying causes of the army unrest, Pétain concluded that these could be grouped into two separate categories: "those stemming from the very conditions of life at the front, and those due to external influences."[114]

At the front the morale was being undermined by general lassitude, irregular as well as insufficient leaves, drunkenness, and failing leadership. In order to counteract these symptoms of psychological unrest, Pétain personally addressed the officers of more than one hundred French divisions in an effort to inspire them with a rededication to the Allied cause. Furthermore, he sought to strengthen the morale of the *poilus* both by improving the army's furlough policy and by liberalizing food and housing allowances. However, these psychological concessions had to be supplemented by disciplinary measures. Army court martials pronounced a total of 150 death sentences, even though

113. See Blake, *The Private Papers of Douglas Haig*, p. 369.

114. For an authoritative summary of Pétain's handling of the mutinies see King, *Generals and Politicians*, pp. 174–78. The text of General Pétain's report to the Minister of War, dated May 29, 1917, is cited in Carré, *Les Grandes Heures du Général Pétain*, pp. 79 ff. For detailed reports on the causes of the mutinies by seventeen prefects see Malvy, *Mon Crime*, pp. 136 ff.

only twenty-three of the convicted men were executed. Pétain thought that military discipline could not effectively be restored without advertising the harsh cost of mutiny.[115]

Meanwhile Pétain advised the Cabinet that whereas he was perfectly capable of handling internal army problems, only the civil authorities could effectively counteract the "external" demoralizing influences. Pétain complained that since March 1917 the press had incessantly criticized practically every decision of the High Command. Moreover, the morale of the soldiers was being affected adversely by press reports to the effect that Russia's military power was waning, that "a workers' and soldiers' council had been created in Petrograd," and that soldiers' councils were countermanding the orders of Russian officers. In order to prevent the "ferment of subversive ideas" from penetrating any deeper into the army, Pétain insisted that certain newspapers be stopped from heaping praise on the Russian Revolution. Nor should the Government continue to tolerate the distribution of pacifist tracts at railroad stations where furloughed soldiers returned to their battle stations. According to Pétain the CGT was responsible for both the printing and the diffusion of fly leaves proclaiming "Enough Men Killed!," "Long Live Peace," and "Our Wives and Children Want Peace." [116]

In France, as also in Russia, both army and civilian morale were largely a function of the Government's over-all economic, social, and war-aims policy. Just as the depressing stalemate undermined the fighting spirit of the soldiers in the trenches, so wartime privations caused the rear-line industrial workers to become restless. A steep rise in the cost-of-living index without a comparable improvement in real wages was driving thousands of French workers into trade unions.[117] In turn, this accelerated syndicalist growth, which was most

115. Pétain thought it necessary to set an example of punishment in each of the mutinied regiments. See Poincaré, *Au Service de la France,* 9, 161. Two American novelists have probed into the tragedy of these random, exemplary executions: Humphrey Cobb, *Paths to Glory,* New York, 1935; and William Faulkner, *A Fable,* New York, 1954.

116. Carré, *Les Grandes Heures du Général Pétain,* pp. 85, 88. At Dormans soldiers refused to obey the orders of their officers, crying "Long live the revolution! Down with the war!" Poincaré, *Au Service de la France,* 9, 147 f. See also *Les Carnets secrets d'Abel Ferry, 1914–1919* (Paris, Grasset, 1957), p. 178.

117. The cost-of-living index had risen from 1,000 in 1914 to 1,800 in 1917. Arthur Fontaine, *French Industry during the War* (New Haven, Yale University Press, 1926), pp. 56, 65; and Oualid and Picquenard, *Salaires et tarifs,* pp. 347 ff.

marked in basic war industries, inspired the trade union leaders to become increasingly inflexible in labor-management negotiations. Consequently, just as the mutinies weakened France's armed forces, so the production front suffered a series of strikes which in metropolitan Paris alone involved 100,000 workers.[118] Furthermore, the forces of movement proceeded to couple trade union demands with persistent pleas for a reformulation of war aims. Pétain complained that extensive press coverage of the strikes as well as of the SFIO agitation in favor of the projected Stockholm Conference reinforced the spirit of military indiscipline.[119]

How would the Cabinet handle these "external" causes of unrest over which Pétain and the Army had little if any control? With popular expectations for an early victory seriously impaired, war-weary Frenchmen tended to become susceptible to the intensified political, but especially war-aims, agitation of the Left. Presently Painlevé, the Minister of War, reported to the Cabinet that reinforcements reaching the front from the interior of France were infected by the destructive influences of peace propaganda.[120] Furthermore, on May 31 General Pétain cautioned the French War Council that he could not vouch for the morale of the Army in case French Socialists were allowed to discuss peace terms with German Social Democrats at an international Socialist conference.[121] Although Prime Minister Ribot successfully called on the press to play down the news about the industrial strikes, the SFIO–CGT campaign for passports to Stockholm was too widespread and persistent to be choked by censorship.[122]

An increasing number of progressives now considered the strikes and the mutinies as compelling evidence that though it might still be too early for a negotiated peace, nevertheless this was an opportune time to press the Cabinet for a public declaration of war aims. The Petrograd manifesto and formulas, as well as repeated convocations to Stockholm, further justified the French *minoritaires* in

118. Picard, *Le Mouvement syndical,* p. 105; Marcellin, *Politique et politiciens,* 2, 121–29; Oualid and Picquenard, *Salaires et tarifs,* pp. 347 ff.; Malvy, *Mon Crime,* pp. 65–72.

119. Carré, *Les Grandes Heures du Général Pétain,* p. 87.

120. Renouvin, *La Crise européenne,* p. 463.

121. Alexandre Ribot, *Journal de Alexandre Ribot et correspondances inédites, 1914–1922* (Paris, Plon, 1936), p. 138. See also Poincaré, *Au Service de la France, 9,* 149.

122. Marcellin, *Politique et politiciens, 2,* 128; and Paul Allard, *Images secrètes de la guerre* (Paris, Illustrés Françaises, 1933), p. 46.

the war-aims campaign. In turn, sensitive to these mounting pressures from their left and from Petrograd, many leading Social Patriots became vocal in their criticism of the Government's war-time diplomacy. They realized that domestic unrest was stimulating the rank-and-file's concern with war and peace problems; politically it would be dangerous to leave their dissident colleagues free to capitalize on the threatening popular discontent. The acceptance on May 28 of the Stockholm invitation by a "reunified" SFIO offered concrete evidence of this radicalization.

The forces of order in France were no less worried about the political implications of rising popular impatience and dissatisfaction. However, unlike the Left they refused to acknowledge the part that the exhausting war had in the current crisis. Instead, they blamed the Socialists and pacifists for instigating the labor troubles and the army unrest. Consequently the Right proceeded to launch a concerted political and propaganda drive against all varieties of dissidents, a campaign which incidentally would also remove the few remaining progressives from important policy-making positions in the Government. Before long Malvy, Caillaux's erstwhile protégé, had become their prime target.

Much to the dislike of the forces of order, Malvy had managed since the outbreak of war to maintain himself as Minister of Interior. In this capacity he had jurisdiction over important labor, police, and security questions touching directly on the *union sacrée*. As one of the spokesmen of the Left in the Cabinet—even in the restricted War Cabinet—Malvy had never wavered in his conviction that an effective political truce could be maintained only with the support of labor. Moreover, he believed strongly that just as labor was being asked to make sacrifices in the interest of the war effort, capital and management should shoulder their share of the burden.

For stubbornly refusing to help increase labor's subservience to capital Malvy incurred the wrath of the Right. He promoted collective bargaining as the most effective and equitable instrument for the settlement of labor grievances. This policy, combined with his earlier refusal to apply Carnet B, had enabled Malvy to keep the support of most syndicalist leaders for an effective industrial truce. Because he had thus earned their confidence, in the middle of 1917 Malvy had the invaluable assistance even of Petrograd-inspired labor leaders like Jouhaux and Merrheim as he sought to restore industrial peace in

the face of serious labor unrest. The Right, however, not only was
angered by Malvy's obvious sympathy for labor but also objected to
his leniency toward pacifists, revolutionary agitators, and Socialist
Internationalists. First through General Nivelle and then through General Pétain, the Army also had tried to get the Minister of War to
take stern measures against dissident elements.[123]

Though Premier Ribot was far from insensitive to these anti-Malvy
pressures, he was more immediately concerned by the danger of the
threatening radicalization of the SFIO. He rightly feared that the dismissal of the Minister of Interior might bring about a further consolidation of the forces of movement. For it was no secret that these
forces strongly endorsed Malvy's contention that the Government
could not afford to "break with the working class"; also, they applauded the Minister of Interior's refusal to "porter la main sur les
organisations ouvrières." [124]

As a consequence the Right intensified its attacks against all "disloyal" elements. Maurice Barrès, the guiding spirit of the Ligue des
Patriotes, and Léon Daudet of l'Action Française became the right-extremist shock troops of this campaign. Before long their vituperative
newspaper crusade against all Internationalists merged with Clemenceau's political offensive against the forces of movement at the Palais
Bourbon. Clemenceau so framed his indictment as to link Malvy with
all the pacifist and Socialist elements which were not altogether unqualified in their support of the war effort, and whose political attention presently was focused on the war-aims issue. The Right was
suspicious of Malvy's continuing contacts with certain political and
editorial leaders of the restless Left. They were particularly concerned
by his real or rumored relations with Caillaux, whom they had never
ceased to distrust both because of his prewar attempts at Franco-German conciliation and his aggressive advocacy of progressive taxation. Caillaux now was charged with trying to take advantage of the
domestic crisis in the hope of staging a political comeback: by sponsoring a conciliatory war-aims program he might establish a connection
with the Socialists as a first step to a popular-front coalition. On the
front page of l'Action Française Léon Daudet published successive

123. Malvy, Mon Crime, pp. 65–72; Marcellin, Politique et politiciens, 2, 121–29;
Picard, Le Mouvement syndical, pp. 105–12; Carré, Les Grandes Heures du Général
Pétain, pp. 159 ff.
124. Cited in Renouvin, La Crise européenne, p. 462.

articles warning of "The Hour of Caillaux," "The Caillaux Clan and Germany's Aims," and "The Delegates of Mr. Caillaux." [125]

Obviously, the crusade for strong executive government and the opposition to war-aims reform were two facets of one and the same political campaign. The Right convincingly portrayed the supposed Malvy-Caillaux axis, supported by the restless Socialists, as the domestic extension of the supposedly German-inspired Stockholm movement. In order to keep the war-aims agitation from scoring a significant success, the Left had to be checked. However, anxious to keep the Social Patriots in the Cabinet, Ribot decided to continue Malvy in office for the time being. Nevertheless, as victory failed to come into sight, the incipient French version of the stab-in-the-back legend won many adherents.

In Great Britain the war weariness and labor crisis did not affect the military establishment. However, the continuing war put heavy strains on a recruiting system which only in the spring of 1916 had been changed from a voluntary to a conscription basis. Unlike France, however, the British Isles did not have a sizable peasantry capable of acting as an important political stabilizer and of providing the Army with a steady stream of peasant recruits. Replacements had to be drawn from industry rather than from the farms. Under the dilution system, the work benches inevitably began to be staffed by a growing proportion of unskilled men and women. In the light of existing wage controls, the wage differentials between diluted and regular workers tended to give rise to serious friction. Until recently the War Cabinet, through its Labour Members, had succeeded in enlisting Labour as well as trade union support for the vital recruiting drive as well as for a moderate but effective industrial relations program. Yet at this time food shortages and attendant distribution inequities began to strain the political truce. Furthermore, the cost-of-living index threatened to get out of hand.[126]

Pressures for an upward revision of wage rates were mounting

---

125. Maurice Barrès, *Chronique de la grande guerre* (14 vols. Paris, Plon-Nourrit, 1920–24), *10*, 16–18, 192–208, 225–35, 251–56, 272–360; Georges Clemenceau, *L'Antipatriotisme devant le sénat: Discours prononcé le 22 juillet 1917* (Paris, Payot, 1917); *l'Action Française*, June 2, 3, and 4, 1917. In Malvy's judgment these were the beginnings of a concerted effort to "find causes of a political nature for the unrest which occurred in the army during June 1917." Malvy, *Mon Crime*, p. 20.

126. See A. W. Kirkadly, ed., *Industry and Finance* (London, 1917), chap. 2; and Humbert Wolfe, *Labour Supply and Regulation*, Oxford, 1923.

when the reports from Petrograd further intensified the mood of popular dissatisfaction. "The political truce was well kept till 1917, when both an extensive strike and peace movement made themselves noticeable in the ranks of Labour owing largely to the news of the Russian Revolution." In March and April 1917 work stoppages involved nearly 200,000 men causing the loss of 1,500,000 working days, "more than the total of men affected and days lost in the engineering and shipbuilding trades between the outbreak of the war and the eve of the strikes." The shop stewards were actively exploiting the discontent among the industrial workers, especially on the Clyde, where the influence of extremist Socialists was considerable.[127]

However, even though the Labour party and the Trades Union Congress now increased their collective bargaining demands, both groups contributed substantially to the restoration of industrial peace. Nevertheless, the Government realized that unless the basic causes of unrest were removed, recent labor-management settlements would only be temporary. Therefore in June nine Commissions of Industrial Unrest were appointed not only to investigate past grievances but to recommend future policies. While emphasizing the continuing loyalty of both workers and employers in his summary report to Lloyd George, George Barnes, the Labour Minister of Labor, insisted that further adjustments of wages to food prices were necessary and the system of food distribution still was in need of serious improvement.[128]

These strikes in the munitions and engineering industries were influenced by a revival of political activity on the Left and by events in Russia. In order to bolster their minority position the Independent Labour party and the small Socialist party [129] sought to capitalize on the strikes as well as on the Russian Revolution. They summoned a joint convention to meet at Leeds on June 3 in order to "begin to do for this country what the Russian Revolution has accomplished in Russia." Under the title "Follow Russia" the widely disseminated cir-

127. Max Beer, A History of British Socialism (London, Allen and Unwin, 1948), pp. 383 ff.; Lloyd George, War Memoirs, 2, 1145–52; Christopher Addison, Four and a Half Years: A Personal Diary from June 1914 to January 1919 (2 vols. London, Hutchinson, 1934), 2, 381–88.

128. See eight regional reports in Commission of Enquiry into Industrial Unrest, Command Papers 8662–69, London, H.M.S.O., 1917.

129. Under the leadership of H. M. Hyndman a majority of members had left the antiwar British Socialist party and formed the prowar National Socialist party. Frederick J. Gould, Hyndman: Prophet of Socialism (London, 1938), chap. 6.

cular convening the conference boldly proclaimed that recent events in Russia "called for a reply on the part of the British Socialist and Labour Movement." [130]

The delegates at Leeds proceeded to adopt four resolutions: (1) Hail! The Russian Revolution; (2) Foreign Policy and War Aims; (3) Civil Liberties; and (4) Workmen's and Soldiers' Councils. The fourth resolution, calling for the establishment of Soviet-type Councils of Workers and Soldiers—a most un-British proposal—quite conveniently enabled the press to pin the subversive label on the entire Leeds movement. However, the MacDonald-Snowden-Lansbury faction, whose main interest was not immediate sociopolitical revolution but merely the revision of British war aims, easily triumphed over the few Maximalists from the Clyde shop steward movement.[131] According to one report the delegates at Leeds, most of whom were "mentally drunk," were swayed by two emotions: "an emotion towards peace and an emotion towards workers' control." Though Beatrice Webb complained about a marked absence of "coherent thinking," in her view the conference was proof of "the existence of a powerful ferment in the Labour Movement." [132]

Meanwhile the impact of the activation of the Left began to reach into the House of Commons. The Radical and Labour backbenchers were waiting for an opportunity to press the Cabinet for a war-aims pronouncement in a parliamentary debate. On May 16, when the Government came before the House with the third Consolidated Fund bill, the dissidents decided to move an amendment. In their name Philip Snowden called on Commons to welcome

the declaration of the new democratic Government of Russia, repudiating all proposals for imperialist conquest and aggrandizement, and call upon His Majesty's Government to issue a similar declaration on behalf of the British Democracy, and to join the Allies in restating the Allied terms in conformity with the Russian declaration.[133]

130. Lloyd George, *War Memoirs*, 2, 1153; and Philip Viscount Snowden, *An Autobiography* (2 vols. London, Nicholson, 1934), *1*, 449–55.
131. William Gallacher, *Revolt on the Clyde* (London, Lawrence and Wishart, 1936), p. 150. For a discussion of the conflicting factions at the Leeds convention see Graubard, *British Labour and the Russian Revolution*, pp. 36–41.
132. Cole, p. 88.
133. *PD, 93* (May 16, 1917), col. 1625.

This amendment touched off a lengthy debate on war aims, secret treaties, conditions in Russia, and the propriety of raising these questions in an amendment to a credit-for-the-war bill.

In his opening speech Snowden quoted the nonannexationist passages of the Provisional Government's April 10th declaration. He then contrasted these passages with Miliukov's unfortunate covering note of May 1 and reported on the agitated reaction to this note in the streets of Petrograd. In the course of the debate Snowden also asked, without specifying, whether the secret treaties were still valid.[134]

Lord Robert Cecil, Under-Secretary for Foreign Affairs, spoke for the Government. He insisted that there could be "no doubt" that these treaties were "binding upon this country." Cecil added, however, that since the new Russian Government was free to "release the rest of the Allies from any particular understanding," there was no need for action by his Majesty's Government. The Snowden amendment was defeated decisively by 238 to 32 votes. However, judging by the course of the debate, the Snowden proposal might well have gained wider support if it had been presented under different circumstances. On May 23 the Government was asked again whether in view of the new Provisional Government's recent note the Allies would "continue to refuse to consider terms of peace based on" the Petrograd principles? Robert Cecil curtly replied that he had nothing to add to what he had said on the 16th.[135]

The next major debate on war aims took place on July 26. This time MacDonald moved an amendment to the fourth Consolidated Fund bill. The ILP leader immediately excused himself for bringing the July 19th Reichstag Resolution to the attention of the House in the form of an amendment to a crucial money bill. MacDonald complained, however, that the Leader of the House had refused his request to set time aside for a special debate. Bonar Law readily admitted his refusal with the assertion that if he had given the time, "it would have represented a view on my part as to the importance" of the dissident movement "which is out of all proportion to its real weight." While pointing to "the Gentlemen who sit below the Gangway" the Unionist leader assured the House that "these Gentlemen are living in a world of unreality." [136]

134. Ibid., cols. 1627–28.
135. Ibid., cols. 1668, 1731–34, 2273.
136. Ibid., 96 (July 26, 1917), cols. 1479–80, 1521.

Nevertheless, MacDonald had read the entire Reichstag Resolution into the record and had urged the assembled Members to assist the Russian Government in bringing about the inter-Allied Conference for which it had been asking. Even though MacDonald was ably seconded by Trevelyan, Snowden, and Ponsonby, not more than nineteen dissidents voted to support him. The great bulk of the Labour representatives stood with George James Wardle, who firmly supported the Government.[137]

On this occasion only five of MacDonald's supporters were members of the ILP; the other fourteen were Radicals. It seems fair to suggest, therefore, that Commons was really being asked to pronounce itself on UDC policies and proposals. Recently the Council of the UDC had not only passed a resolution welcoming the Petrograd formula, but had also urged the British Government "to respond to the invitation of the Russian Government" to issue in conjunction with the Allies "a restatement of the terms on which they would be prepared to make peace." Whereas the ILP tended to make common cause with the international Stockholm movement, the UDC Executive Committee appealed to President Wilson for help. In a letter declaring that "the war aims of the Russian Provisional Government . . . accurately embody the real ideals of the democracies of the world," the UDC urged Wilson to take action "with the object of securing a general declaration by all belligerent states renouncing aggressive aims." [138]

On July 24 Henderson returned from Petrograd firmly convinced that a restatement of war aims could serve the dual function of reinforcing Kerensky's position vis-à-vis the Bolsheviks and of further weakening the German Burgfrieden. Under pressure from the Independents and the rank and file, and prompted by Henderson's "UDC mood," the Labour party and Trades Union Congress now prepared to take an even more public and positive Stockholm position. Incidentally, in Britain the rightist campaign against the consolidating Left never reached the same intensity as in France, possible because

137. Ibid., cols. 1481–1510. An amendment to the fifth Consolidated Fund bill had the support of 31 Members. See ibid., 98 (November 6, 1917), cols. 2007–51.

138. Swanwick, Builders of Peace, pp. 85–86; and Seymour, Intimate Papers, 3, 139. The UDC letter was sent through Colonel House, who withheld it from the President for some time because he did not "altogether agree with the purpose." In England a special UDC leaflet set forth in parallel columns the major Soviet pronouncements and the UDC program. UDC, Free Russia and the Union of Democratic Control, Leaflet 37b.

the Channel put a safe distance between the home front and the battle
lines.

Few, if any, of the prominent Socialist leaders were blind to the
gravity of the Entente's military and economic situation. Cognizant
of the crisis, they stressed the importance of enlightening the citizenry
about the purposes for which it was asked to make redoubled efforts.
In *l'Humanité* Cachin declared that more than ever since the outbreak of war "words counted and have become acts: men also listen
to voices other than those of canons." Norman Angell admitted that
the changes in Russia had temporarily weakened the Allied military
effort; however, these same changes "so far improved the diplomatic
position that with proper management, the military disadvantages
might in large part be offset." Similarly, Ramsay MacDonald declared
that the Russian Revolution had been of purely moral value to the
Allies. Even Lloyd George predicted that the Revolution would "ensure victory more exalted than any one could have contemplated
before." [139]

With the Revolution the diplomatic and ideological posture of the
Entente changed radically. Heretofore the Russian Foreign Office had
advanced the most ambitious annexationist claims. Now, under the
Petrograd Soviet's persistent prodding, of all the Allied and Associated
governments the successive Provisional governments gradually became the most relentless sponsors of liberal war aims. On most Allied
Socialists, however, the daring war-aims pronouncement of the Petrograd Soviet made a more profound impression than the carefully restrained foreign-policy pronouncements first of Miliukov and then of
Tereshchenko. Soon the Soviet's alluring peace formula of May 15—
"peace without annexations or indemnities, on the basis of the self-
determination of peoples"—succeeded in becoming a major and decisive diplomatic guidepost not only for Europe's forces of movement,
but also for all the foreign offices.

Even though Wilson and the Petrograd Soviet were in essential agreement on the general principles which should guide the Allies in the
formulation of a nonannexationist war-aims program, and even though
both eventually became the standard bearers for the rapidly expanding progressive forces, at this time they were worlds apart on one
crucial point. Assuming the peace principles were defined, should the

139. *L'Humanité*, July 18, 1917; Norman Angell, *War Aims* (London, Headley,
1917), p. 37; *PD*, 96 (July 26, 1917), col. 1491; *Liberal Magazine*, 24 (1917), 287.

war be fought on to victory, or was the time ripe for the exploration of a peace without victory? On the one hand there was Wilson, speaking as a war leader engaged in transforming the endless material and human resources of a vigorous and wealthy nation into a powerful fighting machine; he was going to the rescue of America's Allies who were trapped in a dangerous military, economic, and political stalemate. On the other hand was the Petrograd Soviet, the most articulate spokesman of Russia's and Europe's war-weary masses. Whereas this heretofore inattentive public became increasingly responsive to peace slogans and to the idea of a negotiated peace, it was little concerned with questions of military strategy and with balance-of-power calculations.

In brief, whereas the President now was committed irrevocably to a crusade which would achieve peace through victory, the Petrograd Soviet became the foremost exponent of Wilson's earlier peace without victory.[140] With Russia free and Wilson on their side, many progressives who heretofore had been lukewarm in their support of the Allied cause turned into passionate crusaders: now they eagerly wanted a peace through victory on the basis of the Petrograd formula. This sudden conversion tended to make many of these enthusiastic ideological warriors insensitive to the spreading military and economic disintegration which continued to augment the peace hunger in Russia.

As soon as the Entente was cleared of the tsarist stigma the Allied crusade for democracy began to take shape. President Wilson inaugurated the crusade in his War Message of April 2. First, he indicated clearly that the Allies proposed to foster the German forces of movement in opposition to the Berlin Government. Second, he championed a partnership of democratic nations one of whose major postwar aims would be the establishment of a League of Nations to which only democratic states would be admitted. The ultimate aim of the surging crusade was to make the world safe not only for democracy but also for self-government. In a letter of April 9, 1917, Colonel House wrote that Wilson had "always held these convictions, but until Russia joined the democratic nations he [had] not [thought] it wise to utter them."[141] Throughout the remainder of the war the President and the Allied forces of movement had to fight hard against

140. On May 24 W. H. Buckler wrote to House that the Russians now seemed to have adopted "our peace without victory formula." See Wilson Papers.

141. Cited in Seymour, *Intimate Papers*, 3, 36.

the Entente Traditionalists to get their democratic program accepted. That they eventually succeeded may be gathered from Clemenceau's retrospective and reluctant admission that "alas, one must have the courage to say it, but we did not enter the war with a liberation program." [142]

After March 1917 all official war-aims pronouncements had to be weighed with extreme care because of the accelerated tempo of psychological warfare and the precariousness of the political truce. Henceforth, Allied war-aims pronouncements ideally should seek (1) to undermine the political truce in the Central Powers, (2) to bolster the Russian Provisional governments, and (3) to placate the Allied parties and factions of movement.

How would the Allies go about "breaking down the German Government by building a fire back of it within Germany?" [143] Moreover, how would they stir up the suppressed nationalities against Vienna? On Easter 1915 the Annual Conference of the ILP had sent fraternal greetings to Liebknecht; at the time MacDonald hardly anticipated that the center-right war cabinets would eventually also begin to fraternize with the German Maximalists.[144] However, as of July 1916 the French Air Force sporadically dropped air leaflets assuring the German soldiers and workers that "Liebknecht's cause" was their cause.[145] After the Russian Revolution the opposing propaganda machines became even less restrained in their exploitation of the class-warfare theme. The sealed train which brought Lenin to Russia and Germany's encouragement of the Russian Bolsheviks until November 1917, stand out as the most dramatic episodes in psychopolitical warfare during World War I.

The Entente, however, was not to be outdone by the Germans. Free from the autocratic handicap, the Allies now were able to urge the German proletariat to press for Western-type political institutions as the necessary stage in their advance first toward peace and then toward a

142. Georges Clemenceau, *Grandeurs et misères d'une victoire* (Paris, Plon, 1930), p. 159.

143. House Diary, March 28, 1917, in the Edward M. House Collection, Sterling Memorial Library, Yale University.

144. Fenner Brockway, *Socialism over Sixty Years* (London, Allen and Unwin, 1946), p. 133.

145. George G. Bruntz, *Allied Propaganda and the Collapse of the German Empire in 1918* (Stanford, Stanford University Press, 1938), p. 139.

Socialist commonwealth. In the press and in air leaflets the Allies constantly emphasized the universal trend toward democratic institutions, and called on the German people to overthrow their Emperor and Government in order to be admitted to the community of free nations. The French propaganda service did not shy back from extending a helping hand to the Spartacists. Moreover, as of April 1917, once the USPD had seceded from Scheidemann's party, Hugo Haase, Oscar Cohn, Eduard Bernstein, and Kurt Eisner—in addition to Karl Liebknecht—were repeatedly hailed as democracy's most faithful champions in Germany. The French Air Force occasionally covered enemy lines and certain sections of Germany with leaflets assuring the workers that a three-day general strike not only would bring the war to a quick end but also would assure "the victory of the proletariat over their exploiters." [146]

Whereas the democratization and class themes were used in propaganda aimed at Germany, self-determination pronouncements were calculated to weaken the Dual Monarchy. "The event which transformed the whole relation of the belligerents to the national question was the Russian Revolution." [147] Only now that the Allies were liberated from the tsarist connection could they envisage a clear recognition of the self-determination principle (as applied to Europe!). In this sphere the First Provisional Government took the lead; and not even its refusal to renounce Russia's claim to the Straits lessened the full impact of this initiative. Both Beneš and Masaryk testify to the decisive influence of the Revolution on the nationalities policy of the Entente. In answering a congratulatory telegram from his friend Masaryk, Miliukov declared that he subscribed fully to the proposition that free Russia would make a strong contribution to the ultimate transformation of Central and Southeastern Europe.[148] On April 8 Miliukov made an official pronouncement which clearly foreshadowed

146. Hans Thimme, *Weltkrieg ohne Waffen: Die Propaganda der Westmächte gegen Deutschland, ihre Wirkung und ihre Abwehr* (Stuttgart and Berlin, J. B. Gotta'sche, 1932), pp. 142–43; and Ernst Drahn and Susanne Leonhard, eds., *Unterirdische Literatur im revolutionären Deutschland während des Weltkrieges* (Berlin, Gesellschaft und Erziehung, 1920), pp. 126–27, 181–82.

147. Alfred Cobban, *National Self-determination* (Chicago, University of Chicago Press, 1947), pp. 11–12.

148. Beneš, *Souvenirs de guerre, 1*, 348; and T. G. Masaryk, *Die Weltrevolution: Erinnerungen und Betrachtungen, 1914–1918* (Berlin, Reiss, 1925), p. 133.

the independence of Poland, Czeckoslovakia, and Yugoslavia. Indeed, it would seem that "until this time no Allied statesman had used such unequivocal language in an official declaration." [149]

Though the Foreign Minister of the First Provisional Government was a more reluctant partner in the nationalities enterprise than was the Petrograd Soviet, he nevertheless continued to command the allegiance of the *New Europe*.[150] Miliukov was firmly committed to the Entente and fought against every attempt to bring about a separate or negotiated peace. Confident that within a few months the principle of self-determination would become the backbone of Allied war aims, Masaryk and Beneš, as well as the other nationalities' leaders, turned into the most ardent sponsors of the crusade for democracy. They were violently opposed to a peace without victory precisely because it would serve to maintain the Dual Monarchy in its *status quo ante* position. "No Annexations and *la victoire finale*" [151] now became perfectly compatible; and the *New Europe* gave its enthusiastic support to the Second Provisional Government, which relentlessly but gently pressed the Allies for a revision of war aims.

The Russian situation mirrored the full complexity of the political crisis which faced the Entente in mid-1917. Consequently, it is of great interest to note the analysis of the causes of the Revolution and the proposed remedies for the Eastern crisis which the major political factions advanced. For these are relevant to the great debate not only about the crisis in Russia but also about the crisis confronting all of Europe at this historic juncture. Though only Russia was in revolt and on the brink of revolution, the specter of the Russian turmoil reaching over into the West took on an ominous reality—especially with the waning prospect for an early victory.

The Allied Right tended to be completely insensitive to the Socialist aspects of the Russian Revolution, and failed to grasp the ideological and sociological dynamics of the revolutionary movement. They understood and encouraged the Provisional Governments only insofar

149. Beneš, *Souvenirs de guerre, 1,* 329–39.

150. Miliukov's continued claim to the Straits caused sharp criticism in the Soviet and in the oppressed nations; it also served German propaganda. Many of the exiles, however, felt that since a New Russia would gain control of the Dardanelles, this "strategic" control would no longer necessarily imply "russification." *New Europe* (April 19, 1917), p. 18.

151. Title of the lead editorial in the *New Europe* (May 24, 1917), pp. 161–71. See also Mamatey, *The United States and East Central Europe,* pp. 95–100.

as these consolidated the "liberal-democratic" revolution, promoted the Duma, and prosecuted the war.[152] They expected that in the faithful pursuit of this triple aim, the Russian Socialists would accept the same dictates of political truce by which the majority Socialists had thus far been guided in England and France. With this cooperation of the loyal Social Patriots, the Revolution could be stopped at will and the opportunities for German-inspired Bolshevik subversion would be destroyed. It was hoped that the Petrograd-bound British and French Socialist delegations, in pressing these views on their Russian comrades, could help to check the influence of both the Petrograd Soviet and the Stockholm movement. In the late summer of 1917 the success of the British and French governments in dealing with their own internal crisis closed their minds to left-wing "reform" arguments, whether domestic or Russian.

In France and Great Britain the agitated Left pressed the cabinets to support the Social Revolutionaries and the Mensheviks as potentially the most powerful pro-Allied elements in Russia. According to Cachin, as well as Albert Thomas and Arthur Henderson, the cabinets could extend this assistance by officially proclaiming liberal war aims. Though such a pronouncement might irritate the Cadets who continued to cherish tsarist foreign-policy ambitions, it would have the merit of unifying the restless forces of movement in Russia by bringing the aggressively independent Petrograd Soviet into closer cooperation with the Provisional Government. Partly, possibly largely, because the Allied governments tended to support the Cadets—who in addition to their imperialist ambitions were committed to an all-out prosecution of the war—the war-aims schism between the Provisional Government and the Soviet kept widening.

The Allied war-aims forces listened ever more attentively to the Petrograd Soviet, chiefly because Wilson seemed to have suspended the war-aims offensive which he had initiated in December 1916. The "revisionist" initiative passed first into the hands of the Petrograd

---

152. "We will measure the beneficial aspects of the Revolution by the extent to which it will increase the military power of the Entente." Charles Benoist writing in the *Revue des Deux Mondes,* April 1, 1917. Similarly, to judge by Clemenceau's newspaper writings, he was unable to assess the Russian Revolution by any other standard than by its contribution to the defeat of the *Boches.* On April 11, 1917, President Poincaré sorrowfully recorded in his diary that "Russia forgets the war more and more in order to think about its own Revolution." Poincaré, *Au Service de la France,* 9, 110.

Soviet, and eventually into those of the Second Provisional Government.

Wilson's cablegram of May 26, 1917, introducing the Root Mission to Russia, carried little of the idealism of the earlier "peace without victory" speech; instead, it was a fighting document. Wilson reacted to the Petrograd formula—the new standard by which all diplomatic pronouncements were being judged—with the following words of caution: "Practical questions can be settled only by practical means. Phrases will not accomplish the result. Effective readjustments will, and whatever readjustments are necessary, must be made." [153] Many Allied progressives who had hoped that Washington and Petrograd would join hands in the war-aims enterprise now had visions of Wilson enlisting in the ranks of the Traditionalists. That the President was aware of the latter's continuing hold on the Paris and London cabinets is clear from a letter in which Wilson inquired how he could formulate his war-aims program "without seeming directly to contradict Cecil and Ribot if I am to add, as I feel I must, the terms (in general phrases, as in the address to the Senate) upon which we in this country think that a settlement should be made when we win?" About a month later, on July 21, Wilson again wrote to House that "England and France have not the same views with regard to peace that we have by any means. When the war is over we can force them to our way of thinking . . . but we cannot force them now." [154] This was the voice not only of Wilson the war leader but also of Wilson the diplomatist, who recognized that American policy henceforth would have to be formulated in a coalition framework.

It is clear, then, that the reopening of the war-aims debate was directly connected with the Revolution in Russia and its repercussions abroad. For the time being the British and French governments managed to avoid committing themselves publicly to specific war aims—partly because they had stemmed the attack of their own parties of movement, partly because Wilson was not yet prepared to take the diplomatic initiative, and partly because of an overly optimistic estimate by Allied leaders of Russia's ability to remain a trusted ally in a "traditional war."

153. Baker and Dodd, *The Public Papers of Woodrow Wilson*, 5, 51.
154. Cited in Charles Seymour, *American Diplomacy during the World War* (Baltimore, Johns Hopkins Press, 1942), pp. 269–70; and Baker, *Woodrow Wilson, Life and Letters*, 7, 180.

By the end of July, 1917 the political truce in Paris and London, even though considerably shaken, was still in effect. Albert Thomas and Arthur Henderson pressed their fellow Cabinet members to make verbal war-aims concessions in order to prevent the defection of the increasingly impatient Socialist majority; simultaneously they sought to calm their critical party colleagues with the assurance that, particularly since Kerensky was also pressing for war-aims revision, the cabinets could not postpone a liberal diplomatic pronouncement much longer.

Meanwhile, however, both Allied cabinets were also subject to intensified anti-Socialist pressures from the vigilant Right; similarly, the Independents stepped up their attacks on the compromising Social Patriots as well as on the spokesmen of the latter in the cabinets. As the next chapter will show, within a few weeks this hardening of the Right and the Left contributed heavily to the resignation of Thomas and Henderson, which was occasioned by the Stockholm controversy. Thus the breakdown of the French and British political truce followed the collapse of the German *Burgfrieden* by only a few weeks.

In Germany the consolidation of the forces of movement had been completed with the July 19th Reichstag Resolution; in turn, the Right reacted by consolidating its hold over the Reich Government. In France and in Britain, however, throughout July and August the forces of movement were still in the process of consolidating their position. They did so by capitalizing on the increased restlessness of the Allied proletariat, on the taxing military stalemate, on Kerensky's repeated requests for an inter-Allied conference,[155] and on the mounting antiwar movement in Russia. In effect, the expanding forces of movement sought to gain maximum political advantage from these causes of Allied weakness, while at the same time emphasizing the underlying kinship of their own ideological position with the Petrograd formula, Wilson's April 2nd address, and the Reichstag Resolution. Caught between relentless internal and external pressures for war-aims reform, how much longer could Paris and London afford to "stand pat diplomatically" without endangering their diplomatic

155. See dispatches of Ambassador Francis to Secretary Lansing in *FR, Russia, 1918, 1,* 52–53, 66, and the dispatches of Ambassador Page from London on July 6 and Ambassador Sharp from Paris on July 23, in *FR,* 1917, Supplement 2, *1,* 119, 144–46. See also the *New Europe* (May 10, 1917), pp. 114–17; (June 21, 1917), p 293; (July 19, 1917), p. 1.

and their domestic unity, as well as the effectiveness of their ideological onslaught on the Central Powers? [156]

156. *New Republic* (May 19, 1917), pp. 62–63. Charles Beard thought that the Allies must break the union of the Hohenzollern military caste and the German masses whose radicals are Social Democrats . . . and must convince the Russian revolutionists that the things they hold dear are really at stake in the eastern trenches." *New Republic* (June 2, 1917), p. 137. See also H. N. Brailsford's article "The Russian Peace Formula," ibid. (June, 23, 1917), pp. 207–9.

4. BEYOND TRADITIONAL DIPLOMACY

INSPIRED and encouraged by the Petrograd Soviet, between March and September 1917 the renascent Left inside each of Europe's belligerent nations eventually agitated for a conference of Allied, Central, and neutral Socialists. This war-time conclave of the Second International was to meet in Stockholm for the purpose of producing agreement on war aims between and among all its members. In turn, this agreement on war aims was to be the basis for concerted pressure by all Socialist parties and factions on their governments in favor of a negotiated peace.

For five tense months in 1917 this proposed yet still-born Stockholm Conference agitated not only the various factions of each national Left but also all the belligerent governments. Whereas within the Allied Left the Stockholm issue served to convert many Social Patriots from silent condoners of the Old Diplomacy to vocal enthusiasts for the New Diplomacy, within the Allied governments this same issue produced a new awareness of the domestic and diplomatic hazards of party intrusion into the making of foreign policy. Even though the German and Austro-Hungarian governments for reasons of state encouraged the Stockholm movement at home and abroad, they were nevertheless apprehensive of the internal political implications of Socialist success in the realm of diplomacy. From this vantage point of domestic politics, in both Berlin and Vienna the diplomatic initiative of the Vatican looked much less risky than that of the Socialist International. On the other hand, for primarily diplomatic and secondarily political reasons the Allied governments were equally hostile to Socialist and Vatican meddling in diplomacy, even at the cost of alienating influential Social Patriots and the Provisional Government in Petrograd.

Prior to the military stalemate and the weakening of the political truce in Europe only a small group of dissident Socialists had gathered, first in Zimmerwald (1915) and then in Kienthal (1916). At both congresses the delegates were inspired by long-standing antiwar resolutions which advocated instant revolutionary action by the proletariat in case of war. However, even at these two wartime conclaves a majority favored an essentially nonrevolutionary interpretation of the civil-war summons. Invariably the left-revisionist war-aims faction outnumbered the Leninist adherents of civil war.[1]

However, now, in the middle of 1917, similar attempts to revive the International would be inspired not only by recollections of pre-war resolutions, but also by certain wartime developments. Above all, from Russia came the First Proclamation of the Petrograd Soviet declaring that the time had come for the people to start "a decisive struggle against the intentions of conquest" of all belligerent governments by taking "into their own hands the decision of the question of war and peace."[2] Despite the fact that the three major wings of the Socialist movement were far from agreed on any one strategy in connection with the impending drive for a revival of the International, all three were equally animated by the successive pronouncements of the Petrograd Soviet.

Even though the Stockholm Conference was "the natural offspring of the Stuttgart and Copenhagen congresses" it was precipitated by the Russian Revolution.[3] In February 1915, before the momentous changes in Russia, the inter-Allied Socialist Conference in London had expressed the hope that the proletariat of the industrial nations might soon find themselves united against "militarism and capitalist imperialism."[4] Presently, with the recent success of the Russian Revolution before them, many European Socialists concluded that such a re-

1. See Angelica Balabanoff, *Die Zimmerwalder Bewegung, 1914–1919* (Leipzig, C. L. Hirschfeld, 1928); and Gankin and Fisher, *The Bolsheviks and the World War*, chaps. 4–6.

2. *RAR*, pp. 7–9.

3. Comité Organisateur de la Conférence Socialiste Internationale de Stockholm, *Stockholm*, p. v. The preface (pp. iii–xxii) to this collection of documents is a chronological account of the Stockholm movement up to January 13, 1918, by Camille Huysmans. This Belgian Socialist was secretary both of the Bureau of the Second International and of the Stockholm Committee.

4. Cited in Parti Socialiste, *Réponse au questionnaire* (Paris, 1917), p. 3.

union might actually be possible while the war was still in progress. On April 15, 1917, the Dutch Socialists took the initial step to bring about a meeting of Socialists from neutral countries as well as from both belligerent coalitions. In his plans to establish a special committee of neutral Socialists in Stockholm, the pro-German Dutch Socialist P. J. Troelstra was assured of the cooperation of Camille Huysmans, Secretary of the Bureau of the Socialist International. On April 22, over the signature of Huysmans, a first invitation was issued. This invitation summoned all parties, factions, and groups affiliated with the Second International to participate in an "examination of the international situation." [5]

The French and British Social Patriots immediately turned down the invitation because, among many other reasons, they suspected Troelstra's motives. Meanwhile, however, on May 3 the Dutch-Scandinavian Committee had been formally organized in Stockholm. On this Committee the pro-Entente Swedish Socialist H. J. Branting counterbalanced the pro-German elements. Furthermore, the initiating group realized that the objections of the British and French Socialists could be overcome only if the Russian Socialists would join the Stockholm Committee. Therefore, the efforts of the Dutch-Scandinavian Committee "were directed towards its own transformation into a Russo-Dutch-Scandinavian Committee." [6]

By now it was evident that the task of organizing a meeting of Socialists from enemy nations during wartime would be difficult, if not impossible. The Committee recognized the need for nonbinding, preliminary consultations with various delegations. Therefore, it announced that the full-fledged Conference could not meet before June 10. This was the first of a series of frustrating postponements. [7]

In addition to the opposition of the Allied war cabinets, within the Left of each Allied nation a bitter struggle broke out among the anti-Stockholm faction, the pro-Stockholm faction, and the pro-Zimmerwald faction. In England and France, where the Maximalist factions were negligible, the anti-Stockholm Social Patriots easily triumphed over the pro-Stockholm Independents in the first round of this internecine struggle. In Russia the conflict raged between the pro-Stockholm

5. For the entire text of this initial invitation see Comité Organisateur, *Stockholm,* p. viii.
6. Ibid., pp. viii–ix.
7. Ibid., pp. x–xii.

Left and the pro-Zimmerwald Bolsheviks. However, the nonrevolutionary Internationalists in the Petrograd Soviet rejected an invitation to a third Zimmerwald conclave. Instead, on May 9 the Executive of the Soviet issued its own invitation for a general conference to be held in a neutral country.[8]

Consequently there now were two proposals for a non-Maximalist international conference which, to be effective, had to be fused. For this purpose a delegation from the Petrograd Soviet was expected to come to the Swedish capital. However, this Soviet delegation did not arrive in Stockholm until July 4, when the Russo-Dutch-Scandinavian Committee was finally constituted.[9]

During the intervening weeks neither the Huysmans Committee in Stockholm nor the Soviet in Petrograd was inactive. On May 10 the Dutch-Scandinavian Committee began to draft the famous Stockholm questionnaire through which it sought to elicit the views of all affiliated Socialist groups on both their minimum conditions and their proposed agenda for the scheduled Conference. Within a week, on May 18, this questionnaire was sent out together with a manifesto explaining the current activities and the future projects of the Committee.[10] With this questionnaire as a basis, the Dutch-Scandinavian Committee started detailed preliminary meetings and letter-exchanges with neutral, Allied, and Central Socialist groups which were not completed until November.

But whereas the Stockholm questionnaire was instrumental in bringing about a detailed clarification in left-wing war-aims thinking, recent actions of the Petrograd Soviet provided new ideological and political momentum.

On May 15 the Soviet issued its history-making appeal to the "Socialists of All Countries." This appeal launched the memorable Petrograd formula together with a renewed invitation for an international conference.

> Peace without annexations or indemnities on the basis of the self-determination of peoples is the formula adopted unreservedly by the proletarian mind and heart. . . .
>
> The Russian Revolutionary Democracy appeals first to you,

8. Balabanoff, *Die Zimmerwalder Bewegung*, p. 66; and Golder, pp. 339–40.
9. Comité Organisateur, *Stockholm*, pp. x, xix.
10. For the text of this questionnaire and manifesto see ibid., pp. 381–83.

Socialists of the Allied countries. You must not permit the voice of the Provisional Government of Russia to remain the only voice in the Entente.

You must force your Governments to state definitely and clearly that the platform of peace without annexations or indemnities, on the basis of the self-determination of peoples is also their platform. . . .

The Russian Revolutionary Democracy appeals to you, Socialists of the Austro-German alliance: You cannot allow the Armies of your Governments to become the executioners of Russian liberty. . . .

In order to unite these efforts, the Petrograd Soviet . . . has decided to take the initiative in calling for an international conference of all the Socialist parties and factions in every country.[11]

Henceforth the foreign-policy pronouncements of the Petrograd Soviet never ceased to influence the pace and direction of the Stockholm movement.

By May 18 the Dutch-Scandinavian Committee received a telegram from Petrograd which indicated that it could count on the intensified cooperation of the Soviet.[12] Then, on June 1, the Executive Committee of the Petrograd Soviet sent out a new appeal. In this appeal it (1) reiterated the Petrograd formula, (2) claimed that the new Provisional Government had accepted this formula, (3) confirmed its earlier manifestos of May 9 and 15, and (4) summoned the International Conference to meet in Stockholm on July 8. This latest Soviet message concluded with the assertion "that the principal aim of this Conference must be to realize an agreement among the representatives of the Socialist proletariat to completely liquidate the policy of 'national unity' . . . which excludes the possibility of a struggle for peace." [13]

Naturally this announcement of a planned assault on the *Burgfrieden* inside the belligerent nations gave the Stockholm summons a more radical tone than heretofore. Quite appropriately this radicalization was recommended by the Russian Left, which thus far had refused its

11. *RAR*, pp. 22–23.
12. Comité Organisateur, *Stockholm*, p. xvi.
13. For the entire text of this appeal see ibid., pp. xvii–xviii. Cf. Gankin and Fisher, *The Bolsheviks and the World War*, p. 582.

unconditional support to the Provisional Government. Furthermore, successive delays of the Conference assured the restless but determined Soviet of increasing influence in the Stockholm Committee. When still another postponement became necessary, on July 11 the newly formed *Russo*-Dutch-Scandinavian Committee rescheduled the Stockholm Conference for August 15.[14]

"The Bolsheviks from the very beginning came out against participating in the Conference." [15] In their view, even though successive appeals had called on the Socialists to exert pressure on their governments to revise war aims along democratic lines, there had been no reference to the prewar Stuttgart and Basle manifestoes which had summoned the proletariat to turn the impending international conflict into a Europe-wide civil war. Since the Maximalists insisted that a peace based on the Petrograd formula could never be concluded among the bourgeois-capitalist governments, now that the imperialist Russian Government had been overthrown they called on the European proletariat also to embark on revolution as the shortest and safest road to a lasting peace. In fundamental disagreement with the voluntarist conception behind the projected Stockholm Conference, the Maximalists held that without a prior proletarian revolution a negotiated peace could not possibly amount to anything more than a temporary accommodation among Bethmann-Hollweg, Czernin, Lloyd George, Miliukov, and Ribot.[16]

The Maximalists focused their attack on the Independents, who seemed to be spearheading the Stockholm drive. Precisely because the Independents could "pose" as revolutionaries, they threatened to interfere with the growth of a genuine revolutionary movement. Lenin was convinced that the European stalemate would gradually drive the war-weary masses into the Bolshevik ranks, provided the minds of these masses were not fired with deceptive hopes of either a negotiated settlement or a liberating ideology. The Maximalists suggested that since the majority Socialists were completely subservient to the war cabinets, a Stockholm meeting of Social Patriots could never materialize unless popular pressure would force the governments into a search for a negotiated peace. However, since the war cabinets were

14. For the entire text of this invitation see LP, *Report of the Seventeenth Annual Conference* (Nottingham and London, 1918), pp. 43–44.

15. Lenin, *Works, 21*, Pt. I, p. 119.

16. *Spartakusbriefe*, No. 4 (April 1917), pp. 73–76.

still able to withstand this pressure from below, the moment for a direct confrontation was not yet at hand. According to the Maximalists, the governments meanwhile were nevertheless anxious to engage in a preliminary exploration of possibilities for a negotiated settlement; and in this exploratory search they would be forced to have recourse to the Independent Socialists as a bridge. From this analysis followed the Maximalist conclusion that the Independents could best help to strengthen the rising revolutionary tide by refusing to serve as a diplomatic vehicle for the war cabinets. Conversely, however, by going to Stockholm the Independents allowed themselves to be exploited as diplomatic tools by both the war cabinets and the treacherous Social Patriots.[17]

This struggle inside the Socialist movement is important because of its intimate connection with both the domestic tensions and the diplomacy of all the belligerents. Lenin maintained that the Stockholm proposal was a diplomatic maneuver of German imperialists who thought the moment opportune for a negotiated settlement. However, instead of risking a straightforward peace move, the Reich resorted to the services of the "Danish Plekhanovs." [18] Curiously enough this Leninist interpretation coincided with *le Temps'* contention that because Germany was waking up to her ultimate defeat, she was trying to substitute a "pacifist offensive for the one Hindenburg was [being] forced to abandon." [19] Similarly, Czernin now issued passports to his Austrian Social Democrats. He did so not only because he wanted to strengthen Austria's wartime political truce but also because he was anxious to gain the confidence of the Left, whose political pressures in the immediate postwar years might force the ruling classes "to practice Socialist politics." [20]

As stated previously, in the spring and summer of 1917 Germany, and more especially the Dual Monarchy, were in a very precarious economic position. Hence even in certain right-wing quarters in Berlin and Vienna the idea gained ground that by paying lip-service to Socialist peace principles the Central Powers might induce the Menshe-

17. Balabanoff, *Die Zimmerwalder Bewegung*, p. 79. For authentic documents revealing the anti-Stockholm position of the Zimmerwald factions see Gankin and Fisher, *The Bolsheviks and the World War*, pp. 647–62. See also Fainsod, *International Socialism and the World War*, pp. 149–57.

18. Lenin, *Works, 21*, Pt. I, p. 289.

19. *Le Temps*, May 9, 1917.

20. Czernin, *Im Weltkriege*, pp. 228–29.

viks and the Social Revolutionaries in Russia to become more amenable to a separate peace.[21] In order to counteract this diplomatic strategy in which the Scheidemann Socialists were about to be assigned a central role, the German Spartacist Mehring urged Chkheidze, the President of the Petrograd Soviet, to recognize the delegates from the Liebknecht-Luxemburg faction as the only legitimate spokesmen of German Socialism.[22]

In the context of the war-aims debate it is noteworthy that the April issue of the leading German Maximalist organ attacked the USPD position under the provocative title, "Wilson's Socialism." According to the *Spartakusbriefe,* there was nothing specifically Socialist about the Stockholm initiative, since to all appearances its program was an exact replica of President Wilson's earlier mediation offers. After all, Wilson also had called for mutual understanding, publication of war aims, abandonment of violence, commitment to arbitration, and limitation of armaments.[23] Consequently, while boycotting this "Wilsonian" diplomacy in Socialist disguise, the Zimmerwald faction issued its own invitation for a rival third Zimmerwald Conference at which the *Kampf gegen den Burgfrieden* would receive if not exclusive at any rate preferential consideration.[24] In the meantime, since German imperialism judged the present moment opportune for participating at Stockholm, whereas British imperialism deemed it inopportune, Maximalist propaganda prepared to "expose English imperialism and utilize the conflict between it and the English proletarian masses to deepen their class consciousness, to intensify the propaganda of internationalism." [25] Although in Russia this type of propaganda eventually proved very successful, inside the other belligerent nations it proved relatively ineffective.

The opposition of the Traditionalists to the emerging Socialist peace diplomacy crystallized no less rapidly. Would the working class, potentially the largest and most effectively organized sector of the electorate, lend its support to the Stockholm Conference? According to the Right, the Internationalists threatened to deprive legally constituted governments of the fundamental responsibility and prerogative of defining and

21. V. Potiemkine, *Histoire de la diplomatie* (3 vols. Paris, Médicis, 1946), 2, 319. Cf. Helfferich, *Der Weltkrieg, 2,* 152.

22. Balabanoff, *Die Zimmerwalder Bewegung,* pp. 64–65.

23. *Spartakusbriefe,* No. 4 (April 1917), pp. 73–76.

24. Balabanoff, *Die Zimmerwalder Bewegung,* pp. 57–60.

25. Lenin, *Works, 20,* Pt. I, p. 125.

defending the national interest. Aware of the revolutionary nature of this political onslaught, the Traditionalists maintained that no international conference of like-minded parties, any more than any one national political party, could be licensed either to interpret or to dictate war aims to the sovereign body politic. By sanctioning Stockholm the war cabinets would actually recognize, if not reinforce, the class principle, thereby encouraging the majority Socialists to shift their allegiance from the nation-state to the renascent International. The domestic implications of the Internationalist initiative loomed large in the minds of the Traditionalists, especially since they had visions of a resumption of the intensive anti-status-quo pressures which had beset the prewar political arena.

Thus Ribot soon told the *Chambre* in Paris that the major objection to the Stockholm initiative was that the SFIO, which was far from being the sole representative of the nation, was seeking to supersede France's legally and legitimately established Government. The Premier also wondered whether if the Socialists were free to proceed to an "international" examination of war aims, the Catholics of all countries could not also claim the right to meet internationally? With the "red" and the "black" internationals making diplomatic policy, "what would become of the functions of Government?" [26] Further over to the Right on the French political scene, President Poincaré also insisted that "not a party, but only the Government would be empowered to negotiate peace in the name of France." [27]

In Great Britain similar protests were being voiced. In Commons Halford J. MacKinder warned against "an international Socialist conference which shall cut at the roots of nationality in Europe, and which shall give us in Europe a distinction, a horizontal distinction, instead of the distinction which we have between the nations." Since such horizontal distinctions were "hostile to the established system of society" MacKinder opposed the issuance of passports to Ramsay MacDonald: in his view no British delegation ought to be licensed to travel abroad unless it represented the English democracy "as a whole." [28] The view that Socialist delegations were unrepresentative of the entire nation was also shared by Secretary of State Lansing in Washington,[29] Luden-

26. Marcellin, *Politique et politiciens*, 2, 131.
27. Poincaré, *Au Service de la France*, 9, 224.
28. *PD*, 93 (May 16, 1917), cols. 1652–53; and 94 (June 11, 1917), cols. 725–26.
29. *FR, Russia, 1918, 1*, 111.

dorff in Germany,[30] and Counts Tisza and Andrassy in the Dual Monarchy.[31]

Not only the Socialist leaders but the war cabinets as well realized that a breakthrough on the Stockholm front would encourage and help the Socialist movement to repair the debacle of 1914. The *New Republic* rightly suggested that "to accept the Socialist and labor parties as peace intermediaries would be tantamount to a recognition of a revolutionary shift in the equilibrium of political power, to the advantage of the working class elements." Having taken the leadership in war time, the forces of order certainly had "no mind to permit minority parties to snatch from them the price of peace." [32] Furthermore, in the revolutionary cauldron in Russia the political implications of the war-aims and peace agitation gradually crystallized in sharper outlines. Under Maximalist pressure, and suffering from continuing military disintegration, the successive Provisional governments turned into ever more ardent yet ineffective "war-aims champions," until at last the Maximalists themselves had succeeded in identifying the peace clamor with their own political program.

The Stockholm proposal compelled each Allied Government not only to consider the domestic dimension of its war-aims policy, but also to embark on a more systematic exploration of coalition diplomacy. Forced to contend with a growing dissident movement, Paris and London were anxiously watching the signals from across the Atlantic. For should Wilson decide to take a pro-Stockholm position, the war cabinets could expect to withstand the revisionist pressure only with great difficulty. Fortunately, however, Washington quickly, firmly, and irrevocably opposed the Conference. Because America's home front was less agitated than either Britain's or France's the State Department had less cause to waver as it steered its anti-Stockholm course. Particularly since America now developed a sharp sensitivity to the political problems of her transatlantic partners, Ribot and Lloyd George were assured of Washington's rigid opposition to the Conference.

30. Ludendorff, *Meine Kriegserinnerungen*, p. 357. Certain right-wing papers in Germany applauded Ribot for having refused passports to the French Socialists. The *Berliner Neueste Nachrichten* praised the French Premier for "speaking as we could wish that Herr Bethmann-Hollweg had ever spoken in the Reichstag." Cited in *DR*, *EPS* (June 14, 1917), p. 180.

31. Michael Graf Karolyi, *Gegen eine ganze Welt: Mein Kampf um den Frieden* (Munich, Verlag für Kulturpolitik, 1924), pp. 289–90.

32. *New Republic* (August 18, 1917), p. 58.

Henceforth Paris and London were able to coordinate their Stockholm policies with only marginal concern for the Wilsonian variable.

In their efforts to prevent the Internationalists from taking an independent course, the governments were at first able to rely confidently on the services of the Social Patriots. On April 26 and May 11 respectively, the Executive of both the SFIO and the Labour party had decided against Stockholm.[33] However, as the war-aims initiative shifted to the Petrograd Soviet, policy decisions affecting Russia and the Stockholm Conference soon were affected by the gradual radicalization of the Left.

On May 10 through regular diplomatic channels Miliukov forwarded an invitation from the Soviet Executive to all Socialist factions of Great Britain, France, and Italy for an exploratory Petrograd conference. This invitation specifically expressed the hope that the war cabinets would not stand in the way of minority delegations which might want to attend this meeting. The Allied Governments now had to decide whether to honor the request that minority Socialists like Longuet and MacDonald be allowed to travel abroad.[34] Realizing that "a direct refusal would irritate the Russian extremists and perhaps discourage their moderate colleagues," Lloyd George urged Paris and Rome to join him in an encouraging yet altogether noncommittal reply to Petrograd.[35]

In France, meanwhile, the original decision of the SFIO Administrative Commission simply to decline the Stockholm invitation provoked bitter criticism from all dissidents. Over the explicit objections of the Majoritarian leaders, all the left-dissident Socialist factions promptly summoned a meeting for May 6. At this meeting they first hailed the Russian Revolution and then defiantly voted a unanimous endorsement of the Stockholm Conference.

This minority action marked the begining of an intensive internecine struggle within the entire French Left. In order to discuss the issues raised by the Russian Revolution and the Stockholm invitation a meeting of the National Council of the SFIO was scheduled for May 27–28. In the intervening weeks an extensive political and press debate took place between the pro- and anti-Stockholm factions. Their disagree-

---

33. Le Parti Socialiste, *La Guerre et la paix*, pp. 162–65; and Lloyd George, *War Memoirs*, 2, 1119.

34. Poincaré, *Au Service de la France, 9,* 137.

35. Lloyd George, *War Memoirs, 2,* 1119–20.

ment was so sharp that the editorial column of the majority-controlled *l'Humanité* had to be thrown open to the *minoritaires*. A spirited battle of words ensued which lasted until the very eve of the scheduled Council meeting.[36] "Why We Must Go to Stockholm" was the unambiguous title under which Jean Longuet began to propound the minority position which in subsequent articles was also supported by Pressemane, Mistral, and Degense. The Social Patriots, who refused even to consider meeting with enemy Socialists and who shared the official view that the Stockholm meeting was German-inspired, advanced their arguments over the signature of Dubreuilh, Rouger, Grenier, Poisson, and Bracke.

At this juncture Cachin and Moutet returned from their mission to Russia. Whereas in early April they had left France as trusted Social Patriots, they now became leading spokesmen for war-aims revision and for Stockholm. When they addressed the National Council on May 27 Cachin and Moutet claimed to represent the views of Kerensky and of the majority of the Petrograd Soviet. Both of the latter expected the French and the British Left to press their governments for a declaration of nonannexationist terms and to secure the passports which would enable them to join Russia's Socialists at Stockholm. Cachin and Moutet were applauded vigorously, undoubtedly partly because many of the Council members had already heard the first rumors about certain scandalous secret treaties which their comrades had uncovered in Petrograd.[37]

Sensing the marked pro-Stockholm mood of the assembly, Pierre Renaudel, who thus far had been expediently noncommittal, decided to endorse Cachin's and Moutet's position. As the influential political editor of *l'Humanité*, Renaudel had originally been opposed to Stockholm. He had hoped that the Cabinet would issue the war-aims declaration which the Russian Government requested, thereby deflating the internationalist campaign. Renaudel had urged the Government to take advantage of this "magnificent opportunity" to launch a diplomatic offensive: "America is on your side with her idealism and Russia has freed you from all that might disquiet you in the way of

36. From May 14 until May 26 *l'Humanité* almost daily carried an article by either a proponent or an opponent of Stockholm. See *l'Humanité* of May 14–18 and 23–26, 1917.

37. *L'Humanité*, May 28, 1917. Cf. *Les Carnets secrets d'Abel Ferry, 1914–1918*, p. 183.

imperialism and ambition. . . . Russia is calling you. Do not hesitate; answer her appeal." [38] However, this appeal, like so many others, went unheeded, while the pro-Stockholm faction inside the SFIO rapidly gained in strength.

By pronouncing himself in favor of Stockholm Renaudel hoped to exercise a moderating influence on the excited Internationalists and to retain the all-important editorial control of *l'Humanité*. Actually Cachin's and Moutet's speeches enabled him and his followers to rationalize their sudden reversal without too much difficulty: whereas German-inspired neutrals had originally summoned the Stockholm Congress, now the invitation originated directly with the Allied Russian Socialists.[39]

On May 28 the National Council enthusiastically voted to participate in the Stockholm Conference "which had been initiated by the Russian Revolution." [40] In *l'Humanité* Renaudel explained that Cachin's and Moutet's "factual information about the Russian Revolution, its development, its internal greatness, and its Stockholm position" restored the unity between the two major factions of the SFIO. Evidence for the rapprochement of *majoritaires* and *minoritaires* can be gathered from the fact that the Stockholm resolution which was accepted by acclamation was drafted by Auriol and Pressemane and was introduced by Renaudel and Mistral.[41] Even Loriot endorsed the resolution. However, he and his colleagues made it unmistakably clear that by Stockholm they understood a third Zimmerwald Conference.[42]

Even though they agreed in principle to an international conference, the Social Patriots nevertheless tried to lay down rigid conditions under which French Socialists would participate in the Stockholm discussions. Specifically, confident that Germany's aggression would be condemned, they insisted that the question of war guilt would have to be on the conference agenda. However, since the *minoritaires* rejected the unilateral war-guilt thesis, they sought to keep this issue off the agenda in the hope of avoiding acrimonious and disruptive debates. These and similar issues were fought out in three subcommissions

38. See Renaudel's articles in *l'Humanité*, May 17 and 18, 1917.
39. Cf. *l'Humanité*, May 29, 1917.
40. Le Parti Socialiste, *La Guerre et la paix*, pp. 3, 167–69.
41. *L'Humanité*, May 29, 1917.
42. Guilbeaux, *Le Mouvement socialiste et syndicaliste français pendant la guerre*, p. 31.

which were set up to draft an answer to the different sections of the Stockholm questionnaire. The membership of all three subcommissions was carefully balanced between both major factions. Meanwhile, Renaudel and Longuet were to request passports in order to be able to proceed to Stockholm for preliminary consultations. The Soviet was informed that these two emissaries would leave "just as soon as the material difficulties of their trip were overcome." [43]

On May 30, in preparation for the impending parliamentary debate on the diplomacy of the war and on the passports, first Moutet and then Cachin reported to the SFIO parliamentary delegation. On this occasion Cachin spoke at some length about the secret treaties and agreements of which the Russian Socialists were so very critical. Apparently Albert Thomas had approved Cachin's plan to inform his colleagues about the existence of the Doumergue and other agreements; however, both were agreed that these revelations would have to be treated with great discretion.[44] The group decided, therefore, to send a small delegation to call on Premier Ribot in order to discuss this explosive issue as well as broader questions like war aims and passports.

The delegation which met with Ribot was heavily Internationalist, since besides Renaudel and Varenne it included Cachin, Moutet, Prévot, Longuet, Mayéras, Pressemane, and Mistral.[45] These nine Socialist spokesmen informed the Prime Minister that they knew about the Doumergue negotiations, called on the Government both to publish and repudiate all secret treaties, and requested passports to Stockholm. Moreover, they warned Ribot that the Cabinet could "count on our total support for a war of principles, as well as for national defense; however, the day this war becomes imperialist, we will inform you that you should no longer count on us." [46] In the face of this left-wing threat the Premier was at first hesitant. He maintained that the Doumergue agreement did not have the legal quality of a treaty; he was equally evasive on the passport issue. Therefore, in an effort to win concrete concessions, the Majoritarians sought to assure him, through informal channels, that should Renaudel and Longuet get their pass-

43. For the membership of each of the three subcommissions see *l'Humanité*, June 7, 1917. See also ibid., June 26, 1917.

44. Bourgin, *Le Parti contre la patrie*, pp. 218 ff.

45. Ibid., p. 222.

46. Le Parti Socialiste, *La Guerre et la paix*, pp. 98–101; and *Comité Secret*, p. 517.

ports they could be relied on not to have any dealings with enemy Socialists for the time being.[47]

At this juncture Ribot seems to have been sensitive to Renaudel's contention that in order to exercise a restraining control over the Europe-wide Internationalist movement, the French Government should allow the impetuous minority Socialists to function under the watchful eye of their more trustworthy majority colleagues.[48] From his new post in Petrograd, Albert Thomas pressed similar advice on both the French and the British prime ministers. He cabled that the Allies should "carry on the struggle in the field of international Socialism"; moreover, should Paris give its agreement, he had "decided to go to Stockholm at any cost." [49] These and similar opinions were instrumental in leading Lloyd George to caution Ribot on May 29 not only that it was dangerous to leave the Russians and the Germans alone at an international conference but also that it was important for the Allied cause to appear in a favorable light to the European Socialist movement.[50] Even Charles Maurras, one of the Socialists' most vociferous enemies, warned of the danger of taking the Internationalist stirrings too lightly. He advanced the proposal that Albert Thomas be commissioned by his Government as well as by his party to accompany the Russian Socialists to Stockholm.[51]

Precisely because Maurras and l'Action Française recognized that the "manipulation of public opinion was part of total war" [52] they were less prone than other right-wing papers to criticize the Left's, particularly the Social Patriots', adventures into diplomacy. However, le Temps vehemently attacked the Council's decision as a "total capitulation by the majoritaires to the revolutionary and Internationalist minority." It referred to the "brutal disavowal of the majority's heretofore loyal attitude" as one of "the most miserable comedies to which

47. Bourgin, Le Parti contre la patrie, p. 223; and Poincaré, Au Service de la France, 9, 151.

48. Marcellin, Politique et politiciens, 2, 141.

49. Cited in Hamilton, Arthur Henderson, p. 132.

50. Ribot, Journal de Alexandre Ribot, pp. 136–37; and Lady Algernon Gordon Lennox, ed., The Diary of Lord Bertie of Thame (2 vols. London, Hodder and Stoughton, 1924), 2, 132.

51. L'Action Française, June 2, 3, 4, 5, and 10, 1917.

52. Charles Maurras writing in l'Action Française, May 10, 1917. In this article Maurras spoke of the need to "socialize and nationalize the war." To achieve this he proposed, among other things, to guarantee each poilu a share of postwar reparations and indemnities.

political leaders could lend themselves." According to *le Temps* the surrender of the Socialist leaders to the Russian revolutionaries revealed such a "basic absence of political sense" that henceforth worse betrayals could be expected.[53]

These and similar judgments led the Right to marshal its parliamentary and cabinet forces in an effort to prevent the Premier from yielding to the Socialists.[54] The threatened resignation of Maginot, Desplas, Bourgeois, and Painlevé frightened Ribot into mounting the rostrum of the Chamber at 3:00 P.M. on June 1 in order to announce publicly that passports would not be issued.[55] Evidently only by aligning himself further with the forces of order did Ribot succeed in postponing, though not in preventing, a major Cabinet crisis. He did so, however, at the cost of alienating the Socialist Ministers from their Cabinet colleagues.

This refusal of passports merely rendered the position of the Social Patriots, especially of their cabinet ministers, increasingly precarious *vis-à-vis* the rebellious Independents. Therefore, to deny the latter a monopoly on virtue, Marcel Sembat hastened to criticize Ribot's decision, and Renaudel bluntly declared that French Socialists "would go to Petrograd and Stockholm. The Russian Revolution calls us. We will go towards it." [56] But before French Socialists would travel abroad in the face of their Government's formal opposition, their Cabinet colleagues would probably have to resign; in brief, the *union sacrée* would have to be broken. Was Renaudel actually prepared to take this responsibility? In turn, what concessions was the Right willing to make in order to prevent the loyal Social Patriots from drawing closer to the *minoritaires?*

The conflict between the Socialists and the Cabinet was now brought before Parliament. On June 1, 1917, the Chamber went into the sixth secret session of the Republic's history and that of the war in order to listen to and discuss Moutet's and Cachin's reports. The heated debate about secret treaties, war aims, Stockholm, passports, mutinies, and strikes, which Ribot had tried so hard to put off, lasted for a full three days.

53. *Le Temps,* May 30 and June 2, 1917.
54. Cf. *le Temps, le Gaulois, la Victoire,* and *le Figaro.*
55. *Le Temps,* June 1, 1917, and *Les Carnets secrets d'Abel Ferry, 1914–1918,* p. 183. Cf. *l'Humanité,* June 2, 1917.
56. *L'Humanité,* June 2 and 3, 1917.

Moutet spoke first. He gave a general summary of developments in revolutionary Russia as well as of his mission's activities there. He reported that the Soviet had cautioned the Provisional Government to count on its support only as long as the Government adhered to the Petrograd formula. According to Moutet the Soviet also was pressing the Provisional Government to apply pressure on the Allied governments in order that they, too, should revise their war aims. Both from general observation and from his conversations with the special commission appointed by the Soviet to negotiate with the Allied missions, Moutet concluded that the war-aims question was the primary concern of the Russian Left. Furthermore, Moutet and his colleagues were repeatedly asked "not to let the Russians face Scheidemann all by themselves in Stockholm." [57]

Moutet spoke enthusiastically of the fighting potential of Russia's armies which in his and Cachin's optimistic judgment now had adequate supplies and materiel.[58] He repeatedly stressed that above all the Russian army desperately needed a new moral purpose before it could effectively take the offensive. According to Moutet the Russian Socialists asked the French and British Socialist emissaries to convince their Governments to bring about the war-aims revision which would greatly contribute to this revival of their army's fighting spirit. In concluding, Moutet revealed that he and Cachin had promised their Russian colleagues to "do what you ask of us. . . . We made this promise in our personal name as well as in the name of our Socialist party." [59]

Cachin's speech, which followed, was decidedly policy- and action-oriented. In the course of his address he repeated the Socialist request for passports, for a revision of war aims, and for the publication of the secret treaties. First, however, he reminded his very attentive audience that if the Revolution had not taken place in Russia, by now the Tsar and his advisers would certainly have betrayed their Allies. Anxious to overcome the anti-Soviet suspicions of the majority of the Chamber,

---

57. *Comité Secret*, p. 497. Extensive but nevertheless very incomplete selections from the record of the sixth *Comité Secret* are conveniently available in Allard, *Les Dessous de la guerre*, chap. 5.

58. Curiously enough the returning Socialists gave an altogether exaggerated estimate of the supplies and the organization of the Russian armies. A Radical Socialist deputy, M. Lancien, who had also recently come back from Russia, gave a much more pessimistic report about the material conditions in the Russian army. Augagneur, the former Minister of Navy, concurred in Lancien's judgment.

59. *Comité Secret*, p. 499.

Cachin made the following appeal: "Out of patriotism we Socialists gave our total unquestioning support to tsarist Russia. Today, will you refuse your support to Revolutionary Russia which is beset by so many difficulties?" [60] Then, after reiterating the demand for a nonannexationist war-aims pronouncement, Cachin turned to what he termed the "delicate part" of his speech.[61]

In Russia he and Moutet were told that whereas there was a popular, liberating current behind the Allied war effort, "other ambitions had been grafted onto these noble aspirations which have not been submitted and continue to be unknown to the people." Then, turning toward Aristide Briand, Cachin inquired what mandate he, as Prime Minister, had given to Gaston Doumergue when he went to Russia last January. "Well, is it true that he went there to ask for us the left bank of the Rhine—or, if you prefer, to talk about it? Is it also true that with other Allies . . . we negotiated about territorial aspirations in Asia Minor which we [i.e. Socialists] qualify as excessive . . . and that each Allied Power claimed its share?" Without hesitation Briand uttered a heavy, unequivocal "Oui!" which provoked enthusiastic applause on the right and in the center of the house, while producing loud protests among the Socialists. When the noise finally subsided, Cachin proclaimed that at the time Doumergue was in Russia "he negotiated with the Tsar's Government; now, the new Russian Government believes it necessary to revise the treaties which have been signed, the war aims, and I ask you whether you are disposed to do so?" In Cachin's view, now that Russia was renouncing Constantinople this revision had become an "historic necessity." [62]

It was the first time that the secret negotiations and agreements about Constantinople and the left bank of the Rhine had been discussed and questioned on such an authoritative platform. Neither Briand nor Ribot could afford to ignore the Socialist challenge, especially since all deputies were sworn to secrecy.

The following afternoon Briand had the floor.[63] The House was tense; the Socialists were unruly. At first Briand was evasive. He spoke of the way in which Germany was trying to shift the battle from the

60. Ibid., p. 499.
61. Ibid., p. 501.
62. Ibid., pp. 502–3.
63. The following discussion of Briand's first speech during the Comité Secret is based on the verbatim account in ibid., pp. 509 ff.

trenches to the diplomatic realm, and warned of the dangers of the current "peace offensive." But soon Pressemane, with Briand's permission, interjected a brief but pointed question: "What are the treaties and engagements which present-day Russia does not want to respect?"

After a brief recess Briand began to discuss "the accord which gave Constantinople to Russia." According to the former Premier, at the time it was not only a question of satisfying Russia's demands; other "perfectly respectable preoccupations" had to be considered by the French Government: Specifically, France could not afford to ignore the dissolution of the Turkish Empire, especially in view of England's "traditional aspirations" in the Orient. "Hence, the spheres of influence of our country had to be determined, and we settled them."

Thus far Briand had not referred, even indirectly, to the Doumergue episode. However, toward the end of his speech he did refer to France's eastern borders, in whose settlement the Allies would have to promise France a preponderant voice. But he was careful not to mention the left bank of the Rhine.

In the meantime Moutet had returned to the rostrum to read, *in extenso,* the Petrograd Soviet's manifesto of May 15, whose letter and spirit conflicted so blatantly with the legacy of the Old Diplomacy which was being exposed. Curiously enough, Charles Benoist and other Conservatives impatiently criticized the interruption, because "this manifesto was being dragged through all the newspapers"; Briand also admitted that he was not "unfamiliar with this document." [64]

No sooner had Briand finished his far from candid exposé than Renaudel came back to the charge. "Do not hide the truth from us! We will no longer be satisfied with vague words! As responsible parliamentarians we demand to know what negotiations Mr. Gaston Doumergue carried out in Russia! On whose initiative? What about? What has been signed? What letters were exchanged?" Only after the *Chambre* has these facts and texts, Renaudel continued, can it undertake the revision of war aims with Russia as well as with the other Allies. In conclusion Renaudel declared that once these war aims had been revised the trip of two Socialists to Stockholm could no longer be injurious! [65]

Since the Ribot Administration had not denounced or modified any of France's international obligations, it was the Premier's turn to answer Renaudel's hard questions. Incidentally, Ribot himself had had

64. Ibid., p. 511.
65. Ibid., p. 518.

serious reservations about the Doumergue mission, possibly because his rival Briand had been one of its chief architects.

Ribot began his speech with the bold assertion that he had "nothing to hide." [66] According to the Premier the division of Asia Minor was initiated not by France, but by tsarist Russia. Also, England had made constant progress in the area, having arrived in Mesopotamia and in Baghdad. France could not be "disinterested" in these developments. Still according to Ribot, Syria was "ours" because of her peoples' affection for France; at any rate, Syria was in France's zone of influence.

Next Ribot turned to French aims in Europe. On January 12, 1917, at the request of the British Government, the French Government specified certain vital war aims in a letter to Paul Cambon, Ambassador at the Court of St. James. Accordingly France asked for the restoration of Alsace-Lorraine with the "original" borders of before 1790. This restoration would give the Republic "the geographic and mineral basin of the Saar whose possession is essential to our industry." Furthermore, in the view of the French Government "Germany should no longer have a foothold this side of the Rhine." Consequently the Allies should envisage the neutrality and autonomy of the left bank, which could then serve as a buffer between Germany and France, thus permitting the nation to live in "relative security." But above all, this letter insisted that "being most directly interested in the territorial status of this area France must have a preponderant voice in the examination of the settlement of this vital question." Before being sent to Cambon, this letter had been discussed in the Cabinet; subsequently it served as instructions for Doumergue.[67]

In Russia, Doumergue then received unhesitating approval for these proposals from the Tsar and his Government. Like Briand, Ribot reluctantly admitted that new Russia was free to renounce the Doumergue agreement, just as France could simultaneously withdraw her assent to Russian control of Constantinople. Should such a mutual renunciation materialize in later negotiations, the French Government "would not consider it . . . a rupture of the alliance." Mr. Renaudel,

66. The following account of Ribot's speech is based ibid., pp. 519 ff.

67. In the course of these debates neither Briand nor Ribot hesitated to remind the Social Patriots that three of their colleagues were members of the Cabinet when most of the wartime diplomatic agreements were made. They were careful to note, however, that the Doumergue question was discussed at a Cabinet session from which Albert Thomas, completely fortuitously, was absent.

however, "suggests that we revise *all* war aims. . . . Undoubtedly he proposes that we go tell Italy, who entered this war trusting in the conventions which we signed with her, and of which your [Socialist] friends who were then in the Cabinet were the most ardent partisans [68] . . . that these conventions exist no longer because they do not fit a formula which has just been found in Petrograd. If this is how you understand the New Diplomacy of which you speak, permit me to feel some regret for the old one."

The Socialists were incensed by this belligerent, self-justifying defense of the methods and objectives of the Old Diplomacy. They now began to probe still further in an effort to show that such transactions could only be the product of secret diplomacy unchecked by parliamentary controls. Were these matters sufficiently discussed in the Cabinet? Is it not true that Doumergue received instructions from Philippe Berthelot, a high official of the Quai d'Orsay whose brother had financial interests in Asia Minor? Why was neither Wilson nor Lloyd George informed of the Doumergue negotiations?

Briand now was challenged to assume full responsibility for the diplomatic negotiations of his administration which he had failed to describe in his first speech.

> Gentlemen, I implore you to recognize that the life of any Government . . . forces it to register facts together with their consequences and to take precautions and guarantees. It is indispensable that in its hands the Government should have pledges, or, if you prefer, securities, which it will or will not use, depending on the circumstances. . . . The closer we come to the end of the war the more likely it is that we will have to gather around a table . . . to discuss . . . the details of problems. . . . In its application the formula "Alsace-Lorraine" entails conditions on which, in order to avoid a sad spectacle, one must agree before hand; Frenchmen have economic, ethnic, geographic, and security-military views which might be contested by the British, the Italians, or the Russians! It would be stupid not to reach a preliminary understanding. . . . You know that in all negotiations . . . one must possess elements with which to bargain. . . . This is what you call . . . secret diplomacy. But diplomacy can only be se-

68. Earlier in the war Cachin had been to Italy on a mission to help fire the war enthusiasm of the Italian Left.

cret. . . . It is possible that at the end of this war . . . an international organization might not afford all the essential guarantees, especially insofar as sanctions are concerned. Therefore, to secure reparations, there may be need for temporary occupations. . . . And for the future . . . with the agreement of other peoples, a neutralized buffer state between the two nations might have to be established.[69]

In these eloquent words the former Prime Minister came once again to the defense of France's wartime diplomacy.

Two interrelated political questions, one diplomatic and one domestic, were posed as a result of these revealing, exciting, and tumultuous secret debates. First, should the Cabinet under Socialist and Soviet pressure revise French war aims as a first step in a broad-scale revision of Allied war aims? This revision should provide the Russian armies with the reputedly all-essential moral primer, and was likely to have the issuance of passports as a corollary. Second, assuming that Ribot shared the Socialists' view about the vital importance of this revision for the Russian as well as Allied war effort, could he undertake this revision at the behest of political parties and factions which controlled at best one-fourth of the Assembly votes? Furthermore, since the SFIO was far from unified on these and kindred issues how would the Right react to a policy-change which denied the entire diplomatic heritage of the Third Republic? A major diplomatic reversal carried out under minority left-wing threats might well bring in its wake an altogether exaggerated leftward shift in the internal balance of power.[70]

On June 4, after a Sunday recess, the Chamber was called upon for a vote of confidence. A total of twelve *ordres du jour* were introduced, all of which, according to law, would have to be voted on in public sessions. Hence, before declaring the secret session closed, the Right especially was anxious to achieve a maximum degree of unity.

69. The remainder of this account of the debate in which Ribot, Briand, Renaudel, Sembat, and Moutet were the most active participants is based on ibid., pp. 521 ff., esp. pp. 521–23, 527–28, 532–37.

70. Later in the year, using the victory of Russia's Bolsheviks as evidence of the ill effects of the opposition to Stockholm, Cachin and Moutet accused the Right of having been excessively influenced by domestic political considerations in their passport policy. Both Socialists charged that the Right was afraid that the French Left might emerge considerably strengthened from a successful Stockholm conference. JO (December 27, 1917), p. 3617.

Therefore, eight *ordres du jour* were withdrawn in favor of a new one introduced by the moderate Radical Charles Dumont with the backing of the Administration.[71] After asserting that France had no designs on either foreign lands or peoples, and after reiterating France's inalienable right to Alsace-Lorraine and to reparations, this new text declared that France would seek "to obtain lasting guarantees for peace and for the independence of peoples, large and small, through the organization of a league of nations, which was now being prepared." Unlike this text, the resolution sponsored by the majority Socialists sent "expressions of sympathy and firm confidence" to the Russian Revolution and criticized the machinations of "irresponsible secret diplomacy"; however, it did not request the controversial passports.[72]

Apparently the Cabinet had received preliminary indications that leading Social Patriots like Renaudel, Compère-Morel, and Sembat might also abandon their *ordre du jour* in the interest of national unity. At any rate, in the public session Renaudel rose to declare that he was prepared to endorse the Dumont text. However, numerous appeals for unanimity before the nation and the enemy failed to impress the *minoritaires*. Instead Cachin, who by now had noticeably moved toward a centrist position, persisted in his plea not so much for a change in the wording of the Dumont text as for a reversal of the Cabinet's passport decision. "Give us the passports, allow us to go to the Conference." Make this concession, Cachin continued, "and we are prepared to take the necessary step to meet you." [73]

Yet Ribot and his supporters stood firm. They knew that Charles Benoist would vote for the text, not out of agreement with either its letter or spirit but because of his determination to strengthen the War Cabinet. Renaudel's support was secured both because of his reluctance to weaken the defense effort and because of his belief that even though the resolution was far from satisfactory, it did mark an advance in war aims as a "direct and necessary consequence" of Socialist pressure.[74] Clearly, there was no need to make further concessions; the two resolutions sponsored respectively by Pressemane and Brizon could safely be ignored.

71. For the twelve texts see *Comité Secret*, pp. 537–39.
72. Ibid., p. 539.
73. Ibid., p. 541.
74. *L'Humanité*, June 6, 1917. See also *Les Carnets secrets d'Abel Ferry, 1914–1918*, p. 185.

Actually forty-seven Socialist deputies registered a negative vote, among them Auriol, Bedouce, Bouisson, Brizon, Cachin, Laval, Longuet, Mayéras, Mistral, Moutet, and Pressemane.[75] Notwithstanding this unwelcome protest vote *le Temps* justifiably hailed the outcome as a "vote for victory." However, *le Temps* could not resist the temptation of critically commenting on the "pure and simple verbiage of assemblies" which appeared in the resolution as an "unnecessary concession to the Socialists." [76]

After a brief secret debate the members of France's Upper House unanimously voted a war-aims resolution which was altogether free of such "empty verbiage." Since no dissidents sat in the august *Sénat*, not even a passing allusion to either the principle of self-determination or a league of nations was thought necessary. Instead, in good Old Diplomacy style, the French Senate simply declared that "a durable peace [could] only result from the victory of the Allied armies." [77] President Poincaré had good reason to rejoice over the "excellent session" of the Senate, whose statement was "much more unyielding than that of the Chamber." Likewise *le Temps* praised this "vote de clarté" which "proved once again, as in the days of *boulangisme* and nationalism, that the good sense of the Upper House showed the correct way." [78]

At first the British Government had also decided against Stockholm. However, the mounting dissident pressures at home and the danger of Russian and German Socialists meeting alone in Stockholm caused the War Cabinet to reconsider the issue on May 21. By this time, acting on the Soviet's earlier invitations, the ILP and the British Socialist party had applied for passports for MacDonald, Jowett, and Inkpin. These three flaming dissidents had made no secret of their intention to stop at Stockholm en route to Petrograd. The Cabinet felt that if these minority Labourites were to go abroad, "a strong delegation of the British Labour party ought to go as well." On May 21 in a cable requesting Albert Thomas' judgment the British Prime Minister expressed his own apprehension that unless the Allied cause be forcefully repre-

75. *L'Humanité*, June 6, 1917.
76. *Le Temps*, June 6, 1917.
77. For a translated text of this *ordre du jour* see *FR*, 1917, Supplement 2, *1*, 88–89.
78. Poincaré, *Au Service de la France, 9*, 158; and *le Temps*, June 8, 1917.

sented at Stockholm a "bad impression may be produced on the Russian Socialists." [79]

It would seem that far from accepting either the spirit or the letter of the Petrograd formula, Lloyd George nevertheless was determined to explore the possibility of using the contemplated Conference to lessen political tensions inside both England and Russia. As part of this exploration, on May 23, the War Cabinet decided to send Arthur Henderson to Russia on a mission similar to the one which the French Government had entrusted to Albert Thomas. Obviously, Henderson was expected not only to help stem the peace tide in the Petrograd Soviet but also to advise London on the Stockholm question. At the time of his departure Henderson was still uncommitted on the Stockholm issue. He seems to have felt that provided the Stockholm Conference were limited to a restatement of nonannexationist war aims it might exert a healthy influence on the excessively rigid war cabinets. Henderson himself now was instrumental in persuading the British Cabinet to switch from outright opposition to watchful waiting.

Would Stockholm cause a breach in Allied diplomacy? Whereas the French Government had just decided against issuing passports to both majority and minority Socialists, the British Government had granted a travel permit to Ramsay MacDonald. Immediately the British Conservatives protested the Cabinet's decision to allow a leading "pacifist" to go abroad. First Robert Cecil and then Bonar Law assured Commons that MacDonald was going to Petrograd, not to Stockholm, and that he would not consort with "enemy subjects." Both Government spokesmen begged their colleagues to be considerate of Russia's needs. Cecil revealed that the "Russian Government had strongly and repeatedly expressed the desire that the representatives of the minority as well as of the majority . . . should be allowed to visit Petrograd." Moreover, according to Bonar Law, the Cabinet had received similar requests from Sir George Buchanan, Arthur Henderson, and Albert Thomas. On June 6 Buchanan and Henderson had wired that they were "strongly of opinion that it would be a mistake to refuse permission." [80]

In Washington the British Ambassador informed Secretary of State Lansing that the issuance of passports had become "inevitable as con-

79. Lloyd George, *War Memoirs*, 2, 1121; and Hamilton, *Arthur Henderson*, pp. 130–32.

80. *PD*, 94, (June 8, 1917), cols. 494–95; (June 11, 1917), cols. 720–25.

ditions in Russia have changed so rapidly." [81] MacDonald and Jowett would certainly have been on their way if the fervently Social Patriotic leaders of the National Seamen's and Firemen's Union had not come to the Government's rescue; unsolicited, they decided that the dockers and sailors of their union would refuse to load and man the ship on which the dissidents were scheduled to sail.[82]

Meanwhile, shortly after his arrival in Petrograd on June 2, Arthur Henderson had realized that Sir George Buchanan's reports on the Russian situation were exceptionally competent and realistic. Henderson and Buchanan concurred that the ominous peace mood which was settling over the war-weary industrial and peasant proletariat threatened to undermine Russia's war effort permanently. Even while serving as Cabinet Minister, Henderson had never ceased to be interested in UDC's war-aims proposals. Consequently he was ideologically prepared to consider sympathetically the war-aims arguments of the non-Bolshevik Socialists both in the Soviet and in the Second Provisional Government. Presently Henderson concluded that a rapid and decisive revision of Allied war aims, which Stockholm could both accelerate and influence, was one of the only steps which might contribute to a stabilization of the Eastern front. Even though Sir George also warned London on July 12 that a further postponement of the official war-aims conference, which Tereshchenko had proposed a month earlier, would "discourage Russia from continuing her active participation in the war," [83] still unlike Henderson the Ambassador was skeptical of the constructive role the Allied forces of movement could play in the present diplomatic impasse.

By the time he returned to London on July 24 Henderson seemed to have concluded that there were two major reasons for advocating the revision of war aims and passports for Stockholm. First, both issues were of vital importance to the dangerously weak Provisional Government. Second, since he had gained renewed confidence in Socialist foreign-policy principles in Petrograd, Henderson was prepared to use both internal and external pressures in favor of a policy change. According to Henderson, Labour had always claimed that there was "nothing to fear by a clear, definite, frank statement of . . . the aims

81. *FR*, 1917, Supplement 2, *1*, 741–42.
82. See *PD, 96* (July 26, 1917), cols. 1532–33.
83. Buchanan, *My Mission to Russia, 2,* 151.

for which we entered the war and for which we are continuing the war." [84]

Even after accepting a Cabinet post, Henderson openly remained Secretary of the Labour party. Until now this dual allegiance had not produced any conflict in loyalties. After his return from Petrograd, however, Henderson was in a difficult position. On the one hand he wanted to promote the Stockholm project both in the interest of Kerensky and in the interest of Labour. On the other hand, he knew that his Cabinet colleagues were not likely to share his enthusiasm for an international conference, even if this conference were purely consultative.

At any rate, on July 25 Henderson met with the Labour Party Executive. On the strength of his recent experiences he quite naturally was asked to express his views on developments in Russia and on the proposed conference. After finishing his report, Henderson advised his colleagues to place the entire Stockholm question before a special National Labour Conference on August 10. Furthermore, he recommended that British Labour should welcome a Stockholm meeting, provided the meeting was strictly consultative.[85]

After accepting Henderson's advice by a vote of 5 to 2, this same meeting of the Executive decided to engage in preliminary discussions about Stockholm with Allied Socialists. A wire had just been received from the SFIO inviting a Labour delegation to accompany representatives from the Petrograd Soviet to Paris for such consultations. The Executive replied that MacDonald, Wardle, and Henderson would join the Soviet delegates who were in London just then.[86]

Both at the meeting of the Executive and in the meeting with Allied Socialists, Henderson acted in his capacity as Secretary of the Labour party. Nevertheless, in view of his continued membership in the War Cabinet, his activities were likely to be viewed with suspicion by the Right. The Conservatives and Liberals felt, and with considerable justification, that Henderson's Cabinet affiliation meant either that Lloyd George approved of his policies and activities or that there was

84. *PD*, *96* (August 1, 1917), col. 2195. See also LP, *Report of the Seventeenth Annual Conference* (Nottingham and London, 1918), p. 4.

85. *PD*, *97* (August 13, 1917), col. 910.

86. Ibid., *96* (August 1, 1917), cols. 2187–99; (August 13, 1917), col. 910. See also LP, *Report of the Seventeenth Annual Conference* (Nottingham and London, 1918), pp. 44–46.

an irreconcilable conflict between Henderson's two jobs. Soon Henderson was faced with the alternative of resigning either his Cabinet post or the secretaryship in the party.

Henderson's Cabinet colleagues were especially concerned by reports that one of their fellow ministers was about to be closely associated with MacDonald. Twenty-four hours before leaving for Paris, Henderson met with the Cabinet in a special meeting in order to explain his proposed course of action. In the face of strong opposition to his endorsement of a "nonbinding" Stockholm Conference as well as to his trip to Paris, Henderson offered to resign from the Cabinet.[87]

However, since Lloyd George was in Paris for the Balkan Conference, his Ministers could not do more than voice their strong disapproval. According to Bonar Law, the Cabinet knew of Henderson's intention to accompany MacDonald and the delegates of the Soviet, "but only after everything had been settled." Therefore, the Cabinet "could only have stopped him and his colleagues by denying passports."[88]

However, even if Lloyd George had been in London, the Cabinet might not have prevented Henderson from going on this journey. How could His Majesty's Government have issued a passport to Henderson to represent them in Russia, and now deny him the right to meet with Allied Socialists in an Allied capital? Such a refusal, probably followed by Henderson's resignation, would have been ill received both in Petrograd and in the British Left.

Henderson left for Paris after advising the Prime Minister of his decision by telegraph. Even though Lloyd George may not have been shocked by the news, according to the British Ambassador in Paris, he was "nervous about the military situation and the possibility of the Pacifists, British, French, and Russian, forcing an unsatisfactory peace." After discussing the impending arrival of the Anglo-Soviet delegation with Ribot, Lord Bertie, who also knew his own Prime Minister's mind, told Albert Thomas "j'espère que vous les empêcherez de faire des bêtises."[89]

In the light of their conversations with Kerensky and Tereshchenko, as well as in view of the radicalization of their own parties, Thomas and Henderson could not refuse to consider the Stockholm project. How-

87. *PD*, 97 (August 13, 1917), col. 911.
88. Ibid., *96* (July 30, 1917), cols. 1727–28.
89. Ibid. (August 13, 1917), col. 911; Lloyd George, *War Memoirs*, 2, 1127–28; Lennox, *The Diary of Lord Bertie*, 2, 161–62.

ever, both preferred that it should be "a consultation rather than a Conference." Hence they entered these Paris conversations "with the determination to do everything" in their power "to turn the Conference into a consultative assembly rather than a binding assembly." [90]

The Soviet delegation, composed of H. Ehrlich, J. Goldenberg, N. Rusanov, and E. Smirnov, arrived in the French capital in the morning of July 28, accompanied by Henderson, MacDonald, and Wardle. A committee was immediately appointed to draft a resolution on the Stockholm question. On this committee MacDonald, Longuet, and Ehrlich defended the Independent view, while Wardle, Renaudel, and Goldenberg took the Majoritarian position. The resolution which was adopted on July 31 accepted the Stockholm invitation, endorsed the participation of minority parties and factions which were independently organized, and confirmed the call for a preliminary inter-Allied Socialist Conference in London on August 28–29.[91] Also, the Allied Socialists declared that in view of the London meeting they could not be ready for a Stockholm Conference until some time between September 9 and 16. While the *minoritaires* agreed to this postponement, they did not accept the Henderson-Thomas proposal that the decisions of the Stockholm Conference should not be binding.[92]

On July 27 Ambassador Page advised Washington that with Henderson's return from Russia, British Labour had taken a pro-Stockholm turn. However, simultaneously he and Ambassador Sharp reported that in both London and Paris official feeling was consolidating against the Socialists.[93] While the domestic crisis was ebbing in France and Britain, the Reichstag's Peace Resolution indicated that even in Germany's own judgment the German U-boat campaign had failed. Consequently, whereas the Central Powers seemed to be heading toward far-reaching economic dislocations, the Allies confidently banked on the expected contribution of the American war effort.

Upon his return to London on August 1, Henderson immediately saw the Prime Minister in order to inform him of his latest activities and views. After telling Lloyd George that he would continue to fight for a consultative conference, the Prime Minister invited Henderson to

90. *PD, 96* (August 1, 1917), col. 2195.

91. *L'Humanité,* July 29, 30, and 31, 1917.

92. Le Parti Socialiste, *La Guerre et la paix,* pp. 180–82.

93. *FR,* 1917, Supplement 2, *1,* 749–52. See also Poincaré, *Au Service de la France, 9,* 223; and *PD, 97* (August 13, 1917), col. 931.

a special Cabinet meeting that afternoon at four. The entire Right, especially certain leading Cabinet members, pressed the Prime Minister to rebuke Henderson for his recent association with MacDonald. That afternoon the unfortunate "doormat incident" occurred which strained relations still further between Henderson and the rest of the Cabinet.[94]

Nevertheless, in the interest of national unity, Lloyd George was reluctant to break with Henderson. In the evening the Prime Minister himself went before Commons in order to defend his Cabinet colleague. He proclaimed that, since the outbreak of war, of all Labour leaders Henderson had made the greatest contribution to the war effort. Furthermore, on numerous previous occasions Henderson had associated with MacDonald, but then as now always in an effort to counteract the influence of pacifists in the Left. "Do let us show some gratitude for past services," Lloyd George continued. Also, the House should note that not only the British but also the French, Italian, and Belgian governments "thought it desirable that members of their Governments should retain their association with these Labour and Socialist organizations, in order to prevent a great hostile organization growing up outside, which would mobilize skilled and organized labour with the interests of a premature peace." It should not be forgotten either that at the recent meeting in Paris one of the participants had been Albert Thomas, "a man who has rendered greater services to the prosecution of the War in France than almost any other Minister there." The House recessed under the impression that whereas the Prime Minister agreed that Henderson should not have gone to Paris, he asked that Henderson be forgiven because of his past services.[95]

Even though Lloyd George was anxious to prevent a break with Henderson, he was no less determined to prevent Labour delegates from attending a Stockholm Conference. At a private meeting on Au-

94. PD, 97 (August 13, 1917), col. 913. When Henderson arrived for the War Cabinet meeting he was kept waiting in an antichamber for the best part of an hour while his Cabinet colleagues discussed his recent trip to Paris. Finally, G. N. Barnes, a Labour member of the Cabinet, came out with a message which Henderson indignantly refused to accept. Whereas the other Cabinet members insisted that by making him wait they were trying to spare his feelings, Henderson maintained that as long as he was a Minister in good standing this procedure was unforgivable and unprecedented.

95. Ibid., 96 (August 1, 1917), cols. 2206–9.

gust 7 the Prime Minister made his position quite clear to Henderson, who pleaded that the special Labour Conference should be left free to make its own decision on August 10. Moreover, Henderson insisted that in case this decision should be in the affirmative, the Government should allow a Labour delegation to go to Stockholm, provided no members of the Government were members of that delegation. The following day, on August 8, the Cabinet met and discussed the issue again. A statement was read which indicated that, according to the Attorney General, it would be illegal for any British subject to associate with enemy subjects during wartime. It was decided, however, that no announcement about the legal aspects of foreign encounters should be made until after the August 10th Conference. The Cabinet meeting ended, but not without planting the seeds for future misunderstandings. Henderson left the meeting on the understanding that he would go before the special Labour meeting as Secretary of the Labour party and plead for a consultative Stockholm Conference. On the other hand, Lloyd George and the other Ministers carried away the impression that Henderson, in his combined capacity of Cabinet Member and Labour Secretary, would counsel his colleagues and followers against any kind of Conference.[96]

No wonder the Cabinet was startled to learn that upon addressing the special Labour Conference on August 10 Henderson had delivered an eloquent address in favor of Stockholm. Moreover, in the Cabinet there now developed unconcealed resentment over the Nabokoff incident.

On August 3, at the suggestion of the British Government, the Russian chargé in London, Constantin Nabokoff, advised Tereshchenko by cable that Downing Street was opposed to Stockholm. In this same cable, after mentioning that the position of the American Federation of Labor was reinforcing the anti-Stockholm Left, Nabokoff asked that he be authorized to declare that from the Russian point of view the Conference was "a party concern and not a matter of state." Tereshchenko's reply reached London at 4:00 P.M. on the 9th and was immediately forwarded by Nabokoff to Lloyd George. It stated that "although the Russian Government do not deem it possible to prevent Russian delegates from taking part in the Stockholm Conference,

96. Ibid., 97 (August 13, 1917), cols. 914–15, 925–30. Cf. Graubard, *British Labour and the Russian Revolution,* pp. 30–32.

they regard this Conference as a party concern, and its decisions in no wise binding upon the liberty of action of the Government." [97]

Lloyd George rushed a copy of this cable to Henderson in the evening of August 9, and again the following morning. However, much to the dismay of Lloyd George and his Ministers, notwithstanding this document, Henderson refused to change his strongly pro-Stockholm speech materially. Instead, in his address to the Labour Conference, Henderson only casually admitted "that such evidence as I have, though it is very slight, suggests that there has been some modification of the position of the new [Russian] Government as compared with the old, on the question of the proposed Conference." [98] Evidently not even Tereshchenko's cable had changed Henderson's estimate of Russia's military prospects, of the swelling peace sentiment in the Petrograd Soviet, and of Labour's ability to press for a revision of war aims without seriously endangering the political truce.

Therefore, Russia's repeated demand for a reformulation of war aims remained central to Henderson's brief. His motion that "the invitation to . . . Stockholm be accepted on condition that the Conference be consultative and not mandatory" was then adopted by a resounding vote of 1,846,000 to 550,000. [99] This three-to-one majority in favor of Stockholm surprised the Labour world, including Henderson, quite as much as it angered the press and the Cabinet, both of whom had anticipated its rejection. However, since the Miners' Federation immediately moved an amendment seeking to prevent minority Labourites from joining the Stockholm delegation, the Henderson victory seems, on close examination, less staggering. Disagreement on this issue of minority representation caused this special Labour Conference to be adjourned until the 21st. By that time Lloyd George had publicly announced that no passports would be issued, thereby strengthening the anti-Henderson forces. Consequently on the 21st the Miners' amendment was carried by an overwhelming vote of 2,124,000 to 175,000, while a protest against the Government's refusal of passports won by a bare 3,000 votes. [100] Still, the amendment ex-

97. Constantin Nabokoff, *The Ordeal of a Diplomat* (London, Duckworth, 1921), pp. 134–39. Cf. *PD*, 97 (August 13, 1917), cols. 927–30; and Hamilton, *Arthur Henderson*, pp. 145–48.

98. For the entire text of Henderson's address see LP, *Report of the Seventeenth Annual Conference* (Nottingham and London, 1918), pp. 47–51.

99. Ibid., pp. 4–5.

100. Ibid., p. 7. Although the vote within the Miners' Federation had been

cluding the ILP, the British Socialist party, and the Fabians [101] from
the projected Stockholm delegation violated the terms, as well as the
spirit, of the Petrograd Soviet's invitation.

In view of the outcome of the special Labour Conference, Henderson could no longer expect to find the Prime Minister on his side.
Lloyd George promptly informed him that his "retention of the position of Secretary of the Labour Party was no longer compatible" with
his "remaining a member of the War Cabinet." Henderson had no
choice but to hand in his resignation, which, "as everybody knows
. . . has arisen out of the Stockholm Conference." [102]

The Prime Minister now set out to prevent this resignation from
alienating too many Labourites. In a public letter, as well as in Commons, he insisted that Henderson had known of the Cabinet's opposition to Stockholm, and that he had refused to inform the Labour
Conference of the Provisional Government's change of heart. Meanwhile, the Premier had received Nabokoff's permission to publish the
"party concern" message in the hope of further undermining Henderson's position in the eyes of Labour.

However, whereas in England this publication did little except to
exacerbate the Lloyd George-Henderson feud, in the Petrograd Soviet
it caused a veritable furor. Insisting that the cable had not been meant
for publication, Kerensky and Tereshchenko severely reprimanded
Nabokoff. Also, they urged that out of consideration for their own
internal difficulties the British Government should not refuse the passports in question.[103] In an interview with Arthur Ransome, Petrograd
correspondent of the *Daily News*, Kerensky stated rather defensively
that he was not opposed to the Conference. "No. I have insisted again
and again that any opposition offered to it by the Allied Governments
. . . is simply playing into German hands . . . It is an entirely wrong
deduction to say that we are opposed to the Conference." [104]

---

very close, by the block system of voting the entire 600,000 Miners' votes were
cast against Stockholm. The setback of the Internationalists was, therefore, not
nearly so drastic as the vote indicated. *Labour Leader*, August 23, 1917.

101. The Executive Committee of the Fabians had not only appointed its delegates but even invited contributions to cover their expenses. Fabian Society,
35th Annual Report, p. 4.

102. *PD*, 97 (August 13, 1917), cols. 909–10.

103. Nabokoff, *The Ordeal of a Diplomat*, pp. 151–56; and Buchanan, *My
Mission to Russia*, 2, 163–64.

104. Ramsay MacDonald brought this Ransome interview to the attention of
the House of Commons. *PD*, 97 (August 16, 1917), cols. 1501–2.

The weak Provisional Government had tried to help its Ally in a domestic tangle at considerable risk to itself. Meanwhile Kerensky waited in vain for the reformulation of war aims which conceivably might contribute to the consolidation of Russia's own home front. *Le Temps* might as well have spoken for all the Allied foreign offices when it observed that Stockholm was a question not of doctrine but of expediency. The British and French governments did not consider it wise to surrender to the requirements of the Russian Revolution. Less restrained than France's semi-official paper, Sir Robert Cecil proclaimed that he "would as soon send a child of three up in control of an aeroplane as agree to the Labour party sending delegates to Stockholm." [105] Kerensky, however, could not afford this Cecilian rhetoric; he issued passports because in Russia a refusal would have been "impolitic." [106]

The inter-Allied Socialist Conference met in London on August 28 in an atmosphere of accentuated Government hostility. However, since this Conference had received the formal blessings of the War Cabinet, Lloyd George sought to strengthen its loyal Social Patriotic participants by securing the attendance of an American delegation. But the Prime Minister's efforts to involve Gompers in internationalist meetings were no more successful than Henderson's.[107] Hence, out of seventy attending delegates from eight countries, forty-six were British.[108]

The first act of this Conference was to issue a unanimous protest against the refusal of passports by the Allied and Associated Powers, and to ask that they immediately be granted to majority as well as to minority delegates.[109] Hereafter the proceedings were marked by continuous disagreements. Since the battle lines were drawn along majority and minority lines, rather than along national lines, the inter-Allied Socialist and Labour Conference clearly foreshadowed the difficulties which were bound to beset the even less homogeneous

105. *Le Temps,* August 12, 1917; and *PD,* 97 (August 16, 1917), col. 1510.
106. National Archives, Document 763.72119/736.
107. See *FR,* 1917, Supplement 2, *1,* 751; and American Federation of Labor, *Labor and the War: The American Federation of Labor and the Labor Movement of Europe and Latin America, 1914–1918* (1918), pp. 271–76.
108. *Labour Leader,* September 6, 1917.
109. LP, *Report of the Seventeenth Annual Conference* (Nottingham and London, 1918), pp. 9–10.

Stockholm conclave. In the French delegation the struggle between the Social Patriots and the Independents was particularly apparent. Determined to use this opportunity to stem further inroads by the *minoritaires* inside the SFIO, the Renaudel-Thomas faction took a very rigid nationalist stand. Only a threat to dissolve the Conference finally decided the French Social Patriots to participate in the deliberations of the Stockholm subcommittee, which met under the chairmanship of Ramsay MacDonald. However, the disagreements between the Social Patriots and the Independents were too strong to be overcome. The Stockholm committee failed to agree on the tactics to be followed by the Allied Socialists at Stockholm. Likewise, Sidney Webb, chairman of the committee dealing with general conditions of peace, reported the complete failure of his committee to agree on a text for a unified war-aims declaration.[110]

In the hope of resolving these differences the Conference appointed a standing committee which would work out some agreement in preparation for a later meeting. Meanwhile, however, even the official communiqué about these London proceedings confessed that "it could not be disguised that the outcome of the Conference was wholly disappointing." [111] Since Beatrice Webb had been close to the Conference, she may well have had good reason to speak of a "fiasco" which made her wonder "what Stockholm would have been like!" [112]

Judging by Woodrow Wilson's previous diplomatic pronouncements, the Internationalists undoubtedly were justified in counting on the President's support. After all, even the debates in the Soviet which had culminated in the Petrograd peace formula had drawn inspiration and guidance from the President's erstwhile peace without victory slogan. At this time, however, the American policy on the Stockholm Conference had to be formulated within a coalition framework. On May 9, while in Washington, Arthur James Balfour wrote to Secretary Lansing that should the French Government permit its minority Socialists to go to Stockholm, the British Government could expect great pressure from its own Socialists. Balfour informed the Secretary of State that in his view the Allies ought to adopt a common policy; accordingly he had cabled the Foreign Office in London

110. Ibid., p. 8; and *l'Humanité*, September 3 and 4, 1917.
111. Cited in Snowden, *An Autobiography, 1,* 479.
112. Cole, pp. 94–95.

"proposing that the question should be discussed with Mr. Page and the French Ambassador in London." [113] Upon seeing this letter, Wilson advised Lansing on May 11 that he "did not like the movement among the Socialists to confer about international affairs." Evidently Wilson feared that they would "make a deal of mischief, especially in connection with affairs in Russia." Nevertheless, confident that American Socialist delegates would either "make themselves hated or ridiculous," the President at first took a rather permissive view by recommending that the State Department "should neither give them leave nor seek to restrain them." [114] On May 19, however, Lansing informed Wilson that Paris and London felt that should America issue "passports to our Socialists," they would "be forced to do the same." [115] Three days later, with Wilson's agreement, Lansing cabled Ambassadors Page and Sharp that "under direction of the President, no passports [would] be issued to Socialists intending to attend the Stockholm Conference." [116]

Within a week Branting and Huysmans, in the name of the Stockholm Committee, sent Wilson a cable expressing the hope that America's refusal was based on a misunderstanding, since the Conference was convoked "on principles laid down in your Senate speech." Wilson and Lansing were equally unimpressed by this reference to the President's former pronouncement.[117]

Washington's rigid stand led Ramsay MacDonald to express his concern in a letter formally addressed to Buckler at the American Embassy, but destined for both House and Wilson. According to the ILP leader, all progressives were "amazed at the attitude taken by your government regarding the Stockholm Conference, as they expected that America, with its republican and democratic traditions, would have stood for the rights of the peoples." According to MacDonald, one of the most deplorable consequences of America's entry into the war had been the decided "hardening of the dominating opinion" in Allied countries at the very time when the political truce was least stable. Consequently, he anticipated more troublous rather

113. Balfour to Lansing, May 9, 1917, Wilson Papers.
114. *FR, Lansing Papers, 2,* 17.
115. Lansing to Wilson, May 19, 1917, Wilson Papers.
116. *FR,* 1917, Supplement 2, *1,* 739.
117. Ibid., pp. 739–40; and National Archives, Documents 763.72119/631 and /646.

than easier times for the dissidents, as well as a dangerous neglect of Russian opinions and interests. Through the same channel, Charles Trevelyan, one of the moving spirits of the UDC, expressed the fear that Wilson might contribute to "one of the most tragic reverses in history" by endorsing the diplomacy of the war cabinets and thereby driving Russia into either anarchy or a separate peace.[118]

Paris and London never ceased to be concerned by the continuing efforts of their own, as well as American, Socialists to change the minds of policy-makers in Washington. Following the meeting of French and British Socialists with the delegation from the Petrograd Soviet in Paris, Ambassador Sharp cabled that Cambon had "expressed the hope that President Wilson would not look with favor upon Socialist representatives from the United States attending the Stockholm Conference." Again, five days later, on August 7, Sharp reported that according to Cambon not only was "France . . . unalterably opposed to . . . Stockholm, but England and Italy would also pursue the same course."[119] Then, on August 11, Ambassador Spring Rice saw Secretary Lansing in Washington with a note to the effect that Britain would refuse the passports, as would Paris and Rome, and that provided the United States supported this course, a "unanimous coalition position" would be achieved. Thereupon the Secretary of State reassured the British Ambassador that "we had again refused passports and should continue [the] same policy."[120] A few days later the State Department received still another reminder that U.S. foreign policy henceforth could only be made with constant regard for Allied policy. In reporting Kerensky's view that by refusing passports the Allies were giving the Stockholm "deliberations weight which they otherwise would not carry," Ambassador

118. Both letters are cited in Allan Nevins, *Henry White—Thirty Years of American Diplomacy* (New York, Harper, 1930), pp. 343, 345–46. Huysmans concluded that "the United States, instead of remaining true to her liberal traditions, violently swung over to the other side and supported the policy of refusal." Comité Organisateur, *Stockholm*, p. xxiii.

119. National Archives, Documents 763.72119/702 and /711.

120. Ibid., Document 763.72119/791—½. Morris Hillquit, member of the National Executive Committee of the dissident Socialist Party of America and its representative in the International Socialist Bureau, on the strength of a cable from the Chairman of the Petrograd Soviet on July 20 again applied for a passport. On August 7 Paris and London were informed that his request had been turned down. Ibid., Document 763.72119/693a.

Francis recommended that Washington follow the lead of Paris and London, or of London alone.[121]

Even though the *New Republic* did not favor Stockholm, it felt that the denial of passports appeared to be "questionable diplomacy." Like their progressive colleagues in Europe, the editors were deeply concerned about the future of the Russian Revolution, and sought to counteract the rapidly spreading and officially generated belief that the Conference was merely a German plot.[122] Woodrow Wilson, however, was far from blind to the political battle which was raging in Petrograd. As he prepared to dispatch the Root Mission, having decided it ought to include two labor delegates, he realized that because Gompers and his associates were "known to be pronounced opponents of Socialism, they would hardly be influential in the ruling circles in Petrograd." [123] Yet in order not to weaken the AFL *vis-à-vis* the politically ineffective American dissidents and in order to send a delegation representative of American labor, Washington could not send a Socialist. Furthermore, Wilson's cablegram introducing the Mission to Russia was a "crisp and uncompromising fighting document." In it he charged the German Government with seeking a restoration of the status quo ante through a negotiated peace; he also maintained that since the war had issued from that status, it "must be altered in such fashion as to prevent any such hideous thing from ever happening again." [124] Thus even though the Provisional Government and the majority of the Soviet were primarily concerned with securing a revision of war aims—to which Stockholm could make a contribution—Wilson was apprehensive lest these efforts lead to a premature peace (without victory!).

In his Flag Day address of June 14 the President tried to expose the Stockholm movement as Germany's new "intrigue for peace." He declared that because the Reich Government realized "what immense strength the forces of justice and of liberalism [were] gathering out of this war," they were using "liberals . . . socialists, the leaders of labor, the thinkers they [had] hitherto sought to silence" in this peace enterprise. "Their present particular aim is to deceive all those who

121. Ibid., Document 763.72119/763.
122. *New Republic* (June 2, 1917), p. 119.
123. Cited in Baker, *Woodrow Wilson, Life and Letters,* 7, 28–29.
124. For the text of this cable see Baker and Dodd, *The Public Papers of Woodrow Wilson,* 5, 50. For editorial comment see the *New Republic* (June 16, 1917), p. 171.

throughout the world stand for the rights of peoples and the self-government of nations." [125] Was Wilson concerned lest the Central Powers really succeed in posing as the sponsors of what looked like a rapidly growing movement for a definition of purpose and a peace by understanding, thereby competing with the Allied-sponsored crusade for democracy?

There is considerable evidence that in the summer of 1917 many important officials in Berlin, including the Kaiser, were seriously weighing the advisability of having recourse to this ideology in their search for a negotiated settlement. Neither the SPD nor the Independents encountered difficulties when they applied for passports to go to Stockholm. The peace pressure from Vienna was even stronger, and Czernin dispatched the Austrian Social Democrats to the Swedish capital with the certainty that they would give a status-quo-ante interpretation to the Petrograd peace formula. Thus far, however, the July 19th Peace Resolution had been the only indication of waning confidence in important circles in Berlin and Vienna. Then followed the Pope's peace message, dated August 1 and published on the 15th.

Actually, even though the Papal message was timed to commemorate the third anniversary of the outbreak of war, its genesis reached back about three months.[126] On May 13 Cardinal Pacelli had been nominated by the Pope to replace the Papal Nuncio in Munich who had recently passed away. After arriving in the Bavarian capital in late May 1917, Pacelli presented his credentials to King Ludwig III of Bavaria. He also met with Erzberger, who in all likelihood informed him not only of the growing war-aims movement inside Germany, but also of Austria-Hungary's intensified longing for a negotiated peace.[127] There is no way of accurately reconstructing the Pacelli-Erzberger conversations. Suffice it to say, however, that the Pope's representative conferred with the political leader of Germany's Catholic Center party who also had intimate relations with the Government of the Catholic Austro-Hungarian Empire. Even though both *Germania* and the *Osservatore Romano* subsequently denied that any one of the Central

125. Baker and Dodd, 5, 65.
126. For a detailed, pro-Vatican account of the Holy See mediation attempt see Friedrich Ritter von Lama, *Die Friedensvermittlung Papst Benedikt XV*, Munich, J. Kösel and F. Pustet, 1932. A more compact discussion of this episode can be found in Humphrey Johnson, *Vatican Diplomacy in the World War*, Oxford, Blackwell, 1933.
127. Cf. GFM, Container 1123.

Powers had been in any way instrumental in either the drafting or the timing of the message, the Allied press could not be stopped from labeling it an enemy-inspired diplomatic maneuver. Curiously enough, inside Germany the overwhelmingly Protestant Pan-Germans, as well as the right wing of the National Liberal and Progressive parties, accused the Pope of having allowed himself to be used by the Allies. Likewise, the German Supreme Command looked upon the Vatican's preliminary feelers as part of the political offensive inside Germany which soon culminated in the July 19th Resolution. Parallel to the peace campaign of the Second International, the diplomatic initiative of the Catholic international found both friends and foes inside each of the two belligerent camps.[128]

Even if the Pope's message was not directly inspired by Vienna or Berlin, there was nevertheless a good basis for Allied suspicion. At the time Paris and London knew little about Pacelli's diplomacy.[129] However, since then it has been established that when the new Nuncio presented his credentials to Bethmann-Hollweg in Berlin on June 26, 1917, he conveyed the impression to the Chancellor that for the first time since the beginning of the war the Vatican now saw the possibility of peace; furthermore, he sought to induce the German Foreign Ministry to communicate its war aims to the Holy See so that they could be used as a guide in a mediation offer to be launched at a psychologically propitious moment.[130]

Three days later, as a follow-up to this exploratory Berlin conversation, Pacelli had an audience with the German Kaiser at General Headquarters in Kreuznach. On this occasion Wilhelm II, who did not seem hostile to the Vatican initiative, expressed his concern about the fact that thus far Social Democracy had been the only great international organization to have both the wisdom and the courage to explore peace opportunities. The Kaiser thought that since it might be fatal if international Socialism were allowed by default to reap the credit for this relentless peace search, it was in the interest of the Catholic Church, the other major international force, also to take up

128. Von Lama, *Die Friedensvermittlung Papst Benedikt XV*, p. 85.

129. Cf. *The Peace Proposals Made by His Holiness the Pope to the Belligerent Powers on August 1, 1917, and Correspondence Relative Thereto*, London, H.M.S.O., 1919.

130. Bethmann-Hollweg, *Betrachtungen zum Weltkriege*, 2, 211.

the peace struggle.[131] During the first three weeks of July, however, as the new Reichstag majority pressed its political offensive, the crisis in Germany made it inopportune for the Nuncio to pursue his efforts. But once the July 19th Resolution had been passed and Michaelis was in office, Pacelli renewed his diplomatic explorations. From July 24 to July 26 he tried to get the new Chancellor and the Foreign Office to confirm their agreement with both the spirit and the letter of the Reichstag Resolution. Above all, Nuncio Pacelli, as also Scheidemann and Czernin, was anxious to have the German Government unequivocally renounce Belgium, since a negotiated peace was inconceivable on any other basis. Michaelis, however, was too heavily mortgaged to both Ludendorff and the General Staff to make this concession.[132]

Nevertheless the Holy See persisted in its plan to undertake a mediation effort, possibly encouraged by Vienna, which now had even less to expect from Michaelis than heretofore from Bethmann-Hollweg. Although the Pope's message called for a straightforward restoration of Belgium and the evacuation of French territory in exchange for a restitution of German colonies, it made no reference to the principle of self-determination.[133] Indeed, the Vatican was calling for a status-quo-ante-bellum peace favorable to the Dual Monarchy. No wonder both Beneš and Masaryk vehemently denounced the Pope as an agent of Czernin.[134]

Notwithstanding this striking neglect of the self-determination gospel, the Vatican message otherwise strongly registered the 1917 impact of the New Diplomacy. For example, the Pope touched on the freedom of the seas, the limitation of armaments, arbitration courts, economic cooperation, and the Balkan and Polish problems. Indeed, it would seem that this incipient *rerum novarum* for international diplomacy was issued by the Church not only as part of a relatively narrow and desperate pursuit of Austro-Hungarian salvation but also in answer to the forces of movement which currently professed their conversion to the New Diplomacy. The Vatican called for postwar

---

131. Ibid., pp. 213–14; Erzberger, *Erlebnisse im Weltkrieg*, p. 274; Philipp Scheidemann, *Papst, Kaiser und Sozialdemokratie in ihren Friedensbemühungen im Sommer 1917*, Berlin, Verlag für Sozialwissenschaft, 1921.

132. See Michaelis, *Für Staat und Volk*, pp. 337–38; and Ludendorff, *The General Staff and Its Problems*, 2, 477 ff.

133. For the complete text of the Pope's message see Dickinson, pp. 47–50.

134. Beneš, *Souvenirs de guerre, 1*, 523.

arbitration and disarmament because "a new social order was going to emerge from this war which [would] give a moral guarantee against the recurrence of such catastrophes." [135] Moreover, Rome concluded that "everybody [was] extremely worried about the constantly more threatening economic conditions which the continuing war was creating in the belligerent countries." Finally, at the Holy See the "parties of order" were thought to be justified in their concern for the simmering social unrest which was likely to follow the war. The official organ of the Vatican actually queried whether in addition to reducing the dangers of another war, the savings accruing from reduced armaments expenditures could not serve to mitigate these anticipated social upheavals.[136]

Regardless of the Holy See's claim that the Pope's message was not calculated to be a piece of "popular" diplomacy but was meant exclusively for the Government Chancelleries, the fact remains that once it was published in the Italian and British press it became an inseparable part of the wider war-aims agitation. Indeed, l'Humanité sarcastically commented that "Benedict XV now also had answered the Stockholm questionnaire." [137] Actually the Vatican's representative in Bern boasted that "just as the Dome of St. Peter dominates its surroundings, so the Papal proclamation overshadows the confused peace efforts of the Second International." Furthermore, Monsignore Marchetti-Selvaggiani suggested that the Pontiff's prescription coincided with the "no annexations, no indemnities" formula of the Russians.[138] Inside Germany the Vossische Zeitung commented that the Pope might have spoken "partly in order to supplement the Socialist efforts, partly, however, out of anxiety at the threatening overweight of Socialist tendencies." Similarly, the Berliner Tageblatt held that "the Pope, in the name of religion, [was] trying to do what Stockholm, in the name of democracy [had] failed or [would] fail to do." [139]

Especially because the Pope's diplomatic initiative also reflected his moral and humanitarian preoccupations, it would certainly have re-

135. Quoted from an article in the August 20, 1917, issue of the Osservatore Romano cited in von Lama, Die Friedensvermittlung Papst Benedikt XV, pp. 85–86.
136. Loc. cit.
137. L'Humanité, August 17, 1917.
138. Cited in Scheidemann, Papst, Kaiser, und Sozialdemokratie in ihren Friedensbemühungen im Sommer 1917, p. 21.
139. Vossische Zeitung, August 18, 1917, and Berliner Tageblatt, August 16, 1917, cited in DR, EPS (August 30, 1917), p. 514.

ceived Woodrow Wilson's blessings if launched prior to February 1917. One-half year later, however, the President's response would have to be more restrained because of his dual position as war leader of America and as diplomat of the Allied Coalition. As in the case of the Stockholm invitations, inter-Allied consultations would have to precede any official, public reaction. Consequently, on August 18, 1917, on Wilson's suggestion, Secretary Lansing instructed all United States diplomatic missions in Allied countries to "ascertain the views of the Government to which [they were] accredited in regard to the Pope's recent peace communication." [140] In the meantime the French War Cabinet had already decided that, because of the unsatisfactory nature of the Pontiff's manifesto, France, as well as her Allies, ought to ignore it.[141] According to Balfour, even though the British Cabinet was more favorably disposed toward a reply than its French counterpart, it dreaded the "idea of any joint endeavor of composing an elaborate document dealing with complex problems necessarily looked at from somewhat different angles by each belligerent." [142] Hence both Paris and London counseled Washington either to ignore the Pope's message or to react in an altogether casual fashion.

From other sources, however, different advice was being pressed on Wilson. Especially Colonel House was quick to realize that the President was caught between an emotional attachment to his prewar peace without victory diplomacy, and the harsher dictates of war diplomacy. Consequently, in the hope that a careful analysis of this new phase in war-aims politics might help his Chief reach a prompt decision, Colonel House wrote three letters to the White House. In the first one, dated August 15, he confessed that in his own view the situation was "full of danger as well as hope." The danger areas were France, where difficulties of getting through another winter loomed large, and Russia, which was "so eager to get at her internal problems that she will soon, almost certainly, insist upon peace on a basis of status quo ante." [143]

Above all, House continued to be concerned by the dangers of Germany's penetrating deeper into Russia. Presently he thought it more

140. National Archives, Document 763.7219/737a.
141. Poincaré, *Au Service de la France*, 9, 251.
142. Seymour, *Intimate Papers*, 3, 155–56. About ten days earlier, through William Wiseman, Balfour had initiated a request for the President's views on the Pope's appeal. Ibid., pp. 151–52.
143. Ibid., p. 153.

important "that Russia should weld herself into a virile republic than
it [was] that Germany should be beaten to her knees." Because should
the Russian "disorder reach a point . . . where Germany can intervene, it is conceivable that in the future she may be able to dominate
Russia both politically and economically." On the other hand, should
Russia become "firmly established in democracy"—and an adroit war-
aims statement could strengthen this trend—"German autocracy would
be. compelled to yield to a representative Government within a few
years." [144] Moreover, the answer to the Pope might be so phrased as
"to leave the door open," while at the same time accelerating the
breakdown inside Germany. Thus House recommended that the President state that it was "hardly fair to ask the people of the Allied
countries to discuss terms with a military autocracy." Likewise, Secretary Lansing, in agreement with the Russian Ambassador in Washington, wrote Wilson that "to make peace by accepting guarantees
from the military rulers of Germany would only be to postpone the
struggle, not to end it." [145]

Two days of reflection caused House to write Wilson a more decisive
letter on August 17. He now called on the President

> to take the peace negotiations out of the hands of the Pope and
> hold them in your own. . . . Badly as the Allied cause is going,
> Germany is in a worse condition. It is now a race of endurance.
> . . . Germany and Austria are a seething mass of discontent. The
> Russian Revolution has shown the people their power and has
> put the fear of God into the hearts of the imperialists. A state-
> ment from you regarding peace aims of this country would bring
> about almost revolution in Germany in the event the existing
> Government dared to oppose them. . . . You can make a state-
> ment that will not only be the undoing of autocratic Germany,
> but one that will strengthen the hands of the Russian liberals
> in their purpose to mould their country into a mighty republic.[146]

House also referred to the danger of labeling every peace move
"German-inspired," and re-emphasized the importance of seeking to
enlist the new Reichstag majority into the Allied crusade for democracy. After a conversation with the Russian Ambassador, House

144. Ibid., pp. 153–54.
145. Lansing to Wilson, August 20 and 21, 1917, Wilson Papers.
146. Seymour, *Intimate Papers, 3,* 156–57.

reported in a third letter that, according to Bakhmetieff, "success or failure in Russia" might depend on the President's answer to the Pope, especially since the Allies had "made a mistake in refusing passports to the Stockholm Conference." [147]

About this same time Lincoln Steffens arrived from Russia. He carried a message from Kerensky for the President to the effect that the secret treaties were the "hub" of the situation. After delivering this message to Wilson on June 26, Steffens wrote Colonel House that, provided the Allies revise their war aims, the Russians could "be made to fight"; he felt compelled to add, however, that even that "may be an illusion." [148] Since the *New Republic* shared Bakhmetieff's and Steffens' primary concern for Russia, rumors that the European Allies proposed to ignore the Pope's proposal caused it to warn that Wilson's silence would alienate Russia. This liberal periodical also suggested that a negative or merely barren reply might magnify popular discontent with the refusal of passports for Stockholm.[149]

When Wilson's reply to the Pope finally appeared on August 29, 1917, it was very carefully worded and fell short of a comprehensive war-aims pronouncement. Nevertheless, it went one step beyond all preceding Allied statements by declaring forcefully that "we cannot take the word of the present rulers of Germany as a guarantee of anything that is to endure." [150] Hence as of now the distinction between rulers and peoples became central to the official crusade ideology. In connection with his reply, Wilson admitted that even though he "tried to indicate the attitude of this country on the points discussed in the socialistic and other camps," he did not think "it wise to say more or to be more specific because it might provoke dissenting voices from France or Italy." [151]

In the Allied governments Wilson's reply was received with great favor, particularly because it confirmed the President's tremendous

147. Ibid., pp. 157–58.

148. *The Autobiography of Lincoln Steffens* (New York, Harcourt, Brace, 1931), p. 765; and Ella Winters and Granville Hicks, eds., *The Letters of Lincoln Steffens* (2 vols. New York, Harcourt, Brace, 1938), 1, 399–400.

149. *New Republic* (August 18, 1917), p. 57; (August 25, 1917), p. 99.

150. The American Ambassador in London approvingly commented that this was "of course *the* necessary condition of peace." Hendrick, *The Life and Letters of Walter H. Page*, 3, 408. For the complete text of the President's reply to the Pope see Baker and Dodd, *The Public Papers of Woodrow Wilson*, 5, 93–96, esp. p. 96.

151. Cited in Baker, *Woodrow Wilson, Life and Letters*, 7, 231.

war enthusiasm. The British Foreign Office immediately advised Lord Bertie and Sir George Buchanan that "in view of the note sent to the Pope by President Wilson, no further reply of any kind to the Vatican [was] required." [152] Indeed, it seems that since both Rome and Paris [153] took the same position, this was the first occasion on which the American President had spoken authoritatively for England, France, and Italy.[154] Gradually, both the initiative and the direction of Allied war-aims diplomacy were shifting to Washington. Ambassador W. H. Page even reported that in British opinion "the leadership of the war" was now "definitely and confessedly" transferred to Wilson.[155] Meanwhile, in Germany, whereas the Right complained of Wilson's impudent meddling with the Reich's internal affairs, the Reichstag majority had now found additional grounds for pressing its democratization campaign.[156]

All along the Stockholm debate had continued unabated in all the Allied nations. The Vatican initiative had merely served to expand further the political sectors which were taking an active part in the highly intensified war-aims dialectic. Both Stockholm and the Holy See were serving a similar function: they sharpened the challenge to the Old Diplomacy and its traditionalist approach to wartime diplomacy as well as to peace planning. However, since the Socialist legions were better organized than the Church members, and since the Petrograd Soviet had taken the initiative, the Stockholm Conference left a more permanent mark on wartime politics than did the Pope's manifesto. Since it was the Stockholm issue which had effected the posing of the war-aims problem in its full political complexity, no degree of censorship, however strict, could possibly remove it from the agenda of public debate. Furthermore, throughout Europe, Stockholm had succeeded in pointing up the ever-growing interaction between foreign and domestic policy.

152. *British and Foreign State Papers, 1917–1918* (London, H.M.S.O., 1921), *111*, 582.

153. French press reactions were almost unanimously favorable. See *DR*, APS (September 12, 1917), pp. 449–50.

154. Through the Russian Embassy in Washington, Tereshchenko also indicated his approval of Wilson's message. National Archives, Document 763.72119/816.

155. Page to Wilson, September 3, 1917, Wilson Papers.

156. For an extensive survey of the German press reaction see *DR*, EPS (September 13, 1917), pp. 595–98.

In both Paris and London "war had broken out between those wanting to go to Stockholm and those who wanted to prevent them from going." [157] The denial of passports proved once again that the supremacy of the forces of order could not be challenged as long as the leaders themselves were convinced, and convinced the general public, that a military victory could be won. First in England and then in France, major cabinet changes ensued. In Britain Arthur Henderson vacated his place in the War Cabinet in favor of G. N. Barnes—who hereafter loyally served the center-right Government headed by Lloyd George. Likewise in France, Albert Thomas sacrificed his ministerial portfolio for Stockholm.

The political crisis in Paris was delayed until September 7, when the Ribot Cabinet tendered its resignation. President Poincaré invited Ribot to try to work out a new ministerial combination. However, the Socialists as well as the Caillaux Radicals refused their support to the former Prime Minister. Both were resentful of his failure to support Malvy effectively, of his adamant refusal of passports, and of his apparent readiness to sanction repressive measures against dissenters.[158]

Painlevé was next to try to form a coalition government. In the Permanent Administrative Commission of the SFIO the Renaudel-Thomas faction advocated conditional participation: the SFIO would enter the Painlevé Cabinet provided civil liberties and workers' rights were protected and provided the procedures of secret diplomacy were abandoned. On the other hand, the Pressemane faction maintained that the SFIO's continuing support of the war effort did not require ministerial participation. The Social Patriots would undoubtedly have carried the day in the Commission if Painlevé had not insisted that Ribot become his Foreign Minister in the new Cabinet.[159] Quite as much as Painlevé was determined not to disavow his predecessor's foreign and domestic policies, the Socialists were not prepared to abandon their opposition to a mere cabinet reshuffle. Painlevé's Cabinet was invested on September 13 by 368 votes, with 131 abstentions. Among these abstentionists, eighty-six were Socialists and forty-five were Radical Socialists.[160]

157. *Journal de Genève*, August 11, 1917.
158. Bonnefous, *Histoire politique de la Troisième République*, 2, 307.
159. *L'Humanité*, September 8 and 13, 1917.
160. Bonnefous, *Histoire politique de la Troisième République*, 2, 308.

Hence in France the *union sacrée* was broken, even though the SFIO neither voted against Painlevé nor threatened to oppose subsequent war credits. It was no secret to anyone that the Left asserted its hostility to Ribot and Painlevé because both "had opposed the trip of the French Socialist delegates to Stockholm." [161] Furthermore, since this was the first wartime Government in which Malvy was absent from the Ministry of Interior, the Socialists and the left wing of the Radical Socialists were also defeated in the realm of domestic policy.

It should be noted that the Social Patriots' opposition to the new Cabinet was strengthened by their concern with developments inside the SFIO. They knew that at the National Congress, which was scheduled to meet in Bordeaux from October 6 to 8, 1917, the *minoritaires* had decided to stage a powerful drive for control of the party. For fear of being accused of being more interested in a few ministerial posts than in the principles and programs of Socialism, the Majoritarians could not afford to appear any less anti-Government than their rivals.

At the Bordeaux Congress the majority resolution in favor of Stockholm, national defense, war credits, and conditional cabinet participation gathered 1552 votes; however, three minority motions managed to collect a total of 1337 votes.[162] Pressemane's resolution, the mildest of these three, won the support of 834 *minoritaires* by opposing cabinet participation, and by seeking to spell out concrete war-aims conditions for all future war-credit votes. Three weeks later a comparably enlarged opposition was evident at the Congress of the Radical Socialists.[163]

But Clemenceau's rise to power could not be delayed any longer, partly because this dissent could not be allowed to take still greater proportions. In the face of another taxing winter campaign, there was great need for a strong, effective administration and leadership. In anticipation of this need, Clemenceau had for many months prepared his candidacy. Now, on November 16, 1917, he could count on the support of the overwhelming majority of the *Chambre*, even though

161. *Le Temps*, September 13, 1917; and *l'Humanité*, September 13, 1917.

162. The most complete record of the proceedings at Bordeaux is in *l'Humanité*, October 7 to 11, 1917. Cf. *le Temps*, October 11, 1917; and Guilbeaux, *Le Mouvement socialiste et syndicaliste français pendant la guerre*, pp. 34–35.

163. Marcel Laurent, *Nos Gouvernements de guerre* (Paris, Alcan, 1920), pp. 166–68; Armand Albert-Petit, *La France de la guerre* (3 vols. Paris, Bossard, 1918–19), 3, 70–71; *le Temps*, October 29, 1917.

after the investiture debate sixty-four Socialists voted against him, while twenty-five Socialists and fifteen Radical Socialists abstained.[164] Henceforth, Clemenceau headed a pronounced right-wing, though predominantly Radical Socialist, Cabinet, with the enthusiastic encouragement of Barrès, Daudet, and Maurras. Also, President Poincaré congratulated the new Premier for taking the reins of power with "the strong determination to repress defeatist propaganda and to punish all crimes of treason."[165] On November 20, 1917, the Tiger boldly told the Lower House that "if you ask me about my war aims, I reply: my aim is to be victorious."[166]

In both England and France the Right was more firmly in political control of the cabinets than at any other time during the war. As a result, the prospects for a war-aims revision were less encouraging than in the summer. After a meeting with Lloyd George on November 16, Colonel House informed Wilson that it was "useless to try to get either the British or the French to designate terms," and that neither could meet the Petrograd formula.[167] The Clemenceau Cabinet unequivocally declared through the semi-official le Temps that French "demands [would] depend quite logically on the conditions in which Germany [would] be vanquished." Furthermore, le Temps complained that the Socialists were blind to the facts of life largely because they were "obsessed by an ideal formula of a League of Nations which, if successful, would subject the whole world to the control of the Workers' International."[168] Also, Clemenceau now supplemented his motto je fais la guerre with the insistence that not a utopian league but a permanent preponderance of military power was the only guarantee of a lasting peace.[169]

Just the same the Stockholm imbroglio not only had fortified the progressive forces but also had led to a clarification of the peace strategy and aims of the major dissenting factions. Above all the policies of the Second as well as of the Second-and-a-Half Internationals began to emerge in clearer contrast to those of the Third International. Until recently the Internationalist movement had been seriously handi-

164. Bonnefous, Histoire politique de la Troisième République, 2, 351.

165. L'Action Française, November 17, 1917; and Joseph Caillaux, Mes Mémoirs (3 vols. Paris, Plon, 1947), 3, 361.

166. Cited in Bonnefous, Histoire politique de la Troisième République, 2, 349.

167. Seymour, Intimate Papers, 3, 233.

168. Le Temps, October 13, 1917.

169. Cf. Journal de Genève, November 30, 1917.

capped by the many Socialists who had become prisoners of the war cabinets.[170] For quite some months before their actual resignation, both Henderson and Thomas must have been aware that without any major say in policy they had served as hostages for the good behavior of the Left. Now the passport issue served to point up the influence, or rather the lack of influence, of the majority Socialists.

As the "Cabinet left Mr. Henderson on the mat, it placed Labour on the map." In his war-aims campaign, Henderson had started to work closely with both the ILP and the UDC; moreover, he soon "determined to create an independent political party, capable of becoming H. M. Government." [171] The Fabian Society estimated that Henderson's resignation may have been the most "noteworthy result" of the still-born Stockholm Conference, especially because he was left free "to devote his energies to the urgent work" of preparing the Labour party for the next General Election.[172] Consequently, though Stockholm might have been expected to cause an irreparable split in British Labour, it "proved a starting point of an irresistible movement towards consolidation": Lloyd George unwittingly had "galvanized the Labour Movement into new life." [173]

Likewise in France, as a result of the struggle over passports, "the Socialist party, followed by certain Radicals, sought to recapture its political virginity by taking a systematic opposition attitude towards the Government." [174] Once Henderson and Thomas had failed to wrest any war-aims concessions from the cabinets, they could stay on as ministers only at the grave risk of thereby accentuating the radicalization of the Labour party and the SFIO. By leaving the cabinets they and their supporters were able to share the leadership of the organized Left with the Independents. However, in so doing they were forced to subscribe with progressively fewer reservations to the war-aims platform of the Independents.

The defeat of Stockholm left the Maximalists in a highly equivocal position. On the one hand, they were jubilant over this failure of reformist, bourgeois internationalism. Along with their jubilation, they propagated the idea that since the denial of passports had succeeded in undermining the project, it should now be clear to all Socialists

170. Louis, La Crise du socialisme mondiale, p. 59.
171. Cole, p. 94; and Brockway, Socialism over Sixty Years, p. 158.
172. Fabian Society, 35th Annual Report, p. 4.
173. New Republic (December 1, 1917), p. 117.
174. Goguel, La Politique des partis sous la IIIe République, pp. 162–63.

that the entire enterprise was being sponsored by government-inspired Socialists. Thus the Maximalists presented those Internationalists who had built their expectations on this peace initiative with a partly justified "we told you so," implying that the only road to an effective Stockholm was a proletarian revolution. On the other hand, however, for intraparty consumption, the extreme Left continued to label Stockholm as "voluntary preparatory work for the future congress of government diplomats." Accordingly, the Independents and the Social Patriots were accused of assisting the bourgeoisie in preparing a peaceful accommodation among capitalist governments, instead of promoting the cause of class warfare. According to the *Spartakusbriefe,* it was only thanks to the Petrograd Soviet's peace formula that the Stockholm promoters had managed to maintain a Socialist appearance.[175]

These tensions inside the Socialist movement again foreshadowed the eventual split in the Second International, with the two major factions attracted to Wilson's New Diplomacy, and the smallest faction enrolled in Lenin's Third International. Since in the fall of 1917 the overwhelming majority of the growing dissident movement refused to embrace the civil-war gospel, it was clear that its growing and continuing pressure would be exerted in favor of a revision of war aims. In October 1917 the UDC proclaimed that the Petrograd peace formula had "given new life and inspiration to all the democratic forces everywhere which [were] working towards a permanent peace. . . . While the governments [had] not yet been able to evolve a policy which they [dared] publish to the world, the democracies of the belligerent countries had taken the lead and expressed in clear and emphatic terms their determination to secure a Peoples' Peace."[176] Certainly it would have been "a most dangerous delusion to suppose that the 'turning down of Stockholm' [meant] that the vast popular current flowing towards a more democratic Europe [had] ceased to flow."[177] On the contrary, the popular currents continued to expand, and it was up to the governments to bring about the revision of war aims. Whereas this revision would be completed too late to help stem the Bolshevik tide in Russia, the November Revolution itself was destined to make a powerful contribution to the liberalization of Allied war-aims diplomacy.

175. *Spartakusbriefe,* No. 6 (August 1917), p. 114.
176. UDC leaflet entitled *The Basis for a Peoples' Peace.*
177. *New Europe* (August 30, 1917), p. 198.

SECOND PHASE: EUROPE AND THE
BOLSHEVIK REVOLUTION

5. THE NOVEMBER REVOLUTION

AND THE PEACE DECREE

BOTH before and during the war many articulate theoreticians of "socialist-pacifism" had emphatically branded war as evil and ruinous. All along, however, a less numerous though no less articulate group of Marxist publicists had speculated hopefully about the "revolutionary-progressive" consequences which a major European conflagration was likely to engender. No sooner had Lenin returned to Russia in April 1917 than he concluded irrevocably that the World War was the most dynamic and trusted ally of the unfolding Russian Revolution. As the outstanding exponent of "revolution through war," Lenin unequivocally declared before a Bolshevik caucus in Petrograd on April 17 that "the basic question is our attitude towards the war." Lenin soon crystallized the Bolshevik attitude in the first of his April Theses: [1] notwithstanding the prevailing support by the great majority of the Russian proletariat and peasantry of the defensist Provisional Government, "not the slightest concession must be made to revolutionary defensism" by the Maximalists. In all of Europe, but especially in Russia, the treacherous war was bound to keep propelling more and more workers, peasants, and soldiers into the revolutionary movement. Lenin urged his followers to promote the revolution in every possible way, while at the same time warning them to be careful not to preach revolutionary defeatism too openly in order to avoid being labeled German-inspired or German-controlled agents.[2] The Bolsheviks would have to use great care as well as skill in explaining to the

1. For the text of the ten April Theses see Lenin, *Works, 20,* Pt. I, pp. 95–103.
2. Ibid., *21,* Pt. I, p. 138.

masses the inseparable connection between capitalism and the imperialist war; the workers, peasants, and soldiers had to be convinced that "without the overthrow of capital it is *impossible* to conclude the war with a really democratic, non-oppressive peace." [3]

Moreover, by insisting that to ignore "the whole of international relations" would be tantamount to committing a grave error in political strategy,[4] Lenin proved his daring but perceptive insight into the necessary relationship of the Russian—as well as the all-European—peace issue to the simmering revolutionary crisis. In ever-increasing numbers the Russian masses were focusing their hopes and aspirations on every proposal which seemed to promise an early, if not an immediate, end to the war. Consequently Lenin proceeded to fashion his peace call into "a clear-cut political issue"; soon his peace program emerged as the focal point of his entire revolutionary program as well as strategy.[5]

Now Lenin considered it his primary political duty to impress ever wider sectors of both the educated and the uneducated public that "in order to make an end to this war, all power must pass to the revolutionary class." [6] Lenin knew that in the other belligerent nations the Maximalists also were participating in peace campaigns. However, whereas the most that the German and French left-extremists could achieve in the middle of 1917 was a further impairment of the political truce, in Russia, because of the revolutionary crisis and the precarious dual-power relationship between the Provisional Government and the Petrograd Soviet, the Bolsheviks could realistically nurse much greater ambitions. To begin with, they could see to it that a defensist *Burgfrieden* would be given neither the time nor the opportunity to consolidate. Furthermore, since the Revolution had recently endowed Russia with a greater "degree of freedom" than was in evidence in any other belligerent nation just now, Lenin insisted that the Bolsheviks draw every possible advantage from this new-found liberty of political action. In his view, Russia's peculiarly favorable political conditions placed the "responsibility before the International proletariat" for a daring peace offensive squarely on the shoulders of his party.[7]

3. Ibid., *20*, Pt. I, p. 95.
4. Ibid.
5. Ibid., p. 315.
6. Ibid., p. 280.
7. Ibid., p. 95, and *21*, Pt. I, p. 272.

The Bolsheviks proceeded to build their propaganda program around simple and straightforward slogans. They appealed to the war-weary masses with such uncomplicated formulas as "war is evil, peace is a blessing." [8] Given the critical conditions of 1917, this kind of slogan not only made many converts to their revolutionary ranks in Russia but also established an ideological bridge with the non-Bolshevik peace agitation which was sweeping the rest of Europe. From April to October 1917 "it was the spoken or unspoken assumption in the Bolshevik camp that the Bolshevik Revolution in Russia, the ending of the war with a 'democratic' peace, and the proletarian revolution in Europe were parts of a single process and in practice inseparable from one another." [9] In this context of all-European revolutionary politics, the rigid doctrinal and tactical position of the Russian and German Maximalists in relation to the Stockholm movement appears paradoxical. Even though the Social Patriots and the Independents of Central and Western Europe had fatally strained the delicate bonds of Socialist internationalism, at this time they were trying to restore them under political conditions which were by far more stable than those in Russia. Would it not have been wise to throw the full weight of the Maximalists behind the Stockholm movement in order to increase the strength and unity of these anti-status-quo peace forces? Or did Lenin calculate that once the Bolsheviks had set the revolutionary example in Russia, with the help of a swiftly expanding peace mood in Europe all the forces of movement would place themselves under the banner of the Maximalists?

As early as March 25, 1917, in his *Fourth Letter from Afar*, Lenin clearly had indicated how, once in power, the Bolsheviks would undertake to liquidate the war:

1. [the Petrograd Soviet] . . . would immediately declare that it was not bound by any treaties concluded by either the tsarist monarchy or by the bourgeois governments.

2. It would forthwith publish all these treaties in order to expose to public obloquy the predatory aims of the tsarist monarchy and of all bourgeois governments, without exception.

3. It would immediately and openly propose to all the warring nations that an armistice be concluded forthwith.

4. It would immediately publish . . . our conditions for peace:

8. Ibid., *20*, Pt. I, p. 297.
9. Carr, *The Bolshevik Revolution, 3*, 6–7.

the liberation of all colonies; the liberation of all dependent, oppressed, and non-sovereign peoples.[10]

In denying completely Russia's treaty obligations, Lenin liberated himself from the most serious foreign-policy impediment which was complicating Kerensky's frantic search for political stability. Unlike the Social Revolutionaries and the Mensheviks, Lenin coupled his fiery denunciation of the predatory aims of German imperialism with no less vigorous indictments of Allied secret treaties. Free from any of Kerensky's responsibilities of power, Lenin adjusted both his foreign and his domestic program in the light of swiftly changing local conditions. Whereas in October 1915 Lenin had still been committed to following up the seizure of power with an extensive military-revolutionary campaign into Europe,[11] now with Russia's armies in desperate chaos he propounded the urgent necessity of immediate peace. Moreover, in view of the threatening decomposition of the multinational Empire, the Bolshevik platform on self-determination was amended specifically to champion "the right of all nationalities which are now part of the *Russian* state freely to separate and to form independent states."[12] Lenin's tactical flexibility also became evident with the emergence of the "peace and land" slogan which indicated that the Bolsheviks were prepared to sponsor a radical redistribution of land. Just as this last promise was calculated to attract the land- and peace-hungry peasantry, the other parts of the Leninist program sought to win over the tired soldiers and the disgruntled nationalities.

Certainly the swiftly spreading decomposition of the Russian army, polity, and economy was in great measure self-generated. Lenin's revolutionary defeatism merely accelerated a process which was well under way. His indefatigable organizing genius helped to strengthen and consolidate the revolutionary legions in a political "field" which otherwise was almost completely unorganized and unstructured. In both domestic and foreign policy he followed the route charted in *State and Revolution*,[13] by-passing and undermining all traditional conventions and allegiances which guided the political actions not only of the Allies, but of Kerensky as well.

Kerensky never stepped outside the confines of traditional Western politics and diplomacy; his revolutionary doctrine and temperament

10. Lenin, *Works*, *20*, Pt. I, pp. 60–61.
11. Rosenberg, *A History of Bolshevism*, p. 55.
12. Lenin, *Works*, *20*, Pt. I, p. 338.
13. Ibid., *21*, Pt. II, pp. 147–247.

were too tempered to allow him to adopt further drastic reforms, now that the Tsar was overthrown. Once this goal had been achieved, he proceeded according to the Socialist formula which had been worked out on the basis of an analysis of Western European, more especially of German, conditions. According to this formula, before the next step in the direction of the equalitarian society could be taken, the bourgeois revolution would have to be consolidated and industrialization carried forward. Outside the small but hard core of Bolsheviks there was only a marginal awareness that the war might defy every attempt to follow this "leisurely" doctrinal timetable. Eventually, whereas Lenin came to realize that the war crisis might allow Russia to play leapfrog with history, Kerensky became incapable of visualizing more than one step at a time. In brief, Kerensky's commitment to theoretical social democracy tended to blind him to the realities of power and politics in wartime Russia.

This blindness was further compounded by the Allies' incessant and urgent pleas for an immediate offensive on the Eastern front. Kerensky's continuing contacts with the special emissaries of the Allied Social Patriots served to anchor him still deeper in his defensist position; these consultations lessened his sensitivity to the specifically Russian elements in the revolutionary crisis which almost exclusively concerned an ever-growing number of delegates in the Petrograd Soviet. It is not without significance that at the peak of the short-lived success of the July offensive, the Allied Socialists claimed considerable credit for Kerensky's triumph. In Paris, Marcel Sembat declared that the Russian offensive "was the result of the vigorous efforts of Albert Thomas, Vandervelde, Henderson, as well as of their precursors Cachin, Moutet, and Lafont." Even *l'Action Française* suggested that without the persevering activities of Albert Thomas, the offensive could never have been staged.[14]

And yet the influence of these external pressures should not be exaggerated. Kerensky himself emphasized the "inevitability" of a major military undertaking in July, given the dynamics of Russia's domestic situation. Kerensky readily conceded that "the insistence of the Allies would have been of no avail if the necessity for the offensive had not been dictated by our own political considerations."[15] With the Bolsheviks cunningly exploiting the military and civilian

14. *L'Humanité*, July 7, 1917; and *l'Action Française*, July 11, 1917.
15. Kerensky, *The Catastrophe*, p. 207; and Harper, *The Russia I Believe In*, p. 108.

chaos due to inevitable shortages and administrative failures, the Second Provisional Government was threatened by a gigantic wave of anarchy. Under the circumstances, while Lenin was prepared to continue the Revolution in order to crush the war, Kerensky was almost forced to continue the war in order to crush the (Bolshevik) Revolution. The fact that Kerensky's domestic reform policy, more especially his agrarian platform, was much more timid than the Bolshevik promises further aggravated the difficulties of the Provisional Government. Although the Cadets in the Coalition agitated against a daring and imaginative land policy, the responsibility for excessively prudent reforms cannot entirely be shifted to them. For on the peasant question, much of the Russian Left, including many Bolsheviks, had long been the prisoner of a "foreign" doctrine. Western European Socialist thought, which thus far had dominated the minds of Russia's Socialists—excepting the Socialist Revolutionaries—was peculiarly unconcerned with the peasant question in "underdeveloped" nations like Russia. Hence Kerensky's appeal for continuing war and limited land reform had to compete with Lenin's more popularly attractive proposal for immediate peace and drastic land redistribution.

Meanwhile the campaign for a broad revision of war aims had been building up in the Soviet—and henceforth was to continue unabated until November 1917. By May 16 the American Ambassador reported to Washington that because neither the American nor the new Russian Government was a party to the old agreements whose provisions were secret, the moderate wing of the Soviet was pressing for an inter-Allied conference. According to Francis, "the Soviet did not demand that the treaties be made public"; instead, it suggested that the Russian and American Governments be acquainted with their content and, provided they approve, subscribe to them. The chief of Britain's military mission in Petrograd now also reported an "increase of socialistic and peace influence" in Russia. Consequently General Knox asked London whether it was "not possible to reconsider our agreements with the Allies in order to show that our vital aims in the war are something that even Russian Socialists could fight for." [16]

Before long the Allied and Associated Ambassadors were forced to report about pressures for war-aims revision not only in the extragovernmental Soviet but also in the Provisional Government. True, no sooner had Tereshchenko replaced Miliukov as Foreign Minister

16. *FR, Russia, 1918, 1,* 66; and Major General Sir Alfred Knox, *With the Russian Army, 1914–1917* (2 vols. London, Hutchinson, 1921), 2, 621–22.

than he publicly censured those who were advocating the immediate publication of all secret treaties. In his view such a step would lead to the disastrous "isolation of Russia." [17] However, he was prepared to use his office to explore all diplomatic steps which might help to galvanize revolutionary Russia into an effective and reliable partner in the Entente. A separate peace was never considered a possible alternative.

Both before and after the July offensive, Kerensky and Tereshchenko spared no effort to create those material and psychological conditions which would support an effective war policy. Among their advisers, there was almost universal agreement that in view of the Bolshevik-generated peace propaganda—which the Germans cheered enthusiastically—something had to be done to revitalize the morale and the moral purpose of Russia's soldiers, workers, and peasants. The Provisional Government, the majority of the Soviet, the Allied and Associated ambassadors, the special emissaries of Allied Socialism—all seemed to agree that a redefinition of Allied war aims could make a distinct contribution to this ideological and psychological recovery. Such a revision, however, would have to be the product of inter-Allied negotiations.

In Petrograd the British, French, and Italian ambassadors made a first unsuccessful attempt to draft a war-aims statement which might be acceptable both to the Russian Foreign Minister and to their own reluctant foreign offices. Ambassador Francis reported that in the face of such failures Tereshchenko remarked that a war-aims message from President Wilson "at the present time would be . . . far more valuable even than his promise to assist her with money and munitions, which are of the utmost importance and value." [18]

During his stay in Russia Albert Thomas had become convinced of the need for immediate and courageous diplomatic action. Therefore, shortly before his departure, on June 13, Tereshchenko handed Thomas an official note for transmission to his Government. While once again excluding the "possibility of a conclusion . . . of a separate peace," this note proposed that "as soon as there are favorable conditions" an inter-Allied conference be called to reconsider "the agreements concerning the ultimate aims of the war." [19] On June 15 Thomas promised the Russian Cabinet that he would become "the protagonist

17. *FR, Russia, 1918, 1,* 76.
18. Ibid., pp. 90, 92.
19. *RAR,* pp. 26–27; and *l'Humanité,* June 24, 1917.

of your ideas" in France and in Britain and that he would prepare their favorable reception "by supporting your request for a conference." [20] The following day the note of June 13 was formally dispatched to the other Allies.

Tereshchenko's proposal seemed altogether reasonable, especially since on June 8 the British Government had advised him that they were "quite ready, with their Allies to examine, and, if need be, to revise" the agreements made thus far.[21] Both Briand and Ribot had expressed themselves along these same lines in the Comité Secret a few days earlier.

But in view of the Allied Cabinet's prevailing concern with the pressures of their own forces of movement, the Russian request reached Paris and London at a politically inopportune moment. It seemed most unlikely that Lloyd George and Ribot could agree to a liberal war-aims pronouncement which would satisfy the Russian Government without at the same time encouraging the left-wing forces at home. Moreover, in order not to endanger Allied unity, the British and French Cabinets sought an indefinite postponement of a full-blown inter-Allied war-aims debate which was likely to give rise to serious policy divergences. In the House of Commons spokesmen for the war-aims dissidents repeatedly posed questions about the Provisional Government's request both for a joint statement and an inter-Allied conference. Cecil, Balfour, and Bonar Law took turns in answering these questions evasively.[22] Consequently Sir George Buchanan warned in vain that the Russian atmosphere was such that Kerensky could no longer "venture to appeal to the troops to fight for victory, but only for the speedy conclusion of peace" and that the Allies could ill afford to be accused of "prolonging the war for imperialist aims." [23]

Meanwhile, an inter-Allied conference had been scheduled to meet in Paris in mid-July for the specific purpose of considering certain Balkan problems. In view of recent developments, however, such a conference was likely to deal also with the Russian problem. In this expectation the Provisional Government was anxious that America should be represented at this meeting; Tereshchenko hoped that Wash-

20. See the dispatch by the Agence Havas from Petrograd in l'Humanité, June 16, 1917.

21. British and Foreign State Papers, 1917–1918, 111, 544–47.

22. Cf. FR, 1917, Supplement 2, 1, 119; Lennox, The Diary of Lord Bertie, 2, 158; PD, 93–97, May 16 and 23, June 7 and 21, July 12, August 16, 1917.

23. Buchanan, My Mission to Russia, 2, 151.

ington would be particularly understanding of Petrograd's plight. The critical diplomatic situation also led Balfour and Cambon to intensify their efforts to convince Wilson of the urgency of America's participation in high-level inter-Allied consultations. However, still determined to emphasize its Associate status, the American Government decided not to be represented.[24]

Informed of this negative decision, the French Government nevertheless sought to ascertain Washington's views in time for the opening of the conference on July 25. Accordingly, on July 23 Ribot instructed Cambon to request Ambassador Sharp to telegraph certain questions to the State Department. One of these questions asked the United States Government's opinion about Petrograd's proposal "to submit to a future conference the examination of the Allied objects of the war." Furthermore Ribot inquired about the American Government's view on "questions concerning Asia Minor" which had been "at several times the object of agreements between the Allies." [25]

Apparently the Quai d'Orsay never received an answer to these questions. However, after studying them carefully, the President composed an answer in shorthand. Wilson was of the opinion that "if the Russian Government should propose a conference for the common formulation of the objects of the war against Germany . . . the suggestion could not wisely be rejected." Moreover, "with regard to the agreements concerning Asia Minor" the President felt that "it would be exceedingly difficult now to conclude peace on any terms which would mean arrangements in Asia Minor for the benefit of particular nations rather than merely for the benefit and protection of the peoples of that part of the world." These notes were never translated into a state paper in spite of Wilson's conviction that "the sentiment of the world is now aggressively democratic, and will have to be met half way." [26]

24. Lansing to Wilson, July 3, 1917, and W. H. Page to Lansing, July 2, 1917, Wilson Papers. Page was greatly disappointed with the decision not to send an American delegate. See entry of July 16, 1917, in Page, Diary.

25. National Archives, Document 763.72119/685.

26. Baker, *Woodrow Wilson, Life and Letters*, 7, 204. It is not without interest that in Parliament UDC spokesmen repeatedly tried to find out whether America was invited to this conference, and if so, whether the U.S. accepted the invitation. Even though Cecil and Balfour finally disclosed that the U.S. "preferred not to accept the invitation," they reminded their interlocutors that their "questions are not in the public interest." *PD, 96* (July 26 and August 1, 1917), cols. 1408-9, 2060.

In the absence of Russian and American delegates, the Allies extensively discussed the Russian situation, its impact on Allied strategy and diplomacy, and the import of Michaelis' restrictive interpretation of the recent Reichstag Resolution. However, neither Tereshchenko's request nor Thomas' report nor Henderson's dispatches nor the nearly concurrent meeting in Paris of Allied Socialists with representatives of the Soviet moved the assembled statesmen to action. They were as unresponsive to Russia's pleas as they were firm in their resolve to check their domestic war-aims agitation.

At the next inter-Allied meeting in London on August 7 the Allied Governments issued a statement which could hardly have been calculated to help Kerensky. After expressing satisfaction that in recognition of "the necessity of national defense . . . all forces of Russia [were] consolidating around the Government," the Allies not only reiterated their confidence in Kerensky's controlling authority but also expressed a combined hope and/or demand for the re-establishment of "strict discipline which is clearly indispensable to all armies, but above all to the armies of free nations." [27]

As time went on, many Allied statesmen and generals began to be skeptical of the continuing emphasis on the importance of war-aims revision for the redemption of the Russian armies. For soon it became evident that the restoration of discipline and the rekindling of the fighting spirit would have to be supported by a basic renovation of Russia's entire military and economic establishment.

It may have been symptomatic of this reassessment of Russia's position that on September 3 Lloyd George told Douglas Haig that "Russia was in all probability quite finished" and that "she would be of no further help to the Allies in the war." [28] Less surprising still was the decision of the British War Cabinet four days later to consider a Russian appeal for additional guns as "part of the general question as to whether we were to continue to support Russia in view of the lack of discipline that prevailed and the serious economic situation there." [29] When the War College in Washington confronted similar problems in October, it concluded that "the English and the French,

27. Cited in Lloyd George, War Memoirs, 2, 1537.
28. Blake, The Private Papers of Douglas Haig, p. 253. In an interview with the Prime Minister in early October, Bernard Pares got the impression that Lloyd George "had simply lost all interest in Russia as a working factor in the success of the Allies." Pares, My Russian Memoirs, p. 480.
29. Lloyd George, War Memoirs, 2, 1537.

rather than the Russians, are our natural allies." [30] Likewise, Secretary of State Lansing, notwithstanding the "optimistic" report of the Root Mission, thought that henceforth American policy "should be based on the hypothesis that Russia will go from bad to worse." [31] Especially because of widespread fears of Ludendorff's determination to successfully exploit the Russian debacle, no one suggested (as yet) that Russia be left at Germany's mercy.

In the last quarter of 1917 Russia's situation had to be judged in the light of the over-all military and political exigencies facing the Allies as they planned for a fourth year of total war. In these calculations Russia represented the most uncertain variable. General Foch presently concluded that unless Russia recovered her strength with dispatch, the Allies would have to delay their grand offensive until some time in 1919. Meanwhile, should Russia suffer a decisive defeat by the Central Powers, how many German troops would be released for an all-out attack on the Western front? Would Germany be able to organize effectively her "one-front" war before the arrival of American reinforcements? Furthermore, to what extent could the Central Powers hope to break the Allied blockade by drawing essential foods and raw materials from German-occupied Russia?

Certainly there were compelling strategic reasons for assisting the Provisional Government in its efforts to maintain an effective Eastern front. Still, in considering the question of material assistance in a total strategic context, the question arose whether Russia's disintegration had not already reached such a critical point that no amount of aid, material or otherwise, could substantially improve her condition. Perhaps not only the Allies, but also Russia, stood to gain more from maximum military concentration on the Western and Balkan fronts rather than from the supply of costly and scarce war materiel to a phantom Russian army which in any case was not likely to regain sufficient strength to effectively countervail Germany's modern war machine.[32]

The unrestrained enthusiasm with which General Kornilov was hailed in the Allied capitals indicates that in their assessment of Rus-

30. Cited in Williams, *American-Russian Relations*, p. 101.

31. "Memorandum on the Russian Situation and the Root Mission, August 9, 1917," in Lansing Diary (Blue Boxes, Box 2, Confidential Memoranda and Notes, pp. 106–7).

32. Gen. Maxime Weygand, *Foch* (Paris, Flammarion, 1947), pp. 172–73.

sian developments the Allies were primarily concerned with the *fact* of war.[33] The praise and support from Allied reactionary and conservative parties was prompted quite as much, if not more, by Kornilov's military promise as by his outspoken anti-Socialism. On the other hand, in Liberal and Socialist circles he was immediately denounced as a dangerous counterrevolutionary leader, not exclusively for ideological-political reasons. Even though Europe's progressives throughout the war tended to neglect the strategic-military aspects of war in favor of ideological and political considerations, in this instance their political outlook may have been militarily justified. With much cogency they pointed to Kornilov's inability to win the allegiance of Russia's radicalized masses for any major military campaign and warned of the danger that Kornilov might defame the entire crusade for democracy.

With the defeat of Kornilov, Allied hopes of rehabilitating Russia sank to a new low, especially in light of the enhanced power and prestige with which the Bolsheviks emerged from this latest crisis. In early October Ambassador Jusserand informed Secretary Lansing that his Government "was greatly disturbed over the situation in Russia"; moreover, the French Ambassador reported that a new inter-Allied conference was being called tentatively for October 16 in Paris to consider "what means might be adopted to aid Russia and prevent further disintegration." [34]

Secretary Lansing himself realized that the Russian situation "is certainly critical and that everything should be done that can be done to give stability to the Government there." Hence, whereas earlier requests for American participation in Allied diplomatic conferences had been rejected, in view of Russian developments Lansing now thought it advisable to send at least an observer to the projected Paris Conference.[35]

This Conference, which was scheduled for October 16 but did not convene until November 29, was in large measure summoned in response to Tereshchenko's repeated representations. However, before the end of November not only was the Provisional Government swept into oblivion by the Bolsheviks but the Allies had taken certain diplo-

---

33. For a detailed and well-balanced picture of official and unofficial Allied attitudes to Kornilov see Warth, *The Allies and the Russian Revolution*, pp. 123–32.
34. *FR*, 1917, Supplement 2, *1*, 222.
35. Baker, *Woodrow Wilson, Life and Letters*, *7*, 290–91.

matic steps which ran counter to the spirit of Tereshchenko's proposal. As of the last week of September the British, French, and Italian Ambassadors in Petrograd were in possession of instructions from their respective home offices to deliver a stern note to the Provisional Government demanding an early military offensive. In the absence of specific instructions Ambassador Francis repeatedly inquired by cable whether the State Department wanted him to participate in this diplomatic *démarche*. Since he remained without an answer, the three Allied ambassadors presented their joint note, without Francis' signature, on October 9, one day after Kerensky had formed his new Government. Locked in a life-and-death struggle with the extreme Left, the Russian Premier was outraged at this undiplomatic and unrealistic démarche; as a symbolic protest he hastened to express personally his appreciation to Francis for not having signed the note. Forced to recognize that this note was a serious blunder, and suddenly aware of the magnitude of Kerensky's duel with Lenin, Rome and London promptly instructed their ambassadors to extend official apologies to Kerensky. However, Joseph Noulens, the new French envoy, reported that his Government stood by its original view.[36]

But even before these apologies had reached the Russian capital, Kerensky nevertheless affirmed his allegiance to the Entente once again. On October 10, in announcing Russia's participation in the forthcoming Paris Conference, he declared that "in addition to an agreement with our Allies regarding common war aims" the Russian delegates will endeavor to effect an agreement on the basis of the Petrograd formula.[37] This relatively vague statement merely served to heighten the rebellious mood of the Petrograd Soviet, which now sought to undermine the Provisional Government's continued subservience to the Allied foreign offices. The Soviet defiantly appointed its own delegate to the announced inter-Allied Conference in Paris; moreover, it worked out a set of detailed diplomatic instructions for him. Accordingly, Michael Skobelev was to proceed to Paris as a member of the Russian delegation with the following interpretation of the Petrograd peace formula: (1) no annexations and indemnities, with right to self-determination; (2) evacuation of all Russian territories occupied by German troops; (3) Poland, Lithuania and Latvia "to determine their own political organization"; (4) plebiscite in Alsace-Lorraine;

36. *FR, Russia, 1918, 1,* 196–98, 203, 207–8, 219.
37. Ibid., pp. 211 f.

(5) restoration of Belgium; (6) "return" of German colonies; (7) "return" of Greece and Persia; (8) neutralization of Suez and Panama Canals; (9) peace plenipotentiaries to the Peace Conference to be democratically elected by parliaments; (10) secret diplomacy to be abolished; (11) gradual disarmament; (12) compulsory participation by all nations in President Wilson's league of peace. Even though there is much that is Wilsonian in this program, the daring initiative of the Soviet as well as the wording and the spirit of the Skobelev instructions pointed to the gradually accelerating ascendance of the Bolsheviks.[38]

Both the Allies and the Provisional Government were deeply disturbed by this provocative representation of the Petrograd Soviet. When the Allies inquired about the status of Skobelev and his instructions, Tereshchenko reassured them that the Soviet instructions were not binding on his Government. Moreover, in view of the domestic conflict with the Soviet, the Foreign Minister asked that the Paris Conference be postponed until November 15. Meanwhile, on October 29, Tereshchenko publicly declared that since Russia had "to go on with the war in coalition with the Allied Powers, it [was] reasonable to demand that a coordination of our views as to the aims of the war with our Allies . . . should take place" and that consequently "the question of an inter-Allied conference [had] been raised." The Foreign Minister added, however, that Russia would have to come to that conference as "one united whole . . . with a unity of purpose and point of view." [39] Skobelev knew he was disavowed and resigned from the delegation.

In Russia Miliukov chastized the Skobelev instructions for being full of "Stockholm ideas," [40] while the Allied ambassadors were

38. Ibid., 1917, Supplement 2, *1*, 279. For the text of the Skobelev instructions see *Rech*, October 20, 1917, cited in *DR*, APS (November 21, 1917), p. 79; or Dickinson, pp. 79–80.

39. Cited in James Bunyan and H. H. Fisher, eds., *The Bolshevik Revolution, 1917–1918: Documents and Materials* (Stanford, Stanford University Press, 1934), pp. 40–41. The critical reaction to the Skobelev instructions of both Tereshchenko and the Allied Governments is discussed in Warth, *The Allies and the Russian Revolution*, pp. 150–52.

40. *FR, Russia, 1918, 1*, 217. According to one report Tereshchenko himself is supposed to have considered the Skobelev instructions as "contrary to the interests of Russia, because the right to self-determination for Poland, Lithuania, and Latvia would endanger the work of Peter the Great." Cited in Smilg-Benario, *Von Kerenski zu Lenin*, p. 269. Because of the "peace without victory" connotation

alarmed because the proposed Conference threatened to reinforce the swelling peace faction instead of serving Kerensky's defensism. Consequently, on October 22 and again on the 26th Ambassador Francis, in a cable to Washington, expressed grave doubts about the wisdom of carrying through the Conference at this juncture; actually, he recommended that it be temporarily abandoned. In an effort to reassure Francis, Lansing instantly replied that the proposed Conference was "one to discuss vigorous and successful prosecution of the war and not to discuss peace terms or war settlements" and that he "may so state to officials . . . and publicly if necessary." The Secretary of State also advised Ambassador Page in London that "it cannot be too strongly urged that it [will be] a war conference, and nothing else." [41] Rumors that the Russian crisis was forcing the Allies to revise their diplomacy likewise drove Bonar Law to declare in the British House of Commons that the Paris Conference would not "discuss the aims of the war at all, but only methods of conducting it." [42]

The Allies were sharply confronted by the Russian crisis as they assembled at Rapallo in early November to complete the organization of the Supreme War Council and of inter-Allied planning agencies. Since Russia was still an ally, should (must) she not be admitted to these councils? Quite clearly the risk of confiding military secrets to a government as unstable as that of Kerensky's seemed too great. Nevertheless, Lloyd George wisely cautioned that Russia's participation posed a delicate problem which would have to be handled with a great deal of tact. Likewise, General Smuts reminded his colleagues that in view of her internal difficulties, Russia might be looking for a grievance like this proposed exclusion from the Supreme War Council to justify the repudiation of her international obligations. At last the meeting agreed that even though Russia under present circumstances could not be admitted as a regular member of this new-born Council, the constitution of the Council should be so drafted as to enable a stable Russian Government to join at a subsequent date.[43]

In the meantime President Wilson had decided, largely upon the

---

of the Skobelev instructions, and because of a disregard of the nationalities outside the Russian sphere, Masaryk cabled a protest to the Petrograd Soviet. Beneš, *Souvenirs de guerre, 1,* 353.

41. *FR,* 1917, Supplement 2, *1,* 279, 284, 286, 295–96.

42. *PD,* 98 (October 29 and 31, 1917), cols. 1187, 1447.

43. L. Aldrovandi-Marescotti, *Guerre Diplomatique, 1914–1919* (Paris, Gallimard, 1939), pp. 114–15.

urging of Lloyd George, that an American mission, led by Colonel House, should proceed to Europe not only to participate in the impending inter-Allied Conference but also to lay the foundations for regular consultations in the future. Although this mission arrived in London on November 7, because of essential preliminary consultations and other major developments the Conference could not convene for another three weeks. On October 24 the Allies had suffered a serious set-back when the Italian armies were routed at Caporetto. No less disquieting and possibly of even greater consequence for the strategic and diplomatic conduct of the war was the complete change of Russia's political landscape on November 7, 1917. Now that the Bolsheviks ruled in Petrograd, the delegates to the Paris Conference would have to engage in a long-distance diplomatic dialogue with Lenin and Trotsky instead of negotiating in person with Kerensky's delegation. Notwithstanding Lansing's and Bonar Law's categoric denials, the Conference would have to deal with the basic political aspects of a coalition in crisis.[44]

Only Lenin seems to have had an accurate measure of the near exhaustion of the entire Russian nation. But because Lenin was considered highly irresponsible and anarchistic, both inside Russia and outside, his warnings and intentions were not taken seriously. In the West Ramsay MacDonald's admonition that there was "no analogy between the Russia of today and the struggle of France at the time of her Revolution" fell on deaf ears.[45] In July even as staunch a Conservative as Bonar Law had strongly suggested that "anyone who remembers the history of the French Revolution, who remembers what a terrible force those men became when they were fighting for their liberties, had some reason to hope that under proper guidance the New Russia may be a real help to us." [46] However, the anticipated and hoped-for recovery failed to materialize. Naturally enough, this failure was blamed on Russian "traitors" working in the interest of, as well as under orders from, German agents. Henceforth only Kornilov's strong discipline, not the revolutionary enthusiasm of the people, was widely looked upon as the essential key to the salvation of the Eastern front. All along, most Traditionalists had persisted

44. House Diary, November 9 and 15, 1917; and the *New Republic* (November 19, 1917), p. 60.
45. *PD, 94* (June 11, 1917), col. 723.
46. Ibid., *96* (July 26, 1917), col. 1520.

in their belief that a restoration of military discipline would enable Russia to challenge Germany's armies. It was only in restrospect that General Knox, who had favored a revision of war aims prior to encouraging Kornilov, concluded that "the rot in the Russian army had gone too far and no appeal to any idealism would have induced the men to fight." [47] In looking back, even Ambassador Noulens recognized that "all of Russia, without exception, aspired to an immediate end of hostilities." [48] He thereby concurred with le Temps that the Bolshevik Revolution succeeded because "Kerensky personified the prolongation of the war, while Lenin personified immediate peace." [49]

Among Liberals and Socialists comparable miscalculations of Russia's power and resources were no less current. It was not until October 22 that Raymond Robins, the liberal American Red Cross agent in Russia, reluctantly recorded in his diary that "the war [was] dead in the heart of the Russian soldier." [50] Until then he had counseled and assisted William Boyce Thompson in a three-months' effort to convince the Russian people that the Petrograd formula could triumph only under the combined banner of Kerensky and the Allied crusade for democracy.[51] Likewise Henri de Man, the brilliant young Belgian Socialist who had accompanied Vandervelde to Russia, continued in the belief that "the publication of the secret treaties and a frank common statement of democratic, non-imperialistic war aims by the Entente Powers would have put Kerensky in a position to crush Bolshevism more effectively than any terrorist dictatorship could have done." [52] The Liberal pro-Allied Journal de Genève expressed similar views; it bluntly suggested that for the Russian revolutionaries democracy meant peace while reaction meant war.[53] The New Republic interpreted the Bolshevik insurrection as a German political victory

47. Knox, With the Russian Army, 2, 622.
48. Joseph Noulens, Mon Ambassade en Russie Soviétique, 1917–1919 (2 vols. Paris, Plon, 1933), 1, 168.
49. Le Temps, December 17, 1917.
50. William Hard, Raymond Robins' Own Story (New York, Harper, 1920), p. 46.
51. For an account of the Thompson-Robins Red Cross and propaganda mission see Williams, American-Russian Relations, pp. 94–112; and Herman Hagedorn, The Magnate: William Boyce Thompson and His Time, 1869–1930 (New York, Day, 1935), pp. 182–230.
52. Henri de Man, The Remaking of a Mind (London, Allen and Unwin, 1919), p. 228.
53. Journal de Genève, November 19, 1917.

for which "the attitude of certain Western Powers towards Kerensky and towards the Russian demand for a more definite inter-Allied political program was partially responsible." [54] In a similar vein, President Wilson suggested that if Allied war aims "had been made plain at the very outset, the sympathy and the enthusiasm of the Russian people might have been once and for all enlisted on the side of the Allies." [55]

Whether the attitude of the West was the determining factor in the struggle between Russian moderates and extremists will forever remain debatable. With hindsight Bruce Lockhart, and eventually Kerensky, concluded that Russia could only have been saved from Bolshevism if the Provisional Government had sought an immediate peace. [56] But during the two months preceding Lenin's triumph no authoritative Allied leaders advocated a *total* peace without victory. It seems even more inconceivable that Paris, London, and Washington would have given their blessings to a separate Russo-German accommodation. Furthermore, the continuation of the war as well as of Allied support was at all times essential to Kerensky's anti-Bolshevik consolidation policy. Only Lenin was prepared and free to take an independent peace course.

The Bolshevik uprising occurred on the morning of November 7, 1917, the day fixed for the meeting of the Second All-Russian Congress of Soviets. As the Bolsheviks spread their control over Petrograd, the Congress convened only to witness the walk-out of most Social Revolutionaries and Mensheviks. The following day, at a second session, this emasculated Congress approved the formation of the Council of People's Commissars with Lenin as President, Trotsky as Commissar for Foreign Affairs, and Stalin as Commissar of Nationalities. Next it unanimously approved the twin decrees which indicated that the Bolshevik party had every intention of using its proclaimed principles as a guide to government action. The Decree on Land abolishing the private ownership of the soil was an unconcealed bid for the support of the peasantry in the proletarian-led campaign to consolidate the Revolution.

But the Decree on Peace proposing "the immediate opening of negotiations for a just and democratic peace" was of more direct and

54. *New Republic* (November 17, 1917), p. 61.
55. Cited in Frederick L. Schumann, *American Policy toward Russia since 1917* (New York, International Publishers, 1928), pp. 63–64.
56. Lockhart, *British Agent*, p. 168.

decisive consequence for the diplomacy of the war.[57] Clearly the
self-assurance of this initiative contrasted sharply with the hesitant
diplomacy of Kerensky and Tereshchenko. The Provisional Government would never seriously have considered such a move, nor would
it have taken any other major diplomatic step without prior consultation with the Allied foreign offices or their representatives in Petrograd. Moreover, both Miliukov and Tereshchenko had been equally
concerned with restraining the Soviet. Now Lenin transformed the
Petrograd formula into formal government policy: the revolutionary
Government called for the peace which "has been demanded by the
Russian workers and peasants since the overthrow of the Tsarist monarchy." The Bolsheviks emphatically refused to be the heirs of the
Provisional regime; instead, they sought to represent themselves as the
legitimate and faithful spokesmen and instrument of the Petrograd
Soviet.

Above all, the Decree marked a sharp break with Allied diplomacy.
In commenting on the November 21st decision of the Central Executive ordering General Dukhonin to propose an armistice to the Central Powers, Trotsky unequivocally stated that not being "bound by
the formal obligations of the old governments" the Soviet Government made its appeal "independent of the approval or disapproval
of the Allied Governments." [58] Thus, though the country lay prostrate
before the Germans, Lenin and Trotsky served notice on the Allies
that the militarily weak but ideologically renovated Russia had ceased
being a junior partner in the coalition. Notwithstanding her manifest weakness, henceforth revolutionary Russia would strive to re-
establish her diplomatic equality with the other major powers.

Whereas heretofore the Russian chaos had enabled the Bolsheviks
to promote successfully their revolutionary defeatism, now that they
were in power it was their turn to become ardent defensists.[59] The
Bolsheviks had to improve the military and economic position of their
mortally weakened state, more particularly because they soon realized
that the legacy of widespread disintegration would seriously handicap
their efforts to get a favorable settlement for Russia.

Even though the material resources at the disposal of the Soviet

57. All quotations are taken from the translated, complete text of the Decree
on Peace, in Degras, 1–3.
58. RAR, pp. 52–53.
59. Lenin, Works, 23, 27.

Government were woefully limited, its ideological armory fortunately was extremely well stocked. No wonder that Lenin and Trotsky now sought to consolidate the power of Russia and of the Revolution by shifting the discourse as much as possible from the military to the ideological level.

To begin with, the November 8th Peace Decree espoused a negotiated—not a separate—peace settlement. In proposing a general peace conference, the Bolsheviks became the champions of Wilson's January proposal for a peace without victory. However, their version should have been amended to read "peace without *military* victory"— because the Bolsheviks confidently believed that such a peace would be the first step in the political triumph of Socialism throughout Europe.

Especially in their party capacity the Soviet leaders were convinced that since "an overwhelming majority of the workers and the labouring classes of all the belligerent countries" were longing for an immediate peace, all the belligerent governments would be subjected to irresistible pressure for negotiation. In turn, like in Russia, this peace issue would be instrumental in paving the way for the equalitarian revolution in Western Europe. It is not accidental that the Bolshevik Peace Decree appealed first to "all belligerent peoples" and only in the second place to "their governments." Furthermore, in a closing paragraph, this same manifesto made a special plea "to the class-conscious workers of the three most advanced nations of the world and the three mightiest states taking part in the present war: England, France, and Germany." Henceforth, the Wilsonian and Leninist diplomacy were equally determined to emphasize the distinction between the people and their rulers. However, whereas Wilson relentlessly pressed this distinction in the hope of building a republican or possibly a social democratic fire in back of the autocratic German Government, Lenin incited the Western proletariats to exploit the peace issue as part of their campaign to enthrone revolutionary regimes. The war had defied all Socialist predictions: instead of occurring in one of the politically and industrially most advanced countries, the Revolution had swept over the most backward and least European nation. Like all orthodox Marxists, Lenin and Trotsky were convinced that developments in Russia had outrun the political consciousness of the masses. Therefore, in order to save the Russian Revolution from a combination of internal weakness and foreign strangulation, the Bolshevik leaders called the class-conscious proletariat of Western Europe to their rescue.

Even though the Peace Decree "was far more Wilsonian than Marxist in language and inspiration, and deserves to be regarded not as some remote descendant of the *Communist Manifesto*," [60] the political context into which it was introduced left little doubt as to its calculated intent and its anticipated consequences. True, the Decree was designed to impress the growing "progressive coalition." Henceforth, however, both Wilson and Lenin would seek to enlist fellow travelers for their respective peace programs: Wilson would consciously converse with the entire Left, while Lenin would court the pacifists, Radicals, and non-Bolshevik Socialists.

In the context of the Wilson-Lenin dialectic it must be noted that the Decree not only clearly stated that the Soviet "Government abolished secret diplomacy" but also expressed its "firm intention to conduct all negotiations absolutely openly before the entire people." By promising the immediate publication of all secret treaties as well as by denouncing offhand all their provisions, the Bolsheviks were certain to win the sympathy of all Western Socialists and Liberals who both before and during the war had advocated parliamentary control of foreign policy. No less attractive to these same circles was the unqualified rejection of both territorial annexations and financial indemnities. Lenin and Trotsky, while accepting the Petrograd formula, attached their own interpretation of "annexation." They expanded the Petrograd formula by opposing any forcible annexation regardless of when it took place and regardless of whether it involved territory in Europe or "in distant lands beyond the seas." [61] It may be suggested that while "land redistribution" was the Russian amendment to the Central and Western European Socialist domestic reform program, self-determination for the colonies was the Russian amendment to the Socialist foreign-policy platform.

Since the Soviet Government declared that it did not regard "these conditions as in the nature of an ultimatum," [62] it apparently hoped to get a response from that group of belligerents which, at this juncture, might want to explore a negotiated peace. Contrary to Trotsky's naive expectation, the Foreign Commissar could not merely "issue a

60. Carr, *The Bolshevik Revolution*, 3, 10.
61. Degras, p. 4.
62. Ibid., p. 5.

few revolutionary proclamations to the peoples and then close up shop"; the revolutionary state would have great need for skillful and imaginative diplomacy.[63] The stage was set for the Brest-Litovsk drama.

63. Deutscher, *The Prophet Armed*, p. 327.

6. REACTION AMONG THE BELLIGERENTS

THE NEW Soviet Government pressed all the belligerents not only to subscribe programmatically to the Petrograd formula but also to accept it forthwith within a "peace without victory" context. Because of the long-standing war-aims campaign within their own nations, the Allied governments were familiar with this Petrograd program. However, whereas heretofore legitimate minority parties had been its political carriers, now the illegitimate Bolshevik Government became its fiery sponsor. Trotsky rightly emphasized that the promulgation of the Peace Decree by his Government "was unexpected for the old routine habits of thought of the European bourgeois world, and the Decree was first taken as a party declaration rather than as a definite act of State Power." [1]

During the summer the Allied governments had tried to handle the passport issue with circumspection in order to prevent any serious damage to their domestic political truce. In handling the new Petrograd proposals, they would have to be equally cautious in the hope of minimizing the military and diplomatic repercussions of a major ally's impending defection. Moreover, in view of the pronounced ideological dimension in the Russian Government's diplomacy, all the ideological issues raised at the height of the Stockholm imbroglio would have to be faced again, both nationally and internationally.

In evolving their policy toward the Bolshevik Government, the Central Powers, quite as much as the Allies, were guided primarily by calculations of national interest. According to Trotsky, "the ambiguity in the attitude of the Central Powers was that as Germans

1. Degras, p. 4.

and Austro-Hungarians they were ready to rejoice, but as bourgeois propertied classes they had cause to fear."[2] True, Trotsky encouraged the German proletariat to overthrow their rulers, thereby contributing to a considerable revival of the July 19th coalition. But the danger of internal conflict was small compared to the tremendous military advantages to be gained from a separate peace with an outspoken yet weak revolutionary regime.

Such a separate peace with Russia would give the Central Powers two distinct military advantages: the liquidation of the Eastern front, and supplies from the Ukraine. Furthermore, they might score a considerable though temporary propaganda victory by giving the impression that, unlike the Allies, Germany readily accepted Trotsky's bid for a negotiated settlement of the war. In turn, success in this direction eventually might also contribute to a consolidation of the *Burgfrieden* in both Germany and Austria-Hungary.

Whereas Germany could only benefit from Russia's further collapse as well as from the resulting Bolshevik peace offensive, these same developments were certain to injure seriously the Allied war effort.

The repeated proposals by a major ally for an immediate armistice to be followed by a negotiated peace was bound to put the Entente on the diplomatic defensive. First the Bolshevik Government had unilaterally issued the November 8th Peace Decree. This step in itself was welcomed by the Central Powers because it pointed to a sharp divergence on war aims in the Allied camp. In quick succession the Bolsheviks took other diplomatic steps which were as embarrassing for the Allies as they were helpful to the enemy. On November 21 the Soviet Government proposed an immediate armistice to the Central Powers. A day later Trotsky defiantly announced the publication of the incriminating secret treaties. On November 28 a preliminary cease-fire was signed between Russia and her enemies.[3]

At the request of the Soviet delegation this cease-fire agreement was combined with a five-day postponement of all further negotiations. The purpose of this suspension was "to give the Allies time to define their attitude to the question of peace negotiations."[4] By drawing the Allies into the negotiations the Bolsheviks hoped to strengthen their position. The Central Powers nevertheless readily granted this re-

2. Ibid., p. 5.
3. See ibid., pp. 3–4, 8–9, 11–12.
4. Ibid., p. 11.

quest in the justified expectation that the Soviet inquiry would increase the Entente's diplomatic and political discomfort. In pursuit of these same objectives on December 6 and 28 the Central Powers agreed to two other such postponements.[5] The Allies now were forced to assess the military consequences of the Russo-German negotiations while at the same time formulating their diplomatic response.

The Supreme War Council immediately recognized that the Allies "were confronted with a fundamental if not a permanent change in the conditions upon which their strategy had to be based." From Petrograd General Knox advised his superiors in London that "whatever happens politically in Russia, the bulk of the Russian army refuses to continue the war."[6] In turn, first General Pershing and then General Bliss reported to Washington that the military crisis was "largely due to the collapse of Russia as a military factor and to the recent disaster in Italy." Bliss anticipated that this crisis might culminate "not later than the end of next spring, in which case, without great assistance from the United States, the advantage will probably lie with the Central Powers."[7] General Foch summarized the apprehensions of the military leaders with the cryptic assertion that "la situation russe domine tout pour 1918."[8]

These military prognoses were carefully studied by political leaders. Clemenceau presently recommended that military planning for 1918 should proceed on the assumption that "Russia cannot be counted on to render any effective military assistance." Apparently even the Tiger was sufficiently shaken by the recent turn of events to suggest that "it may be that victory will be achieved by endurance rather than by military decision." Similarly, from the discussions at the inter-Allied Conference in Paris, House concluded that "unless a change for the better comes, the Allies cannot win, and Germany may." In his view, "for six months or more the ground has been steadily slipping away from the Allies."[9]

Quite apart from the bitter hostility with which the Bolshevik Government was greeted in Paris, London, and Washington, Lenin's vic-

5. For the text of the statements in which Trotsky announced both these postponements see respectively ibid., pp. 17–18; and Dickinson, pp. 104–6.

6. Lloyd George, *War Memoirs*, 2, 1631, 1540.

7. *FR*, 1917, Supplement 2, *1*, 386–87; and John J. Pershing, *My Experiences in the World War* (2 vols. New York, Stokes, 1931), *1*, 249–50.

8. Weygand, *Foch*, p. 173.

9. Lloyd George, *War Memoirs*, 2, 1650; and *FR*, 1917, Supplement 2, *1*, 356.

tory did much to shake Allied confidence in the recovery of Russia's war machine. Instead of hoping for an early Russian offensive, the Allies now lowered their military and diplomatic objectives to limiting Germany's penetration eastward, and to perpetuating some sort of Eastern front. In this pursuit they might be able to profit from a connection with the Bolshevik regime, which they refused to recognize either *de facto* or *de jure*.

Even before it was decided to take official steps in this direction, certain Allied representatives in Petrograd independently approached Trotsky. One such representative was Jacques Sadoul, a French agent of Socialist convictions who was attached to the French Embassy. In addition to being in constant correspondence with Albert Thomas in Paris, he was in close contact with General Niessel, chief of the French military mission in Petrograd. However, without instructions from either, Sadoul went to see Trotsky, whom he knew well, in the hope of impressing him with the long-run dangers of agreeing to an onerous peace with Germany. However, instead of criticizing the Bolshevik armistice proposal, Sadoul urged Trotsky to confront the Germans with certain conditions. In the forthcoming negotiations Trotsky should insist on "the continuation of fraternization and of revolutionary agitation, the prohibition of transporting troops from one front to another, negotiations on neutral or Russian soil, very disadvantageous military conditions for the Germans, etc." [10] Raymond Robins, Sadoul's American counterpart, pressed similar pro-Allied suggestions on Trotsky.[11]

Because of their declared agreement with many of the basic socioeconomic aspirations of the Revolution, both Sadoul and Robins were open-minded about Bolshevik objectives and policies. Realizing Russia's desperate need for peace, they were impressed by the skill with which Lenin had combined the peace with the reform issue. Also, they were too well versed in recent Russian affairs to fall for propaganda campaigns which accused all Bolsheviks of being German agents. Since the Bolsheviks and the Allies were equally anxious

10. Capt. Jacques Sadoul, *Notes sur la Révolution Bolchévique* (Paris, Sirène, 1919), esp. pp. 120 ff.; and General Niessel, *Le Triomphe des Bolchéviks et la paix de Brest-Litovsk* (Paris, Plon, 1940), pp. 98–99, 111.

11. Williams, *American-Russian Relations*, p. 115; U.S. Senate, Committee on the Judiciary, *Bolshevik Propaganda* (Washington, 1919), p. 790; National Archives, Document 763.72119/1070.

unofficially to influence each other's decision-making, Sadoul and Robins became useful in their fellow-traveling capacity, to both sides.

On the one hand, despite their unqualified hostility to the Bolshevik regime, Buchanan, Francis, and Noulens used Sadoul and Robins in the hope of influencing, through them, policy-making at Smolny headquarters. On the other hand, should he be forced into separate negotiations with Germany, Trotsky was anxious to strengthen his bargaining position. He could hope to accomplish this only by threatening to seek increased military assistance from the Allied and Associated Powers. Hence, since he had to give at least the appearance of contact with the Allied embassies and military missions, Trotsky welcomed Sadoul's and Robins' services.[12]

On November 27 Trotsky even went beyond these unofficial channels. He summoned the Chiefs of the Allied military missions in order to assure them that "as evidenced by all our steps, we are striving for a general and not separate armistice"; should the Allies persist, however, in "closing their eyes before the facts," Russia might be forced to a separate armistice. The Foreign Commissar strongly emphasized that the hostility with which the Russian initiative was being met in Allied circles could not in the slightest change Bolshevik policy.[13] Even though nothing was accomplished at this meeting, the Allied representatives nevertheless resolved to continue their efforts to temper Bolshevik diplomacy.

In pursuit of this minimum policy, Francis cabled Lansing on November 26 that, barring contrary instructions, he would ask the chiefs of the Allied military missions to recommend to the Soviet Government that a separate armistice be conditioned on the opposing armies remaining in status quo.[14] Three days later the head of the United States military group, General Judson, saw Trotsky in an "unofficial effort to influence armistice terms." After the interview, which was suggested by Robins but had the approval of Francis, Judson reported to the War Department that the points bearing on the transfer of troops and the liberation of German prisoners appealed to the Foreign

12. See chap. 5 in George F. Kennan, *Russia Leaves the War* (Princeton, Princeton University Press, 1956), for an exhaustive account of the official and unofficial contacts between the American Embassy and the new regime during the four weeks following the access to power of the Bolsheviks.

13. *FR, Russia, 1918, 1,* 250.

14. Ibid., pp. 252–53.

Commissar, and "had already been in his [i.e. Trotsky's] mind." [15] Judson's visit was publicly interpreted by Smolny as the first "official" intimation that, should Russia refuse to surrender to Germany's excessive demands, the Allies might be prepared to support the Soviet Government.[16]

The specter of German domination of the Eastern European rimland and the Eurasian heartland continually discouraged a complete break with the revolutionary regime. The British Foreign Secretary wisely recognized that it was to Allied "advantage to avoid, so long as possible, an open break with this crazy system." According to Balfour, since the Bolsheviks were in a position "to fight neither Germany nor anyone else," the Allies ought to devote all efforts to preventing their aiding Germany. Moreover, he warned that even though Germany in all probability would strengthen her troops in other theaters of operation, this reinforcement in manpower was likely to be less important than her ability to use "the large potential resources of Russia to break the Allied Blockade." Balfour insisted, however, that it would take considerable time before Germany could effectively supply her needs from Russian sources; the Allies should, therefore, seek to make "that period as long as possible by every means in [their] power and no policy would be more fatal than to give the Russians a motive for welcoming into their midst German officials and German soldiers as friends and deliverers." [17]

In Germany, meanwhile, military and political leaders were not in agreement as to whether military operations or diplomatic negotiations would most speedily and decisively advance the cause of the Central Powers. Ludendorff proudly maintained that "the Revolution in Russia was no lucky accident, but the natural and necessary conse-

15. Ibid., p. 279. Gradually Ambassador Francis began to question the independence with which Robins and Sisson carried on their contracts with Bolshevik leaders. On December 15, 1917, he cabled Lansing for clarification whether he, Francis, or Robins-Sisson, were to make and recommend policy. See Wilson Papers.

16. When confronted with Trotsky's interpretation, General Judson told Francis that it was "incorrect, but not as much so as feared." Meanwhile Judson's visit produced strong protests in Allied diplomatic circles in Petrograd and in the Allied press abroad. FR, Russia, 1918, 1, 282–83; Williams, American-Russian Relations, p. 115; Kennan, Russia Leaves the War, pp. 118–19.

17. For the complete text of Secretary Balfour's "Notes on the Present Russian Situation" which the Prime Minister considered one of Balfour's most notable state papers, see Lloyd George, War Memoirs, 2, 1545–47.

quence of our conduct of the war."[18] He tended to ignore the ideological aspects of the Russian Revolution as well as their possible repercussions on Germany's domestic scene. Like so many Western observers the Quartermaster General underestimated the hold which the Bolsheviks were gaining over Russia. Also, his view that with little effort the Wehrmacht could wrest the political scepter from the revolutionary Government was widely shared in both coalitions.[19]

In Germany the scope of the foreign-policy debate transcended the immediate problems arising from the Russian collapse and the Soviet peace initiative. A new version of the *Mitteleuropa* scheme began to gain favor in certain political quarters. Reshaped to encompass East European areas, Naumann's plan now gathered many supporters in those circles which before the war had advocated an eastward foreign-policy orientation as being less likely to clash with the vital interests especially of England, but also of France.[20] In the prewar decades Germany's economic interests in overseas areas had been relatively marginal; the bulk of her investments was concentrated in Russia, the Dual Monarchy, Turkey, Bulgaria, and Rumania. The bold naval rivalry with England proved, however, that the economic, political, and military factions favoring commercial and political expansion into overseas areas had triumphed. Now that Germany's navy had been checked decisively, and the sea power of the United States had reinforced England's naval advantage, could this be the occasion for a basic reappraisal of German foreign policy? Might not the growing popular unrest, which was bound to draw encouragement from the Soviet regime, make the Allies amenable to a negotiated peace that would give Germany a free hand in the East in exchange for her renunciation of all ambitions in the West and in Africa?

At any rate, the Allies were deeply concerned by the military and economic implications of a Russo-German bloc: 44 per cent of Russia's imports and 40 per cent of her exports had been with the Reich. Raymond Robins held that Russia was "the greatest possible field for commercial enterprise, the investment of capital and the consumption of manufactured products": even though American investments might

18. Cited in Lutz, *Fall of the German Empire*, 1, 768.
19. Seymour, *Intimate Papers*, 3, 234.
20. Henry Cord Meyer, *Mitteleuropa in German Thought and Action, 1815–1945* (The Hague, Nijhoff, 1955), pp. 270–80.

"for the time being seem to have been wasted," the future offered un-parallelded prospects. Just as Robins suggested that good relations with Russia would "pay in the next fifty years $100 for every dollar contributed," so *le Temps* argued that France could not afford to be excluded from the economic development of Russia which was "the great task for the Europe of tomorrow." [21] Moreover, it is not without significance that in the middle of December the American *Inquiry*, a quasi-governmental organization designed to formulate United States war aims, planned a special study "of Russo-German relations, with a view to indicating methods by which the economic penetration of Russia, due to political weakness, may possibly be prevented." [22] Ac-cordingly, since Russia was in no condition to continue the military struggle, the Allies realized that "both to the immediate conduct of the war and to postwar relations" nothing could be more fatal than Russia's developing into a German colony.[23]

Even assuming the Allied governments had wished to extend ma-terial help to the Bolsheviks, from November 1917 to January 1918 their Supreme War Council was in no position to order an immediate and effective military intervention in Russia. Nor could the Allies af-ford to divert sizable quantities of scarce supplies to an army which no longer wanted to be an army. Meanwhile, the Caporetto disaster also reminded them that they had better prepare for increased German pressure on the Western front, especially since American men and materiel had not as yet reached the Continent.

These strategic and balance-of-power considerations constitute the basic framework within which official and unofficial Allied reactions to the November Revolution as well as to the Soviet diplomatic offensive must be viewed. The Entente was left with less than marginal scope for direct military and economic intervention in the East. The Allied and Associated Powers were forced, therefore, to rely increasingly on di-plomacy and on psychological warfare in their desperate efforts to

21. Robins quoted in Williams, *American-Russian Relations*, p. 99; and *le Temps*, December 19 and 24, 1917.

22. *FR, Paris Peace Conference, 1919, 1*, 38. On November 21, 1917, Trotsky told the Central Executive Committee that "America does not aim at territorial conquests; America can be tolerant with regard to the existence of the Soviet Government, since it is satisfied with the exhaustion of the Allied countries and Germany. Apart from that America is interested in investing capital in Russia." Degras, p. 7.

23. Lloyd George, *War Memoirs*, 2, 1547.

repair a dangerous, possibly even a fatal, breach in their coalition. However, even in this field they had unmistakably lost the initiative both to the Central Powers and to the Bolshevik regime.

By cheerfully agreeing to successive postponements for the purpose of inviting the Allies to armistice and peace negotiations, Germany emerged as the most conciliatory of the major belligerents. Furthermore, until the actual peace negotiations unmasked her real intentions, Germany successfully used the secret treaties to discredit the Allied war-aims record. Also, the Central Powers did nothing to interfere with Bolshevik peace propaganda, provided it was directed against the Entente.

Even without German encouragement the Bolsheviks had every intention of deriving maximum benefit from their ideological offensive. They did not claim or suggest that their war aims were of Bolshevik origin. In their desperate power predicament, Lenin and Trotsky did not hesitate to exploit foreign-policy principles which during the preceding decade had gradually become central to the reform program of Western Radicals. Presently they sought the support of the Allied forces of movement which, without Maximalist help, had sponsored these principles since the outbreak of the war, particularly since March 1917. In view of the long-standing campaign for war-aims revision by Allied progressives, the *New Republic* bitterly complained that there had been no good reason why the publication of the secret treaties "should have been permitted to figure as a trump in the hands of the Bolsheviki." [24]

The Allied and Associated Powers were not yet prepared to revise their war aims. Nevertheless, like the Central Powers, within limits they now also encouraged the Bolsheviks to exploit the Petrograd formula. But whereas Germany wanted Trotsky to practice the New Diplomacy in order to embarrass the Allies, the Entente wanted him to direct his psychological warfare against the Central Powers. The Allies hoped that Germany's inability or refusal to make peace on a "democratic" basis would (1) make the Maximalists suspicious of Germany's motives and intentions, (2) increase the opposition inside Germany to a predatory peace, and (3) convince the Allied peoples of the ruthlessness of German imperialism. Eventually, on December 22, France and Great Britain, at the suggestion of Balfour, decided to refrain carefully "from any word or act condoning the treachery of the

24. *New Republic* (December 1, 1917), p. 105.

Russians in opening peace negotiations with our enemies." Meanwhile, however, the Entente would take every occasion to reiterate its readiness to accept the Petrograd formula and to "press on the Bolsheviks the importance of not being satisfied with empty phrases from the Germans." [25]

In the dawning battle for the minds of men, all the governments had recourse to one and the same New Diplomacy gospel and practice. This widespread yet strictly expediential use of intrinsically noble and promising ideas could not fail to worry Wilson. He may have been familiar with a recent study by the research staff of the Inquiry which warned of an intensification of enemy peace propaganda "calculated as accurately as possible to allure the groups of the Allied Left" by approaching "more and more the verbal form of their war aims." [26] On December 4, in his address to the joint session of Congress the President publicly admitted his concern about the "unfitting" patronage under which the New Diplomacy was being expounded.

> You catch, with me, the voices of humanity that are in the air. They grow daily more audible, more articulate, more persuasive, and they come from the hearts of men everywhere. They insist that the war shall not end in vindictive action of any kind; that no nation or people shall be robbed or punished because the irresponsible rulers of a single country have themselves done deep and abominable wrong. It is this thought that has been expressed in the formula, "No annexations, no contributions, no punitive indemnities." Just because this crude formula expresses the instinctive judgment as to the right of plain men everywhere it has been made diligent use of by the masters of German intrigue to lead the people of Russia astray—and the people of every other country their agents could reach—in order that a premature peace might be brought before the autocracy has been taught its final and convincing lesson, and the people of the world put in control of their own destinies.
>
> But the fact that wrong use has been made of a just idea is no reason why a right use should not be made of it. *It ought to be brought under the patronage of its real friends.*[27]

25. Cited in Lloyd George, *War Memoirs*, 2, 1550; and in *FR, Russia, 1918, 1,* 330–31.

26. *FR, Paris Peace Conference, 1919, 1,* 27.

27. Baker and Dodd, *The Public Papers of Woodrow Wilson*, 5, 130 (italics mine).

The Russo-German peace offensive probably reminded Wilson of his diplomatic initiatives as well as of his peace principles of late 1916 and early 1917; he may even have felt that the misfortunes of war had cast not only Trotsky but also Czernin in a role which had really been destined for himself. By going above governmental channels in addressing their appeals to the "peoples of the belligerent countries" Lenin and Trotsky sought to converse with the same "voices of humanity" which had reached Wilson's ear. The President would not stand by idly while others dispensed "his" program; within a few weeks he would try to bring it under Allied patronage.

Meanwhile, various attitudes toward the Bolsheviks had started to crystallize among the Allied peoples. The right-wing press lost no time in blaming Kerensky's overthrow exclusively on the sinister machinations of Bolshevik leaders, all of whom were said to be in the pay and service of Germany. However, an understanding of—even a sympathy for—Bolshevik actions prevailed in the various sectors of the forces of movement.

At first the censors systematically tried to suppress the Bolshevik Peace Decree. However, both the Central Powers and the Allied dissidents gradually managed to pierce this censorship curtain. A furious condemnation of Soviet diplomacy immediately followed. *Le Temps* assailed the Maximalist peace program for being "as vague and perfidious as though it had been drawn up in the *Wilhelmstrasse*"; in the editor's view "one does not make peace with cut-throats." An even more stinging, but no less representative, editorial indictment of the proposed "Leninist Armistice" appeared in the London *Times*.

> It would be undignified for the Allies to expend words of reprobation on this step. . . . They know that the Maximalists are a band of anarchists and fanatics who have seized power for the moment, owing to the paralysis of the national life. . . . They know that Lenin and several of his confederates are adventurers of German-Jewish blood and in German pay, whose sole object is to exploit the ignorant masses in the interest of their employers in Berlin. . . . While the Bolsheviks are tolerated at the head of affairs, Allied help to Russia is out of the question.[28]

It would seem that these and other respectable Allied papers and most of their devoted and influential reading public had little under-

28. *Le Temps,* November 11, 1917; and the *Times* (London), November 23, 1917.

standing or knowledge of the "social aspects of the second revolution." [29] Especially in right-wing circles, Trotsky's New Diplomacy
was looked upon as merely another facet of a perfidious military betrayal. Their hostility increased still further when the Foreign Commissar, upon publishing the Allied secret treaties on November 22,
declared that "the abolition of secret diplomacy [was] the primary
condition for an honest, popular, truly democratic foreign policy."
Incidentally, Trotsky hastened to assure the Allies that he was certain
that "when the German proletariat enters the revolutionary path leading to the secrets of their chancelleries, they will extract documents
no whit inferior." [30] But this assurance by one of Europe's leading
heretics was not likely to stop the Allied press from denouncing the
treaties published in *Izvestiya* as enemy propaganda. The editors of
the London *Times*, in order "not to inconvenience the British, French
and Italian governments," maintained silence about the treaties and
curtailed "as far as possible" the dispatches on this subject from their
Petrograd correspondents.[31] Even though on November 27 and 28
le Temps gave brief summaries of some of the most important documents published by the Bolsheviks, hereafter *le Temps* and the rest
of the Parisian press also joined the conspiracy of silence under the
rigid control of the French censor.[32]

But whereas the Allied Right was merciless and brutal in its denunciation of the Soviet Government, the non-Bolshevik Left made
every effort to view the causes for Lenin's success dispassionately. Moreover, the forces of movement renewed their agitation for war-aims re-

29. *The History of the Times*, 4, Pt. I, p. 367.
30. Degras, p. 9.
31. *The History of the Times*, 4, Pt. I, p. 361.
32. *Le Temps*, November 27 and 28, 1917. Even a lengthy editorial justifying
the treaties was banned from the front page of *le Temps* by the French censor.
Marcel Berger and Paul Allard, *Les Secrets de la censure pendant la guerre* (Paris,
Portiques, 1932), p. 248. On November 30, 1917, in a cable to the U. S. Minister
in Sweden, Lansing asked for the text of the treaties whose publication was being
prevented by Allied censors. Ira N. Norris cabled a summary of the published
documents from Stockholm on December 5. That same day Francis transmitted
the actual texts to Washington; his dispatch, however, apparently did not reach
the State Department until December 27. *FR*, 1917, Supplement 2, *1*, 327, 446–
47, 493–507. "On the front page the *New York Times* carried a report from Petrograd announcing the beginning of the publication of the Allied secret treaties . . .
and summarizing briefly the first few documents released. Thereafter the *New
York Times* dropped the whole matter": Mamatey, *The United States and East
Central Europe*, p. 168, n. 58.

vision. In Kerensky's time they had asked for this revision in order both to strengthen the Provisional Government and to inspire the Russian army with enthusiasm for the Allied cause; now they claimed that only a war-aims revision was likely to prevent the Bolsheviks from signing a separate peace.

In the meantime, while bluntly and energetically censuring all the pro-German actions and proposals of the Bolsheviks, Allied progressives held their own governments largely responsible for the most recent aggravation of the Russian crisis. In the French Chamber, Mistral charged that "the Maximalist access to power was made possible by Allied policy vis-à-vis Russia"; the repeated denial of passports and the stubborn refusal to revise war aims had helped German and Bolshevik propaganda, thereby weakening Kerensky's position. The same charge was leveled by Ponsonby and Trevelyan in the House of Commons.[33] Naturally the enlarged and emboldened forces of movement now pressed the Allied governments to repair their past errors.

Lenin and Trotsky eagerly watched this renewal of the war-aims campaign in the Entente nations. Actually, the Peace Decree as well as the publication of the secret treaties was calculated to quicken dissident tempers. Even though the Bolsheviks had highly exaggerated estimates of the strength of foreign revolutionary forces, they were largely justified in expecting a favorable response to their diplomatic offensive. In England the Labour party and its allies were galvanized into such concerted action that within a few weeks they distinctively influenced a major official diplomatic pronouncement. At first the Right sought to dismiss the Bolshevik-published treaties as enemy propaganda. Then, under Radical and Labour pressure, Lord Balfour stated that "the documents in question ought not to have been published, and I do not propose to republish them." However, even though the Cabinet turned down left-wing demands that the Government open its archives, the documents could not be kept out of the dissident press.[34]

The UDC considered the Soviet documents as valuable though no less shocking evidence for its three-year old crusade against the Old Diplomacy. Its Executive Committee immediately resolved to urge the Radical and Labour press to publish the treaties, and before long

33. JO (December 27, 1917), p. 3619; and PD, 100 (December 19, 1917), cols. 2001, 2069–70.
34. PD, 100 (December 12, 1917), cols. 1152–54.

lengthy excerpts from these documents appeared in the *Manchester Guardian*, the *New Europe*, the *Labour Leader*, and the *Herald*.[35]

In France, because of rigorous censorship, the secret treaties were not exposed in the press; instead, the Socialist party decided to air them in a public session of the Lower House. When a Conservative deputy criticized Marius Moutet "for giving scandalous publicity to the treason of Trotsky and Lenin," Moutet replied that his exposé of the secret treaties was based on information published "in the newspapers of the entire world."[36] On December 27, in the name of the SFIO, Longuet, Mistral, Pressemane, Moutet, and Sembat once again called on the Government to publish and repudiate the secret treaties, and to revise war aims. Even though this request was refused, it did win the support of 99 deputies.[37] But meanwhile the SFIO parliamentary delegation had sent an appeal to Russia's Socialists asking them not to weaken their country's defenses, and promising that Allied war aims would soon be revised.[38]

Caught between Petrograd's open and repeated appeals and the threat of a renewed assault on the political truce in France and Great Britain, Allied statesmen were forced to reconsider their diplomacy. How much longer could they limit their war-aims revision to unofficial dispatches passing back and forth among their diplomatic chancelleries, or to timid and indirect intimations to Smolny that the Entente looked favorably upon the Petrograd formula? Lenin and Trotsky, as well as the Allied forces of movement, kept insisting on a public clarification of Entente diplomacy.

The rising specter of revolution and the dangerous uncertainties of an indefinite stalemate now began to worry even certain influential traditionalist leaders. Prior to the outbreak of war, some of the leading spokesmen of European Socialism had warned of the cataclysmic consequences which were likely to arise from a major world conflict. Primarily because the Second International had so dismally failed to stage its threatened civil war in July–August 1914, Europe's ruling

---

35. UDC, *Minutes of the Executive Committee*, December 11, 1917. The earliest and most complete translations of the principal secret treaties were serialized in the *Manchester Guardian*, December 12, 1917, January 18 and 19, February 1, 7, 8, and 22, and March 12, 1918; and in the *New Europe*, December 20 and 27, 1917, and January 17, 1918.

36. JO (December 27, 1917), pp. 3612–14.

37. Ibid., p. 3632; and *l'Humanité*, December 28, 1917.

38. For the text of this appeal see *l'Humanité*, December 19, 1917.

classes immediately forgot the warnings of the Stuttgart and Basle congresses. Even so, at this time some of these earlier Socialist admonitions threatened to turn into prophecies. The acceleration of history in which Lenin trusted so profoundly was serving the revolutionary cause; and the mutual exhaustion of which Rosa Luxemburg and Romain Rolland had written so eloquently began to stare European statesmen in the face. Could it be that by giving birth to the Russian Revolution and by consecrating a new balance of world power, the war would also gnaw away at those social, religious, and political foundations in whose defense the Allied sword had been drawn? Was there any truth to Trotsky's charge that the European governments were "no longer concerned with the realization of their initial aims, but with the liquidation of this enterprise with the least possible damage to their rule?" [39]

The Pope's August 1st message had offered evidence of the Holy See's sensitivity to the quickening disintegration of Europe.[40] Even though one of the primary aims of the Vatican's mediation effort may have been to assist the predominantly Catholic Dual Monarchy in her search for survival, the text of the Holy See's message reveals that the Pope was also concerned by more far-reaching dangers: "Must the civilized world become nothing but a field of death? And Europe, so glorious and flourishing, is she, as though carried away by a universal madness, to rush into the abyss and aid in her own suicide?" [41] Another prominent Catholic who shared the Holy Father's apprehensions, Joseph Caillaux, also was anxious to help bring about a peace which would not désarticuler Europe's internal and external structure. Caillaux thought that Europe's statesmen now "were very surprised to find that they had erred, since the disease went deeper than they had thought." [42]

Likewise, even a few months earlier, James Bryce had anticipated "a pretty bad time between Labour and Capital after the war"; after helplessly watching the spectacle of the hideous breakdown of an attempted democracy in Russia, by late October he "thought that Socialism was likely to gain a majority." [43] Though this type of apprehension

39. Degras, p. 7.
40. See above, pp. 229–36.
41. Cited in Dickinson, p. 48.
42. Joseph Caillaux, Mes Prisons (Paris, Sirène, 1921), pp. 39–40; and Caillaux, Mes Mémoirs, 3, 257.
43. Fisher, James Bryce, 2, 165, 167, 176.

was not current in the general public, it gradually appeared in certain traditional leadership circles. This new concern with the preservation of European civilization, which on many points coincided with an anxiety for the existing socioeconomic order, cannot be ignored. Eventually the American Inquiry, in preparing the American peace dossier, speculated whether one of the motives which would probably "control all others in the minds of European statesmen" would be how to obtain "the means of recuperation, because unless these were found, 'revolutionary discontent' would accompany demobilization." [44]

It is curious that Trotsky should have considered the British Government the most hostile of all to his peace maneuvers,[45] since it was actually in England that certain influential Traditionalists were beginning to question the wisdom of a fight to the finish. Ever since the March Revolution Lord Milner had been full of misgivings about the future, and by early October a member of Lloyd George's Secretariat, Thomas Jones, reported to the Webbs that Milner, as the most alarmed member of the War Cabinet, was hankering "after peace by agreement with the Hohenzollerns lest worse befall the British and German Junker class alike." [46] Milner thought that British diplomacy heretofore had been too timid to listen to any of the peace proposals, but that under the new circumstances the Allies "ought to listen to every peace whisper." [47] That other Conservatives shared Milner's apprehensions is evident from the Lansdowne Letter which appeared in the Daily Telegraph on November 29, 1917. The man who now published a counsel of moderation had been, in previous years, Viceroy of India, Governor General of Canada, War Secretary, Leader of the Tory party —and Foreign Secretary.

Even though Lord Lansdowne had negotiated the Anglo-French Entente in 1904 as foreign minister in an all-Conservative Government, he became in late 1917 the foremost public spokesman for those Traditionalists who were dedicated to the "conservation" of the European order. Fearful lest a further prolongation of the war "spell ruin for the civilized world," Lansdowne questioned what the value of the blessings of peace would be "to nations so exhausted that they

44. FR, Paris Peace Conference, 1919, 1, 31.
45. See Degras, p. 6.
46. Cole, pp. 96–97; and D. Chapman-Houston, The Lost Historian (London, Murray, 1936), pp. 268–69, 278–79.
47. Report by W. H. Buckler on a conversation he had had with Milner on November 3, forwarded from London by Colonel House to President Wilson, Wilson Papers.

can scarcely stretch out a hand with which to grasp them?" Hence, he thought the time had come to submit a program on the basis of which the war could "be brought to a close in time to avert a world-wide catastrophe." [48]

Lord Lansdowne did not publish his Letter without first sounding out certain Cabinet members. On three separate occasions in November he pressed his views on Balfour; but the Foreign Secretary felt that this "was not a very suitable time to discuss peace matters." [49] Apparently Lansdowne also discussed his project with some of his Peers, among them Lords Loreburn, Morley, and Curzon. Though not all of them agreed with every aspect of his program, they seem to have been sufficiently of one mind to encourage him in his enterprise.[50] Moreover, in a talk with Colonel House, who was in London just then, Lord Lansdowne not only spelled out six definite war aims but also "thought that it was time for the British to realize that in the settlement they need not expect to get . . . 'twenty shillings to the pound.'" This conversation led House to conclude that "Conservative that he is, we scarcely disagreed at all." [51]

Before submitting his Letter to the *Daily Telegraph,* Lord Lansdowne had sought to have it published in the London *Times.* However, access to the pages of Britain's most influential newspaper was politely yet firmly denied to him.[52] Immediately after the Letter had appeared in the *Telegraph,* in an editorial entitled "Foolish but Mischievous," the editors of the *Times* explained that they had "felt obliged, in accordance with [their] policy, to refuse, because [they] believed it to reflect no responsible phase of British opinion." [53] While the *Morning Post* joined in a violent attack on the eminent Tory leader, and the *Daily Mail* proclaimed that if Lord Lansdowne raised the white flag, he was "alone in his surrender," [54] a good number of other traditionalist papers around the British Isles supported the Letter.[55]

48. Cited in Dickinson, p. 88.

49. Blanche E. C. Dugdale, *Arthur James Balfour* (2 vols. New York, Putnam, 1937), 2, 182–83. Cf. Crosby, *Disarmament and Peace,* pp. 53–54.

50. George Allendice Riddell, *Lord Riddell's War Diary, 1914–1918* (London, Nicholson and Watson, 1933), p. 298.

51. Cited in Seymour, *Intimate Papers,* 3, 232–33.

52. *The History of the Times,* 4, Pt. I, p. 336.

53. *Times* (London), November 30, 1917. Cf. John Evelyn Wrench, *Geoffrey Dawson and Our Times* (London, Hutchinson, 1955), pp. 156–57.

54. *Daily Mail,* November 30, 1917. Cf. *FR,* 1917, Supplement 2, 1, 327–28.

55. See *The History of the Times,* 4, Pt. I, p. 342; and Lord P. C. Newton, *Lord Lansdowne: A Biography* (London, MacMillan, 1929), p. 470.

Even the *New Europe*, which was one of the most ardent champions of the crusade, warned that the Letter was "a symptom which only malice could misread." [56] A significant sector of the Liberal press also endorsed it, especially after former Prime Minister Asquith declared that Lord Lansdowne had sought merely to bring about a clear statement of war aims.[57]

Judging by the pages of the *Manchester Guardian* and the *Daily News*, British Radical and Labour circles were Lansdowne's most ardent supporters. Prominent members of the forces of movement organized a special Lansdowne Committee, of which F. W. Hirst, former editor of the *Economist*, was Honorary Secretary, and Lord Beauchamp chairman, and which counted Earl Loreburn, Gilbert Murray, and Ramsay MacDonald among its members. This Committee immediately worked in close unison with the Union of Democratic Control. The UDC "very heartily welcomed Lord Lansdowne's movement both in London and in the provinces," and circularized about 1500 copies of the November 29th issue of the *Daily Telegraph* to its Branch Secretaries "for distribution to Liberals and Conservatives." [58] Meanwhile, in Paris, Pierre Renaudel also praised Lansdowne's efforts to elicit a clarification of Allied war aims.[59]

Even before all this support had crystallized, the British War Cabinet was fearful lest both at home and abroad the wrong interpretation be placed upon Lord Lansdowne's initiative. After all, Bonar Law and Lansing had recently taken great pains to declare that the forthcoming inter-Allied Conference would not discuss war aims. Now, the very day that this Conference convened in Paris, an Allied public figure of Lansdowne's eminent stature broke into print with a highly controversial revisionist statement. In order to counteract those interpretations which might identify the Letter with official policy, the Government persuaded Reuters to insert a communique in the *Times* to the effect that Lansdowne "only spoke for himself," that he did not con-

56. *New Europe* (December 6, 1917), p. 228.

57. H. H. Asquith, *A Clean Peace and National Reconstruction*, speech delivered at Birmingham on December 11, 1917 (published by the Liberal Publication Department, n.d.); and the *New Republic* (December 15, 1917), p. 160.

58. Francis W. Hirst, *The Consequences of the War to Great Britain* (London, Oxford University Press, 1934), p. 17; Swanwick, *Builders of Peace*, p. 88; UDC, *Minutes of the Executive Committee*, December 4, 1917; Newton, *Lord Lansdowne*, p. 473.

59. *L'Humanité*, December 4, 1917.

sult with any Member of the Government, and that His Majesty's Ministers read the Letter "with as much surprise as did everyone else." [60]

However, neither the invectives of the *Times* editorial nor the Reuters interpretation could conceal the fact that Lansdowne "represented a powerful and growing section of the people not only in social, but also in industrial circles." [61] W. H. Buckler immediately hailed the Letter as "a fit climax to the events of the month"; its political effect had been "suddenly to crystallize what was formerly in solution." Within less than a month Buckler informed Colonel House of the emergence in Parliament of a new group of twenty-nine moderates "untarred by the brush of pacifism" who supported Lord Lansdowne, and among whom "Baring, Brunner, and Holt represent large financial interests." [62] According to the parliamentary correspondent of the *Westminster Gazette*, the Letter expressed "a great body of public opinion which had been so far inarticulate in order not to embarrass the Government," but which had now found a leader.[63] Similarly, W. H. Page thought that the Letter was having the effect of enormously increasing "the demand in all quarters, except in Government quarters, for a simpler and clearer explanation of the aims of the war, an explanation that laboring men, the men in the trenches, the men in the street, can understand." [64]

In the Central camp Erzberger took the Lansdowne utterance as proof that "the signs of the times all point in the same direction," and that it was particularly gratifying "for men of insight in *both camps*" that the Letter coincided "with the Russian proposals." [65] Germany's Secretary of State von Kühlmann, a leading adherent of the eastern

---

60. Cited in Dugdale, *Arthur James Balfour, 2,* 183–84; and in the *Liberal Magazine, 25* (December 1917), 575.

61. Lloyd George, *War Memoirs, 2,* 1491.

62. See Buckler's reports to House dated November 30, December 10, and December 21, 1917, William H. Buckler Papers, in the Edward M. House Collection, Yale University. "Particularly by the autumn of 1917 certain industrialists and financiers began to see the importance of a moderate peace movement. There were seventeen M.P.s who were industrialists, merchants, or bankers among the Liberals . . . [and] practically all of these sat for constituencies in the north of England." Crosby, *Disarmament and Peace,* pp. 64 and (appendix B) 166.

63. *Westminster Gazette,* November 30, 1917.

64. Page, *Diary,* December 1917.

65. Quoted by the Berlin correspondent of the *Nieuwe Rotterdamsche Courant,* December 3, 1917, cited in *DR,* (December 6, 1917), p. 280.

foreign-policy school, also considered the Letter a hopeful sign that the more moderate forces were gaining ground in England.[66] Many influential German and Austro-Hungarian Traditionalists worried about the impending repercussions of the Russian Revolution on the Central Powers; furthermore, they were abandoning all hopes of winning a decisive military victory. As the Allies learned from the Smuts-Mensdorff conversations in Switzerland, certain elements in Germany—and certainly Czernin—might be willing to negotiate a settlement which would give the Reich a free hand in Central and Eastern Europe.[67] Among these Traditionalists Delbrück, Helfferich, von Kühlmann, Solf, and Prince Max of Baden figured most prominently. Especially Prince Max, who in his memoirs devoted two chapters to his "dialogue with Lansdowne," was anxious to tell Lord Lansdowne "that the German party in favor of understanding which it was his aim to encourage, was quite ready for negotiations with the *better* England which he represented, but equally determined to fight the knock-out Government to a finish." [68] Likewise in Vienna, on November 30 and again on December 4, the authoritative *Neue Freie Presse* considered it "almost a duty that a word should be addressed from Austria to the British nation as to whether a conversation (*Aussprache*) would not be possible." [69]

It was against this complex background—the Soviet ideological challenge, the military crisis in the East and at Caporetto, the impending renewal of the assault on the political truce, and the split in the forces of order—that the inter-Allied Conference finally assembled in Paris. Notwithstanding all protestations, the war-aims question was bound to be at the top of the agenda. Indeed, everyone felt that because the Russian problem was the most formidable of the moment, it would have to be examined under all aspects; and "the means of meeting it [would] be the chief object of the deliberations." [70]

This much-postponed Conference, which owed its origins to the hopeless but persistent pleas of the Second Provisional Government, had an unusually difficult assignment. On October 24, in what proved to be Kerensky's last appeal to the Russian people, the Premier had

66. Helfferich, *Der Weltkrieg*, 2, 356.
67. See Lloyd George, *War Memoirs*, 2, chap. 19, 1477 ff.; and Richard von Kühlmann, *Erinnerungen* (Heidelberg, Lambert Schneider, 1948), pp. 475 ff.
68. Prince Max of Baden, *The Memoirs*, 1, 169 ff., 231 ff.
69. Cited in *DR*, FPS (December 4, 1917), pp. 262, 279.
70. *Liberté*, November 28, 1917; and *Echo de Paris*, November 28, 1917—both cited in *DR*, APS (November 30, 1917), p. 231.

announced that Russia's representatives would attend the Paris Conference in order to work out an agreement with the Allies on the basis of the principles proclaimed by the Revolution.[71] Subsequently, as soon as the Bolsheviks were in power, Lenin and Trotsky, basing themselves on the same Petrograd formula, called for an immediate peace; furthermore, instead of continuing Kerensky's subservience to Allied policy, the new regime asked whether the Allies were "agreeable to support *our* initiative" toward peace or whether they demanded "other measures." [72]

The Soviet initiative could not be ignored. On November 29, Lloyd George discussed the Trotsky summons at a meeting of the British War Cabinet; however, he informed his colleagues that England "could not act alone, the subject was one which should be referred to the Conference now meeting in Paris"—where the Lansdowne Letter remained "uppermost in the mind of the British Prime Minister." [73] In the French political arena even Briand now made considerable efforts to convince French leaders that Clemenceau's slogan *vaincre pour être juste* should be recast to read *être juste pour vaincre*.[74] By the time Colonel House reached the Conference, he was determined to exploit every possible revisionist pressure in order to achieve the long overdue clarification of Allied diplomacy. Presently House's determination was reinforced by a cable from Boris Bakhmetieff, the Ambassador of the (defunct) Second Provisional Government in Washington, who insisted that the Soviet armistice proposal could not "remain unanswered," since evasion would simply strengthen the Bolsheviks and help them create an atmosphere in Russia hostile to the Allies; moreover, "any formal protest against Lenin's policy or any threats" were likely to have the same effect.[75]

Consequently House, with prior approval from President Wilson, submitted the following war-aims resolution to the Conference:

> The Allies and the United States declare that they are not waging war for the purpose of aggression or indemnity. The sacrifices they are making are in order that militarism shall not continue

71. Francis, *Russia from the American Embassy*, p. 172.
72. Degras, p. 10.
73. Lloyd George, *War Memoirs*, 2, 1541–42; and FR, 1917, Supplement 2, 1, 353.
74. Georges Suarez, *Briand: Sa vie—son oeuvre* (6 vols. Paris, Plon, 1938–52), 4, 326; and Seymour, *Intimate Papers*, 3, 279–80.
75. *FR, Russia, 1918, 1,* 254.

to cast its shadow over the world, and that nations shall have the right to lead their lives in the way that seems to them best for the development of their general welfare.[76]

Even though his draft proposal was much more vague and noncommittal than the Lansdowne Letter, Colonel House could not persuade the Conference to adopt it. Allied opposition to this mild declaration becomes even more puzzling when compared either with the Petrograd program or with President Wilson's subsequent attempt to bring the New Diplomacy under the "right" patronage in his Fourteen Points address.

But at this time traditionalist diplomacy still reigned supreme in Allied councils. It can be seen from Colonel House's diary entries as well as from his cables to the President that whereas England was "passively willing" to back his declaration, "France was indifferently against it, Italy actively so.[77] Even before the Conference convened, a preliminary exploration of Allied war-aims intentions had led House to inform Wilson that he would refuse to be drawn into any of the Allied controversies, "particularly those of a territorial nature." [78] He was not surprised, therefore, that throughout the deliberations especially Clemenceau and Sonnino persisted in their rigid determination not to make any concessions to the New Diplomacy. Clearly, the Paris Conference was the first head-on diplomatic confrontation between the European Allies, which were mutually enmeshed in a network of international obligations, and the United States, which was diplomatically as free by historical legacy as Soviet Russia was by unilateral declaration.

Even though formally not represented, Russia continued to be the central concern of the Conference. The rejection of House's first draft was followed by consultations with the (defunct) Second Provisional Government's Ambassador to France, V. A. Maklakoff, who also thought that a statement was necessary. Maklakoff insisted, however, that since there was no recognized government in Petrograd, Russia's citizens should be assured that the Allies would "proceed to a revision of war aims together with Russia, so soon as there shall be a government aware of its duties to the country and defending the interests of the country and not of the enemy." [79] A statement with such a marked

76. Seymour, *Intimate Papers*, 3, 281–82.
77. Ibid., p. 285.
78. Ibid., p. 281.
79. Ibid., p. 290.

anti-recognition slant was not likely to move the Bolsheviks to reconsider their expediential peace strategy. Therefore House demurred.

Lloyd George also was anxious not to affront the Bolsheviks for fear of exacerbating their anti-Allied prejudices. The British Prime Minister's cautious attitude was influenced not only by Balfour but also by a recent dispatch from the British Ambassador in Petrograd. Sir George Buchanan advocated that without dealing with the revolutionary regime, the Allies should leave the Bolshevik Government free "to decide whether they will purchase peace on Germany's terms or fight on with the Allies." In Buchanan's view the only policy which "could tempt Russia to make one more effort" would be to release the Bolsheviks from all obligations to the Allies. The Ambassador argued that an unqualified release from the no-separate-peace Agreement of September 5, 1914, might "take the wind out of their sails, as they will no longer be able to reproach the Allies for driving Russian soldiers to the slaughter for their imperialistic aims." On the strength of this and similar advice, Lloyd George drafted a declaration which was calculated to reconcile the House and Maklakoff proposals.[80]

However, this compromise failed because for Colonel House the Prime Minister's draft was too inconsiderate of Russia's plight, whereas for Sonnino it lacked the requisite toughness. Consequently the initial effort to promulgate a joint war-aims declaration and to give a collective answer to Trotsky's summons was abandoned. Instead, at the suggestion of Lloyd George, it was decided that separately the Allied and Associated Ambassadors in Petrograd would "let it be known" that their Governments "were willing to reconsider their war aims in conjunction with Russia . . . as soon as she had a stable government with whom they could act." [81] The omissions in the Conference communique were "so eloquent" that Renaudel labeled this decision "the new mistake." [82] A fresh or common diplomatic policy had failed to materialize, even though the inter-Allied consultations produced a broad, far-reaching, and effective coordination of military, naval, and economic resources and activities.

But it would be wrong to write the Conference off as an unqualified

---

80. For the text of the Ambassador's dispatch see Buchanan, *My Mission to Russia*, 2, 225–26. See also Lloyd George, *War Memoirs*, 2, 1543; 3, 284, 290.

81. Seymour, *Intimate Papers*, 3, 285, 316–17; Lloyd George, *War Memoirs*, 2, 1543; *FR*, 1917, Supplement 2, 1, 352.

82. *L'Humanité*, December 6, 1917.

diplomatic failure simply because all concrete achievements were confined to the realm of military and economic coordination.[83] This had been the first full-scale inter-Allied diplomatic consultation since the overthrow of the Tsar. Moreover, "while Russia disappeared, the United States for the first time participated in an Allied conference. . . . Under the double impact of the Russian collapse and of the American intervention the center of gravity of the world conflict was moving westward in some measure."[84] Undoubtedly this westward movement was largely due to America's becoming the critical storehouse of Allied military, economic, and ideological power. However, though Russia was impotent in the first two forms of power, the Soviet regime had a potent ideology at its disposal. And even though they lacked the material power with which to support their ideological offensive, the Bolsheviks nevertheless contributed as much as Woodrow Wilson to the onslaught on the Old Diplomacy.

The continuity in mood, procedures, and objectives of 19th-century diplomacy was being totally disrupted by two newcomers to world politics—Bolshevik Russia and Wilsonian America—which were equally convinced that the war had sent the peoples in search of a new gospel. Because of their deep commitment to the Old Diplomacy, Europe's statesmen could not be expected to react instantaneously and coherently to the challenge of the New Diplomacy, especially since the respective proposals from Petrograd and Washington only gradually revealed their new directions. In the meantime, however, the Paris Conference had served to remind the Allies once again that for both diplomatic and domestic reasons the war aims of the coalition would have to be clarified. It was becoming increasingly evident that whereas without this clarification the Allies might manage to continue the war successfully, they might not be able to continue a convincing crusade for democracy.

83. For the view that this Paris Conference "marked the decisive crossroads in the path to Allied victory" because of its achievements in economic and military coordination, see Seymour, *American Diplomacy*, pp. 239–44.

84. *Le Temps*, November 29, 1917.

THIRD PHASE: THE NEW DIPLOMACY

7. BREST-LITOVSK AS CATALYST

IN HIS semi-official interview with Trotsky, General Judson had assured the Foreign Commissar that "the time of protests and threats . . . [had] passed." [1] Even without this unauthorized assurance, the Bolsheviks were bound to observe carefully the inter-Allied Conference in Paris in the hope that some pro-Soviet decisions might be announced. Trotsky's disappointment must have been great when this Conference terminated its diplomatic labors with a stony silence.

Nevertheless, since a general peace continued to look more promising for the Russians than a separate peace, the Bolsheviks could be expected to make every effort to delay the final reckoning with the Central Powers. Therefore, on December 6 Trotsky informed the Allied Ambassadors that at the request of the Soviet delegation the conference at Brest-Litovsk had once again been suspended for one week in order to inform the Allied peoples and governments "of the fact of negotiations and the course they have taken." [2] In an obvious bid for Allied support, Trotsky declared that "as a condition of the armistice no troops are to be transferred from one front to another." The Foreign Commissar stated, furthermore, that "with regard to war aims, the delegates of the opposing side decline to give a definite reply" and also claim "that they had no authority to consider the question of an armistice with countries whose delegates were not taking part in the negotiations." [3] Evidently Trotsky sought to prevail upon the Allies to surpass the Central Powers by endorsing Soviet war aims

1. Degras, p. 15.
2. Ibid., p. 17.
3. Ibid., p. 18.

and by declaring their readiness to negotiate peace on this basis. In his view, by adopting such a policy the Allies would place Germany's rulers before two equally unattractive alternatives: either they would agree to a nonannexationist peace or they would have to face dangerous revolutionary pressures from Germany's class- and peace-conscious proletariat. In other words, in Germany as in Russia the peace issue would also pave the road to revolution.[4]

In closing his December 6th message, Trotsky emphasized that by the time negotiations had resumed on December 12 more than a month would have elapsed since the initial Peace Decree had been issued. He concluded, therefore, that the Allies could hardly claim not to have had ample "opportunity to define their attitude to the peace negotiations." In brief, by December 6 the Petrograd summons which the inter-Allied Conference at Paris had found impossible to honor had again been served. That same day Sadoul, in a hasty note to Albert Thomas, pleaded desperately that he could no longer go to Smolny without some Allied commitment to the Petrograd formula which had become the basis of his "conversations with Trotsky, Lenin and all their associates."[5]

While the Allied foreign offices were engaged in their agonizing reappraisal, on December 15 a separate armistice was signed at Brest-Litovsk. Especially in Allied right-wing quarters, but also among the forces of movement, this news caused deep consternation. Instantly both Radical and Socialist leaders interpreted the armistice as a pressing diplomatic ultimatum. Consequently, they prepared to intensify their war-aims campaign. Trotsky and Lenin must have noted that whereas the war cabinets maintained their silence, the forces of movement became increasingly articulate.

The Bolsheviks then concluded that by helping the forces of movement to increase pressure on their own reluctant governments they might be able to influence official policy. Hence their next major foreign-policy pronouncement was addressed to the "Toiling, Oppressed, and Exhausted Peoples of Europe." Trotsky justified this revolutionary appeal with the assertion that, since the "existing capitalist governments" were incapable "of making a democratic peace," he

4. Cf. testimony by Raymond Robins in U. S. Senate, Committee on the Judiciary, *Bolshevik Propaganda*, pp. 785–87.

5. Sadoul, *Notes sur la Révolution Bolchévique*, p. 99.

would turn for support to the Allied as well as to the enemy peoples.[6]

In December 1917, as well as in subsequent months, whenever they were exposed to Allied intransigence and to the realities of German power, Lenin and Trotsky ceased to act as diplomats and instead spoke as "soldiers of the revolution." According to Trotsky, in the course of the Brest-Litovsk negotiations he and his fellow delegates "never forgot for a single instant that we were the representatives of the revolutionary class. Our speeches were directed to the workers of all the nations oppressed by the War. . . . While speaking with Kühlmann and Czernin we thought of our friends and partisans: Karl Liebknecht and Fritz Adler." [7]

The Soviet regime used traditional and revolutionary diplomacy in varying degrees and combinations. Perhaps the most striking departure from accepted practice was the December 3rd appeal to the "Moslems of Russia and the East," renouncing Russia's claim to Constantinople, voiding the partition of Persia, and announcing the impending withdrawal of Russian troops from Persia. After asserting that even far-off India was raising the standard of revolt, the appeal continued: "Moslems of the East! Persians, Turks, Arabs and Hindus. . . . It is not from Russia and its revolutionary government that you have to fear enslavement, but from the European imperialist robbers, from those who laid waste your native lands and converted them into their colonies." [8] This unrestrained and provocative communication to the natives of the Entente's colonial realms did as much to arouse Allied anti-Bolshevik and anti-Russian feelings as did the appeal to Europe's toiling, oppressed, and exhausted masses.[9] Both appeals, however, went above the heads of governments in a frenzied effort by the new rulers of Russia to hasten a general peace, through helping "the working class in all lands to overthrow the rule of capital and to seize political power." [10]

On November 30 Trotsky had told the Petrograd Soviet that in future negotiations with either the Allies or the Central Powers the Bolsheviks would not permit any distortion of the Revolution's gen-

6. Degras, p. 19.
7. Deutscher, *The Prophet Armed*, p. 371; and Léon Trotsky, *De la Révolution d'octobre à la paix de Brest-Litovsk* (Geneva, 1918), pp. 3–4.
8. Degras, pp. 15–17.
9. E.g., see Buchanan, *My Mission to Russia*, 2, 233–37.
10. Degras, p. 19.

eral peace principles. Moreover, he had promised "that the prosecutor, in the person of the Russian revolutionary delegation" would in due course "make a thunderous speech for the prosecution on the diplomacy of *all* imperialists."[11] Whereas this frontal assault on the prevailing international order reduced Russia's chances of winning any kind of support from the Allied governments, it was a necessary outgrowth of Trotsky's and Lenin's deep revolutionary convictions— convictions which made them prisoners of the doctrinal prophecy according to which Europe's class-conscious proletariat was about to mount the barricades.

The first plenary session of the Brest-Litovsk Peace Conference met on December 22, 1917.[12] In the absence of the Allies, the Soviet delegation was bound to launch the anticipated ideological offensive. Realizing that every word would be "taken down and reported by radiotelegraph to all nations," the leader of the Russian delegation notified the opposing delegations that, in the present negotiations his Government would stand by the principles enunciated in the November 8th Peace Decree. Accordingly, Adolf Joffe, the head of the Russian delegation, submitted the following points as the essential basis for negotiations:

1. Not to allow any forceable annexation of territory seized during the war. Troops occupying these territories to be withdrawn in the shortest possible time.

2. To restore in full the political independence of those nations deprived of their independence during the present war.

3. National groups not enjoying political independence before the war to be guaranteed an opportunity to decide freely by means of a referendum whether to adhere to any given State or to be an independent State. This referendum to be organized as to guarantee complete freedom of voting for the entire population of the given territory, not excluding emigrants and refugees.

11. Ibid., pp. 12–13.
12. For a masterful though Entente-oriented study of the Brest-Litovsk Peace Conference see J. W. Wheeler-Bennett, *The Forgotten Peace: Brest-Litovsk, March 1918*, New York, Morrow, 1939. For a particularly perceptive analysis of Trotsky's diplomacy see Deutscher, *The Prophet Armed*, pp. 346–404. See also Czernin, *Im Weltkriege*, pp. 291–347; von Hoffmann, *The War of Lost Opportunities*, pp. 203–32; and von Kühlmann, *Erinnerungen*, pp. 518–68.

4. In regard to territories inhabited by several nationalities, the right of minorities to be protected by special laws, guaranteeing them cultural national independence, and, as far as practicable, administrative autonomy.

5. None of the belligerent countries to be bound to pay other countries so-called "war costs": indemnities already paid to be returned. Private individuals who have incurred losses owing to the war to be compensated from a special fund, raised by proportional levies on all the belligerent countries.

6. Colonial questions to be decided on the lines laid down in points 1, 2, 3, and 4.

As a supplement to these points the Russian delegation proposes that the contracting parties should condemn the attempts of strong nations to restrict the freedom of weaker nations by such indirect methods as economic boycotts, economic subjection of one country to another by means of compulsory commercial agreements, separate customs agreements, restricting the freedom to trade with third countries, naval blockade without direct military purpose, etc.[13]

Notwithstanding the absence of a specific mention of open diplomacy, the Joffe program must be assessed in the light of the Bolsheviks' commitment to this principle. Immediately after taking power, they had declared their "firm intentions to conduct all negotiations absolutely openly before the entire people."[14] Furthermore, since then they had published the Allied secret treaties and strengthened their belief in the potential usefulness of open-diplomacy procedures.

Henceforth this six-point program, combined with the practice of open diplomacy, was to serve as a policy guide to the Bolshevik delegates at Brest-Litovsk. Moreover, it soon became the foreign-policy manifesto of the unfolding World Revolution. In this second capacity Joffe's Six Points were soon to be confronted by Wilson's Fourteen Points. Consequently, the Joffe program should not be compared to the peace prescription which called for the re-establishment of the Concert of Europe. Instead, it should be compared to the Radical-Socialist program, which was also founded on a confused yet intense aware-

13. Degras, pp. 21–22.
14. Ibid., p. 2.

ness that the war was contributing to the birth of a new world—both national and international.

Once the Joffe declaration is viewed from this broad perspective, it is seen to coincide with two major tenets of the UDC-Wilson platform, namely open diplomacy and liberalization of trade. Furthermore, points one through four indicate that the revolutionary program shares with the progressive platform the growing concern for self-determination, even though point six, which insists that self-determination also applies to colonial areas, is a major deviation from the Western program. On the other hand, three points which are central to the UDC theses are conspicuously missing from the Bolshevik declaration: (1) arbitration; (2) disarmament; and (3) world organization.

It was through Bolshevik insistence at Brest-Litovsk that self-determination became "a dominant interest" for the diplomacy of the war.[15] For many years Lenin had realized that although Western statesmen and reformers were thinking about the possible and probable application of this principle, they did so within a purely European context. Both as a citizen of the major Eurasian Power and as a soldier of the Revolution, Lenin pursued his investigations of self-determination—fully convinced that only an "historical and economic study of the national movement" could suggest a realistic approach. By November 1915 he concluded that it seemed senseless to seek a solution to the problem of self-determination in Europe without also considering the non-European world where "for every four inhabitants of the great nations, there are five inhabitants in their colonies." In Lenin's view, a careful analysis of trends toward self-determination pointed "toward the Orient, Asia, Africa, the colonies, where this movement is not a thing of the past but of the present and the future." [16] Since Lenin's ideas on self-determination crystallized while he was engaged (from 1915 to July 1916) in the writing of his *Imperialism, the Highest Stage of Capitalism,* these ideas may well be connected with the basic thesis of this work. More specifically, it may be suggested that his theses on self-determination are the political extension of Lenin's primarily economic analysis of imperialism.

In early March 1916, Lenin completed his *Theses on the Socialist Revolution and the Right of Nations to Self-Determination,*[17] which

15. Cobban, *National Self-determination,* p. 12.
16. Lenin, *Works, 18,* 223, 367.
17. See ibid., *19,* 47–60.

henceforth served as a basic guide to all Bolshevik discussions on self-determination. In bold and imaginative strokes he divided the world into three distinct areas where the function and dynamics of self-determination differed radically:

> First, the advanced countries of Western Europe and the United States of America. In these countries the bourgeois, progressive, national movements came to an end long ago.
>
> Secondly, Eastern Europe: Austria, the Balkans and particularly Russia. Here it was the twentieth century that particularly developed the bourgeois-democratic national movements and intensified the national struggle. The tasks of the proletariat in these countries—in regard to the consummation of their bourgeois-democratic reformation, as well as in regard to assisting the socialist revolution in other countries—cannot be achieved unless it champions the right of nations to self-determination. In this connection the most difficult but most important task is to merge the class struggle of the workers in the oppressing nations with the class struggle of the workers in the oppressed nations.
>
> Thirdly, the semi-colonial countries, like China, Persia, Turkey and all the colonies, which have a combined population amounting to a billion. In these countries the bourgeois-democratic movements have either hardly begun, or are far from having been completed. Socialists must not only demand the unconditional and immediate liberation of the colonies without compensation —and this demand in its political expression signifies nothing more nor less than the recognition of the right to self-determination—but must render determined support to the more revolutionary elements in the bourgeois-democratic movements for national liberation in these countries and assist their rebellion—and if need be, their revolutionary war—AGAINST the imperialist powers that oppress them.[18]

Clearly, Lenin struck out in two directions which were foreign to the main body of the Western self-determination doctrine. First, he established the inextricable connection between the national movements and the class struggle; second, he posited the right of national self-determination as a universal principle. In introducing these modi-

18. Ibid., pp. 54–55.

fications Lenin undoubtedly was influenced by the historic and geographic legacy of the Russian Empire. The western borderlands of
Russia "were inhabited by peoples who, whether Slav or non-Slav,
stood within the wide circle of European civilization," thus fitting into
Lenin's second geographic area. Moreover, Russia's eastern borderlands "meaning the lands of the Volga basin and of the northern slopes
of the Caucasus, and Central Asia east of the Caspian Sea" not only
offered a colonial setting but also touched on the semicolonial countries and reached into the colonial possessions of the third geographic
area.[19]

The World War, involving India, China, Japan, and the United
States, precipitated a one-world—as against the Europe-centered—
view of international politics which Lenin sought to incorporate into
Bolshevik revolutionary doctrine and strategy. Even in 1914 Lenin
had queried whether the Bolsheviks should seek for an answer to the
self-determination problem in legal definitions deduced from all sorts
of "general concepts of law," or whether they should "seek an answer
in the *historical* and economic study of the national movements?" [20]
It would seem that, whereas in Lenin's Marxist framework colonialism
was a function of the *Highest Stage of (Western) Capitalism,* in his
framework of international politics this same colonialism was an integral part of an historically conditioned yet waning world-power con-
figuration. Russia's debacle in the Russo-Japanese War had awakened
Lenin to the impact which the economic and military maturation of
non-European nations was having on the changing global balance
of power. According to Lenin, while Japan had been growing about
"ten times faster than Russia," the United States was developing so
rapidly that in comparison "Europe as a whole signifies economic
stagnation." [21] He expected the war, this unequaled accelerator of
history, to give a decisive impetus not only to the ripening of the
revolutionary crisis in Europe but also to the development of non-
European power centers and to the colonial awakening (or, stating
it negatively, the weakening of the European Powers). Even though
other leaders in either the Allied or the Central camp were not un-

19. Carr, *The Bolshevik Revolution, 1,* 314–15.
20. V. I. Lenin, *The Right of Nations to Self-determination* (Moscow, 1947),
p. 9.
21. Lenin, *Works, 18,* 271.

aware of these trends, nevertheless, unlike Lenin, they were not likely to favor and promote them.

Traditionalists and Liberals alike were concerned exclusively with the self-determination problem as it developed in Lenin's second geographic area. Before long Lenin, Wilson, and Clemenceau converged in Eastern Europe, each statesman raising the national self-determination banner in the pursuit of different objectives. Against great odds Lenin sought to connect the East European nationalist movements with the class struggle and the Third International. On the other hand, with greater chance of success, while seeking to arouse the nationalities against their Austro-Hungarian masters, Wilson also tied these movements to the Central European bourgeois-democratic revolution and the League of Nations. As for Clemenceau, his ambitions were basically very traditional: he encouraged the formation of the small Eastern European nation-states primarily in the hope that these new states would take the place of Russia as France's partner in an alliance calculated to keep Germany at bay.

In Eastern Europe the national independence movements had already made great strides under bourgeois-democratic leadership. Even though Lenin suggested that the Eastern European Socialist revolutions could not be achieved without championing the right to self-determination, he was far from convinced that the proletariat could wrest control of the nationalities movements from the firmly entrenched bourgeois leaders. Many of his colleagues, among whom Rosa Luxemburg was the most articulate, soon warned Lenin that by sponsoring the self-determination cause, and thereby making the proletariat a supporter of nationalism, the Bolsheviks were helping the bourgeois leaders to pervert the self-determination campaign into a counterrevolutionary instrument. In Luxemburg's view, the war had done nothing to invalidate the Socialist contention that nationalist appeals were useful to the forces of order in their efforts to deflect attention from basic economic and political issues. Even at the risk of playing into bourgeois hands, Lenin nevertheless continued to promote unqualified self-determination, primarily because he was convinced that the war would compel both the Dual Monarchy and the Russian Empire to surrender to the force of nationalism.

During both Lvov's and Kerensky's regimes the Maximalists had criticized the reluctance and the limitations with which the New Russia had "freed" Finland, Poland, and the Ukraine. Given the refusal of Europe's belligerents to sponsor self-determination, the Bolsheviks may have calculated that by recognizing and promoting the "inevitable" they might be able to make decisive inroads into the Eastern nationalities movements. Consequently, as soon as they were in power Lenin, Trotsky, and Stalin consciously pursued a vigorous nationalities policy. They gave complete freedom to Finland, even though the bourgeoisie was bound to gain control of the country; the promises made to the Poles and the Ukrainians were no less radical. Then, at Brest-Litovsk, the Soviet Government became the foremost champion of self-determination, partly because, as even Rosa Luxemburg recognized, it had little else "to oppose to the display of force by German imperialism." [22]

A comparison of Joffe's declaration with Lenin's March 1916 theses reveals the actual extent to which the Bolsheviks amended their ideological program to fight their first critical diplomatic battle. All earlier references to the class struggle now were submerged in a detailed exposition of the "nonrevolutionary" self-determination program. This program was calculated to accentuate the nationalities pressure on Austria-Hungary, one of the major participants at Brest-Litovsk, as well as to impress not only Europe's fellow travelers but also President Wilson. It was in pursuit of either a general peace or the least onerous separate peace that the Maximalists engaged in this doctrinal compromise.

The compromise, however, had many other far-reaching implications for the diplomacy of the war. By their obstinate propagation of "nonrevolutionary" self-determination the Bolsheviks unwittingly turned into the most effective advocates of the Radical-Socialist war-aims program. In actual fact, by subduing or almost suppressing the revolutionary aspects of his nationality platform, Lenin came dangerously close to "parroting" the bourgeois-democratic self-determination thesis. Indeed, it would seem that Rosa Luxemburg was justified in concluding that "the phrases concerning self-determination and the entire nationalist movement . . . experienced an extraordinary strengthening from the Russian Revolution and the Brest negotiations." By coupling the League of Nations and disarmament with self-determination, Wilson eventually formulated the only effective ide-

22. Rosa Luxemburg, *The Russian Revolution*, trans. Bertram D. Wolfe (New York, Workers' Age, 1940), p. 24.

ological program—largely in response to Lenin's all-out sponsorship of self-determination. With considerable justification, Rosa Luxemburg soon accused the Bolsheviks of having supplied "not alone the ideology for the strangling of the Russian Revolution, but even for the plans for settling the entire crisis arising out of the World War." [23]

Insofar as this accusation is based on Joffe's first four points, it cannot be refuted, except to insist that Lenin probably had made a realistic estimate of the inevitable triumph of self-determination in Eastern Europe. Lenin, however, stood his revolutionary ground by persisting in his advocacy of self-determination for the semicolonial and colonial areas. He was convinced that regardless of developments in the second geographic area, the third area would henceforth be of crucial importance, both to the Revolution (Russia) and to Western Europe. It is perhaps symptomatic of this clash of the Western and the Eastern *Weltanschauung* that the Europe-oriented peace program of the Entente eventually brought the issues of arbitration, disarmament, and world organization into a focal position; on the other hand, Lenin's Eurasian perspective led him to look at Europe not only in relation to the developing equalitarian revolution but also in relation to the shifting picture of *world* power and politics. Consequently, as agents and sponsors of these twin historical forces, the Bolsheviks never envisaged a diplomacy of peaceful change. In brief, while the Entente peace program would be geared to securing a Europe-dominated, relatively "static" world order with machinery adequate for the peaceful adjustment of minor diplomatic disputes, the Russian Bolsheviks were devoted to a policy calculated to promote a major shift in internal as well as external power both in Europe and in Asia.

According to Albert Sorel, during the early stages of the French Revolution "the idea that order [was] necessary to the coexistence of nations vanished, and instability became the essence of progress." [24] In assessing the impact of the Bolshevik Revolution, Secretary of State Lansing was one of the first statesmen to contrast the despotism of Berlin and of Petrograd by suggesting that "one, at least [had] the virtue of order, while the other [was] productive of disorder and anarchy." [25] He was particularly disturbed because Lenin's program threatened not only the "existing social order in all countries" but also

23. Ibid., p. 31.
24. Sorel, *L'Europe et la révolution française*, 1, 134.
25. FR, *Lansing Papers*, 2, 253.

the stability of the future world order by applying the self-determination principle to the colonial world. Lansing contended that "however justified may be the principle of local self-government, the necessities of preserving an orderly world require that there should be a national authority with sovereign rights to defend and control the communities within the national boundaries." [26]

Even though the Joffe declaration was calculated to reach the diplomatic chancelleries as well as the peoples of all the belligerents, the Central Powers, having agreed to the peace negotiations, became its primary audience. Since the Allies were likely to abide by their refusal to come to Brest-Litovsk, von Kühlmann and Czernin prepared to exploit the Allied predicament in favor of their diplomacy. As of November 10, 1917, the Austrian Foreign Minister proceeded on the assumption that the peace-hungry Bolsheviks would succeed in maintaining themselves in power. According to Czernin, the Central Powers had every interest in helping Lenin to implement his proposed peace *fait accompli* which could easily mark a decisive turning point in the war. In Czernin's view, since the Allies would refuse to enter into peace negotiations, the Triple Alliance could quite safely take a benevolent attitude toward Lenin's proposals. After the Allied refusal the Central Powers could then meet the Russians on the basis of the July 19th Resolution and various Czernin pronouncements, all of which were sufficiently flexible to allow for a favorable outcome. On November 17 Czernin had flatly predicted that the rigidity of Paris and London in the face of the Bolshevik peace offensive would enable the Central coalition to split Russia from her Allies.[27] At Brest-Litovsk he and von Kühlmann now tried to implement this prediction.

It seems that both enemy foreign ministers realized that by flagrantly violating the liberating self-determination gospel in favor of Ludendorff's naked expansionist demands, the Central Powers would risk losing the ideological and moral initiative to the Bolsheviks. Furthermore, both agreed that a harsh treatment of Russia, in addition to strengthening the diplomatic position of the Entente would stir the parties of movement in Germany and the Dual Monarchy. It is noteworthy that with their daring peace program the militarily impotent Bolsheviks succeeded in throwing the militarily victorious Central Powers on the diplomatic defensive. Though most immediately

26. Ibid., pp. 247–48.
27. Czernin to von Hertling, November 10 and 17, 1917, GFM, Container 1123.

concerned with Vienna's near-starvation, Czernin was no less apprehensive of the corroding effect of the Soviet delegation's nationalities
program. Moreover, before long the German Chief of Staff reported
to the Kaiser that the open diplomacy at Brest-Litovsk was undermining the morale of the Wehrmacht.[28] This impairment of army morale
was particularly prevalent on the Eastern front, where the first armistice
agreement had actually sanctioned fraternization between German and
Russian troops. In the meantime, as part of their ideological offensive,
the Bolsheviks were dropping revolutionary fly-leaves signed by Lenin
and Trotsky over German lines. These tracts promised that Russia
would continue to press her general peace offensive, urged the German
soldiers to let Liebknecht be their inspiration, and called on the German
proletariat to help secure a general peace by rising against their
rulers.[29]

In spite of their appreciation of the importance of not leaving the
ideological initiative to the Russians, the German and Austro-Hungarian foreign ministers felt uncomfortable on this highly unconven-
tional diplomatic battlefield. The unorthodoxy of both the behavior
and the composition of the Soviet delegation put additional strains
on this first face-to-face encounter of the Old and the New Diplomacy.
Heretofore von Kühlmann and Czernin had been accustomed to negotiating in an atmosphere of grave decorum and expedient secrecy.
Now, in order to match the performance of their public-conscious
Soviet opponents, they were called upon to talk simultaneously to their
Soviet interlocutors as well as to the Allied and Central peoples. There
must have been numerous occasions when von Kühlmann and Czernin
inclined toward abandoning their resistance to the undiplomatic, imperialist German Supreme Command, which pressed relentlessly for
immediate and complete control of the resources of the Ukraine and of
Courland.[30]

Nevertheless, on December 25 Czernin tried to create the impression
that Joffe's principles were acceptable to the Central Powers. However,
this acceptance was conditional: "all the powers now participating in
the war must within a suitable period, without exception and without

28. A. D. Schwertfeger, *Entstehung, Durchführung und Zusammenbruch der
Offensive von 1918* (Berlin, Deutsche Verlagsgesellschaft für Politik und Geschichte, 1925), p. 103.
29. See GFM, Container 1123.
30. Erich Ludendorff, *Kriegsführung und Politik* (Berlin, Mittler, 1922), pp.
236–38; and Noulens, *Mon Ambassade en Russie Soviétique, 1,* 207–8.

any reserve, bind themselves" to this program.[31] Even though this adroit diplomatic maneuver was accompanied by a statement which indicated that the Quadruple Alliance had no intention of abandoning Poland, Lithuania, or Courland,[32] it nevertheless scored a decisive success in the struggle for the minds of men. Allied statesmen were embarrassed still further when on December 28 the Central Powers agreed to still another postponement of negotiations in order to enable the Bolsheviks to send their third invitation to the Entente.

On December 29, after consulting with the Central Executive Committee of the Soviets, Trotsky issued this third invitation in the form of an open appeal to both the Allied peoples and governments. In his latest message the Foreign Commissar contrasted the Soviet and the Central program, both of which had just been outlined at Brest-Litovsk. He insisted that only a combination of adverse military conditions and growing political pressures by the German proletariat were forcing the Central Powers to make a few reluctant concessions.

> If the Governments of the Allied countries would express their readiness, together with the Russian government, to found a peace upon the complete and unconditional recognition of the principle of self-determination for all peoples in all States, if they would begin by giving this right to the oppressed peoples of their own state, this would create such international conditions that when the inherently contradictory programs of Germany and especially Austria-Hungary, were shown in all their weakness, objection would be overcome by the pressure of all the interested people.[33]

Assuming Trotsky was truly anxious to enlist the help of the Allies, might he not have been well advised to eliminate all references to popular pressures and to the colonial question? Or was Trotsky sufficiently astute to realize that his ideological forays were not likely to interfere with Allied national-interest calculations? At any rate, like the two preceding messages, this one also failed to elicit an immediate, favorable response from the Allies. Russia seemed doomed to confront her powerful enemies all by herself at the peace table.

This renewed refusal to enter into peace negotiations also accen-

---

31. For the translated text of Czernin's statement see Dickinson, pp. 101–2.
32. Cf. Czernin, *Im Weltkriege*, p. 311.
33. Cited in Dickinson, pp. 104–6.

tuated the stalemate of Allied diplomacy. By refusing to participate in
the Brest-Litovsk debates, the Allies lost favor with public opinion both
at home and abroad.[34] The Allied Powers could not refute Trotsky's
charge that they had not even "advanced that one step toward peace"
which the Central Powers had been obliged to make. Nor could they
disagree with Trotsky's repeated insistence that it was "necessary to
state clearly what is the peace program of France, Italy, Great Britain,
and the United States." [35] Above all, the situation called for some sort
of public pronouncement by the Allies.

In the meantime, in Paris on December 22, 1917, the French and
British governments—represented respectively by Clemenceau and
Pichon, Milner and Cecil—had formally agreed on the expediency of
repeating their "readiness to accept the principle of self-determination
and, subject to that, of no annexations and no indemnities." However,
at this same meeting two other policy decisions were made which, under
the circumstances, had to be kept strictly secret. The first of these
decisions was unofficially but deliberately to promote the Sadoul-
Robins type of contracts: each government was to "at once get into
relations with the Bolsheviki through unofficial agents, each country
as seems best to it." [36]

Secondly, anticipating further German incursions into Russia, the
French and British statesmen decided that it was "necessary to keep in
touch as far as we can with the Ukraine, the Cossacks, Finland, Siberia,
the Caucasus, etc., because these various semi-autonomous provinces
represent a very large proportion of the strength of Russia." Furthermore, they agreed that "besides finance, it is important to have agents
and officers to advise and support the provincial governments and their
armies," though this would have to be done "as quietly as possible so
as to avoid the imputation—as far as we can—that we are preparing to
make war on the Bolsheviks." According to the Milner-Cecil Memorandum, which embodied this program, whereas the Ukraine was assigned
to France the British took the responsibility for "the other south-east

34. Walter Lippmann, *Public Opinion* (New York, Harcourt, Brace, 1922), p.
210.
35. Degras, p. 25.
36. The entire text of this Milner-Cecil Memorandum, incorporating the
decisions of these discussions, is reproduced in Lloyd George, *War Memoirs*, 2,
1550–51; and in *FR, Russia, 1918, 1,* 330–31. See also Kennan, *Russia Leaves
the War*, pp. 178–79.

provinces." Moreover, since these Allied leaders "understood" that
the United States would "assist" these efforts financially, they forwarded this Memorandum to Lansing on December 29.[37]

Obviously, neither the Allied peoples nor their elected representatives were to be informed of this hastily projected intervention. In the
absence of any official response to the Brest-Litovsk summons, the
forces of movement redoubled their war-aims pressures. Also, the
Allied peoples read all dispatches about the Russo-German diplomatic
duel with silent prayer.

Possibly upon official request, even *le Temps* and the London *Times*
temporarily repressed their hostility to the Bolsheviks in order to feature prominently articles dealing with the apparent success with which
the Soviet delegation was embarrassing the enemy. The following
front-page head lines in the New York *Times* may be considered in-
dicative of the perspective with which the Brest-Litovsk Conference
was being both reported in the press and viewed in official quarters:

> December 23—"Russia Won't Bow before Kaiser, Trotsky Insists"
> December 26—"Trotsky Protests against German Shifting Troops"
> December 27—"Report Lenin Gives Germans Peace Ultimatum"
> December 30—"The Terms of Peace Rouse the Fury of Pan-Ger-
> mans"
> January 3—"Russian Stand Pleases London"
> January 4—"Allies May Now Recognize Lenin"
> January 5—"Trotsky Opened Eyes of Germans"
> January 7—"Bolshevik Stand Shocks the Teutons"
> January 7—"Bolsheviki May Help Allies Best" [38]

In the negotiations at Brest-Litovsk the London *Daily News* detected
something which the world "had not seen since the French Revolution:
. . . a straight fight between a nation armed with an idea and a na-

37. In a letter to President Wilson dated December 10, 1917, Secretary of State
Lansing had already recommended Allied support of "Kaledin and the military
group around him." See Wilson Papers. According to Kennan, Lansing's memorandum was the basis for the American Government's decision to help financially
anti-Bolshevik groups in south and southeast Russia; in turn, this decision "was
taken into account by the French and British statesmen in their discussions."
Kennan, *Russia Leaves the War*, pp. 174–78.

38. Walter Lippmann and Charles Merz, "A Test of the News," in the *New
Republic* (Special Supplement, August 4, 1920), p. 12.

tion armed with diplomatic cunning." This Radical British daily summarized the question which the statesmen of the Allied and Associated Powers had to answer: "Are we to be silent and passive witnesses of this momentous conflict?" [39]

In view of the persistent interest of the forces of movement in the Russian problem, the answer to this question would have to be formulated in the light of both diplomatic and internal political considerations. Hence the decision on whether and how to answer the Trotsky summons would be made not by the foreign offices of the Allied and Associated Nations but by their chief executives. Whereas Clemenceau chose to remain silent, first Lloyd George and then Wilson delivered a major public pronouncement. (The Prime Minister's Trades Union address and the President's Fourteen Points address will be discussed in the next two chapters.)

Of the three Allied statesmen, Clemenceau was perhaps the least flexible. His reactions to the disorderly elements which were threatening to beset the international order were much akin to those of Lansing. However, Clemenceau had made a most down-to-earth evaluation of the military situation in Russia; it has been noted how this realistic estimate may have affected his stand on war aims. But added to his military calculus, in which the potential of the United States army and economy figured so heavily, was his almost complete inability to evaluate the rising political forces ranged to his left. The Tiger, unlike Lloyd George, had completely freed himself from the ideas and aspirations which had guided his earlier political career. He fought this uncompromising military war in order to restore *la belle France*, which had been so mortally wounded. Politics would not be allowed to interfere with war-making: the recovery of the safety and honor of his country would be greatly accelerated and enhanced by the temporary arrest of the parliamentary process, which in any case was none too congenial to his temperament. Also, in a predominantly agricultural country where the peasantry always bore the brunt of the military burden the proletarian masses did not have enough momentum to precipitate major political realignments. Clemenceau was able to assess power in its cruder and short-run manifestations. His estimate of the Russian weaknesses, his reliance on American aid, his insistence on a unity of command etc. all testify that he was at home in this com-

39. Cited in Willis, *England's Holy War*, pp. 246–47.

position of physical power. On the whole, his assessment of the vector of forces tended to suffer from his inability to recognize that even ideas are weapons.[40]

Lloyd George, on the other hand, was much more of a politician; he was so enraptured by the political game that he was often unable to stop short of unscrupulousness. It must be remembered, though, that the Welshman, as compared to Clemenceau, had to contend with a much more complicated situation. His attention had to be tuned as much to a rapidly emerging Labour party as to the increasingly self-assertive Dominions. Lloyd George's prodigious political instincts readily enabled him to detect stirrings and strivings which might eventually find expression in new power configurations. He sought to control these new-fledged forces by dealing them the deathblow of partial recognition. Indeed, throughout the war the accessibility of Lloyd George "to people with whom he did not agree, was one of his greatest assets." [41]

President Wilson, after America's entry into the war, set out momentarily to harness all available power in the service of the Allied cause. Whereas he had at first been the only Western chief executive to articulate the ideological issues which eventually would have to be faced, after April 2 he (reluctantly?) surrendered that function to Petrograd. Moreover, the President came under considerable pressure from London and Paris to build the American industry and army with extreme dispatch. Therefore his forced-draft concern with the fighting of the war overshadowed, for the time being, his passionate devotion to an inquiry into the implications of the coming peace. However, as the year progressed and America's war effort was well on the way, Wilson, always prompted by Colonel House, realized that he should again attempt a discussion of the purposes of the war. In the meantime, although the world had moved in on both the United States and its President, except for Theodore Roosevelt's pugnacious campaign in favor of a peace of victory and not of ideals the American political scene was unagitated. Unlike his two European colleagues, Wilson was free to be a statesman.

40. The following year, after his first pre-Armistice talks with the French Premier in Paris, Colonel House noted in his diary that "the trouble with Clemenceau is that he thinks in terms of the Second Empire. He does not know what all this new thought is about." House Diary, October 30, 1918.

41. Lord Beveridge in introduction to Cole, p. xi.

In late December 1917, then, Clemenceau, Lloyd George, and Wilson were faced with a military, diplomatic, political, and psychological crisis of great magnitude. Irrespective but not independent of domestic politics, all three had to come to terms with the impending liquidation of Germany's Eastern front and Italy's continuing military ineptitude. Diplomatically they were forced to respond to the enemy-applauded Bolshevik challenge to publicize Allied war aims, especially since the diplomatic situation was so structured that a refusal to respond was bound to play into enemy hands. Also, in view of the new-found strength of the forces of movement, in France and Britain the political implications of a call for renewed efforts and sacrifices on the threshold of another winter campaign had to be faced. And then, "in London and Paris, beneath all the embittered tenacity which three and a half years of war had bred, there was an undercurrent of dull apprehension at the realization of the numerical superiority which the Germans would now be able to amass in the West. . . . The long exertion was now taking its psychic toll. Many people were wretchedly overworked and overwrought. Tempers were frayed, sensibilities chafed and tender. There was, in some quarters at least, a loss of elasticity." [42]

Against this somber but by no means desperate background the Allied statesmen took inventory of their military, economic, and ideological resources.[43] In general, even though Germany's concentration on the Western front was greatly feared, two factors gave confidence in the face of this prospect. On the one hand, it was generally held that "this would be Germany's last great effort, and that if it were successfully contained, the worst would be over." [44] On the other hand, as both Lloyd George and Clemenceau looked ahead to spring and summer, unlike the Central statesmen they were able to anticipate fresh replacements for their seriously worn and depleted infantry and materiel.

These replacements would soon arrive from the United States, where the military and economic mobilization efforts of 1917 were about

---

42. George F. Kennan, *The Decision to Intervene* (Princeton, Princeton University Press, 1958), pp. 3–4.

43. "Political power in the international sphere may be divided into three categories: (a) military power, (b) economic power, (c) power over opinion." E. H. Carr, *The Twenty Year's Crisis, 1919–1939: An Introduction to the Study of International Relations* (2d ed. London, Macmillan, 1949), p. 108.

44. Kennan, *The Decision to Intervene*, p. 3.

to bear plentiful fruit. However, the Allied response to the pressing diplomatic and ideological challenge emanating from Brest-Litovsk could not be delayed until the American potential could be translated into actual military power on the Western front. In fact, once the tangible balance of forces had shifted in favor of the Allies, the urgency of countering the ideological offensive would be greatly reduced. Presently, therefore, while taking a power inventory, Lloyd George and Wilson decided that by drawing on certain intangible elements of power which were immediately available to them they might in some degree alleviate the transitory military and economic strain. Among these intangible elements of power, ideology figured most prominently, as is amply evident from the formulation and the text of the British Prime Minister's Trades Union speech and of the American President's Fourteen Points address.

8. LLOYD GEORGE ANSWERS

THE SUMMONS

DURING the last weeks of 1917 and in the first days of January 1918 Lloyd George was surrounded by revisionist pressures, even though only a year before, the advocacy of the knock-out blow had won him extensive support. Because of vocal domestic and foreign demands, the British Premier presently considered the utility and substance of a major diplomatic pronouncement.

Domestically the Labourites, the Lansdowne-ites, and the Milnerites insisted on a clear-cut retrenchment from the knock-out-blow policy. The Cabinet could not fail to notice that the demand for war-aims clarification was no longer limited to the negligible UDC–ILP minority. Even Lord Robert Cecil felt this revisionist pressure in the extended war-aims debate in Commons on December 19, 1917. The subterfuge of refusing to consider the war-aims problem by simply imputing unpatriotic motives to Ponsonby's and Trevelyan's speeches ceased to be effective; Cecil was challenged to answer the speeches of many Members who heretofore had never intervened in debates on the diplomacy of the war.[1]

From abroad, and not without impact on the aforementioned internal pressures, there came the Trotsky summons and indications of an impending diplomatic initiative from Washington. Furthermore, these converging political pressures were not unrelated to the ominous military stalemate.[2] This stalemate, whose dangers were magnified by the

1. *PD, 100* (December 19, 1917), cols. 1993–2097.
2. W. H. Buckler reported that "the growing sentiment in favor of peace by negotiation is making its way in the army on purely military grounds." Buckler to House, December 13, 1917, Buckler Papers.

313

314   THE NEW DIPLOMACY

Brest-Litovsk armistice, now forced the British Cabinet to seek additional recruits. At the very moment when Labour renewed its war-
aims drive, it was asked to help supply additional manpower. Would the
Labour party do so unconditionally, or would it insist on prior war-
aims concessions?

In an annual balance sheet of the war addressed to Colonel House,
W. H. Buckler quoted a member of the War Cabinet as saying that
he was "willing to be blackmailed by Labour for the duration of the
war provided [he could] keep them in it." [3] In a similar vein the staff
of the Inquiry suggested that because of the continuing stalemate in
Western and Central Europe, domestic unity would "involve placating
the moderate Left even at the cost of opposition from the irreconcilable
Right." According to the Inquiry, both European coalitions were likely
to "depend increasingly upon this movement toward the Left"; furthermore the "price of unity is increased in each nation as the liberalism
of the enemy increases." [4] This diagnosis was particularly applicable
to Great Britain at the turn of the year. Lloyd George was concerned
by the increasing liberalism of the enemy as displayed at Brest-Litovsk;
also, he recognized the expediency of placating the moderate Left,
especially since Lansdowne and Milner had reduced the irreconcil-
ability of the Right.

The British Left, which was about to articulate strongly its war-aims
proposals and conditions, had not been crushed or intimidated by the
recent passport refusal. Actually, as early as September 4, 1917, Henderson had insolently proclaimed that even though Stockholm "as a mere
name may be dead," the first steps to secure a revival of the Internationalist project were already being taken.[5] After his resignation
Henderson deliberately proceeded to marshal political support for
a renewed war-aims offensive in Great Britain. With himself as the
new center, the former War Cabinet member enlisted the cooperation
of Robert Smillie and J. H. Thomas on his right, and Ramsay Mac-
Donald and Sidney Webb on his left; together they gradually won
over to the revisionist viewpoint a substantial number of conservative
leaders in both the political and the industrial sectors of the Labour
movement.[6]

3. Buckler to House, September 30, 1917, Buckler Papers.
4. *FR, Paris Peace Conference, 1919, 1,* 29–30.
5. R. W. Postgate, *The International during the War* (London, 1918), p. 50.
6. Maddox, *Foreign Relations,* p. 150.

Meanwhile a combined subcommittee of the Labour party Executive and the TUC Parliamentary Committee began to draft a unified war-aims statement on the basis of the various British programs which recently had been submitted to the August 28th inter-Allied Socialist Conference. With Henderson's political task force in the background this subcommittee made a careful and fruitful study of the comprehensive, yet often conflicting, war-aims programs of the Labour party, the Independent Labour party, the Fabian Society, the British Socialist party, and the Union of Democratic Control. The subcommittee was busily engaged in this task when the news from Brest-Litovsk increased the receptivity of the rank and file to Henderson's war-aims arguments. Gradually the restlessness of labor became so pronounced that it threatened to interfere "seriously with the output of essential war material and equipment." [7]

In mid-December the subcommittee completed the draft of the new Memorandum on War Aims which was to be "recommended for general endorsement by all sections of the British Labour Movement" at a Special Conference scheduled to convene at Central Hall, Westminster, London, on December 28, 1917.[8] In view of the mounting political and labor agitation, the War Cabinet was certain to study this document with great care; also the unrelenting Bolshevik peace offensive helped to secure an attentive official and unofficial audience.

One of the most curious and striking aspects of this very detailed Memorandum was the complete absence of any reference, direct or indirect, to either the November Revolution or the Brest-Litovsk negotiations. Furthermore, the Memorandum did not mention the recruiting issue which now brought the negotiations between Lloyd George and the Labour party to a head. Like Joffe's Six Points, the Memorandum may also have been calculated to transcend the partic-

7. Hamilton, *Arthur Henderson,* pp. 170, 172. For a contemporary, on-the-spot journalistic account by two American Socialists of the radicalization of British Labour during the last year of war see Paul U. Kellogg and Arthur Gleason, *British Labor and the War,* New York, Boni and Liverwright, 1919. See also David Lloyd George, *Memoirs of the Peace Conference* (2 vols. New Haven, Yale University Press, 1939), *1,* 34.

8. The Labour Party and the Trades Union Congress, *Memorandum on War Aims,* London, December 28, 1917. The inside of the front cover of this Memorandum gives a complete listing of the National Executive of the Labour party and of the Parliamentary Committee of the Trades Union Congress. The entire text is conveniently accessible in *International Conciliation,* No. 123 (February 1918), 45–56.

ular political context in which it was brought forth. Whereas the Russian Bolshevik program sought to rally prospective members of the Third International, the British Labour program sought to regroup the scattered forces of the Second International.[9]

Notwithstanding this long-range objective, in November–December 1917 the timing, the mood, and the ideas, of British Labour leaders were decisively influenced by Russian developments. Perhaps the most striking evidence of Petrograd's indelible imprint is manifest in another war-aims memorandum which was drafted by Arthur Henderson, but which was never published.[10] In this unpublished draft-memorandum the Secretary of the National Executive of the Labour party unequivocally asserted that "British Labour welcomes warmly the six main principles laid down by the Russian Government." Accordingly, Henderson sought to assure Lenin and Trotsky that Labour approved their principles "in essentials" and that judging by "his published statements" President Wilson also endorsed them. After exposing the "deceit and false pretense" of Czernin's December 25th proposals bearing on Poland and Lithuania, Henderson's statement continued:

> We accept the principle of self-determination . . . for all peoples, and believe that this can be secured for Egypt and India by a rapid extension of self-governing institutions on Dominion lines.
>
> We accept the principles of no annexations. We will take no territory out of this war. . . . As for indemnities, we want none. But like our Russian comrades we demand reparation according to international law for definite wrongs done to nations or individuals.
>
> We ask our Russian comrades not to believe that the imperialist British press at all represents the real feeling of the British

9. On January 8, 1918, the same day that Wilson delivered his Fourteen Points address, the Stockholm Committee gave the following instructions to Huysmans, who was about to leave for a Labour party conference in Nottingham: "To save the situation the perspective of a separate peace must be changed into one of a general peace, and this is possible, thanks to the tactic which you [i.e. the Labour party] have just adopted. You have formulated your war aims. You will now ask the Allied Socialists to endorse them. Then you will ask that your formula be made the program of the International. Hence, you will bring about the general Conference which can play its historic role on the condition that it will not allow itself to be overtaken by events." Cited in Comité Organisateur, *Stockholm*, p. xxx.

10. This memorandum, entitled *Labour's Peace Terms*, is clearly marked "proof only," and is preserved in the archives of the Labour party, Transport House, London.

people—either soldiers or civilians. If we had been able to meet at Stockholm, or elsewhere, we should by now have learnt to understand one another better.

Henderson's off-the-record answer to the Brest-Litovsk summons then spelled out the relationship between Trotsky's desperate appeals and Britain's own domestic crisis. The British Labour leader maintained that since the Russian debacle had further aggravated the military stalemate, the War Cabinet was compelled to ask Labour "to waive certain pledges and to supply half a million more men." In the light of the new war-induced circumstances which buttressed the bargaining position of the British Left, Henderson concluded that Labour should "state clearly for what and what only it is prepared to fight on." Notwithstanding their full appreciation of this perilous emergency, the leaders of the war-aims faction pressed their offensive inside the Labour world, in parliamentary circles, and before the public at large. The official Memorandum, however, was less dramatic, less direct, and less emotional than Henderson's draft. The Labour war-aims leaders proposed to address not only Lenin and Wilson but also the British War Cabinet, the non-Socialist forces of movement, and the Lansdowne-ites.

Even though the first section of the December 28th Memorandum declared Labour's continued adherence to the economic interpretation of the causes of war, this rededication to Socialist doctrine was largely ritualistic. In the text it served as a preamble to Section II, which set forth the general aims and principles for the coming peace under the heading "Making the World Safe for Democracy." [11] Thus British Labour declared its enthusiastic allegiance to Wilson's ideological crusade, which now became "the fundamental purpose . . . in supporting the continuance of the struggle." The Labour Memorandum did not call for a peace without victory, but for a battle calculated, in the Wells-Shaw-Wilson spirit, to make sure "that there should be henceforth on earth no more war."

Convinced that no matter who triumphs, "the peoples will have lost unless some effective method of preventing war can be found," Labour imaginatively offered its prescription for perpetual peace. Accordingly, the Memorandum enumerated five essential principles on which international politics would have to be based in tomorrow's era of lasting

11. In this discussion all quotations are taken from the document cited in footnote 8 above.

peace: (1) "complete democratization of all countries"; (2) abandonment of every form of "imperialism"; (3) "suppression of secret diplomacy"; (4) limitation of military service and armaments; and
(5) establishment of a League of Nations. Judging by these fundamental requisites, the UDC–Wilson ideas had successfully permeated
the thinking of Labour's drafting committee. For the time being,
Lenin's program was cast in a similar though less pronounced idealistic
nonrevolutionary mold. However, whereas his commitment to international Radical-Socialism was expediential, Labour discarded the revolutionary, internationalist Socialist gospel out of profound conviction.

On the other hand, Labour's embrace of the self-determination principle was less complete than Lenin's. The Memorandum's longest
section merely insisted that all territorial adjustments "be arrived at by
common agreement on the general principle of allowing all peoples to
settle their own destinies." It is not without interest to note that whereas Labour's program bearing on Europe was very moderate, the solutions it envisaged for the Turkish Empire and Tropical Africa were
somewhat more daring.

In accordance with official Allied policy, the British Left insisted
on "complete and untrammeled" independence as well as reparations
for Belgium. However, probably in view of the recent advances of the
minoritaires in the SFIO, the English Labour world advocated a plebiscite in the twin provinces under League auspices without prior transfer to France, instead of calling for the straightforward restoration of
Alsace-Lorraine. Similarly, Labour's support of Italy's claims now were
much less articulate than a few months earlier. In the light of the
recently published text of the Treaty of London, the subcommittee
incorporated a last-minute reservation into the text. While recognizing
the necessity for "securing the legitimate interests of the people of
Italy in the adjacent seas," Labour had "no sympathy with the far-
reaching aims of conquest of Italian Imperialism, and [believed] that
all legitimate needs [could] be safeguarded, without precluding a
like recognition of the needs of others or annexations of other people's
territories."

According to the Memorandum, the rising nationalities of the Balkan peninsula were to safeguard their new freedom by joining not
only a Customs Union but also a Balkan Federation. Though sincere
and devoted sponsors of an enlightened nationalities policy, neither
the ILP nor the UDC ever lost sight of the socioeconomic aspects of

self-determination. Unlike the *New Europe*, Wilson, and Joffe, Labour sought to cushion the economic and political shocks which were bound to result from the disintegration of the Austro-Hungarian and the Turkish Empires. In Labour's view, the legitimate ethnic, religious, and language aspirations of the Balkan peoples could be satisfied only with the help of a common economic and political framework for the cluster of new nation-states.

Next, Labour proclaimed that the peace of the world required "that Constantinople should be made a free port" and that the Straits be neutralized permanently. Furthermore, since it seemed "impracticable" to leave the peoples of the Turkish Empire "to settle their own destinies," the Memorandum insisted that, "conformable with the policy of 'no annexations,' they should be placed for administration in the hands of a commission acting under . . . the League of Nations." Whereas this suggestion distinctly anticipated the Mandates System, the paragraph pertaining to the colonies of Tropical Africa was even more precocious. Disclaiming every sympathy with imperialist ambitions, Labour proposed "the transfer of the present Colonies of the European Powers in Tropical Africa" to the League of Nations and "their administration under the Legislative Council of that authority as a single independent African State." Even though Labour generally shared the Bolsheviks' concern with colonial problems, they were not in accord with the Bolsheviks on geographic perspective. As a leader of Russia, Lenin tended to focus on the colonial areas located on the Eurasian land mass; Labour assigned Africa a central position in its colonial program. This emphasis on the dark continent may have been due to long-standing Labour concern with African problems which had produced severe tensions among the Great Powers since the turn of the century.[12] Also, E. D. Morel's passionate campaign against the cruelties practiced by most, if not all, colonial powers on the African natives may have left its imprint on the Labour document.[13] Eventually the Right pointed to these colonial proposals as most symbolic of the heresies which the New Diplomacy threatened to perpetrate.[14]

12. Cf. Walter Lippmann, *The Stakes of Diplomacy* (New York, Holt, 1915), esp. pp. 87–110.

13. Two of E. D. Morel's major works are *The Congo Slave State* (Liverpool, 1903), and *Africa and the Peace of Europe* (London, 1917).

14. "Could one conceivably imagine, even if only for a moment, that the

No less challenging to the Old Diplomacy, however, were two subsequent sections of the Memorandum entitled respectively "Economic
Relations" and "Problems of Peace." Labour cautioned that "to make
the world safe for Democracy involves much more than the prevention
of war, either military or economic"; it also warned that "it will be a
device of the capitalist interests to pretend that the Treaty of Peace
need concern itself only with the cessation of the struggles of the armed
forces and with any necessary territorial readjustments." These admonitions echoed Rosa Luxemburg's earlier prediction that the victorious Powers would restrict the agenda of peace negotiations to traditional diplomatic questions. But whereas she hoped to exploit this
fatal "capitalist" narrow-mindness to promote the revolutionary cause,
British Labour pointed to these new dimensions of international politics
as part of its search for an integral program of peaceful change, domestic and international. Consequently the Memorandum called both
for free trade and for international labor legislation. Moreover, having
turned into devoted students of War Socialism under Sidney Webb's
guidance, Britain's Labour leaders now suggested that the nationalization, centralization, and rationing upon which the entire war economy
rested could serve not only the transition to peace but also the postwar order.

"In view of the probable world-wide shortage, after the war, of ex-
portable foodstuffs, raw materials and merchant shipping," Labour
proposed that all belligerents continue the necessary government controls "to meet the most urgent needs of the whole community on the
principle of 'no cake for anyone until all have bread.'" Furthermore,
convinced that extensive unemployment would be an inevitable by-
product of uncontrolled reconversion, Britain's Labour leaders declared
that the "restless" mood of the demobilized soldiers and workers could
be satisfied only by equitable measures calculated to minimize the
social and human cost of reconversion. Labour supported its arguments
in favor of government-controlled reconversion with the assertion that
"widespread unemployment in any country, like a famine, is an injury
not to that country alone, but to the rest of the world." Since major
unemployment "is as much the result of government neglect as is any

British Government could approve the queer (*étrange*) colonial program which
the workers' congress sanctioned in London yesterday?" *Le Temps*, December 30,
1917.

epidemic disease," governments should prepare plans for extensive public works to supplement investments by private capital.

Even under Asquith, the War Cabinet had commissioned a Reconstruction Committee to study these nondiplomatic aspects of peacemaking. Later, under Lloyd George, this Committee's assignment had been broadened, partly in the hope of convincing Labour that a genuine *Neuorientierung* would follow the political truce. In this connection the War Cabinet had sought out three Fabians (including Beatrice Webb), and two Labourites (Clynes and Thomas) to serve on this fifteen-member Reconstruction Committee; another Fabian, Arthur Greenwood, and Philip Kerr, of the Liberal-Imperialist *Round Table*, served the Committee in an administrative capacity.[15]

This officially sponsored cooperation of prominent representatives of the forces of movement with leading members of the forces of order served the purpose of keeping the center-right Cabinet abreast of opposition ideas not only on post-war reforms but also on war aims. Consequently, it seems hardly likely that any part of the Labour Memorandum on War Aims came as a shock or as a surprise to Lloyd George and his Cabinet colleagues.

Nevertheless the Prime Minister, even though close to issuing his own war-aims statement, sent a rather cold letter to the December 28th Conference of the Labour Movement. In this letter he maintained that war aims could be revised only in agreement with the Allies, that the problem was constantly kept in view by the Government, and that the delay in revision was largely due to Russia's inability to send representatives to the inter-Allied Conference in Paris a month ago. Although at the Labour Conference a few right-wing Labourites used this Lloyd George letter as a basis from which to criticize the Memorandum, the majority of the delegates resolutely supported the war-aims spokesmen. Consequently, after Henderson reminded the Conference that if the country had listened to him last July, the "present awful Russian disaster" might have been avoided,[16] the Memorandum was accepted by 2,132,000 to 1,164,000 votes.[17]

In their first concerted campaign for a revision of war aims since

15. Lloyd George, *War Memoirs*, 2, 1160; Addison, *Four and a Half Years*, 2, 423, 434, 607, 608–12; Cole, p. 81.
16. Hamilton, *Arthur Henderson*, p. 172.
17. Kellogg and Gleason, *British Labor and the War*, pp. 29–30.

Henderson's resignation, the major factions of the British forces of movement were able to base themselves on a concrete, unified program. Meanwhile, this unmistakable radicalization of the Left, combined with the depressing reports from Eastern Europe, increased the receptivity of top decision-makers to counsels of moderation.

When C. P. Scott, editor of the Liberal *Manchester Guardian,* saw the Prime Minister on December 28, the Brest-Litovsk negotiations "formed the necessary starting point" for their discussion. Presently Lloyd George warned Scott that he was "in a very pacifist temper" and that for some time he had felt that there ought to be a restatement of war aims. Furthermore, he reported that there was a "good deal of feeling in the War Cabinet towards peace—Balfour is not opposed— Milner is the most inclined to peace of anybody. Carson is nothing so violent as he seems. . . . I don't know about Curzon." [18] About this same time a short private talk with Lord Milner confirmed Buckler's earlier "impression as to the conciliatory spirit" in England. After Czernin's speech Buckler also reported that "the *Express* (the organ of Beaverbrook and indirectly of Bonar Law) was deliberately advising the Government to answer the German peace offer." [19]

There can be no doubt that this conciliatory mood in Britain's highest decision-making circles influenced Lloyd George's decision to prepare an important war-aims statement. According to the Prime Minister's own account, he drafted this statement "after full deliberation by the War Cabinet and consultation with the responsible leaders of the Liberal party and the representatives of organized Labour." In recent weeks, many Liberals had expressed their agreement with Lansdowne's request. Now, at a special breakfast meeting with Lloyd George, Lord Asquith and Viscount Grey approved the Premier's 'projected text. Likewise, through General Smuts the Dominions gave their consent.[20]

Nevertheless, undoubtedly the most extensive and least orthodox negotiations were held with the Labour party. Judging by a hasty cable from Balfour to House, the success of these negotiations with Labour for additional recruits "depended mainly on the immediate publication of an official war-aims pronouncement." [21] Since thus far

18. Hammond, *C. P. Scott of the Manchester Guardian,* pp. 221, 223; Riddell, *Lord Riddell's War Diary,* p. 293; *The History of the Times, 4,* Pt. I, pp. 345–46.
19. Buckler to House, December 21, 1917, and January 1, 1918, Buckler Papers.
20. Lloyd George, *War Memoirs, 2,* 1492.
21. Seymour, *Intimate Papers, 3,* 340.

Lloyd George had made no attempt to enter into the inter-Allied consultations which he had mentioned in his message to the December 28th Labour Conference, Balfour's emphasis on Labour's ultimatum may have been calculated to justify the Prime Minister's unilateral diplomatic initiative. It is true, nevertheless, that Lloyd George himself discussed the Labour Memorandum exhaustively with the members of the TUC Parlimentary Committee and the Labour party Executive. According to the London *Times* in this Lloyd George – Labour consultation "a full and frank exchange of views took place not only on the broad question of general policy, but also on the detailed proposal of the [Labour] memorandum." [22] By January 1, 1918, Buckler quoted a prominent Liberal journalist to the effect that the Premier was "now converted, presumably by Labour pressure, to much more moderate views" and that he had "abandoned his opposition . . . to the Labour party's policy of conciliation." [23]

The very fact that Lloyd George chose to make his war-aims pronouncement at the Trades Union Congress in London on January 5, 1918, is conclusive evidence that—to follow the Inquiry analysis—the War Cabinet was seeking "to placate the moderate Left." In the opening paragraph of his speech, Lloyd George candidly stated that in view of recent requests for additional assistance from organized labor, the latter's "representatives are entitled to ask that any misgivings and doubts" about the purposes of the war "should be definitely cleared." [24]

Jacques Bainville, the French right-wing journalist and historian, immediately pointed to the novelty of a Prime Minister deliberately seeking out a labor congress as a place and occasion for a major diplomatic pronouncement. "Besides Parliament, are there other forces which count, and with which one consults and negotiates? . . . Parliament alone no longer counts," Bainville concluded, "and the nation has other representatives in addition to the deputies from geographic districts." [25]

Notwithstanding his decision to address a labor convention, Lloyd George knew that, compared to those with whom he shared the Labour platform, he would have to speak to a more comprehensive and less

22. *Times* (London), January 7, 1918; and Lloyd George, *War Memoirs*, 2, 1510.

23. Buckler to House, January 1, 1918, Buckler Papers.

24. All quotations are drawn from the complete text of the speech in Lloyd George, *War Memoirs*, 2, 1510–17.

25. *L'Action Française*, January 7, 1918.

homogeneous audience. In addition to addressing the English nation, Lloyd George had to speak to the statesmen and peoples of the enemy coalition, as well as to the Bolshevik Government.

Consequently, the Prime Minister had to deal specifically with the Trotsky summons. Albert Thomas, who was on the speaker's platform while Lloyd George delivered his speech, authoritatively reported "that the British Government did not want to let the Brest-Litovsk declarations go unanswered." [26]

Lloyd George now gave the first official and detailed Allied response to the Central as well as to the Bolshevik Government. First he violently attacked Czernin's December 25th statement by declaring that "mere lip service to the formula of no annexations and no indemnities or the right of self-determination is useless." His own program for Eastern Europe, however, was far from a model of clarity. Lloyd George made no "attempt to deal with the question of the Russian territories now in German occupation," justifying his evasion in the following terms: "The Russian policy since the Revolution has passed so rapidly through so many phases that it is difficult to speak without some suspension of judgment as to what the situation will be when final terms of European peace come to be discussed." According to the Prime Minister, in case of a separate settlement in the East these Russian provinces would henceforth be "part of the dominions of Prussia."

Was Lloyd George prepared to abandon Russia to the Central Powers? In his December 28th interview, C. P. Scott had gained the impression that the Prime Minister was seriously thinking of "paying the Germans in the East in order to square them in the West." [27] In rejecting unconditionally Trotsky's Brest-Litovsk summons and in refusing to hold out any hope of Allied assistance to the Bolsheviks, Lloyd George came dangerously close to publicly inviting the Germans to make the best of their opportunities in the East.

> We shall be proud to fight to the end side by side with the new democracy of Russia, so will America and so will France and Italy. But if the present rulers of Russia take action which is independent of their Allies, we have no means of intervening to arrest the

26. *L'Humanité*, January 6, 1918. "The open diplomacy of the Russians is bearing fruit. As a direct result of the conference at Brest, the Prime Minister has restated his war aims." (London) *Nation* (January 12, 1918), p. 473.

27. Hammond, *C. P. Scott of the Manchester Guardian*, p. 232.

catastrophe which is assuredly befalling their country. Russia can only be saved by her own people.

In view of Russia's desperate weakness, the Central Powers could easily interpret this passage as an indication that Britain might be disposed to give them a free hand in the East in the hope that Germany would minimize her demands in the West as well as in the colonial realm. In turn, the Bolsheviks feared that Lloyd George might be preparing the basis for a general negotiated peace at the expense not only of Russia but also of the Revolution.[28]

In proclaiming an independent Poland as "an urgent necessity for the stability of Western Europe," the Prime Minister made his only unequivocal "nationalities" commitment. Though he called for "genuine self-government" for the peoples of the Dual Monarchy, he also insisted that "the break-up" of Austria-Hungary was "no part" of England's war aims. This reassurance was calculated to keep the door open for separate negotiations with Vienna.[29] On the other hand, the restrained treatment of the Eastern European nationalities problems in the Labour Memorandum might also have reinforced Lloyd George's

28. For a compact but well-balanced summary of statements and/or actions which by the Bolsheviks were taken as indices of Allied readiness to consider a negotiated peace with the Central Powers at the cost of Russia and the Revolution, see Carr, *The Bolshevik Revolution*, 3, 23–25, n. 6. See also a cable dated January 6, 1918, from Ambassador Francis in Petrograd, cited in *FR, Russia, 1918, 1,* 425. Especially in Great Britain the project of settling the war at the expense of Russia and the Revolution seemed to gain important adherents between the middle of March and the middle of July 1918. See Cole, pp. 111–16; and *The History of the Times, 4,* Pt. I, pp. 359–62.

29. The Allies still pursued their diplomatic efforts to detach Austria-Hungary from Germany. Recently General Smuts had returned from Switzerland, where he had engaged in an exchange of views with Czernin's representative, Count Mensdorff. Whereas Mensdorff made it quite clear that a separate peace was out of the question, Smuts was equally set to decline any discussion of a general peace. Nevertheless, in these conversations Smuts gathered renewed evidence that Vienna continued to press Berlin for moderation. In turn, Mensdorff was assured that the break-up of Austria-Hungary was not the object of the Allies; according to Smuts it was the aim of the Allies "to assist Austria to give the greatest freedom and autonomy to her subject nationalities" on a dominion pattern. However, the two delegates did not make any advances on specific issues like Transylvania and Dalmatia. Yet their talks were not altogether sterile. By Lloyd George's own admission, his decision to draft a war-aims address was influenced by Mensdorff's suggestion "that we should define our terms before the enemy, and that the enemy should either accept or reject them." For the unabridged text of Smuts' account of these conversations, dated December 18–19, 1917, as well as the Prime Minister's own comments, see Lloyd George, *War Memoirs, 2,* 1478–90.

own reluctance to accelerate the disintegration of the Dual Monarchy without simultaneously proposing a solution capable of preventing chaos in the Balkans. Fully aware of this leniency toward Vienna, the Prime Minister apologetically admitted to Wickham Steed, one of Britain's leading spokesmen for the Eastern European nationalities, that he had "not been able to go as far as you would like about Austria." [30]

The Labour Memorandum very likely also influenced Lloyd George to confine himself to a curt, one-sentence reference to Italy's "legitimate claims." Likewise, since the Prime Minister did not call for the outright return of Alsace-Lorraine to France, the Labour leaders may have been instrumental in limiting England's policy to a "reconsideration of the great wrong of 1871." [31] On the whole, even though he carefully stayed within the traditional diplomatic framework, in response to the Brest-Litovsk developments Lloyd George seemed to be advocating a decidedly toned-down version of the knock-out policy.

Moreover, Lloyd George did make certain hesitant excursions into the New Diplomacy in an effort to meet Wilson, Labour, and the Bolsheviks. Upon leaving the Paris Conference, Colonel House had left the Big Three with the definite impression that Wilson would soon reformulate America's war aims within a distinctly liberal context. Now that Labour, in addition to Wilson, was sponsoring the crusade for democracy, the Prime Minister also proclaimed that "government with the consent of the governed must be the basis of any territorial settlement in the war." However, unlike Wilson, both Labour and Lloyd George failed to advocate specifically the democratization of Germany. The Prime Minister's sponsorship of open diplomacy was hardly more forceful. After recognizing that "the days of the Treaty of Vienna are long past," and without denying the existence of the secret treaties, Lloyd George simply declared that "as new circumstances, like the Russian collapse and the separate Russian negotiations, have changed the conditions under which those arrangements were made, we are, and always have been, perfectly ready to discuss them with our Allies"—but not with the Bolsheviks.

The Prime Minister's limited endorsement of the crusade and of

30. Henry Wickham Steed, *Through Thirty Years, 1892–1922* (2 vols. New York, Doubleday, Page, 1924), 2, 180.

31. Nevertheless, immediately after the text of the address reached Paris, Clemenceau wired his endorsement. For the text of Clemenceau's wire see *l'Humanité,* January 7, 1918.

open diplomacy indicates that the War Cabinet was not convinced of either the intrinsic merits or the present necessity of the New Diplomacy. It would seem that in deploring the "crushing weight of modern armaments" and in agreeing that "a great attempt must be made to establish by some international organization an alternative to war" the Cabinet merely joined Lloyd George in reluctantly making a few verbal concessions to the new *Zeitgeist*.

Perhaps the expediential rapprochement to the "verbal form" of Left war aims emerged most distinctly from those sections of the speech which dealt with overseas problems. Lloyd George declared that in the light of the gradual contraction of the Turkish Empire, Arabia, Armenia, Mesopotamia, Syria, and Palestine were "entitled to recognition of their separate national conditions." Accordingly, the self-determination principles which would guide the reorganization of the Dual Monarchy also should apply to the projected reforms in the Near and Middle East. Moreover, though none of the German colonies would be returned to Berlin, Lloyd George promised that they would be "held at the disposal" of the Peace Conference; there they would be dealt with in accordance with "the general principle of self-determination applicable in their cases as in those of occupied European countries." This promise had an organic connection with an earlier part of Lloyd George's speech in which Czernin's insistence on a restoration of Germany's colonies was attacked for causing the principle of self-determination to vanish "into thin air." Indeed, did the British Cabinet mean to convey the impression that it advocated a stricter application of self-determination in colonial and semicolonial areas than in Eastern Europe?

Notwithstanding the many inconsistencies and expediencies, Lloyd George's TUC address went considerably beyond House's declaration which only four weeks ago had been defeated at the inter-Allied Conference in Paris; his speech was the first comprehensive Allied pronouncement since January 1917. Even though Lloyd George differed extensively with the Memorandum on War Aims, he succeeded nevertheless in winning considerable Labour support. While J. R. Clynes, of the right wing, enthusiastically congratulated the Prime Minister,[32] Henderson expressed his guarded approval to Albert Thomas.[33] Labourites and Radicals to the left of Henderson were especially critical

32. Lloyd George, *War Memoirs*, 2, 1493.
33. Riddell, *Lord Riddell's War Diary*, p. 345.

of the sections dealing with Russia and the crusade. However, the bulk of these dissidents three days later were placated by Wilson's Fourteen Points address. On the other hand, because the Fourteen Points were equally considerate of Vienna they did not counteract the censure of the *New Europe,* which was extremely critical of the Prime Minister's leniency toward the Dual Monarchy.[34]

Naturally the Lansdowne Conservatives were highly pleased, and so was Lord Milner. Anxious to secure the support of the greatest number of both Conservatives and Liberals, Lloyd George explained the occasion and nature of his speech to Wickham Steed, foreign editor of the *Times.* On this occasion Steed was told that in the speech there was "a good deal of tactics . . . and a little Bolshevism." [35] The *Times* now assured its readers that the speech was a necessary reply "to the enemy and the Bolshevists"; furthermore, "the Prime Minister having cleared the ground . . . the paper had no motive for masking the discussion of peace any longer." [36] Apparently Lloyd George justifiably claimed that he had spoken "not merely the mind of the government, but of the nation and of the Empire as a whole."

Nevertheless, since Lloyd George had outlined a program designed not only as an ideological primer for the Allies but also as a possible basis for negotiation with the enemy, his speech seemed to be lacking in clarity as well as simplicity. At Brest-Litovsk the Bolsheviks were fighting their diplomatic offensive with simple slogans and phrases. They had served notice that henceforth the chancelleries would have to talk to the people as well as to each other; in drafting their speeches statesmen would have to remember that millions of bayonets were in search of an idea. Therefore, Woodrow Wilson proposed to counter Joffe's Six Points with his own Fourteen Points.

34. *New Europe* (January 10, 1918), pp. 385–88. See also Beneš, *Souvenirs de guerre, 1,* 548–52.

35. Steed, *Through Thirty Years, 2,* 180.

36. *Times* (London), January 7, 1918; and *The History of the Times, 4,* Pt. I, p. 347.

9. WILSON ISSUES A COUNTERMANIFESTO

ABOUT six weeks before the end of the war, Woodrow Wilson aired his
conviction that "national purposes [had] fallen more and more into
the background and the common purpose of enlightened mankind
[had] taken their place." Wilson conceived of the titanic struggle no
longer as a "statesmen's war" but rather as a "peoples' war," in which
"statesmen must follow the clarified common thought or be broken." [1]

In March 1917 war and revolution had become hopelessly intertwined. Since then these two forces had been deepening the political,
social, economic, and ideological ravages inside the major European
belligerents. Wilson was sensitive to these emerging revolutionary dimensions, just as he also made a sober estimate of the changing balance of world power in which America was destined to figure prominently. Instead of taking a narrow view of the responsibilities of
America as an Associated Power, he successfully capitalized on his
geographic detachment from old Europe in order to view the Great
War from a world perspective. Wilson's analysis of the crisis which
led him to formulate and practice the New Diplomacy was hardly
that of a political idealist or a nonconformist minister whose thought
and temperament were "essentially theological, not intellectual." [2] In
the course of the war the President developed either a dormant or a
new historical acumen which enabled him to make an unusually
perspicacious assessment of both the domestic and the international
tensions generated by the simultaneous waning of an old era and birth
of a New World. Instead of allowing the gigantic scale and complexity

1. Baker and Dodd, *The Public Papers of Woodrow Wilson*, 5, 259.
2. John Maynard Keynes, *Essays in Biography* (New York, Horizon, 1951), p. 21.

of recent developments to frighten him into status-quo thinking, he courageously formulated both his thought and action with a view to steering the onrushing historical forces into orderly channels.

It was in this broad context that Wilson studied the diplomacy of the Allies. Even if he did not know all the details of the secret treaties, he certainly must have been aware of their general sense. There were repeated occasions when he encountered the secret understandings either directly or indirectly.[3]

For example, the President met with Balfour on May 21, 1917, three days after the visiting Foreign Secretary had sent him the text of various agreements, among them the Treaty of London, the Sykes-Picot Agreement, and the Constantinople notes. No one knows whether these treaties were discussed on this particular occasion.[4] However, subsequently the President repeatedly spoke of Allied ambitions in Asia Minor. Meanwhile his closest adviser, Colonel House, discussed these treaties with Balfour, with the help of a map on which the proposed territorial changes were staked out.[5]

On July 23, in eliciting his Government's views on select diplomatic questions, the American Ambassador in Paris referred to "certain of the secret treaties." In reply, Acting Secretary of State Frank Polk asked for information about "agreements between the Allies concerning Asia Minor." On August 2, after a visit with Cambon, Ambassador Sharp wired considerable details about these agreements. In turn, on August 3, Wilson penned the shorthand note in which he spoke of the difficulty of concluding "peace on any terms which would mean arrangements in Asia Minor for the benefit of particular nations."[6]

Still, no one knows whether Wilson actually studied the official *text* of any one or combination of documents. Nevertheless, even in the absence of authentic documentary evidence, the President could not have missed knowing the nature of the territorial aims which England, France, and Italy were pursuing.

Precisely because he was aware of the conflicting aims of America and her Allies, Wilson was careful not to press prematurely for an

3. Seymour, *American Diplomacy*, pp. 266–68.
4. Baker, *Woodrow Wilson, Life and Letters*, 7, 74–75, 80.
5. Seymour, *Intimate Papers*, 3, 39–41, 42–46.
6. *FR*, 1917, Supplement 2, *1*, 151, 155–56; and Baker, *Woodrow Wilson, Life and Letters*, 7, 204.

exchange of views. With House and Lansing he feared that such a review of war aims might lead to dangerous frictions within the coalition at a time when the military situation was far from promising. Whereas Secretary of State Lansing eventually requested Ambassador Francis to send copies of the treaties from Petrograd to Washington, he refused to approach the British and French governments for information about them. As late as March 22, 1918, he advised Representative J. T. Heflin of his "preference, for obvious reasons, not to make this inquiry of them at the present time." [7]

In addition to official and unofficial reports reaching him through conversations, letters, and the press, Wilson was certainly alive to the secret-treaty issue as a result of the long-standing campaign of Radicals and Socialists, both at home and abroad, against secret diplomacy. Finally, toward the end of 1917, Trotsky's pronouncements reached Washington, and summaries and reprints of the secret treaties appeared in the press as well as in diplomatic dispatches.[8]

Perhaps Polk and Lansing spoke for the President when they insisted that "as to the secret treaties . . . the State Department has no knowledge of their existence or of their terms except through reports emanating from the Bolshevik press." [9] In other words, the Department never claimed a lack of knowledge; it merely maintained that its information was gathered from unofficial sources.

At any rate, detailed knowledge of specific secret treaties would certainly have reinforced, not weakened, Wilson's reasoned dissent from the objectives and methods of the Old Diplomacy. He was as convinced that secret diplomacy was one of the root causes of war as he was devoted to popular control as the key to diplomatic wisdom and prudence. Meanwhile, however, Wilson's criticism of the Old Diplomacy also was supported by the sobering fact that America neither was party to any of the secret treaties nor sought physical control over any new foreign territories.

This lack of involvement in the politics of the Concert of Europe was due less to the deliberate designs of American foreign-policy makers than to accidental historical circumstances. Wilson, however,

7. Seymour, *American Diplomacy*, pp. 269–70; *FR*, 1917, Supplement 2, *1*, 327; Baker, *Woodrow Wilson, Life and Letters*, 8, 42–43.
8. See *FR*, 1917, Supplement 2, *1*, 446–47, 493–507.
9. Baker, *Woodrow Wilson, Life and Letters*, 8, 20.

realized that the war was rapidly changing these circumstances. The American economy and navy had reached the kind of stature which, in Wilson's view, would inevitably force policy-makers to acknowledge that the isolationist era in American foreign relations had come to a close. By entering the war, the United States had become an integral part of the historical forces which were challenging Europe's continuing diplomatic supremacy. Since this entrance into the war itself was symptomatic of the overflow of American power into the world community, it is perhaps not surprising that Wilson's unrelenting emphasis on the "unselfishness" of American motives should have encountered lingering suspicion abroad. As an agent of the New World, how could Wilson come forth with a prescription calculated to redress the balance of the Old World? Was not the Wilsonian gospel the diplomatic dimension of the revolutionary domestic program of the Petrograd Soviet? Nevertheless, given their growing dependence on American manpower and materiel in the life-and-death struggle with the Central Powers, both Paris and London gradually were forced to listen attentively to Wilson's messages.

Wartime necessity eventually compelled the Allied war cabinets to declare publicly their verbal adherence to the New Diplomacy. As early as July 21, 1917, Wilson predicted that "when the war is over we can force them to our way of thinking, because by that time they will, among other things, be financially in our hands." [10] The collapse of Russia and the Caporetto disaster increased the dependence of the Allies on the United States.

When Stephen Pichon, the French Foreign Minister, reassured the Chamber of Deputies that the loss of Russia would not be fatal, he claimed that America was a worthy substitute for the failing eastern Empire. According to Pichon, the United States could be counted on to contribute "not only their commercial, industrial, financial, and military power, but also all their moral forces." In the British House of Commons similar ideas were current. Commander Josiah Wedgwood, a nominal Liberal close to the ILP, and genuine Asquith Liberals like Walter Runciman, proclaimed that the alliance with America was "not only an alliance of ideals, but an alliance of necessity." In this view it was therefore "all the more urgent that our speakers here should approach ever more nearly to the terms adumbrated by President Wilson." Lip service to New Diplomacy phrases

10. Ibid., 7, 180.

seemed a small price to pay for desperately needed transatlantic assistance.[11]

Nevertheless, serious distrust of Wilson's diplomacy persisted in right-wing circles, partly because of its acceptance by the internal forces of movement. Many Conservatives apprehensively but helplessly watched both Washington and Petrograd proclaim that while "the masses of men" had become "certain of what it is they are fighting for," statesmen retained "the impression" that they were still "playing a game of power." [12] Wilson, as well as Lenin, stood prepared to harness the progressive forces generated by this otherwise destructive war in the hope of substituting statesmen of "wrong impressions" with "spokesmen of the people." Throughout Europe the strains of the military stalemate and the turnip winter called forth not only an intensified popular yearning for a just and lasting peace but also a growing awareness that domestic reforms were an essential precondition for a stable world order. Henceforth, in Europe, Wilson's vision of the New World and Socialism's vision of the New Society reinforced each other. During the last year and a half of war, while the political distinction between Democratic Socialism and Bolshevism was as yet relatively uncrystallized, the amorphous and syncretic nature of both major progressive ideological poles (Wilsonianism and Leninism) facilitated recruitment to the over-all forces of movement. Uncertain whether they were more heavily sworn to the New Diplomacy than to the Equalitarian Commonwealth, many converts to progressivism seemed to swear a vague but firm allegiance to both.

President Wilson proceeded on the assumption that the Left could be counted on to join the Radical–Liberals in pressing not only for the New Diplomacy but also for an extension of political democracy. Consequently, from April 1917 onward Wilson did not hesitate to fan the opposition fire in back of the German Government, even though he knew that in Germany the Social Democrats, not the Liberals, were the effective backbone of the anti-Hohenzollern forces.

Paris and London, however, were much more reluctant to adopt *officially* a policy of inciting citizens to revolt against their legitimate

11. JO (December 27, 1917), p. 3631; and *PD, 100* (December 19, 1917), cols. 2021, 2084–85. "The deciding voice in the war councils, say dispatches from Europe, is coming more and more to be the voice of America. . . . The war torn Allies rest their hopes upon the fresh and almost illimitable forces and resources of our Republic." *Literary Digest* (January 12, 1918), p. 7.

12. Baker and Dodd, *The Public Papers of Woodrow Wilson, 5*, 259.

rulers. This reluctance was foreshadowed in the Allied skepticism about that part of the President's answer to the Pope in which Wilson had insisted that America would "not take the word of the present rulers of Germany." Many Allied leaders would have preferred that "the President had not insisted so strongly upon what amounted to a revolution in Germany, that is upon an event almost impossible to bring about during war." [13] On December 22, 1917, Ambassador Page impatiently informed the President that the British should "say more plainly and concretely that the only way to security was to overthrow the German military autocracy." [14] Almost as if in reply to Page's letter, on January 3, 1918, the retiring British Ambassador in Washington reported to London about an intimate conversation with Wilson. On this occasion the President noted that the Bolsheviks "were now adopting the same policy" of appealing to the German people "behind the back of the German Government." According to Spring Rice, the President had concluded that in the face of the appeals from Petrograd the Allies could no longer remain silent, because the Bolshevik appeals were addressed not only to the Germans but also to the peoples of the Allied nations. Wilson feared that "if the appeal of the Bolsheviki was allowed to remain unanswered, if nothing were done to counteract it, the effect would be great and would increase." [15] Whereas on January 5 Lloyd George had again refrained from advocating subversion, Wilson's mounting readiness to compete for the allegiance of enemy as well as Allied "popular forces" soon became one of the outstanding characteristics of his 20th-century diplomacy.

It was largely as a consequence of the disagreements which the American reply to the Pope had stimulated among America's Allies that on September 2, 1917, Wilson suggested to House that

> we ought to go systematically to work to ascertain as fully and precisely as possible just what the several parties to this war on our side of it will be inclined to insist upon as part of the final peace arrangements, in order that we may formulate our own position either for or against them and begin to gather the influences we wish to employ—or at least ascertain what influences

13. According to Buckler, Lord Milner held this view. Buckler to House, November 3, 1917, Buckler Papers.

14. Cited in Hendrick, *The Life and Letters of Walter H. Page*, 3, 413.

15. Stephen Gwynn, ed., *The Letters and Friendships of Sir Cecil Spring Rice* (2 vols. Boston, Houghton Mifflin, 1929), 2, 422–25.

we can use: in brief, prepare our case with a full knowledge of the position of all the litigants.[16]

It is of interest to note that in this charter letter of the American Inquiry, President Wilson, the "idealist," thought of the necessity "to gather the influences we wish to employ—or at least ascertain what influences we can use." Could it be that by this time the President, as well as House, was fully apprised of the political struggle in which the war-aims revision in Europe had become enmeshed? Recently the breach between people and government had become irreparable in Russia; moreover, a similar though less drastic breach had developed not only in the Central camp but also in the Entente. Therefore, as the Inquiry proceeded to compile the American peace dossier, in addition to correlating the official declarations of all the belligerents, it also assembled the "significant declarations of policy by opposition statesmen, minority parties, and important social groups." [17] This information was destined to help formulate the American war-aims program and to identify those political forces abroad which could be counted upon to support American policy.

But even before the Inquiry was charted, American war-aims circles were well informed about the programs and actions of the European, particularly of the British, forces of movement. Colonel House was the most influential political figure to take a consistent interest in these developments. Soon House confided to Wilson that he was "thoroughly saturated with information from the other side." [18] How did he get this information?

Undoubtedly House relied heavily on the letters and reports of William H. Buckler, Counselor at the American Embassy in London. With the encouragement of Ambassador Page, Buckler spent much time in "looking up and keeping tabulated all that seems worthwhile about peace terms and proposals, and possibilities, and the feelings and hopes of men worthwhile." [19] Also, the Embassy Counselor maintained close relations with Trevelyan, the Buxtons, Brailsford, Massingham, and Nevinson. At the Embassy and in his constant correspondence with House, Buckler made no secret of his sympathy "with many of the ideas of Lord Lansdowne, Lord Haldane, and Ramsay Mac-

16. Baker, *Woodrow Wilson, Life and Letters,* 7, 254.
17. *FR, Paris Peace Conference, 1919, 1,* 36.
18. House to Wilson, August 17, 1917, Wilson Papers.
19. W. H. Page to Wilson, June 8, 1917, Wilson Papers.

Donald." [20] Before long Colonel House reassured him that "your view-point seems to be unprejudiced and quite similar to our own." [21]

Repeatedly the UDC sought the help of Buckler in getting messages to President Wilson. For example, the letter in which the UDC Executive Committee on May 29, 1917, asked Wilson to issue a war-aims statement was given to Buckler for transmission to House. In turn, this letter, which was signed, among others, by Angell, Charles Buxton, Hobson, Jowett, MacDonald, Morel, Ponsonby, and Trevelyan, eventually was forwarded by House to Wilson with the marginal comment that it was "interesting because of the signatures." [22]

There were other equally revealing communications between Buckler and House. On August 1, 1917, the former drafted a detailed report about the parliamentary debate in which MacDonald, supported by the UDC back-benchers, called attention to the July 19th Reichstag Resolution and renewed the request for passports. Enclosed with this report, Colonel House received not only the verbatim record of these debates, but also favorable newspaper articles from the *Nation,* the *New Statesman, Common Sense, Cambridge Magazine,* and the *Labour Leader.* In acknowledging receipt of these papers, the Colonel assured his faithful correspondent that these were "not only of interest to me but to a number of literary friends" as well. [23]

One such literary figure of considerable prominence was Walter Lippmann, the Socialist-oriented co-editor of the *New Republic,* with whom House had weekly conferences. While House certainly sought

20. Nevins, *Henry White,* pp. 341–42. Judging by his own reports, Buckler saw Ramsay MacDonald quite regularly, especially during the second half of 1917. See Buckler Papers.

21. House to Buckler, January 11, 1917, Buckler Papers.

22. This UDC letter with House's comment is in Wilson Papers. In another letter, also addressed to Buckler but meant for House and Wilson, MacDonald gave expression to the left dissidents' disappointment with America's Stockholm policy. Buckler to House, August 17, 1917, Buckler Papers.

23. Buckler to House, August 1, 1917, and House to Buckler, August 11, 1917, Buckler Papers. Buckler faithfully reported not only about war-aims debates in Parliament (e.g. October 13, 1916, and December 21, 1917) but also about major developments within the Labour party (e.g. August 8 and December 31, 1917). Once, when House had not heard from Buckler "for a long while," House wrote him that he "missed the valuable data and information which you have been sending." House to Buckler, September 28, 1917, Buckler Papers. Actually, on August 28, 1917, Ambassador Page had ordered the Embassy Counselor to stop his reports to House. Buckler did not hesitate to ask House to intervene, and within a few weeks the correspondence was resumed. Buckler to House, October 19 and 26, 1917, Buckler Papers.

to exploit the pages of this influential liberal periodical in the interest of the Wilson Administration, he undoubtedly also absorbed many of Lippmann's and Herbert Croly's ideas.[24] Then, at the request of Colonel House, Lippmann left the *New Republic* in order to become Secretary of the Inquiry, as well as Division Chief in charge of "politics and government, including international cooperation." [25] In justifying his choice of Lippmann, as well as Mezes, for the leading positions in the Inquiry, Colonel House told the President that "the small group around me must be in thorough sympathy with your purposes." [26]

All through the war the *New Republic* welcomed many instructive visitors from England, among them Gilbert Murray, Robert Cecil, the Webbs, Keynes, Brailsford, Ratcliff, Angell, Masefield, and Wells. Alvin Johnson, one of Lippmann's editorial colleagues, was impressed by "the openness and wide reach of their minds" and their "ability to look upon the Great War in an historical perspective." According to Johnson, these Englishmen saw in the war "the culmination of forces over which no single nation had had actual control, in the existing state of international anarchy." [27] Furthermore, British UDC ideas on war aims and postwar problems were familiar to the readers and editors of the *New Republic*, which counted Brailsford, Angell, and Wells among its permanent contributors. Between January 1916 and January 1918 these three left-wing intellectuals contributed twenty-five, eleven, and five pieces respectively; J. A. Hobson, Sidney Webb, and G. B. Shaw also wrote two articles each for Croly's journal. Furthermore, Norman Angell, who saw Colonel House on different occasions, supplied Wilson with a considerable number of memoranda.[28]

24. House referred to his meetings with Lippmann as "briefings." See House Diary, January through August 1917.

25. *FR, Paris Peace Conference, 1919, 1,* 34. Immediately after being appointed to the Inquiry, Lippmann asked to see the texts of the secret treaties. Interview with Walter Lippmann in Washington, D.C., October 15, 1952.

26. House to Wilson, September 20, 1917, Wilson Papers.

27. Alvin Johnson, *Pioneer's Progress: An Autobiography* (New York, Viking, 1952), p. 243.

28. Angell, *After All,* p. 203; and House to Wilson, August 9, 1917, Wilson Papers. Angell made the first of four wartime crossings the day after the sinking of the Lusitania. To judge by his own testimony, Angell "saw a little of Colonel House and his circle (to which indeed the *New Republic* group were fairly close)." Angell, writing in Bell, *We Did Not Fight,* p. 58. According to the House Diary, Angell saw House on October 2, 1917.

Noel Buxton, G. Lowes Dickinson, and Josiah Wedgwood were three
other well-known British dissidents who in the course of the war
were repeatedly in touch with Colonel House and with the *New Republic* circle.[29]   *in Lords*

In brief Buckler, through his correspondence with House, and the
New Republic, through its feature and editorial pages, served to
 strengthen the embryonic bonds between influential quarters in America and the forces of movement in England.

Meanwhile House had taken advantage of his latest trip to Europe
in order to gather first-hand information about the politics of European war aims. In England, after discovering that Lloyd George
"was committed too far to the British Conservatives," House conferred with many spokesmen of the growing war-aims movement,
among them Asquith, Brailsford, Noel Buxton, W. J. Davis, Hirst, Lansbury, Lansdowne, Loreburn, Massingham, C. P. Scott, Strachey, J. H.
Thomas, and Wedgwood. In France, in the face of Clemenceau's
uncompromising attitude, he exchanged views with Moutet, Renaudel,
and Briand.[30] Subsequently, House's failure to win approval for his
timid war-aims resolution at the inter-Allied Conference, about which
he cabled Wilson in great detail, merely accentuated his sympathy
as well as his support for the Allied dissidents.

Before leaving Paris, House telegraphed Wilson suggesting that he
postpone "any statement concerning foreign affairs until I can see
you." On his own carbon copy of this cable, House noted that since
the Conference had failed to agree on a statement, "the next best
thing was for the President to do it."[31] Then, at the White House
meeting of December 18, at which they criticized the intransigence

29. See T. R. Conwell-Evans, *Foreign Policy from a Back Bench, 1904–1918:
A Study Based on the Papers of Lord Noel-Buxton* (London, Oxford University
Press, 1932), pp. 119 ff.; E. M. Forster, *Goldsworthy Lowes Dickinson* (New
York, Harcourt, Brace, 1934), pp. 163–69; Josiah C. Wedgwood, *Memoirs of a
Fighting Life* (London, Hutchinson, 1940), pp. 118–24.

30. Seymour, *Intimate Papers*, 3, 279–80; House Diary, November 12 to 21,
1917; *FR*, 1917, Supplement 2, 1, 243, 347; Suarez, *Briand: Sa vie—son oeuvre*,
4, 332–33.

31. Seymour, *Intimate Papers*, 3, 286. For the American delegation's entire report about the inter-Allied Conference see *FR*, 1917, Supplement 2, 1, 334–445.
Incidentally, the President informed House that he could not "omit foreign affairs" from his December 4th address to Congress for fear that "reticence on my
part at this juncture would be misunderstood and do much harm." Wilson to
House, December 3, 1917, Wilson Papers.

of Lloyd George, Clemenceau, and Sonnino, Wilson and House definitely decided to formulate a major war-aims address.[32]

At the suggestion of Colonel House, the Peace Inquiry Bureau was asked to assemble materials and information which might be helpful in the drafting of this speech. By December 22, 1917, S. F. Mezes, D. H. Miller, and Walter Lippmann, the three top men of the Inquiry staff, had completed an incisive Memorandum on "The War Aims and Peace Terms it Suggests," which Colonel House took to the President on January 4, 1918.[33]

In addition to dealing with specific territorial problems and with general peace principles, this Memorandum dealt extensively with the politics of war aims. First the Inquiry staff noted certain political intangibles which, "if skillfully used," could be counted on the side of the Allies:

> (1) the universal longing for peace, which under the circumstances should not be handed over to Germany as something for them to capitalize: (2) the almost universal feeling on the part of the common people of the world that the old diplomacy is bankrupt, and that the system of armed peace must not be restored. This is a sentiment fundamentally anti-Prussian in its nature and should be capitalized for our side . . . (3) a great hope of a league of nations which has the approbation of disinterested people everywhere; (4) there is the menace of social revolution all over the world, and as a factor in it, a realization by the governing political and financial groups that the meeting of the war debts is virtually insoluable without revolutionary measures about property. In a war fought for democratic aims, these fears should be made to fight on our side.[34]

This forceful analysis offers additional evidence of the interest and care with which circles close to the President studied the psychopolitical landscape of Europe. Furthermore, it reveals the combined influence of Colonel House and European progressives on the American conception of the results to be achieved by a diplomatic pronouncement.

32. Seymour, *Intimate Papers, 3,* 317.
33. House Diary, December 18, 1917, and January 9, 1918. For the entire text of this Inquiry Memorandum see *FR, Paris Peace Conference, 1919, 1,* 41–53.
34. *FR, Paris Peace Conference, 1919, 1,* 46–47.

One such secondary result was spelled out unequivocally in the same Inquiry Memorandum.

> Utterances from the United States . . . will show the way to the Liberals in Great Britain and in France, and therefore restore national unity of purpose. These Liberals will rapidly accept the leadership of the President if he undertakes a liberal diplomatic offensive, because they will find in that offensive an invaluable support for their internal domestic troubles.[35]

Curiously enough, in identifying one of the "influences" about which Wilson had speculated in his letter of September 2, 1917, the Inquiry pointed exclusively to Allied Liberals. It would seem, however, that this "Liberal" label was meant to be stretched to cover the entire progressive bloc which was advocating war-aims reform. In its mid-December memorandum the Inquiry had ventured the prognosis that henceforth the unity of the Allied as well as of the Central coalitions would depend increasingly on a political "movement toward the Left."

The unity in outlook between the Allied forces of movement and President Wilson found further expression in their identical reaction to the Brest-Litovsk summons. Notwithstanding his earlier opposition to Stockholm, Wilson's analysis of Russian developments now coincided with that of the British and French Radicals and Socialists. Ever since March he had looked upon the Russian Revolution as perhaps the most compelling evidence that this was a peoples' war. Furthermore, with both the Petrograd formula and the Joffe declaration before the world, could anyone doubt that the Revolution successfully promoted the revolt against the ways of the Old Diplomacy? During the early stages of Bolshevik rule Wilson maintained his boundless faith in the Russian people, confident that before long they would conquer their war weariness in order to reenlist actively in the great crusade. Moreover, partly because Lenin's peace policies at this time overshadowed his economic and political program, Wilson, like most other Radicals and Socialists, was undisturbed by the revolutionary aspects of Lenin's domestic program. In Wilson's view the Bolsheviks were only temporarily in control of the Petrograd Soviet, which would in any event soon be supplanted by a new popularly elected Constituent Assembly.[36]

35. Ibid., p. 49.
36. Cf. the *New Republic* (December 29, 1917), p. 230.

At the inter-Allied Conference, Colonel House who was confident of the President's support, had prevented, with the help of Lloyd George, Clemenceau and Sonnino from forcing through an overtly hostile policy toward Russia. Though House and Wilson were seriously troubled by the political and military hazards of a Russo-German bloc, neither of them was as yet prepared even to consider, let alone implement, the Milner-Cecil type of military intervention. Instead, much like the progressives who argued that a reformed diplomacy might have saved Kerensky, Wilson and House hoped that a war-aims offensive could forestall a separate peace in the East.

In the December 22nd Memorandum the Inquiry recommended that the best policy toward Russia consisted (1) in showing that we are not unwilling to state war aims; (2) in a hearty propaganda of the idea of a league of nations; and (3) in a demonstration to them that the diplomatic offensive is in progress, and the Allies are not relying totally upon force." [37] As of the middle of December 1917 many prominent officials reached similar conclusions.

On January 3, 1918, Ambassador Francis by cable "respectfully requested" the President to "reiterate in some public manner the noble expression of his address to the U. S. Senate of January 22 last." Francis recommended a return to the peace without victory formula because Russia's "tired people [would] not fight for territory, they need status quo ante." However, since the Russian people might "possibly" struggle for a democratic peace, the Ambassador concluded that "the psychology of war justifies and demands the repetition of the noble humanitarian thoughts expressed in [Wilson's] great message." [38] After his return to America from Russia, Boyce Thompson began to press similar advice on official Washington. In his perceptive "Memorandum of the Present Situation in Russia" dated January 3 and significantly subtitled "Suggested Means to Prevent German Domination of Russia," Thompson advised the White House that neither recognition of, nor direct communication with, the Bolshevik Government was necessary; the President could "speak to the Russian people almost as well through a message to the American Congress." [39]

---

37. FR, Paris Peace Conference, 1919, 1, 43.

38. Ibid., Russia, 1918, 1, 423. This cable reached Washington on January 6 and was seen by the President on the 7th. National Archives, Document 763.72119/1072.

39. Hagedorn, The Magnate, p. 259. Creel forwarded the Thompson Memorandum to Wilson on January 5, 1918. See Wilson Papers.

At the suggestion of Raymond Robins, who had taken over Thompson's functions in Russia, an even more specific prescription originated from Petrograd on January 3, 1918. Edgar Sisson sent a cable to George Creel, his chief in Washington, urging Wilson to "restate anti-imperialist war aims and democratic peace requisites of [America] in a thousand words or less, short almost placard paragraphs, short sentences." [40] Likewise, judging by a rather skeptical report from W. H. Page, another request for "thumb nail catch phrases . . . [which] the man in the street and in the trenches can understand" seemed to be circulating in London.[41] Finally, official Allied encouragement came from Lord Balfour in a cable dated January 5, 1918. The Foreign Secretary conveyed the assurance that should Wilson decide to answer the Bolsheviks, the British Prime Minister was "confident that such a statement would also be in general accordance with the lines of the President's previous speeches." [42] Would Wilson accept the challenge to speak to the Allied and enemy peoples, as well as to the Bolsheviks, even though he confessed to George Creel that "he had never tried his hand at slogans and advertising copy"? [43]

Allied war-aims diplomacy had traveled a long way since March 11, 1917, when the secret Doumergue agreement was signed by France and tsarist Russia. The aims of the war could no longer be spelled out exclusively, even primarily, in secret executive agreements. First the Petrograd Soviet had pressed for public pronouncements; now the new Soviet Government was speaking in popular terms at Brest-Litovsk. It is hardly surprising, therefore, that in drafting his Fourteen Points address Wilson should have been guided by one primary purpose: to answer the Bolshevik demand "for an explanation of the objects of the war" in such a way as to "persuade Russia to stand by the Allies in their defense of democratic and liberal principles according to which . . . the peace settlement must be framed." Colonel House, reassured by a conversation with Russian Ambassador Bakhmetieff, encouraged the President in this resolve.[44]

40. The complete text of the Sisson cable is cited in *RAR*, p. 67. Cf. Edgar Sisson, *One Hundred Red Days: A Personal Chronicle of the Bolshevik Revolution* (New Haven, Yale University Press, 1931), p. 205.

41. Hendrick, *The Life and Letters of Walter H. Page, 3,* 413.

42. Seymour, *Intimate Papers, 3,* 340.

43. George Creel, *Rebel at Large* (New York, Putnam, 1947), p. 168.

44. Seymour, *Intimate Papers, 3,* 331.

Only Lansing cautioned Wilson against responding to Trotsky's "Appeal to the Toiling, Oppressed, and Exhausted Peoples of Europe." [45] On January 2 he warned the President that Lenin and Trotsky were "so bitterly hostile to the present social order in all countries . . . that nothing could be said which would gain their favor or render them amenable to reason." Nevertheless, even the traditionalist Secretary of State presently wondered whether "it may not be expedient at some time in the near future to state our peace terms in more detail than has yet been done." [46]

Whereas Lansing feared that the Revolution was threatening to undermine all governments, the Inquiry suggested that Germany was in markedly greater danger of subversion. According to the Inquiry, since the "anticapitalist feeling would be fully as extreme against German capitalism" the Russian Revolution could be regarded as "a great dissolving force through its sheer example." [47] Similarly in his cable Sisson indicated that he planned to use the "placard paragraphs" as much to encourage the dissenting forces in Germany as to strengthen Russian resistance to the Central Powers. [48] Inside the State Department William Bullitt, who was engaged in a thorough analysis of the opposition forces in Germany, also recognized the dual function of a diplomatic offensive. He saw a "unique opportunity" for the President, with a specific statement of liberal war aims, "to unite Russia against the German Government and to produce a revolt against the Government within Germany." After noting that the effects on the Dual Monarchy "would not be slight" either, Bullitt concluded a special memorandum with the urgent reminder that "Today, the iron is hot!" [49] These references to the political tensions inside Germany merely reinforced Wilson's own determination to encourage the revo-

45. The text of Trotsky's Appeal reached the State Department from Petrograd on January 1, 1918. *FR, Russia, 1918, 1,* 405–8.
46. *FR, Lansing Papers, 2,* 348–49.
47. *FR, Paris Peace Conference, 1919, 1,* 45–46.
48. *RAR,* p. 67.
49. National Archives, Document 763.72119/1269—½. In a recent letter Bullitt himself confirmed that he "worked closely with Colonel House on the question of detaching the German Left from the Kaiser and the Junkers." Cited in John L. Snell, "Wilsonian Rhetoric Goes to War," *Historian, 14,* No. 2 (spring 1952), 199. On January 3, 1918, F. W. Taussig, Chairman of the U. S. Tariff Commission, also urged President Wilson to answer both Trotsky and Czernin. See Wilson Papers.

lutionary forces there. Hence, the "appeal to the German Socialists" became the second major purpose which guided Wilson and House as they drafted the Fourteen Points.[50]

Whereas the British War Cabinet revised its war aims at least partly, if not largely, as a result of insistent pressures by Labour, the Wilson Administration faced no comparable domestic opposition. Above all, the major opposition party in the United States did not agitate for anything like a peace without victory or a public formulation of new war aims. On the contrary, the Republican party, in particular Theodore Roosevelt and Henry Cabot Lodge, called for an unequivocal commitment to unconditional victory over Germany in a language similar to that of the European parties of order. Like its European counterparts, the American Right was most skeptical of the usefulness of utopian phrases and symbols, although it did not hesitate to arouse patriotic emotions. In the fashion of Clemenceau, Roosevelt whipped up popular enthusiasm by summoning the American people to a war of revenge against the brutal Huns. However, unlike Roosevelt, Clemenceau never had to castigate the French Government for its idealism; first as one of the leaders of the Right opposition, and subsequently as Premier, he successfully prevented the forces of movement from imprinting their foreign-policy ideology upon French diplomacy.

On the other hand, since Wilson combined his war message with a summons to a crusade for democracy, American diplomacy immediately took on an idealistic and proselytizing dimension. Even though Roosevelt and his conservative supporters were unsparing in their criticism of Wilson, in view of their long-standing war enthusiasm they could hardly step forward as champions of pacifism. Actually this was their war more than it was Wilson's. Therefore, at best they could claim that they were better qualified to fight the war than the idealist in the White House, and they could try to commend their greater war-making skills and enthusiasm by attacking the lack of realism in Wilson's diplomatic pronouncements.

In the fall of 1917 Roosevelt insisted that America "did not go to war to make democracy safe." Instead, he held that having gone into the war "because we had a special grievance . . . first and foremost we are to make the world safe for ourselves. This is our war, America's war. If we do not win it we shall some day have to reckon with

50. Seymour *Intimate Papers*, 3, 322.

Germany single-handed. Therefore, for our own sake let us strike down Germany." [51] Among the Republicans the knock-out-blow attitude became fashionable just as Lloyd George was about to abandon it, no doubt because unlike the British forces of order the American Right could confidently rely on an immense reservoir of national power.

Even from 1912 to 1915, while heading the Progressive party, Roosevelt had "remained, at heart, a romantic militarist, an aggressive national egoist." [52] Needless to say, as soon as he began to make common cause with Leonard Wood, Elihu Root, Cabot Lodge, and the war-loan interests, and now that he was back in the Republican fold, Roosevelt was bound to intensify his boisterous espousal of national egotism. His long-standing dedication to the national self-interest was also evident in his pronouncements about international organization: like Lords Cecil, Curzon, and Milner in England, he was always careful to insist that the jurisdiction of a future league of nations could not be allowed to impair national sovereignty and territorial integrity.

Meanwhile, in 1916, in his bid for re-election, Woodrow Wilson had reactivated the process of reform which had been "temporarily halted in 1914." The President and his advisers realized that only by winning the Progressives to their side could they hope to defeat the Republicans. They had to "convince Progressives that the Democratic party was an acceptable vehicle of reform of the kind they wanted." [53]

For reasons of both conviction and expediency Wilson now "became almost a new political creature, and under his leadership a Democratic Congress enacted the most sweeping and significant progressive legislation in the history of the country up to that time." The confirmation of Louis D. Brandeis as member of the Supreme Court was followed in quick succession by legislation bearing on rural credit, workmen's compensation, child labor, and the eight-hour work day. Hence by election time Wilson and the Democratic majority in Congress had "enacted almost every important plank in the Progressive platform of 1912." [54]

51. Cited in Robert Endicott Osgood, *Ideals and Self-interest in America's Foreign Relations* (Chicago, University of Chicago Press, 1953), p. 273.
52. Ibid., p. 85.
53. Link, *Woodrow Wilson and the Progressive Era*, pp. 80, 224.
54. Ibid., pp. 222–36. "Clearly, it was not to be a simple matter to frame a militant campaign address against an Administration with such a record." Claude G. Bowers, *Beveridge and the Progressive Era* (Boston, Houghton Mifflin, 1932), p. 491.

Important sectors of the American forces of movement immediately
shifted their allegiance to the President and his party. Among the
converts there were many members of the "informal brain trust of
the Progressive movement," [55] including intellectuals and journalists
like John Reed, Ray Stannard Baker, Lincoln Steffens, Ida Tarbell,
Irvin Cobb, Walter Lippmann, Herbert Croly, John Dewey, Max
Eastman and George Creel. Also, "one by one, the men and women
who had gone into the Roosevelt party in 1912 to fight for principles
and social regeneration rather than to follow a hero, came out for
Wilson—Jane Addams . . . Francis J. Heney . . . John M. Parker
. . . Edgar C. Snyder . . . Bainbridge Colby." No less significant was
the unconcealed adherence of "the railway brotherhoods, the American Federation of Labor . . . the Non-Partisan League . . . and
practically all independent newspapers and periodicals." [56]

But since menacing war clouds overhung the election, neither
Hughes nor Wilson could restrict campaign oratory to questions of
domestic reform. Indeed, "in his frenzy for 'sound Americanism'
Roosevelt subordinated all considerations of domestic reform." Consequently, not only was Hughes denied a progressive domestic platform,
but because of the largely unsolicited and uncontrolled support of
both Roosevelt and Lodge he appeared before the voters as an ally
of the interventionists. Particularly in view of the prominence of
preparedness elements in the Republican ranks, the Democrats cunningly boasted, with Bryan's help, that Wilson had "kept us out of
war" while at the same time accusing the opposition of being the
"war party." [57]

In brief, Wilson's victory proved that he had successfully fused "the
peace cause with the ideal of progressive democracy." Once the returns
were counted, it was clear that the American forces of movement—
the left-Progressives, the pacifists, and labor—had helped Wilson's
candidacy in many states, particularly in the South and the West.
Furthermore, just as in Europe many Socialists looked to Wilson for
guidance not in the field of domestic reform but rather in the area of

55. See Richard Hofstadter, *The Age of Reform: From Bryan to F.D.R.* (New
York, Knopf, 1955), pp. 154–56.

56. Link, *Woodrow Wilson and the Progressive Era*, pp. 239–40.

57. Ibid., pp. 241–47; Goldman, *Rendezvous with Destiny*, p. 245; Walter
Millis, *Road to War: America 1914–1917* (Boston, Houghton Mifflin, 1935), pp.
316–18.

diplomacy, so also in America some half million Socialists abandoned their party in order to vote for the peace-oriented President.[58]

The pacifist elements had also entered the Democratic camp, largely because they were frightened by the interventionist agitation of Roosevelt, the munitions makers, the war-loan bankers, and the Plattsburg movement. Bryan, Jane Addams, Lillian Wald, Oswald Garrison Villard, and David Starr Jordan hoped that once re-elected the President would enforce strict neutrality and would seek to use American influence to arrange an accommodation between the Allies and the Central Powers.[59]

But whereas these antiwarmongers were primarily motivated by a profound pacifism, other components of the forces of movement— La Follette, Bourne, labor, and the Socialists—were anti-interventionist above all because they feared the domestic repercussions of war. Like their European counterparts, "many reformers were leery of intervention precisely because they were reformers"; they were convinced "that war would bring an end to reform." Specifically they were anxious to protect the recent socioeconomic advances of the New Freedom; moreover, like Marcel Sembat in *Faites un roi sinon faites la paix*, they warned about the detrimental impact of war both on civil liberties and on the political struggle against the vested interests.[60]

"No element of progressive thinking was lacking in Wilson's reluctance to go to war." Even though the President was no pacifist, he had a pronounced horror of war. Furthermore, he spoke of the dangers of "illiberalism at home to reinforce the men at the front," of the majority of people going "war mad," of conformity becoming "the only virtue," and of the businessmen dominating "the nation for twenty years after the war comes to an end." [61]

These apprehensions were fully justified. No sooner had war been declared than "reform stopped dead, large-scale business swiftly in-

58. Link, *Woodrow Wilson and the Progressive Era*, pp. 241, 249–51.
59. Millis, *Road to War*, pp. 103, 385.
60. Goldman, *Rendezvous with Destiny*, pp. 236 ff. In *The Age of Reform*, p. 270, Hofstadter notes that "war has always been the Nemesis of the liberal tradition in America." Not only Hofstadter but also Goldman, Millis, Link, and Osgood have failed to note that war has just as often been the nemesis of the liberal tradition in Europe. On the whole, the above-cited studies of the Progressive era are unduly parochial.
61. Goldman, *Rendezvous with Destiny*, pp. 241–48; and Osgood, *Ideals and Self-interest*, pp. 238–42.

creased its profits and its powers, inflation began its ravaging. Civil liberties were twisted, narrowed, virtually abolished . . . the Administration and Congress rushed through sweeping legislation dealing with espionage, sedition, and trading with enemy, and many local governments followed suit." And again, there was nothing peculiarly American about the fact that the "unofficial and the official hysteria fell more and more under the control of conservatives, who were just as interested in silencing reform agitation as they were in suppressing friends of Germany." [62] Charles Beard might as well have had reference to France and England when he noted that in America "the occasion of the war which called for patriotic duties was seized by emotional conservatives as an opportunity to blacken the character of persons whose opinions they feared and hated." [63]

On December 18, 1916, when Wilson had dispatched his Note to the European belligerents inviting them to state their war aims, he had done so partly in the hope of precipitating a negotiated end to the war which, so long as it continued, threatened to engulf America in external belligerency as well as in internal reaction. For implying that both sides seemed to be fighting for the same objectives, Wilson was severely taken to task by Theodore Roosevelt, who denounced this view as being "wickedly false." Furthermore, in unison with the Allied foreign offices, "American champions of the Allied cause denounced Wilson for playing Germany's game and approving Germany's attempt to impose a dictated peace settlement." On the other hand, "the defenders of Germany, the peace element, and the great mass of non-interventionists hailed it as the beginning of the end of the war." [64]

In spite of his disappointment with Germany's belligerently noncommital answer to his Note, Wilson pursued his diplomatic labors. On January 22, 1917, in an address to the Senate, he asserted that a lasting peace would have to be a peace without victory supported by a League of Nations in which, as a new world power, the United States would have to play a responsible role. Once again, not only in America but also in the Allied countries,[65] the President received enthusiastic acclaim from the Left, while the Right registered severe

62. Goldman, *Rendezvous with Destiny*, pp. 254–56.

63. Charles A. Beard and Mary R. Beard, *The Rise of American Civilization* (rev. ed. New York, Macmillan, 1947), Pt. II, p. 643.

64. Millis, *Road to War*, pp. 366–69; Osgood, *Ideals and Self-interest*, pp. 149–50; Link, *Woodrow Wilson and the Progressive Era*, p. 261.

65. See above, pp. 157–61.

protests. In Roosevelt's eyes "Wilson, by his support of a world league and a peace without victory, had become a rallying point for all the pacifists, cowards, and short-sighted fools which had plagued him since the war began." [66]

Presently external conditions cut short the argument between American interventionists and neutralists. The German resumption of unrestricted submarine warfare and the Zimmermann note led to the decision for entering the war on the side of the Allies.

Given his actions and pronouncements as an antiwar progressive throughout 1916 and in the first weeks of 1917, Wilson could hardly have been expected to justify the war in Rooseveltian terms. If the United States had intervened while a conservative administration was in power, the war might have been presented as a war in which America's vital self-interest coincided with honor and righteousness. This was the explanation advanced by the European governments in August 1914, while most European Radicals and Socialists rationalized their support by baptizing the war as a war to end war, a war for civilization, a war for principles.

In America, however, the Chief Executive himself was a convinced and dedicated progressive who in early 1917 enjoyed the support of the major political and intellectual sectors of the forces of movement. In proclaiming that America was fighting for principles and not for self-interest the President articulated a position which was common to the forces of movement on both sides of the Atlantic, particularly after the Russian Revolution. In America the Wilson formula now "became the ideological bridge by which most of the progressive group moved with their leader from neutrality to intervention," [67] just as in Europe at the outbreak of war similar though nonofficial formulas had facilitated the shift from an antiwar to a prowar position by Radicals, pacifists, and Socialists.

Whereas in England, Radicals like H. G. Wells did not join Crewe House until early 1918,[68] in America left-oriented intellectuals eagerly entered government service immediately after the declaration of war. "The men who went to work for George Creel (himself a crusading journalist) in the Committee on Public Information, whose job it was to stimulate public enthusiasm for a war of ideals and principles were

66. Osgood, *Ideals and Self-interest*, p. 150.
67. Goldman, *Rendezvous with Destiny*, pp. 250–51.
68. See below, pp. 378–79.

in so many instances the same men who had learned their trade drumming up enthusiasm for the Progressive reforms and providing articles for the muckraking magazines." [69] In his home propaganda about America's moral crusade Creel enjoyed the cooperation of Arthur Bullard, Harvey O'Higgins, Will Irwin, Wallace Irwin, Ernest Poole, Samuel Hopkins Adams, Louis F. Post, Ray Stannard Baker, and Ida Tarbell—"indeed, it was a roll call of the muckrakers." [70]

Even though the Wilson formula could not win over dedicated pacifists like Jane Addams and unyielding reformers like Randolph Bourne, it did facilitate the adherence of the American Social Patriots. The crusade immediately won the enthusiastic support of Socialists like William English Walling, Charles Edward Russell, John Spargo, Gustavus Myers, and Upton Sinclair. Likewise, with the exception of the numerically insignificant IWW, organized labor endorsed the war with pledges of loyalty and with "no-strike" promises.[71] However, the majority of the Socialist party maintained a strong dissident position. Even though it did not appeal for revolutionary opposition to the war, partly because of the initial vagueness of Wilson's war formula, the Socialist party sought to make its support conditional. The party's National Executive Committee disseminated the following message: "Not a single soldier until we know what we are fighting for." [72] Pending this clarification the party maintained its benign opposition.

On the whole, then, in late 1917 the strength of the antiwar Socialists and pacifists was of little consequence. As for the prowar factions of movement, they were enthusiasts for the Allied cause. Even before the Fourteen Points address Wilson had begun to convince them that the war was an unequaled opportunity for international reform which, in turn, was an essential precondition for the next phase of domestic reform. However, the bulk of the American public, including most Democrats and Republicans, were diligently perform-

69. Hofstadter, *The Age of Reform*, p. 273.
70. Louis Filler, *Crusaders for American Liberalism* (Yellow Springs, Ohio, Antioch Press, 1950), pp. 374–75; and Osgood, *Ideals and Self-interest*, pp. 274, 277–78.
71. Donald Drew Egbert and Stow Persons, eds., *Socialism and American Life* (2 vols. Princeton, Princeton University Press, 1952), *1*, 316–18; and John Spargo, *Americanism and Social Democracy* (New York, Harper, 1918), pp. 145–56, 298 ff.
72. Cited in Alexander Trachtenberg, ed., *The American Socialists and the War* (New York, Rand School of Social Science, 1917), pp. 45–47. See also Morris Hillquit, *Loose Leaves from a Busy Life* (New York, Macmillan, 1934), pp. 165–68.

ing their war duties without concerning themselves with ideological disputations, either national or international.

True, in the *New Republic,* the *Nation,* and the New York *World,* Walter Weyl, John Dewey, Charles Beard, Herbert Croly, and Frank Cobb glorified the war as a struggle against German militarism and a crusade for democracy, self-determination, and a league of nations to preserve a peace of principles. However, "it became increasingly evident that a powerful faction of the people was determined to wage war in the old way, for tangible and self-interest reasons first, and for universal ideals second." Prominent militant patriots like James Harvey of the *North American Review* and Theodore Roosevelt called for "Peace with complete victory! Peace with unconditional surrender!" [73] Simultaneously the great majority of American newspapers were "possessed by a spirit of romantic patriotic militarism"; [74] their editorials may not have been quite so martial and self-righteous as those of the *Morning Post* in London or the *Action Française* in Paris, though they certainly were comparable in language and national egoism to those in the London *Times* and in *le Temps.*

Until December 1917 the major American newspapers did not bother to distinguish between the German people and its government, nor did they actively promote the idea of a league of nations. Instead, the press was instrumental in sharpening both the official and the nonofficial persecution of the far from numerous Socialist, pacifist, and pro-German dissenters. As during the height of the political truce in Europe, all dissident opinions were suspect. Since April 1917 President Wilson had abandoned his "peace without victory" ideas; consequently many superpatriots felt justified in labeling all references to the kindred Petrograd peace formula as treasonable. Little wonder that after a speaking tour through the United States in the fall of 1917 Lincoln Steffens should have run into a war psychosis which made an intelligent public discussion of war aims altogether impossible. [75] Walter Lippmann urged Colonel House to call the President's attention to this dangerous hardening of American opinion. In turn, House told Wilson that even though the attitude of most antiwar Socialists was perhaps deplorable, "more harm may easily be done by repres-

73. Osgood, *Ideals and Self-interest,* pp. 267–73; and William E. Dodd, *Woodrow Wilson and His Work* (New York, Doubleday, Page, 1920), pp. 255–61.
74. *New Republic* (January 12, 1918), p. 293.
75. *The Letters of Lincoln Steffens, 1,* 399–423, esp. 402, 415.

sion [and that] between the two courses, it is better to err on the
side of leniency." [76]

Evidently there was only marginal indigenous American political
pressure for a reformulation of war aims. In America none of the
dissident groups was able to capitalize on war weariness, a turnip
winter, economic hardships, or battle fatigue. Furthermore, the Republican party had not formulated anything like British Labour's
Memorandum on War Aims, nor had it produced a Lansdowne faction. Wilson was free to rely primarily on the Russian imbroglio to
provide the political rationale for his war-aims offensive.

At the turn of the year Wilson nevertheless instructed his Secretary,
Joseph P. Tumulty, to canvass "carefully the editorial comments in
the principal journals of the country." Tumulty's survey revealed that
those papers which favored a reply to Trotsky did so almost exclusively in the light of diplomatic, not of domestic, expediency.
While the New York *Evening Post* concluded that "all the situation
required [was] a discriminating answer," the Springfield *Republican*
insisted that "peace terms [were] as much part of strategy as the
planning of battles"; consequently the diplomacy of the Central Powers
at Brest-Litovsk should be countered in such a way as "to make it
perfectly clear that the real blame for continuing the War, like the
blame for beginning it, does not rest with the Allies." Similarly, the
Baltimore *Sun,* the New York *Sun,* the Newark *News,* and the Boston
Globe agreed that "the Allies must meet the powerful peace offensive
of the Central Powers promptly and courageously with a unified and
high-minded policy." [77]

Thus Wilson's Fourteen Points had an eminently realistic diplomatic
origin. However, in addition to answering the Bolsheviks and to encouraging the German Socialists, the President also sought to force
London and Paris to liberalize their diplomacy and ideology. This intention became evident when, upon hearing of Lloyd George's TUC
address, the President momentarily considered abandoning his own
message; he took this speech as signifying the first welcome step in
the liberalization of Allied diplomacy. However, since his own mes-

76. House to Wilson, October 17, 1917, Wilson Papers.

77. These editorial comments are taken from Tumulty's memorandum to the
President, dated January 3, 1918, in Wilson Papers. Among the major newspapers
which thought that no reply was necessary were the Chicago *Daily News,* the
Philadelphia *Record,* the Washington *Post,* and the New York *Herald.*

sage was in final draft before the complete text of the British Prime
Minister's January 5th speech reached Washington, Wilson, with
House's strong encouragement, decided to proceed with his projected
address to Congress. House did not hesitate to reinforce his encouragement with the flattering prediction that the forthcoming address
would make Wilson "spokesman of the Entente and, indeed, the
spokesman for the liberals of the world." [78]

It appears, then, that even though the President and his advisers
may not have had a complete understanding of the world situation in
late December and early January, they drafted the Fourteen Points
address in full awareness of the seriousness of the Allied crisis.[79]
Furthermore, the address was drafted with the overarching purpose
of preventing a tolerable military and diplomatic crisis from becoming
aggravated by a widespread *crise de confiance*.

It is imperative, therefore, not to separate artificially the Fourteen
Points themselves from the address in which they were delivered to
Congress—and to the world. The oft-quoted fourteen placard paragraphs must be viewed against the political and diplomatic background which Wilson himself traced in his much neglected speech
of January 8, 1918. Certainly the broad context of this speech is essential to the explication of the origins, the objectives, and the methods
of Wilsonian diplomacy.

In the second sentence of the opening paragraph the President unequivocally stated that "parleys have been in progress at Brest-Litovsk
between Russian representatives and the Central Powers to which
the attention of all the belligerents has been invited for the purpose
of ascertaining whether it may be possible to extend these parleys
into a general conference with regard to terms of peace and settlement." [80] As against the British Prime Minister's introduction, which
responded to the Labour pressure, Wilson's introduction was in direct
answer to the Brest-Litovsk summons. Moreover, accepting the ideological challenge no less directly, Wilson asserted that "the Russian
representatives presented not only a perfectly definite statement of
the principles upon which they would be willing to conclude peace

78. House Diary, January 9, 1918.

79. Lippmann, *Public Opinion*, pp. 209–10.

80. This quotation as well as all later quotations are from the text of the Fourteen Points address in Baker and Dodd, *The Public Papers of Woodrow Wilson*,
5, 155–62.

but also an equally definite program of the concrete application of those principles." The conversation between Wilson on the one hand and Lenin and Trotsky on the other had begun.

Even while launching his attack on the imperialist designs of Trotsky's opponents, the President appeared in his revolutionary role. Whereas Lloyd George, with the help of specific examples, censured Czernin for being "deplorably vague" in his endorsement of self-determination, Wilson immediately ascribed the blatant contradictions in the policy of the Central Powers to the growing schism inside their body politic. He maintained that the Russian representatives "were sincere and in earnest" in breaking off the negotiations, because they realized that the "military leaders" of the Central Empires still had the upper hand over "the more liberal statesmen."

Not unlike the Bolsheviks, Wilson seized this perilous opportunity to add fuel to the fire in back of the German Government by asking whether the world was listening to "those who speak the spirit and intention" of the July 19th Reichstag Resolution "or to those who resist and defy that spirit and intention and insist upon conquest and subjugation?" In order to leave no doubt about the purpose of these questions, Wilson went on to suggest that actually the world was listening to both, "unreconciled and in open and hopeless contradiction." After having outlined the Fourteen Points in a later part of the address, Wilson reiterated, as if to provide the necessary emphasis, that as a "preliminary" to any negotiations the Allies must know whether the enemy's representatives speak "for the Reichstag majority or the military party and the men whose creed is imperial domination."

Though Wilson's circuitous exhortation to revolution was not cast in terms of class warfare, it nevertheless blended with the straightforward revolutionary appeals reaching Germany and the Dual Monarchy from Russia. The net political effect of Wilson's tactics was to broaden the scope of the revolutionary call. Whereas the Socialist appeal from the East agitated the left wing of the enemy forces of movement, Wilson's Radical appeal encouraged the non-Socialist elements in the growing Reichstag majority. Nevertheless, it is obvious that in January 1918 Wilson and Lenin alike had exaggerated notions of the intensity of the revolutionary fire in Germany.

But Wilson was primarily concerned with Russia's plight. It is not surprising, then, that Colonel House himself thought that what the

President had said about Russia was "in some respects the most eloquent part of his message." Indeed, Wilson's decisive passage on Russia
speaks for itself:

> There is, moreover, a voice calling for these definitions of prin-
> ciple and of purpose which is, it seems to me, more thrilling and
> more compelling than any of the many moving voices with which
> the troubled air of the world is filled. It is the voice of the Rus-
> sian people. They are prostrate and all but helpless, it would seem,
> before the grim power of Germany, which has hitherto known
> no relenting and no pity. Their power, apparently, is shattered.
> And yet their soul is not subservient. They will not yield either
> in principle or in action. Their conception of what is right, of what
> it is humane and honorable for them to accept, has been stated
> with frankness, a largeness of view, a generosity of spirit, and a
> universal human sympathy which must challenge the admiration
> of every friend of mankind; and they have refused to compound
> their ideals or desert others that they themselves may be safe.
> They call to us to say what it is that we desire, in what, if any-
> thing, our purpose and our spirit differ from theirs; and I believe
> that the people of the United States would wish me to respond,
> with utter simplicity and frankness. Whether their present lead-
> ers believe it or not, it is our heartfelt desire and hope that some
> way may be opened whereby we may be privileged to assist the
> people of Russia to attain their utmost hope of liberty and or-
> dered peace.

Notwithstanding the British Prime Minister's uninspiring conclusion
that Russia could "only be saved by her own people," the President
strained to establish a new bridge between the Allies and revolutionary
Russia. Seeking to impress both ruler and ruled, he did not call for
the overthrow of the Bolsheviks as a condition for renewed cooperation; Wilson even seemed to hold out the faint hope of American assistance to Russia's illegitimate rulers.

Moreover, fully resolved to continue the crusade regardless of all
suggestions for a negotiated peace, Wilson refused to abandon Russia's
borderlands to the mercy of the Central Powers. The first of the
Fourteen Points dealing with Europe's territorial question (Point VI)
leaves no doubt that at this time America went beyond idle words of
good will and friendship:

Evacuation of all Russian territory and such a settlement of all questions affecting Russia as will secure the best and freest co-operation of the other nations of the world in obtaining for her an unhampered and unembarrassed opportunity for the independent determination of her own political development and national policy and assure her of a sincere welcome into the society of free nations under institutions of her free choosing; and more than a welcome, assistance also of every kind that she may need and may herself desire. The treatment accorded to Russia by her sister nations in the months to come will be the acid test of their goodwill, of their comprehension of her needs as distinguished from their own interest and of their intelligent and unselfish sympathy.

There is no need to compare this clear-cut policy statement with Lloyd George's refusal even "to deal with the question of the Russian territories now in German occupation."

Perhaps the moving and confident language of Point VI, as well as of other passages, is the most convincing evidence that Wilson was profoundly impressed with the importance and seriousness of the recently begun regeneration of Russia. It appears that Wilson himself, aided by House, was the main architect of this paragraph. In its December 22nd war-aims Memorandum the Inquiry studiously avoided giving any guidance on the fate of Russia's borderlands. On January 2, 1918, in another memorandum, the Inquiry again refused to take up in any detail questions pertaining to "the future of Russia," primarily because its staff felt that the Russian problems "involve large political considerations and broad political judgment, rather than the study of specific data." [81]

Only the Chief Executive was in a position to decide on questions of major political expediency. Wilson, with the assistance of House, had concluded that it was "part of wisdom" to segregate Russia as far as possible from Germany, and this "could only be done by the broadest and friendliest expression of sympathy and promise of more

81. The Inquiry was concerned primarily with five territorial questions: Alsace-Lorraine, Italian "Irredenta," Poland, the Balkans, and Turkey. The Inquiry staff held that broad political judgments were involved not only in the Russian problem but also in the democratization of Germany and the reorganization of Austria-Hungary. See "A Suggested Statement of Peace Terms (Revised and Enlarged from Part III of the Memorandum of December 22, 1917)" dated January 2, 1918, Wilson Papers.

substantial help." [82] It is difficult to measure the exact amount of political expediency in Wilson's diplomatic offensive. In postulating the treatment to be accorded to Russia by her *sister* nations as the acid test of international friendship and morality, did Wilson intend to subject only the Allies to this test? Or would the Central Powers have to pass the same test? Clearly, this test would be most taxing for Germany and the Dual Monarchy, should the Allies refuse to participate in the Brest-Litovsk negotiations. This refusal was bound to play into the hands of the German General Staff which, far from inspired by sisterly feelings, anxiously waited for this chance to exploit Russia's prostration. Not even Wilson could have expected Germany to sign a fair separate peace with Russia; her generals needed Russian supplies to continue the war against the Allies.

These considerations raise the additional question of the kind of expectations Wilson and House entertained about their ability to re-enlist Russia in the crusade. Were they able to visualize Lenin as a partner in their enterprise? Furthermore, did they side with those Bolsheviks who declared Russia capable of fighting a revolutionary war? Or were they confident that an assurance of American aid was all that was required to tip the scales in favor of the war forces in Russia? At any rate, Wilson and House apparently overestimated Russia's recovery potential, while underestimating the extent to which the self-determinatoin forces had already undermined "Russian" control over the western borderlands.

Neither Wilson nor House failed to recognize the success with which Lenin and Trotsky were practicing open diplomacy. In the true UDC spirit Colonel House told the President that open diplomacy was not only "right" and the "diplomacy of the future," but also would "please, the American people and the democracies of the world." [83] On this score Wilson needed no convincing since he himself had long been concerned with extending the principle of democratic government to include popular control over foreign policy. Had he not been forced to develop his diplomacy in a coalition framework, it is quite likely that on a prior occasion Wilson would have advocated the abolition of secret diplomacy. This assumption seems partly justified by the enthusiasm with which the President now praised the Russian representatives for insisting "very justly, very wisely and *in the true spirit of*

82. Seymour, *Intimate Papers, 3,* 330–31.
83. Ibid., p. 326.

modern democracy that the conference they have been holding . . . should be held within open, not closed doors."

In practicing the open diplomacy, however, the Bolsheviks pursued specific limited revolutionary objectives. They gave no indication that they planned to integrate the open-diplomacy method into their foreign policy, certainly not while their revolutionary state was condemned to live in a hostile international environment. In contrast, Wilson prepared to make open diplomacy a permanent keystone of the New Diplomacy. Curiously enough, a year earlier Wilson had considered a peace without victory necessary for a rational and permanent peace. In January 1917 he had proclaimed that, since "victory would mean peace forced upon the loser . . . it would be accepted in humiliation, under duress . . . and would leave a sting, a resentment, a bitter memory upon which terms of peace would rest, not permanently, but only as upon quicksand." [84] Now, one year later, the President proposed to rely on open diplomacy as a safeguard against the irrationalities of peace-making and peace-keeping. Henceforth, public opinion—the collective power to see "right" through "reason"—would be an iron guarantee against the schemings of traditional diplomacy.

> It will be our wish and purpose that the processes of peace, when they are begun, shall be absolutely open and that they shall involve and permit henceforth no secret understandings of any kind. The day of conquest and aggrandizement is gone by; so is also the day of secret covenants entered into in the interest of particular governments likely at some unlooked-for moment to upset the peace of the world.

Apparently Wilson and the Bolsheviks shared the optimistic notion that no government could ever hope to win the electorate's approval for policies of conquest. Therefore, they seized upon the open-diplomacy method as a safeguard against the adoption of aggressive and expansionist policies.

Certainly, Lenin and Trotsky could hardly have hoped for a more complete and eloquent endorsement of their recently adopted principle than the first of the Fourteen Points: "Open covenants of peace, openly arrived at, after which there shall be no private international under-

84. Baker and Dodd, *The Public Papers of Woodrow Wilson, 4,* 410.

standings of any kind but diplomacy shall proceed always frankly and in the public view."

Nonetheless, Wilson and House were prepared to admit that even public opinion could make mistakes. The second of the Fourteen Points, which proclaimed the freedom of the seas, provided that the world community acting through the League of Nations is empowered to curtail this freedom. The concept of collective security was foreshadowed in the statement that "the seas may be closed in whole or in part by international action for the enforcement of international covenants." True, the fact that the comparatively radical freedom of the seas appeared in second place was symptomatic of America's new naval maturity; but given the President's search for a New World, Point II also reflected his determination to have the New Diplomacy facilitate major power readjustments.

Wilson was perfectly aware that America's growing naval and economic strength was the basis for her imminent rise to world stature. On July 4, 1914, in an address at Independence Hall in Philadelphia, he had formulated two questions which, after more than three years of World War, had an even more pressing urgency: "What are we going to do with the influence and power of this great nation? Are we going to play the old role of using that power for our aggrandizement and material benefit only?" [85] House had been instrumental in sensitizing Wilson to the dangers of commercial rivalry as a major cause of war; in June 1914 House had actually proposed economic development of the world's backward areas by the industrially advanced nations as a means of reducing diplomatic tensions.[86] In November 1917, while House was abroad, Wilson sent Mezes his reactions to a preliminary outline of the subjects with which the Inquiry proposed to deal. Apparently prompted by a lacuna in the Inquiry outline, the President underscored the necessity to "study the just claims of the large states, like Russia and Austria, and Germany herself, to an assured access to the sea and the main routes of commerce not only, but to a reasonable access to the raw materials of the world which they themselves do not produce." [87] There is very little kinship between this approach to postwar economic problems

85. Ibid., 3, 142.
86. Seymour, *Intimate Papers*, 1, 264–65.
87. Woodrow Wilson to Sidney Mezes, November 12, 1917, Wilson Papers.

and the one evolved by the Allies at their Economic Conference in Paris in June 1916. Actually, Point III—advocating "the removal, so far as possible, of all economic barriers and the establishment of an equality of trade conditions among all nations consenting to the peace and associating themselves for its maintenance"—must be looked upon as a multi-purpose formula. While proclaiming America a serious contender for a sizable share of the world market, Point III also pointed out the necessity of providing "institutions" capable of facilitating major impending shifts not only in political power but also in the pattern of world trade.

It was not accidental that, in view of the interrelated growth of American naval and economic power, Points II and III should have dealt with the twin freedoms of the sea and of trade. It will be remembered that the Bolsheviks as well as Labour also invoked the free-trade gospel, though for different reasons. Joffe condemned "the attempts of strong nations to restrict the freedom of trade of weaker nations" as part of a calculated attack on economic imperialism.[88] Labour endorsed the free-trade formula because economic warfare threatened to inflict serious hardship on the proletariat of industrially advanced nations.

In the context of the war diplomacy it must be noted that Wilson proposed to give the benefits of free trade only to nations "consenting to the peace and associating themselves for its maintenance." Apparently the President sought to make the "right" to free trade, as much as the freedom of the seas, conditional upon membership in good standing in the community of nations to which only "democratic" states would be admitted.

Germany had a vital interest in trade and navigation; after the war she would have to find an adequate place for her rapidly expanding economy in the network of international trade. However, under her present form of government, Germany would not be eligible for membership in the Wilsonian League, which proposed to offer not only political but also economic security. According to the Inquiry, the projected League would seek "the attainment of joint economic prosperity, including equal opportunity upon the highways of the world and equitable access to the raw materials which all nations need." Since Germany was thought to be particularly vulnerable on these economic scores, the Inquiry suggested that the Allies had the power

88. Degras, p. 22.

"to compel Germany's assent at the peace conference by our ability to bar her indefinitely from access to supplies. . . . This involves adopting as our policy the reserving of the discussion of economic peace until our political, social, and international objects are attained. . . . No economic peace until the peoples are freed." [89] Here total war and total diplomacy became inextricably intertwined. In Point III Wilson combined his threat to the very existence of the established order in the enemy countries with his promise for a New World. Later, at the Versailles Conference, this diplomatic strategy found new mentors in Foch and Clemenceau. However, by then the German Republic had been born and both Wilson and Lloyd George were apprehensive lest further economic hardships in Germany promote the Spartacist cause.

In the context of a comparison of the Wilsonian and Leninist diplomacy, Point IV, advocating disarmament, is perhaps the most Wilsonian of the Fourteen Points. Disarmament is the realm in which Wilson and Lenin had nothing in common. Though both heralded the birth of the new era, they differed sharply on the method for its delivery. Addressing the forces of movement of the world Wilson invited them to participate in the exciting experiment of building the first international community capable of organizing peaceful change. Lenin, on the other hand, was committed to a social and political revolution in which violence was expected to play a necessary role.

In contradistinction to Lenin's militant assertion that "we are not pacifists" Wilson called for "adequate guarantees given and taken that national armaments will be reduced to the lowest point consistent with domestic safety." This fourth point was a concise summary of all the disarmament formulas which Liberals, Radicals, Pacifists and Socialists had evolved in recent years. Point IV also had been inspired by analyses of the Norman Angell variety which insisted that war had ceased to be an effective instrument of control. In January 1917 Wilson had proclaimed that "the question of armaments . . . is the most immediately and intensely practical question connected with the future fortunes of nations and of mankind." [90] But in early 1917 this statement sounded less daring, even less idealistic, than a year later after war and revolution had made common cause.

In his January 5th speech Lloyd George had made no more than a

89. *FR, Paris Peace Conference, 1919, 1,* 53.
90. Baker and Dodd, *The Public Papers of Woodrow Wilson, 4,* 413.

passing reference to "the crushing weight of modern armaments and the increasing evils of compulsory military service." His advocacy of world organization had been equally vague. The Prime Minister's references to these aspects of the New Diplomacy could not have been any stronger since they were merely calculated to placate the Labour party, which had proposed a drastic limitation of armaments as well as "the entire abolition of the profit-making armaments industry." Both Wilson and the Labour party firmly committed themselves not only to disarmament but also to international organization.

Certainly Wilson was no less dedicated to self-determination than was either Lloyd George or Lenin. And yet, in his address to Congress, he outlined four cardinal peace principles before even mentioning self-determination. Moreover, instead of making self-determination a separate ground rule, the President wove it into his over-all program for territorial adjustments. Perhaps Wilson was anxious to avoid Lloyd George's blanket endorsement of self-determination. In the light of the Bolsheviks' specific renunciation of Persia as well as of their general denunciation of imperialism, Lenin's espousal of "integral" self-determination appeared more genuine than that of Lloyd George. Curiously enough, the first of Wilson's territorial points (Point V) dealt with the colonial problem. Could it be that he was concerned by the restrictions which not only "imperial" holdings but also future colonial ambitions of London and Paris were likely to impose on Allied nationalities diplomacy? In any case, there is evidence that the future of the Ottoman Empire was on Wilson's mind, because in early December 1917 he was troubled by Allied plans "for divisions of territory" in Asia Minor.

In his fifth point the President very cautiously advocated "a free, open-minded, and absolutely impartial adjustment of all colonial claims." There is no way of knowing whether in referring to "colonial claims" he proposed to limit the discussion to the overseas territories conquered from the enemy, just like Lloyd George had suggested that these be settled at the peace conference. But, however broad or narrow the interpretation of what was to be included under "colonial claims," Wilson insisted that their settlement be "based upon a strict observance of the principle that in determining all such questions of sovereignty the interests of the populations concerned must have equal weight with the equitable claims of the governments whose title is to be determined." Compared to the boldness with which Lenin and

Trotsky placed the debate of "colonialism" on the agenda of 20th-century diplomacy, the President gave a conservative interpretation of America's anticolonial tradition. In January 1918, however, even the Bolsheviks were more impressed with Wilson's generous treatment of Russia (in Point VI) than they were critical of his colonial program.

Points VII and VIII deal with Belgium and Alsace-Lorraine respectively. As in London, in Washington there was undivided support for Wilson's insistence that Belgium's sovereignty *must* be completely restored, together with full damages. In the case of Alsace-Lorraine unanimity was less complete on both sides of the Atlantic. Unlike Lloyd George, the British Left was reluctant to return the twin provinces to France without some sort of prior plebiscite. Inside the Inquiry both Lippmann and Mezes, over the objections of the politically less progressive D. H. Miller, expressed "strong sympathy for the French claim" but nevertheless urged that the United States should not become committed to "the demand for complete return." [91] Possibly on the strength of this advice based on apprehensions about French ambitions on the left bank of the Rhine, Wilson declared in Point VIII that the wrong done to France *should* (not must) be righted. On the two major issues pertaining to Germany's western borders American and British policies were in basic accord.

Point IX, relating to Italy, extended this official Anglo-American harmony on Western European problems to include the British Labour party. It was under the latter's pressure that Lloyd George, fully acquainted with the Treaty of London, had limited his advocacy to Italy's "legitimate" claims. Since Wilson apparently was cognizant of Italy's excessive ambitions, he condensed a seven-line recommendation by the Inquiry which was mindful of Italian "defensive and nationalist considerations," to the straightforward proposition that "readjustment of the frontiers of Italy should be effected along clearly recognizable lines of nationality."

That the President, no less than House, was far from convinced that these lines of nationality were readily recognizable emerges from Points X and XI bearing on Austria-Hungary and the Balkans. This geographic bloc is of particular interest since it falls within Lenin's second geographic area.

Point X declared that "the peoples of Austria-Hungary, whose place among the nations we wish to see safeguarded and assured, should be

91. A Suggested Statement of Peace Terms, January 2, 1918, Wilson Papers.

accorded the freest opportunity of autonomous development." Again, Wilson was in full accord with the British Prime Minister;[92] both were skeptical about not only the desirability but also the inevitability of the break-up of the Dual Monarchy. The Inquiry suggested that for reasons of psychological warfare the Allies should stir up "the nationalist discontent"; they should not, however, accept the "extreme logic of this discontent, which would be the dismemberment of Austria-Hungary."[93] The Inquiry recommended this policy in the hope that it might strengthen those elements in Vienna which favored an early negotiated peace as the key to the preservation of the Dual Monarchy.[94] By encouraging the Austrian forces of conciliation, the Allies might drive a wedge between Vienna and Berlin.

The Inquiry's recommendation, however, was not based exclusively on considerations of diplomatic tactics. Like the Labour party's Memorandum on War Aims, the Inquiry's Memorandum expressed the definitive opinion "that in the last analysis economic considerations [would] outweigh nationalistic affiliations in the Balkans, and that a settlement which insures economic prosperity [would be] most likely to be a lasting one."[95] Whereas this economic realism—which for the moment seemed forsaken even in Lenin's nationalities program—prevailed in the Inquiry group, President Wilson tended to neglect the economic aspects of the nationalities problem. While Point X stopped short of a clear-cut endorsement of self-determination by placing the emphasis on the "opportunity for autonomous development," in subsequent pronouncements Wilson gradually became a fiery advocate of unqualified self-determination for the Vienna-oppressed nationalities. According to Walter Lippmann, the Inquiry

92. On January 2, 1918, House had received a cable from Balfour about the Smuts-Mensdorff conversations. According to this cable Mensdorff "received with much sympathy" the assurance of "our strong desire to see the various nationalities of which the Empire is composed given an opportunity for autonomous development." Mamatey concludes that "Balfour's statement that the Austrian nationalities should be given 'an opportunity for autonomous development' appeared verbatim in the Fourteen Points." Mamatey, *The United States and East Central Europe,* p. 175.

93. *FR, Paris Peace Conference, 1919, 1,* 45.

94. "This approach should consist of references to the subjection of the various nationalities . . . but coupled with it should go repeated assurances that no dismemberment of the Empire is intended." *FR, Paris Peace Conference, 1919, 1,* 48.

95. *FR, Paris Peace Conference, 1919, 1,* 51.

repeatedly, but with little success, "tried to slow the President down on self-determination." [96]

But Wilson not only inadequately appreciated the economic problems of Eastern Europe but also was handicapped by his rather cursory geographic and ethnographic knowledge of the entire area. In Point XI, after calling for the evacuation of Rumania, Serbia, and Montenegro, Wilson added the somewhat vague recommendation that "the relations of the several Balkan states to one another should be determined by friendly counsel along historically established lines of allegiance and nationality." In the course of 1918 the American position on Serbia and other new nations became more specific and encouraging, partly because the self-determination movements in Eastern Europe and the Balkans were making such tremendous strides. Whereas they drew much inspiration from Lenin in early 1918, later Wilson became their spokesman and protector.

As for the inevitable liquidation of the Turkish Empire, in Point XII Wilson assured the non-Turkish nationalities of "an absolutely unmolested opportunity of autonomous development." Moreover, in unison with both Lloyd George and the Labour party, Wilson called for the neutralization as well as the internationalization of the Straits. On the other hand, like the British Prime Minister but unlike British Labour, Wilson did not envisage a mandate system for Turkey's non-European possessions.

The outright and unqualified commitment to an independent Poland in Point XIII contrasts sharply with Wilson's hesitant application of the self-determination principle in the preceding six points. It must have been evident to Wilson, as it was to the Inquiry, that the national and language conflicts destined to emerge with the future rebirth of Poland were likely to be no less intense than those of many other nascent successor states. It is noteworthy, therefore, that unlike these other successor states, only Poland was given specific political and economic guarantees. First, Wilson publicly proclaimed Poland to be in need of a "free and secure access to the seas." Secondly, this economic-strategic safeguard was further supplemented by Wilson's proposal that Poland's "political and economic independence and territorial integrity should be guaranteed by international covenant."

This thirteenth point which gives an international guarantee for

96. Interview with Walter Lippmann.

the independence of Poland may be looked upon as the link to the fourteenth point, calling for the establishment of the League of Nations: "A general association of nations must be formed under specific covenants for the purpose of affording mutual guarantees of political and territorial integrity to great and small nations." Though countless millions rallied to the idea of a League of Nations as the essential guarantee for a perpetual peace, it must be noted that Wilson, without even mentioning peace, chartered an association of nations in order to secure "mutual guarantees of political independence and territorial integrity." Peace was the ultimate objective; but the immediate function of the League was the preservation of the territorial arrangements which would emerge from the peace conference. Point II, on the freedom of the seas, anticipated this emphasis of the need to guarantee the stability of a new international order and equilibrium. Just as the Inquiry suggested that a considerable body of opinion in the Dual Monarchy presently favored a league of nations because it was likely to serve as "a guarantee of the status quo," so Wilson was equally concerned with guaranteeing the new "status quo" which would be effectuated by the war.

Nevertheless, the President's advocacy of an association of nations immediately won more converts than the Prime Minister's, primarily because it was part of an over-all diplomatic program untrammeled by the "dead hand of the past." Free from territorial ambitions and secret treaties, America stepped forward to embrace the open diplomacy initiated at Brest-Litovsk. As early as January 1917 President Wilson had spoken of a "community of power" as against the old "balance of power"; now his fourteenth point seemed to incorporate this vision into Allied policy.

This community of power was meant to put small and weak nations on a par with their more powerful neighbors. The association of nations would be a decisive instrument needed to help the rising nationalities to their feet. Point XIV compensated for the lack of precision with which Wilson dealt with self-determination in some of his other "placard paragraphs." The association of nations was meant to be a sort of midwife to nations about to be born; it would help them pass from the precarious stage of infancy, through adolescence, to full maturity—in a new "community of power."

With the Revolution only in its early stage, Lenin could not subscribe to the Wilsonian program, which sought to trace the road to early international, as well as domestic, order and stability. Lenin soon discovered that Wilson's daring proposal for orderly change became the most decisive challenge to his own revolutionary ideology. The war had stirred large masses of people; furthermore, it had shaken the beliefs of large segments of the élite and of the intelligentsia. A large-scale search for new ideological, political, and social moorings was under way. In this search some would eventually turn to Wilson, others to Lenin. In the meantime, however, for a short while the Bolsheviks themselves were grateful for the Fourteen Points.

EPILOGUE: WILSON VS. LENIN

THE ENTENTE had not entered the Great War with the object of liberating subject peoples and democratizing the Central Powers. It was only after three and a quarter years of mutually exhausting military operations coupled with various fundamental politicodiplomatic realignments that the Allies were in the process of crystallizing crusading war aims. Before the Allied military campaign was transformed into an ideological crusade, the Romanovs had been overthrown, America had entered the maelstrom of world politics, the European parties of movement had regrouped their forces, the Petrograd Soviet had articulated the basic tenets of the New Diplomacy, the Bolshevik Revolution had produced the first official practitioners of this New Diplomacy, and President Wilson had transcended his role as American war mobilizer to become a world statesman.

In addition to these historical causes there were certain compelling immediate causes for the review of Allied war aims. Above all, the Russian imbroglio forced the pace of Allied stocktaking. Both the British Prime Minister and the American President realized the importance not only of exploring every possible way of keeping Russia in the Entente coalition but also of denying the psychodiplomatic offensive to the Central Powers; and, if possible, they wanted to capture this offensive for themselves.

On January 3, in commenting on the diplomatic offensive of the Bolsheviks, the *Nation* in New York had suggested that these "wild men" would "put the old-fashioned diplomacy to shame" if they really brought about "the concrete restatement of war aims which Lord

Lansdowne desired, and Mr. Asquith approved." [1] Now that Lloyd George and Wilson had spoken publicly the *Nation's* sister journal, the *New Republic,* approved the restyling of Allied diplomacy in an issue whose cover prominently reported PROGRESS IN WAR AIMS. According to this Wilsonian weekly, the progress was in large measure due to "aid and comfort from Russia": the Allies had not started to clarify their war aims until after the Bolshevik Government had thrown "a flood light on the war aims of the belligerents." [2]

Whereas Wilson praised the Bolshevik diplomacy in his Fourteen Points address, Lloyd George waited until after the war to admit that "it would not be fair to suppress the part which the Bolshevik Government had played in this development." [3] In Paris, Albert Thomas, without for a single instant abandoning his hostility for the Bolsheviks, reluctantly confessed that it was the "honor of the Russian Revolution to have led the Western Powers into cleansing their peace propositions of all imperialism." Moreover, he reproachfully told the French Government that "if the repeated appeals of Kerensky and Tereshchenko had been heeded earlier the political situation in Russia might well be different." However, Thomas insisted that notwithstanding the erratic diplomacy of the Bolsheviks, now that Lloyd George and Wilson had spoken Clemenceau could no longer afford to remain silent. He urged the French Government to take the initiative to get the Allies to issue a joint declaration which would have the additional advantage of harmonizing the demands formulated by the British and American chief executives. [4]

Even though there were marked differences between the two addresses, they had certain basic features in common. Since the entire Allied coalition was confronted with one and the same diagram of diplomatic-military forces, it was perhaps not surprising that, though "drafted absolutely independently," the pronouncements of Lloyd George and Wilson should have coincided on territorial essentials. Both statesmen had felt the need to present opposing declarations to those launched by the Imperial Powers from Brest-Litovsk. [5] They agreed on Belgium, on Alsace-Lorraine, and apparently on the Italian

1. *Nation* (January 3, 1918), p. 4.
2. *New Republic* (January 12, 1918), pp. 295, 297
3. Lloyd George, *Memoirs of the Peace Conference,* 2, 497.
4. JO (January 11, 1918), pp. 38–39.
5. *Journal de Genève,* January 15, 1918.

claims. Furthermore, both statesmen came to terms with the new ideology, though obviously each in his own way: whereas Wilson embraced it enthusiastically, Lloyd George reluctantly acknowledged its existence. Jacques Bainville, therefore, warned them of the dangers of sacrificing so much "to the idols of the day." According to this right-wing historian, both leaders ought to treat the ideas "of democracy and of the League of Nations" with caution because on some future occasion such "ideas and theories might cease to be immaterial." Nevertheless, while criticizing both Wilson and Lloyd George for "playing with fire," Bainville had a great deal more praise for the latter than for the former. Bainville thought that since the British Premier did not "dream up a chimerical reconstruction of Europe," at the peace conference England could be counted on to follow a line similar to the one she had followed at the Congress of Berlin.[6]

The European Left also realized immediately that the Prime Minister's pronouncement was decidedly more traditional than the President's. By maintaining his rigid mistrust of the virtues of both popular control of foreign policy and open diplomacy, Lloyd George proved his continuing faith in the Old Diplomacy. Moreover, in addition to barring an ideological dialogue with the Bolsheviks he failed to make a clear-cut distinction between the governors of Germany and the German people at large.

However, Lloyd George's reluctance to participate in Germany's embryonic civil war was not based exclusively on doctrinal considerations. Unlike President Wilson, the British Prime Minister had drafted a program which was calculated to serve Allied diplomacy in the event of either an immediate negotiated settlement or a future total victory. In pursuit of an early negotiated peace, Lloyd George sought to convince the rulers of the Central Powers that England had abandoned the program of the knock-out blow. This assurance might strengthen the position of the German interlocutors of Lord Lansdowne and Lord Milner. On the likely assumption that a fight to the finish might be necessary, Lloyd George made verbal concessions to the Labourites and to Wilson; the support of both would be absolutely essential if the Central Powers had to be decisively defeated.

Once America had entered the world struggle, Wilson never seriously envisaged either the possibility or the desirability of a peace without

6. Jacques Bainville writing in *l'Action Française*, January 6, 7, 10, and 13, 1918.

total victory. Consequently, now in early 1918 the President's diplomatic and psychological warfare offensive was not going to be blunted by the exigency of compromising with Berlin. Instead, Wilson stepped forward resolutely to embrace the New Diplomacy, to bid the German people to revolt against their rulers, and to proclaim the Allied military effort a part of both a crusade for democracy and a war to end all wars. By now the President confidently trusted in America's tremendous and, for the Allies, crucial military and ideological reserves, and was fully prepared to shoulder the complex responsibilities of leadership in the drive for total victory over German autocracy and militarism. In addition to dedicating himself to the crusade gospel which the Allied and Russian forces of movement had been preaching since March 1917, he now inspired them to help bring about the liberalization of the diplomacy of the entire anti-German coalition. Furthermore, instead of bemoaning the Russian Revolution as a military collapse engineered with the help of German agents, Wilson considered this Revolution as an integral part of the general intensification of the ideological momentum of the Great War.

Profoundly dedicated to the proposition that ideas are weapons, Wilson was unwilling to allow the Germans to make psychological capital out of the Brest-Litovsk negotiations. He was no less determined to prevent Lenin from gaining a monopoly on blueprints for the postwar world, especially since many of Lenin's diplomatic formulations were taken from the arsenal of Western Liberal ideas. As he stepped into the madly raging battle of words, Wilson was able to tie his "placard paragraphs" to a reasonably comprehensive liberal-progressive ideological system of which the defunct New Freedom was the domestic policy dimension. Even though the domestic reform aspects of the President's program were extremely vague or almost nonexistent, his progressive audience in Europe shared the belief that this deficiency would soon be remedied. The President's international program rested on the same dedication to rational and moral progress which was at the basis of social-democratic plans for an equalitarian society in a peaceful world; according to many leftists the synthesis of liberal internationalism and Socialist reform would be consummated under Wilson's tutelage.

At the present juncture not only Wilson but also Lenin placed the major emphasis in their pronouncements on promises for a new world.

Both became daring generalissimos on the novel propaganda front and, as such, emerged as the "champion revolutionists of the age." [7] Because Wilson boldly accepted the challenge of the new *Zeitgeist* in the Fourteen Points address, Colonel House predicted that this address "would so smother the Lloyd George speech that it would be forgotten." [8] And it was forgotten.

If it be true, then, that Wilson set for himself, or the diplomacy of the Great War set for him, such a wide-ranging political task, it would appear that his primary audience was not in the United States but abroad, in Russia, Austria-Hungary, Germany, France, and Great Britain. It was in Europe, and not in any of the forty-eight states of the American Union, that the ravages of the war had been instrumental in weakening the wartime political truce, in dangerously reducing areas of consensus on political beliefs and institutions, and in sending millions of soldiers and workers in search of new ideological and leadership symbols.

Since Wilson considered the Russian people the most receptive, possibly even the most important, sector of his international audience, on January 9, 1918, Secretary of State Lansing sent the following cable to the American Embassy in Petrograd: "President delivered speech Congress yesterday stating war aims and attitude toward Russia. It was cabled to you at once. Have it conveyed unofficially to Trotsky. (Suggest you use Robins). Report results also of measures taken to circulate it." [9] Three days later the Embassy replied that in an interview with Robins, Lenin had "approved of message and thought it a potential agency promoting peace"; furthermore, Lenin had agreed to telegraph the "President's message textually to Trotsky at Brest." [10] Sadoul soon reported to Albert Thomas that the President's address was being hailed with gratitude throughout Russia, and that even in Bolshevik circles there was jubilation. The Maximalists were particularly sensitive to the respect with which the President had treated

---

7. Harold Lasswell, *Propaganda Technique in the World War* (New York, Knopf, 1927), p. 216.

8. House Diary, January 9, 1918.

9. National Archives, Document 763.72119/1072. Meanwhile Creel had sent Sisson a telegram advising him that "wonderful three thousand words are going to you today." Cited in Sisson, *One Hundred Red Days*, p. 206.

10. National Archives, Document 763.72119/1123. See also Kennan, *Russia Leaves the War*, pp. 258–60; U. S. Senate, Committee on the Judiciary, *Bolshevik Propaganda*, p. 566; Sisson, *One Hundred Red Days*, pp. 208–9.

Bolshevik peace principles. They were also struck by Wilson's "friendly tone," which compared so favorably with the incessant anti-Bolshevik denunciations coming from almost all other Allied quarters.[11] Nevertheless, because of both their past attacks on Wilsonian bourgeois-pacifism and their strong doctrinal convictions, the Bolsheviks combined their temporary friendliness toward Wilson with a deep-running distrust of his noble words. In the meantime, however, Lenin and Trotsky were only too anxious to use Wilson's Fourteen Points address in their dangerous diplomatic encounter with the Central Powers. According to Sisson, Lenin hailed the speech "as a great step ahead towards the peace of the world."

It is not surprising, therefore, that the Bolsheviks should have encouraged and helped Sisson in his plans to distribute the speech widely throughout Russia. First the speech had to be hurriedly translated into Russian at the Petrograd offices of the American Committee on Public Information. Then it was printed in the form of posters, handbills, and pamphlets. 100,000 posters were put up on the walls of Petrograd, while nearly 900,000 handbills were distributed in the capital. Moreover, the entire text was published in *Izvestiya* whose close to one million circulation reached far beyond Petrograd. According to Sisson, the editors of this official newspaper allowed him "to blackface the passages we desired—all clauses relating to Russia." All in all, "in its different handbill, poster, and pamphlet forms, the printed issues of the speech totaled 3,463,000 copies issued from Petrograd and Moscow presses, and this sum took no account of the millions of distribution through the *Izvestiya* and other newspapers, nor of handbills printed at Odessa, Tiflis, Kiev, Chita, Omsk, and Ekaterinburg." About one million of these "copies" were disseminated to German soldiers who were in the Eastern trenches or were prisoners inside Russia.[12]

11. Sadoul, *Notes sur la Révolution Bolchévique*, p. 194.

12. Sisson, *One Hundred Red Days*, pp. 206–11; *Complete Report of the Chairman of the Committee on Public Information* (Washington, 1920), pp. 217–18; Wheeler-Bennett, *The Forgotten Peace*, p. 147. Editorially *Izvestiya* proclaimed that "the conditions laid down by President Wilson represent a great victory in the great struggle for a democratic peace, and we may hope to find in the American people an actual ally in that struggle." Cited in Kennan, *Russia Leaves the War*, p. 262. In commenting on this editorial Kennan (ibid.) invites the reader to "note here the reference to the American people rather than to the American Government . . ." Though this reference was undoubtedly symptomatic of the Bolsheviks' efforts to circumvent established governments, it should also be noted that in the Fourteen Points address Wilson himself had extensive recourse to this

Recognizing that Wilson's passages pertaining to Russia were calculated to court a failing ally, the Central Powers immediately sought to expose the President's "hypocrisy." The *Norddeutsche Allgemeine Zeitung* insisted that Wilson was wooing Petrograd primarily because he had not abandoned the hope of fashioning a "new business connection" with the Russians.[13] Though unable completely to restrain its admiration for the new voice from Washington, even the Socialist *Vorwärts* wondered whether the "idealistic verve" of the address was not "merely a diplomatic maneuver" to draw the Russians again into "the bloody morass" of the war.[14] Similarly the *Kölnische Zeitung* upbraided the President for complicating the peaceful enterprise at Brest-Litovsk by trying simultaneously to fortify the weak and demoralize the strong.[15]

Naturally the Central Powers looked with greater favor on Lloyd George's hands-off policy toward Russia [16] than on Wilson's uncompromising pronouncement about Russia's borderlands. The Bolsheviks were equally quick to notice the difference between the Prime Minister's and the President's Russian policies. They feared that Great Britain might be seeking "to have German demands satiated in the East so her requirements be minimized in the West." [17] The Bolsheviks may have had little evidence other than the equivocations of the

---

same circumvention in passages addressed not only to the German but also to the Russian people. *Pravda,* the party organ, published the President's speech under the partisan headline "Wilson under the Mask of an Internationalist." On January 12, 1918, *Pravda's* disparaging editorial comments were cast in uncompromising Bolshevik language reminiscent of Lenin's prerevolutionary attacks on Wilsonian internationalism and pacifism. Cf. ibid., pp. 262–63.

13. *Norddeutsche Allgemeine Zeitung,* January 11, 1918.

14. *Vorwärts,* January 10, 1918. This January 10th editorial can also be found in GFM, Container 1499.

15. *Kölnische Zeitung,* January 11, 1918. For a summary review of German press reaction to Wilson's speech see cable from the American Embassy in the Hague to Lansing, dated January 11, 1918. National Archives, Document 763.-72119/1098. See also Joachim Seeberg, *Wilsons Botschaft der 14 Punkte vom 8. Januar 1918 im Urteil der grossen deutschen Tagespresse von Januar bis zum Oktober 1918,* Berlin, 1936.

16. For German press comments on Lloyd George's speech see *DR* (January 10, 1918), pp. 545–46.

17. *FR, Russia 1918, 1,* 425. As part of his policy of domestic as well as diplomatic conciliation, Lloyd George invited first MacDonald and then Lansbury to breakfast. According to Buckler, who saw MacDonald on January 22, the Prime Minister requested the ILP leader "to undertake a mission to sound out the German Socialists." Buckler to House, January 10 and 22, 1917, Buckler Papers.

Prime Minister's speech to support this apprehension. However, their doctrinal image of the inevitable hostility of the combined capitalist world for the Revolution helped to validate their fear of a general peace to be concluded among all the belligerents at their expense. Lenin and Trotsky would soon use this real or imaginary threat as an additional argument for a speedy separate peace with the Central Powers: to forestall a combined capitalist onslaught on the precarious citadel of world Socialism. On January 11 Sadoul reported Lenin and Trotsky to be equally convinced that preliminary negotiations between Germany and England had been initiated.[18] Then, on January 20, Lenin declared that "in concluding a separate peace we free ourselves *as much as is possible at the present moment* from both hostile imperialist groups, we take advantage of their enmity and warfare— which hamper concerted action on their part against us."[19] A week later, at the third All-Russian Congress of Soviets, Trotsky maintained that Germany's imperialist designs in the East were "silently approved in London."[20]

Even though Russia's Foreign Commissar denounced not only von

18. Sadoul, *Notes sur la Révolution Bolchévique*, p. 191.
19. Cited in Degras, p. 39.
20. Carr, *The Bolshevik Revolution*, 3, 23–25, n. 6; Louis Fischer, *The Soviets in World Affairs, 1917–1921* (2d ed. 2 vols. Princeton, Princeton University Press, 1951), *1*, 50; Suarez, *Briand: Sa vie—son oeuvre, 4*, 315–16. It would seem that Trotsky's fear that a negotiated peace either with the Germans or between the Central and Allied Powers might be to the disadvantage of the revolutionary regime was the "natural" concern of a statesman pursuing the defense of his country's national interest. The fact that this apprehension was expressed in the vernacular of the anticapitalist ideology should not detract from the objective power situation in which the inexperienced Bolshevik leaders were compelled to formulate foreign policy. This is not to deny that their ideology reinforced their suspicion of Allied motives beyond the realities of a diplomatic situation which were far from easy to assess accurately. Kennan's interpretation of Bolshevik foreign-policy pronouncements seems to emphasize unduly their dogmatic ideological foundations, which, in turn, he equates with unlimited and unprincipled expediency. He refers to Trotsky's "cynical view that the Allies were anxious to see the Germans succeed in imposing an onerous and punitive peace on Russia, since this would ease their own problem in arriving at a peace with Germany at Russia's expense." Kennan takes Trotsky's address to the Congress of Soviets as further evidence that "it never occurred to him, any more than to Lenin, to credit Wilson with any good faith in the expression of self-determination sentiments. . . . Thus whatever effect the Fourteen Points may have had on Trotsky they certainly did not decrease his cynicism about American motives or convince him that her purposes had anything in common with those of Soviet leadership." Kennan, *Russia Leaves the War*, pp. 261–62.

Kühlmann, Lloyd George, and Clemenceau but also Wilson, for embracing "the same aims," [21] throughout Europe the President was widely applauded for refusing to sacrifice Russia. The *Journal de Genève* noted that whereas Lloyd George seemed "disinterested" in Russian problems to the point of encouraging German territorial ambitions, Wilson categorically "prohibited" Germany from expanding eastward.[22] Likewise, on January 9, the British Labour movement welcomed Wilson's "demand that Russian territory must be evacuated." [23] Even Maklakoff, the deposed Russian Ambassador to France, contrasted American and British policy toward his country "in words of bitterness." [24]

Unlike the Prime Minister's TUC address, the Fourteen Points were calculated to serve as the basis for a frontal psychological-warfare assault on the Reich. Again with Bolshevik help, Sisson arranged for a German translation of Wilson's speech to be disseminated among the enemy's eastern armies. 500,000 handbills were fed across the northern and southern armistice lines, while 600,000 were distributed among German prisoners who might be returning to the Reich before long.[25]

Inside Germany, Wilson's message accentuated party divisions over the political and diplomatic conduct of the war. Ever since March 1917 both Scheidemann and Haase had incessantly warned the German parties of order of the dangers of not agreeing to a full democratization of Germany. Now their prediction that the Allies would "impose the democratization of Germany as a war formula" was coming true. Neither the tone nor the content of the Fourteen Points address was unexpected for either the leaders or the followers of the SPD and the USPD. While Scheidemann confronted the Right with a highly justified "we told you so," he simultaneously sought to embarrass both Lloyd George and Wilson by asking them to promise also self-determination to Ireland, Persia, and India. But while engaging in such tactical maneuvers, Scheidemann and Haase were wide awake to the

21. Bunyan and Fisher, *The Bolshevik Revolution*, p. 506.

22. *Journal de Genève*, January 11 and 13, 1918. The (London) *Nation* (January 12, 1918), p. 374, complained that "Mr. George's reference to Russia was singularly cold, and has made Russia think that her Western Allies meant to abandon her."

23. See statement published by British Labour Organizations on January 10, 1918, cited in *FR*, 1918, Supplement 1, *1*, 34.

24. *FR*, 1918, Supplement 1, *1*, 19.

25. *Complete Report of the Chairman of the Committee on Public Information*, pp. 216–19.

long-range ideological implications of Wilson's message. Consequently they insisted that in view of the new ideological framework which Lenin and Wilson had set for all peace debates, the German Government could not afford to allow the Supreme Command to dictate with an iron fist at Brest-Litovsk. In late January industrial strikes broke out in various parts of Germany in protest against the high-handed tactics of Ludendorff in the peace negotiations with the Russians.[26]

But even prior to these strikes the forces of order had violently accused the Socialists of promoting the internal disunity upon which Wilson seized with such great skill. The *Vaterlandspartei* condemned the entire forces of movement for doing the work of Germany's enemies by giving the impression that the Allies might eventually be able to deal with the Reichstag's "starvation peace majority and its chosen government."[27] This interference in the Central Powers' internal politics also worried Czernin, who on so many of the war aims was in harmony with the German Left as well as with Wilson. At Brest-Litovsk he "politely but definitely" declined to consider those points of Wilson's speech which counseled the Central Powers to reform their Governments.[28]

Whereas some Allied statesmen and publicists failed to recognize the revolutionary nature of Wilson's interference in Germany's domestic affairs, others were baffled by the subversive aspects of this New Diplomacy. Especially the right fringe of the Allied forces of order protested against any "arbitrary" distinction between the German people and their Government; they charged that all Germans were equally guilty of having plunged Europe into war. On the other hand, the more timid souls in the parties of movement were apprehensive lest the Wilson strategy work too well and contribute to uncontrolled revolution in Central Europe. It would seem, however, that by making common cause with Europe's nonrevolutionary progressives, more especially with those of the Central camp, Wilson was serving enemy

26. Arthur Rosenberg, *The Birth of the German Republic*, pp. 210–16; Mammach, *Der Einfluss der russischen Februarrevolution*, pp. 84 ff.; Walter Bartel, "Der Januarstreik 1918 in Berlin," in Albert Schreiner, ed., *Revolutionäre Ereignisse und Probleme*, pp. 141–83.

27. *Deutsche Tageszeitung*, January 10, 1918, cited in *DR* (January 16, 1918), p. 597.

28. Czernin, *Im Weltkriege*, p. 402. In mid-January 1918 various parts of Austria-Hungary were plagued by food riots, industrial strikes, and political protests. Bauer, *Die Österreichische Revolution*, pp. 63–66; and Jan Opočenský, *Umsturz in Mitteleuropa* (Dresden, Avalum, 1931), pp. 70 ff.

and Allied Governments alike by denying Lenin a monopoly on appeals to the "Toiling, Oppressed, and Exhausted Peoples."

Coupled with his determination to fight on to final victory, Wilson's decision to sponsor a revolution in Germany marks perhaps his most decisive departure from the Old Diplomacy. In the United States "The Friends of German Democracy" now stepped up their campaign against the twin evils of the Hohenzollern autocracy and the military imperialists.[29] Before long the reform of Germany's political system emerged as the central objective of the crusade to make the world safe for both democracy and peace. The hesitancy which temporarily restrained Wilson's appeals to the Eastern European nationalities never interfered with his unrestrained drive against the established order in the Reich.

With "revolution in Berlin" as the inevitable corollary to the crusade, the need for an analysis of the political implications of the hoped-for victory should have been recognized. But in responsible circles little effort was made either to try to visualize the type of revolution which was being encouraged in Central Europe, or to clarify the image of the postrevolutionary political and economic system likely to arise in Germany.

In Great Britain the War Cabinet drafted Lord Northcliffe into government service to map out a new psychological warfare campaign in the light of the recent changes in the diplomatic and ideological situation. It is not without significance that Britain's Conservative newspaper tsar summoned H. G. Wells, a disillusioned Radical who had become a fervent crusader, to assist him at Crewe House in an advisory capacity. In the spring of 1918 Wells suggested that since the Allies did not "want to kill Germany" the only other alternative was to change her.

> If we do not want to wipe Germany off the face of the earth, then we want Germany to become the prospective and trustworthy friend of her fellow nations. And if words have any meaning at all, that is saying that we are fighting to bring about a Revolution in Germany. . . . America, with him [i.e. Wilson] as her spokesman, is under no delusion; she is fighting consciously for a German Revolution as the essential War Aim.[30]

29. *Complete Report of the Chairman of the Committee on Public Information*, pp. 89–90; and Bruntz, *Allied Propaganda*, pp. 35–36.
30. Wells, *In the Fourth Year*, pp. 70–71.

But soon after declaring that "the changing of Germany" had become "the primary war aim for the Allies," Wells cautioned that the process by which Germany was to be changed was "a complex question." "The word *Revolution* is, perhaps, to be deprecated. We do not, for instance, desire a Bolshevik breakdown in Germany, which would make her economically useless to mankind. We look, therefore, not so much to the German peasant and labourer as to the ordinary, fairly well-educated mediocre German for cooperation in the reinstatement of civilization." [31] In brief, would the revolution in Germany be controlled or uncontrolled, would it be a revolution from above or a revolution from below? It was with the course of the Russian Revolution before his eyes that Wells contemplated the overthrow of the Hohenzollerns and the Habsburgs. As he scanned Germany's political horizon, Wells saw quite clearly that the SPD was the only party equipped to lead an extensive and lasting revolt. In order to prevent this SPD-led revolt from leading to the institution of Soviets in Germany, Wells proposed that the Allies enter into an alliance with his kind of Liberals in the Central camp.[32]

In any case, President Wilson, as well as Labour and Wells, reinforced the traditionalist contention that Germany alone was responsible for the outbreak of the war. However, they amended this monolithic interpretation which placed all the blame on German militarism by locating the roots of Germany's imperialist ambitions in her anachronistic political institutions. With this amendment they prepared the ground for the equally oversimplified proposition that whereas democratic states are inherently peaceful, despotic governments of necessity generate tensions leading to war. By incorporating open diplomacy into the Allied peace plank, President Wilson gave further support to this new thesis. He argued that parliamentary control of foreign policy, supplemented by the ever-watchful eye of public opinion, was an essential safeguard against the kind of diplomatic cunning which so often in the past had produced war. This mechanistic view of foreign-policy formulation lacked both an historical and a political dimension; it was insensitive to the need for recurring and basic adjustments in the balance of power. The problems facing the coming peace conference were bound to be so overwhelming and complex that no

31. Cited in Sir Campbell Stuart, *Secrets of Crewe House* (London, Hodder and Stoughton, 1920), p. 80.
32. Bruntz, *Allied Propaganda*, p. 28.

matter how perfect and extensive this democratic control, many problems defied just and lasting solutions. Nevertheless, in the midst of this revolutionary crisis, Allied progressives trusted that parliamentary majorities were endowed with adequate insight, rationality, and unanimity to conclude a perpetual and democratic peace.

In the view of many Traditionalists, much of what Wilson and the UDC—and the Socialists—advocated seemed steeped in Bolshevik and Socialist theory. Locked in diplomatic battle with the Russian delegates at Brest-Litovsk, on January 24 Count Czernin indignantly exclaimed that never, so far as he knew, had peace negotiations been conducted with open windows.[33] Czernin's initial contact with open diplomacy had been through the Joffe and Trotsky manifestoes which sought to circumvent the traditional channels of diplomacy. Now the Entente seemed to engage in the same kind of revolutionary international politics. Czernin's apprehensions foreshadowed the thesis advanced in le Temps shortly after the Armistice in November 1918: that in deciding on secret negotiations Europe's statesmen would act as disciples of Talleyrand; however, should they decide in favor of public negotiations they would be acting under Trotsky's inspiration.[34]

But the negotiations at Brest-Litovsk had done even more to acquaint Czernin with the most extreme formulation of self-determination which in the course of 1918 also was echoed in gradually bolder versions by Paris, London, and Washington. In addition to having been very instrumental in giving the self-determination issue such great prominence, Lenin and Trotsky seemed to be forcing the Allied governments into giving occasional thought to the type of successor governments which were likely to arise from the ruins of the Dual Monarchy.

In Eastern Europe and the Balkans, for which Lenin had created his second geographic category, the Socialist movement was less structured and commanding than in Germany, France, or Great Britain. The predominantly agricultural economies within which scattered pockets of industry had developed presented an unlikely breeding ground for proletarian movements. Furthermore, the fight for national liberation itself tended to dilute even this marginal class-consciousness by diverting the proletariat's attention from class issues. Inside the Dual Monarchy self-determination was the principal political issue around which the battle for succession raged.

33. Czernin, Im Weltkriege, p. 396.
34. Le Temps, November 21, 1918.

All along, the bourgeois elements continued to hold commanding positions of power and control in the nationalities movement, especially because many Eastern European Socialists were half-hearted in their commitment to national regeneration. These Socialists kept warning that the class struggle was in danger of being completely subordinated to the nationalist struggle; accordingly they accused the bourgeoisie of exploiting the emotional appeal of the patriotic slogans in order to check the forces of progress.[35] As a result, the Socialists were ill-equipped to challenge the Liberal patronage of self-determination. Moreover, the extremely influential *New Europe*, Free Serbia, and Regenerated Poland committees in the Allied and Associated capitals were representative of the bourgeois nationalities forces. As these committees drafted the blueprints for the postrevolutionary stage, they were concerned primarily with questions of plebiscites, elections, and civil liberties. The émigrés did not contemplate a balanced national-political-economic-social revolution; they were essentially 19th-century nationalists whose "Liberalism was much too weak and too much undermined by nationalism." [36]

After the Bolsheviks had pressed their bid for the leadership of the nationalities at Brest-Litovsk, the bourgeois leaders began to exploit the specter of a Socialist nationalities revolt in order to win Allied statesmen for their cause. Occasionally they would not hesitate to give unduly exaggerated reports about the strength of the leftist forces in their home countries. In a similar vein, Masaryk never declined to capitalize on the faithful performance of the Czech Legion in Russia. Accordingly, A. J. P. Taylor suggests that the "threatening collapse of Central Europe finally brought success to the émigré leaders; they convinced the Allies that they alone had the 'authority' to stave off Bolshevism." [37]

35. In the Austrian Social Democratic movement the federalist thesis was advocated most persistently by Karl Renner; Otto Bauer became the leading advocate of the unrestrained self-determination thesis. See Rudolf Schlesinger, *Federalism in Central and Eastern Europe*, pp. 232–47; and Bauer, *Die Österreichische Revolution*, pp. 54 ff.

36. Hans Kohn, *Pan-Slavism* (Notre Dame, 1953), p. 210. See also Hugh Seton-Watson, *Eastern Europe between the Wars, 1918–1941* (Cambridge, 1946), esp. p. 141.

37. A. J. P. Taylor, *The Habsburg Monarchy, 1809–1918* (London, Hamilton, 1948), p. 246. Bauer was more modest than Taylor when he claimed that "the victory of the Czechs, the Poles, and the Yugoslavs was a bourgeois revolution which broke the power of the Habsburgs, the German-Austrian bureaucracy, and the Magyar gentry; in the latter's place the Czech, the Polish, the Yugoslav

Even though Masaryk and Beneš had a closer affinity with Woodrow Wilson's New Freedom than with Clemenceau's static republicanism, in early 1918 they turned to Paris for help. At this time not only Lloyd George but also Wilson seemed to be hedging on the self-determination issue, primarily as part of what the nationalities leaders considered an inauspicious attempt to wean the Dual Monarchy away from Germany.[38] Only Clemenceau and Pichon in France and Northcliffe and Wickham Steed across the Channel were committed to a policy of unconditional surrender which included the dissolution of Austria-Hungary. Thus, though otherwise violently opposed to the New Diplomacy, Allied Traditionalists now took the initiative on the national question.

As a student of the March Revolution, Trotsky suggested that one of the Provisional Government's chief functions had been "to short circuit the revolutionary energy of the masses into patriotic wires." [39] A similar process now began in connection with Allied diplomacy. Although the Bolsheviks themselves had made self-determination a focal issue, they were unable to capitalize on it in Lenin's second geographic area. In the meantime, however, the Traditionalists in Paris, London, and Washington who had gradually rediscovered the potency of the nationalist idea, prepared to extend their full backing to the bourgeois-nationalities movements. By the end of 1918 *le Temps* recognized that since communism could not be defeated with "barbed wire" alone it was imperative to oppose it with a rival ideal. Accordingly, with Bolshevism determined to disrupt nations, *le Temps* looked to an inflamed patriotism as the most effective challenge to Socialist internationalism. *Le Temps* proclaimed that Europe's statesmen were about to reach the following crossroads: "One [was] the way of the nationalities. The other the way of classes. . . . Peace of nations or Bolshevism, between these two perspectives a choice [must] be made." [40]

From January 1918 onward, under constant traditionalist prodding, self-determination gradually became the one *new* Allied war aim on which almost the entire political spectrum was in agreement. As Wil-

---

bourgeoisie organized the new national states: and the triumphant national spirit also captured the proletariat." Bauer, *Die Österreichische Revolution,* p. 114.

38. Beneš, *Souvenirs de guerre, 1,* 549–50.

39. Leon Trotsky, *The History of the Russian Revolution, 1,* 288.

40. *Le Temps,* December 26, 1918, and January 9, 1919.

son's crusade for democracy fused with the nationalist crusade in Eastern Europe, this new synthesis was grafted onto the time-tested spirit of romantic nationalism. In the Allied and Associated nations the sponsors of the struggling peoples in Eastern Europe were able to build on a long historical tradition in nationalist aspirations. Moreover, the bourgeois nationalist leaders in Lenin's second geographic area came to rely heavily on this non-Socialist support.

Soon especially the French Government sponsored the European nationalist movements in a pronounced conservative context. However, whereas the Quai d'Orsay eventually became a reliable champion of self-determination, it was at all times highly skeptical of the other aspects of Wilson's war-aims offensive. Certain French officials even felt that Lloyd George had paid too much deference "to the extreme Labour party and Mr. Henderson." [41]

On January 11, 1918, in the *Chambre* the SFIO once again called upon the Government to answer the Soviet peace proposals and to issue a joint war-aims pronouncement with the Allies. However, Clemenceau scornfully refused to participate in the debate. Instead, he left it to his Foreign Minister to ward off this new Socialist interpellation. Stephen Pichon declared that France would continue "to execute her contracts" because she had agreements "which she could not conceive of breaking." For "nothing in the world" would France break her agreements with Italy, Serbia, Rumania, and Belgium." Pichon was utterly unyielding. He spoke "in precise language which conveys the outlines of living reality, and does not lose itself even in the most tempting clouds." [42]

This refusal to liberalize French diplomacy in the face of the Lloyd George and Wilson speeches infuriated the entire Left. Albert Thomas and Pierre Renaudel now spoke for the Social Patriots, while Mayéras intervened in the parliamentary debate in the name of the *minoritaires.*

Renaudel declared that he had listened to Pichon's speech with "considerable sadness." He insisted that Lloyd George had "no distrust" of the Labour party and that President Wilson had courageously answered the Russian summons. Both statesmen were in agreement with the Left and, according to Renaudel, had brought about the war-aims

41. Lennox, *The Diary of Lord Bertie, 2,* 241–42. For a summary of the French press commentary on Wilson's speech see Ambassador Sharp to Secretary Lansing, January 10, 1918, National Archives, Document 763.72169/1099.

42. JO (January 11, 1918), p. 43; and *le Temps,* January 13, 1918.

revision for which the SFIO had been clamoring for so many months. Why was Clemenceau reluctant to come out in support of Wilson's proposals? In Renaudel's view, the French Premier's "entire policy" continued to be "in contradiction with the noble ideas of President Wilson." [43]

As expected, the *minoritaires* were even more incensed than their Majoritarian colleagues. At first their demands included the publication of the secret treaties, the recognition of the Soviet regime, and the readiness to participate in the Brest-Litovsk negotiations. However, Mayéras, Pressemane, and Mistral abandoned their *ordre du jour* in favor of the one sponsored by Bracke, Renaudel, Cachin, Thomas, Varenne, and Lafont. According to this text, the *Chambre* was asked to proclaim "its general adhesion to the words of Mr. Lloyd George . . . and Mr. Wilson." Furthermore, the SFIO wanted the French Government "to insist on the convocation of an inter-Allied diplomatic conference" for the purpose of translating Wilson's Fourteen Points "into a final, joint declaration of war aims." [44]

Even though the uncompromising confidence motion introduced by the opposing forces of order was passed by a substantial majority, this time the forces of movement counted 145 deputies in their own ranks.[45] Nevertheless, unlike Lloyd George, Clemenceau stubbornly continued to refuse to meet the SFIO halfway. Primarily because France was very weak he did not actually voice any criticism of the Fourteen Points address; however, Clemenceau studiously avoided making a pronouncement in support of Wilson's crusade. On the contrary, in early March he reiterated that his domestic and foreign policy were identical: in both spheres "I prosecute the war. . . . At all times I prosecute the war." [46]

As a result of the stubborness of the Right, the entire French Left was galvanized into the President's most ardent supporter in the Entente, and within the SFIO the *minoritaires* soon became the new majority.

Meanwhile, however, self-determination became the only principle of the New Diplomacy to be advocated by the Clemenceau Cabinet. Before long the promotion of the nationalities cause became tied to the

43. JO (January 11, 1918), pp. 44–48.
44. Ibid., pp. 48–49; and *l'Humanité,* January 12, 1918.
45. Loc. cit.
46. Général Mordacq, *Le Ministère Clemenceau: Journal d'un témoin* (4 vols. Paris, Plon, 1930–31), *I,* 123; and JO (March 8, 1918), p. 790.

réligion de la patrie which had never ceased to be the rallying creed of all French Conservatives. Paul-Boncour deplored that by taking self-determination out of its Wilsonian context French leaders "were striving to give this liberation a reactionary orientation." [47] Marcel Sembat cautioned against taking the nationalities principle as an exclusive guide, since without some higher allegiance it might lead to the "états *dés*unis d'Europe." [48] But the *Ministère* Clemenceau had no inclination to embrace the League of Nations or to favor open diplomacy. Instead, *le Temps* accused the Socialists of misusing Wilson's idealism for their own class purposes.[49] With the SFIO under constant fire from the Right, even the Social Patriotic Pierre Renaudel summoned all French progressives to support Wilson against France's own "chauvinists." [50]

In the context of the Wilson-Lenin dialectic, the war-aims battle within the SFIO during the remainder of the war is particularly instructive. Immediately after the last Assembly vote, the *minoritaires* made swift gains at the cost of the Social Patriots. However, Longuet, Bourderon, Merrheim, Mayéras, Mistral, and Pressemane fought their way to control of the entire party on a Wilsonian, not on a Leninist, platform. Before long Loriot and a few Maximalist supporters were hopelessly isolated on the extreme left. They refused to join their former colleagues of the Comité pour la Reprise des Relations Internationales because, in Loriot's view, these colleagues obstinately looked westward in the expectation of "finding Stuttgart in Washington, and Liebknecht in the White House." [51]

On July 28–29, 1918, at a meeting of the National Council of the SFIO, the *minoritaires* were in the majority for the first time. Their Wilsonian motion was supported by 1544 votes against only 1172 votes for the Renaudel-Thomas faction.[52] However, because Clemenceau continued to be unyielding on war aims, both major factions—the new and the old majority—were equally unrestrained in their devotion to

47. *L'Humanité*, August 10, 1918.
48. Ibid., November 28, 1918.
49. *Le Temps*, August 31, 1918.
50. *L'Humanité*, October 15, 1918.
51. Cited in Guilbeaux, *Le Mouvement socialiste et syndicaliste français pendant la guerre*, pp. 40–41.
52. *L'Humanité*, July 29 and 30, 1918. Longuet himself claimed that the resolution which he had drafted together with Mistral and Cachin "had the backing of the great majority of the party." *Le Populaire*, July 31, 1918. Cf. Guilbeaux, *Le Mouvement socialiste et syndicaliste français pendant la guerre*, pp. 49–51.

Wilson. By hailing Wilson instead of Lenin, both Longuet and Renaudel were able to dissent without being disloyal to the crusade for democracy. At the meeting of the National Congress on October 6–8, 1918, the old minority formally became the new majority. Once again, over the objection of the small Loriot faction, the SFIO sent an enthusiastic message to Wilson.[53]

Marcel Cachin and Jean Longuet, who now displaced Renaudel and Compère-Morel as chief editors of *l'Humanité*, found comfort in the fact that Wilson's "ideals were frightening all the Conservatives." Cachin proclaimed that it was to the President's "lasting glory" to have recognized the dawning era of democratic and popular rule. Hence, before completing his own transformation from *majoritaire* to Maximalist, Cachin became an ardent Wilsonian who predicted that "henceforth Wilson would have all democrats and Socialists on his side." [54]

But why not Lenin? Renaudel soon decided that the Bolshevik Revolution was unworthy of serving as a model for France. The mounting violence of the Revolution, combined with the Bolsheviks' defection from the Entente, led Renaudel to proclaim that his Socialist convictions had rejoined those "du Président bourgeois qu'est Wilson." [55] Likewise, Albert Thomas wrote an article in *l'Humanité* under the then novel title "Democracy or Bolshevism." In this article Thomas declared that it was "Either Wilson, or Lenin. Either democracy based on the French Revolution, fortified by the struggles of an entire century, developed by the great American Republic, or the primitive, incoherent, brutal forms of Russian fanaticism. A choice must be made." [56] Shocked by the excesses of the unfolding Russian Bolshevik Revolution, most French Social Patriots, as well as Independents, pre-

---

53. Ferrat, *Histoire du parti communiste français*, pp. 63–64; and Guilbeaux, *Le Mouvement socialiste et syndicaliste français pendant la guerre*, p. 51. As early as March 23, 1918, Tracy Lay, the American Consul in Paris, informed Washington that the mounting unrest within the French Left was due to the fact that the French Government had not subscribed publicly to the Wilson program; he noted, furthermore, that whereas in England the Lansdowne movement could "check and restrain the radicalism of the Socialist faction," in France there was no comparable movement "capable of standing as a buffer between the present regime and Socialism." *FR*, 1918, Supplement 1, *1*, 210–13.

54. *L'Humanité*, August 22, 1918.

55. Ibid., October 14, 1918.

56. Ibid., November 9, 1918. See B. W. Schaper, *Albert Thomas: Dertig Jaar Sociaal Reformisme* (Leiden, Universitaire Pers Leiden, 1953), pp. 173–78.

pared to abandon temporarily the equalitarian gospel and began to
look to parliamentary democracy for guidance.

But was the choice really between Wilson and Lenin, between
"democracy and bolshevism"? Léon Blum, then young in years as well
as in experience, burst forward with a thundering NO, insisting that
these were not the only alternatives: "Je ne choisie ni Wilson, ni Lénine.
Je choisie Jaurès." [57] It was rather tragic that the "candidacy" of Jean
Jaurès was posed as kind of an afterthought, and that none of the
elder Socialist statesmen had come forth in defense of Jaurès' "democratic revolutionary Socialism." Blum's article sounded like a desperate
attempt to recall the existence of the Second International, which was
in the process of being overshadowed on the Right by the League of
Nations and on the Left by the Third International.

But meanwhile *l'Humanité* published a special appeal "To the
French Nation" which was signed by the CGT, the Ligue des Droits
de l'Homme, the Coalition Républicaine, and the SFIO, urging all
Frenchmen "not to listen to the chauvinist excitations" of the French
press which currently was engaged in a propaganda campaign designed "to distort Mr. Wilson's own intentions." [58] All the parties and
factions of movement with the exception of the Maximalists had come
out in favor of Wilson.

In England, notwithstanding the Prime Minister's January 5th war-
aims concessions, Labour also hastened to abandon Lloyd George in
favor of Wilson. On January 9, 1918, in the afternoon following the
President's address, a joint meeting was held by the Parliamentary
Committee of the TUC, the Executive of the Labour party, and the
Cooperative Parliamentary Representation Committee. Over the signatures of C. W. Bowerman, Arthur Henderson, and H. J. May, the British Left issued a statement commending "the moral quality and
breadth of vision" of Wilson's pronouncement. In Labour's judgment,
by speaking "in favour of open diplomacy and [in] support of revolutionary Russia," the President had met the supreme test of statesmanship. After endorsing the moral crusade, the freedom of the seas, and
the protection of Russia's western borderlands, the Labour statement

57. *L'Humanité*, November 15, 1918. For extensive excerpts from pro-Wilson
editorials in the major French Socialist dailies see Van Der Slice, *International
Labor, Diplomacy, and Peace*, pp. 234–47.

58. *L'Humanité*, October 27, 1918. Cf. *le Temps*, October 28, 1918.

concluded that Wilson's "programme [was] in essential respects so similar" to the Labour Memorandum on War Aims "that we need not discuss any point of difference in detail." [59] It is perhaps not surprising that in March 1918 Beatrice Webb should have made the exaggerated claim that "the British Labour party was Wilson's one supporter in Europe." [60]

At the inter-Allied Labour and Socialist Conference held in London from February 20 to 24, 1918, the expanding bonds between European non-Bolshevik Socialism and Wilsonian Liberalism were no less evident. A new inter-Allied Labour and Socialist Memorandum on War Aims which the delegates now adopted was a Wilsonianized version of Labour's December 28th Memorandum.[61] The most striking evidence of the Wilsonian imprint on Allied Socialist war aims was the recognition in this February Memorandum that the League of Nations had given "an entirely new aspect" to all territorial problems. Even though Gompers refused to concert with Socialist Internationalists and Lenin chastized this London Conference for its "renegade" character, it was obvious that through his Fourteen Points Wilson had won a powerful representation in Socialist circles. Since a vote for the February Memorandum was a vote for Wilson, the President was assured of the support not only of right-wing Socialists like Clynes, Renaudel, and Vandervelde but also of fervent Two and Two-and-a-half Internationalists like Henderson, MacDonald, Thorne, Longuet, Bourderon, Merrheim, and Huysmans. Before disbanding, this Conference decided to send a delegation to America "to confer with President Wilson and Gompers." Jouhaux, Cachin, and Huysmans were to be the most prominent members of this still-born mission.[62] Nevertheless, even

59. In cabling the complete text of this Labour statement to Secretary of State Lansing, the U. S. Consul General in London commented that "this unreserved approval of the British Labor Organizations should be noted as a matter of great political importance." Cited in FR, 1918, Supplement 1, 1, 32–34.

60. Cole, p. 115.

61. Inter-Allied Labour and Socialist Conference, Memorandum on War Aims, Agreed upon in London February 20th to 24th, 1918, London, n.d. This pamphlet gives extensive details on the composition of all the delegations as well as on the membership of the various working committees. In the United States the text of the entire Memorandum was published in a special issue of the New Republic, March 23, 1918; and in FR, 1918, Supplement 1, 1, 155–67.

62. L'Humanité, February 24 and March 6, 1918; and FR, 1918, Supplement 1, 1, 151–53. As of late March 1918 the Wilson Administration assured the Allied Governments that it would not welcome the visit of Socialist delegations from abroad. Baker, Woodrow Wilson: Life and Letters, 8, 60, n. 2; and FR, 1918,

without the personal visit of European Socialists, Wilson knew enough about their ideas and actions to conclude that "the labor people in touch with world movement" were the only internationally minded people.[63]

Regardless of whether Wilson consciously sought "to establish himself as leader of labour and radicalism everywhere," as the Washington correspondent of the London *Times* alleged,[64] the net political effect of hi͵ diplomacy was to draw away the rapidly expanding and articulating parties of movement from the Socialist International. That in this fourth year of total war public opinion was particularly susceptible to a program projecting the bases for a lasting peace is not surprising. In Europe, excepting in Russia, even though the Socialist war aims were not more radical than Wilson's diplomatic proposals, the Left could not impose its war-aims program because the parties of order would not accept proposals which they knew to be an integral part of a more far-reaching reform program.

Furthermore, the British and the French parties of movement, more particularly the Labour party and the SFIO, harbored no illusions about the political strength which they might be able to muster in a showdown with the war cabinets. Partly because the popular passions which usually feed revolutionary agitation had been spent in the war, and possibly because the bloodshed of the military engagements acted as a repellent from further violence at the barricades of the Socialist revolution, the British and French Left were destined to proceed along evolutionary lines. Certainly the leadership of both the LP and the SFIO, as well as of the trade unions,[65] was dedicated to exercising

---

Supplement 1, *1*, 171–72. By this time Samuel Gompers was actively exercising his influence in Washington and in the Allied capitals to strengthen the conservative elements in the Allied Socialist and Labour parties. See Gompers, *Seventy Years of Life and Labor* (2 vols. New York, Dutton, 1925), *2*, 403 ff.; *FR*, 1918, Supplement 1, *1*, 189, 198, 250–51, 259, 299, 330–31; Angell, *The British Revolution and the American Democracy*, pp. 21 ff.

63. Cited in Baker, *6*, 241. As late as October 5, 1918, the *New Republic*, p. 271, noted that "the only important body of opinion which hitherto has appraised the League of Nations as the dominant formative principle of the peace settlement has been that represented by the British Labour Party and the Inter-Allied Socialist Conference. The character of the support which this particular emphasis upon the League obtained is a fair indication of the revolutionary changes which its acceptance will force upon the world." The editors of this journal were decidedly too optimistic about the future of the Wilsonian program.

64. Cited in *The History of the Times*, *4*, Pt. I, pp. 440–41.

65. According to the leader of the French CGT, the President's speech "coincided

all its influence in pursuit of a nonrevolutionary advance against the parties of order. But in their search for allies, Henderson and Mac-Donald, as also Thomas and Longuet, were led to turn beyond the geographic borders of England and France respectively. Indeed, as the era of perpetual international civil war seemed to dawn, Wilson commended himself as a natural partner. His language, unlike Lenin's, had much in common with Keir Hardie's and Jean Jaurès'. Moreover, whereas Lenin's extremism alienated most if not all non-Socialist members of the forces of movement, the engaging reasonableness of Wilson's platform actually was bound to lead to a further expansion of the progressive columns. Wilson could win the allegiance of Norman Angell, G. Lowes Dickinson, Gilbert Murray, E. D. Morel, Léon Bourgeois, and Romain Rolland.

Hence, Beatrice Webb soon realized that the war aims on which Wilson and Labour were in broad agreement became " 'the new thing' around which all who are discontent with the old order foregather." [66] Likewise in France the Wilsonian system corresponded so well with the ideology of all the parties of movement that these parties and factions hailed the President as their leader.[67]

Meanwhile, in Russia, Lenin rightly claimed that never before had "Bolshevism been looked upon as a world force." [68] In Central and Eastern Europe, where military defeat paved the way for the domestic victory of the nonrevolutionary forces of movement, food shortages and anarchy fed the Bolshevik cause. Particularly in Germany these disorganizing conditions nursed the growth of the Spartacist party, and emboldened the even more rapidly growing USPD. Whereas in England and France the war cabinets reaped the political fruits of military victory, in Germany and the Dual Monarchy the precariously enthroned democratic successor governments embarked on a policy of political stabilization without this powerful asset. On the contrary, in Central Europe the humiliation of military defeat merely accentuated restlessness, hunger, and dissatisfaction among the laboring and war-weary classes, and among the new nationalities.

In this tense transitional period from October 1918 through June

---

so well with our strongest sentiments that all our sympathy went to him as the statesman whose clear and courageous thoughts broke with all the errors of traditional diplomacy." Léon Jouhaux, Le Syndicalisme et la C.G.T. (Paris, Sirène, 1920), p. 199.

66. Cole, p. 105.
67. See Goguel, La Politique des partis sous la IIIe République, pp. 165, 174.
68. Lenin, Works, 23, 245.

1919 Wilson and the Wilsonian ideology became important instruments of control. Even though many Germans, particularly right-wing Germans, expediently rallied to Wilson's banner primarily because the President was their only ally in the impending peace struggle with the fiercely hostile Allied statesmen and their political-military supporters, many other Germans trusted in him for more constructive reasons. In Berlin the mantle of power had fallen on the Social Patriots who instead of steering a Leninist or national-communist course sought to channel Germany into a policy of cooperation with the Allies. Such a cooperative policy not only would lead to Germany's early admission to the projected League of Nations but would also help Social Democracy in its battle for domestic power and reform. When the Spartacists proceeded to agitate against the predatory ambitions of French, British, and Italian diplomacy, Scheidemann used Wilson's wartime pronouncements to prove that the Spartacist allegations were exaggerated. Thus in Germany, also, Wilson performed the all-important function of serving as a powerful beacon of hope to many Independents as well as to the SPD. Bernstein, Haase, and Kautsky relied on Wilson quite as much as their Allied counterparts.

With his Radical-Socialist peace program the President first delayed and then dampened the politically explosive disillusionment of both the enemy and the Allied Left with the peace of victory which was being fashioned in Paris between January and June 1919.

During the Peace Conference three great influences were at work "which may briefly be described as the Reaction, the Reconstruction, and the Revolution." [69] Clemenceau and Sonnino with determination practiced the Old Diplomacy in pursuit both of national aggrandizement and of the consolidation of the French and Italian Right vis-à-vis the agitated parties of movement. If in Paris, while Central Europe was on the brink of anarchy, the ideology and program of the Old Diplomacy had set the *public* framework for the peace negotiations, then under Lenin's influence the westward-moving revolution might have gained innumerable adherents. Even the growing specter of revolution in Germany, Austria, and Hungary could not move the French and Italian leaders to diplomatic moderation. On the other hand, particularly after Bela Kun's victory in Budapest, Lloyd George actively sided with the forces of Reconstruction.

These forces of Reconstruction were inspired and led by Woodrow

69. Walter Lippmann, *The Political Scene: An Essay on the Victory of 1918* (New York, Holt, 1919), p. x.

Wilson. The President battled for a peace without annexations and indemnities on the basis of the self-determination of peoples, guaranteed by the League of Nations. Just as the Right in France and England opposed his visionary program partly because this program also was the platform of the Left opposition, likewise in the United States Theodore Roosevelt and Cabot Lodge became Wilson's passionate opponents. However, although he was disavowed by the forces of order on both sides of the Atlantic, he had an extensive constituency among the forces of movement in both Allied and enemy nations. These progressive elements were attracted by Wilson's explicit advocacy of the New Diplomacy as symbolized in his League project, and by their self-generated confidence that Wilson's diplomatic program would also serve the cause of basic economic and social reform.

Some dissidents gave their support to the President not so much because they had faith in his positive program as because they hoped that his program might help prevent civil strife. In an open letter Romain Rolland implored the President to "speak, speak to everybody! The world is thirsting for a voice which transcends both national and class borders. And that the future may herald you under the name of conciliator." [70] Rolland wrote this letter because in his view Wilson was the "last remaining dyke," and should this dyke give way, then Europe "was in danger of continuing this bloody game." In private the author of *Au-dessus de la mêlée* not only admitted that he addressed Wilson without deep faith, but also charged that through his "clever lie Wilson was making away with the European Revolution in favor of the liberal bourgeoisie." [71] Meanwhile, however, the attraction of Wilson's vision for the coming peace and its contribution to civil reconciliation—strategically supported by American financial power and economic surplus [72]—kept Rolland as well as many Socialists and Radicals from instantly joining the forces of Revolution.

Under Lenin's resolute guidance these forces of Revolution belligerently proclaimed that the existing capitalist governments were

70. For the complete text of this letter, dated November 9, 1918, see Rolland, *Journal*, pp. 1645–46.

71. Ibid., pp. 1654–61; Rolland, *Les Précurseurs* (Paris, 1920), pp. 216–18; *l'Humanité*, December 14, 1918.

72. A well-documented discussion of the role of American economic resources in the stabilization of Europe during the seven-months' armistice can be found in Herbert Hoover, *The Ordeal of Woodrow Wilson* (New York, McGraw-Hill, 1958), esp. pp. 87 ff.

incapable of concluding a democratic peace. According to the Maximalists a nonpredatory peace would be possible and secure only after the proletarian revolution had been victorious in the major capitalist countries. This revolution was expected to gain much from the war's legacy of misery and unrest, and the nascent Communist parties stood ready to intensify and profit from the prevailing political instability as a first step in the total transformation of European society, both national and international. Lenin's immediate aim was destructive: class war in preparation for the transitional dictatorship of the proletariat. However, his ultimate objective of the classless society in a warless world had the same hopeful and utopian quality as Wilson's search for a peaceful community of sovereign democratic nations of unequal power.

The war had thrown Europe into a profound political, economic, and intellectual crisis, and until 1917 this exhausted Europe faced the future without any hopeful visions. "But in one deed, the only truly great statesman-like deed, the first signal of world improvement rang out: Wilson announced the League of Nations; he foresaw that without it the peoples could no longer carry on their existence. The second attempt at world improvement . . . has been undertaken in Russia, and it is yet too soon to pronounce upon it. . . . There can be no question that *sub specie aeternitatis* . . . Wilson and Lenin will appear merely as men with different methods. It is certain that mankind must make up its mind either for Wilson or for Lenin." [73] Even though Clemenceau eventually triumphed over both Wilson and Lenin at the Paris Peace Conference, Clemenceau and his supporters at best scored a short-lived and pyrrhic victory.

73. The German-born Swiss essayist and playwright Hermann Kesser, writing in the *Neue Züricher Zeitung*, October 27, 1918, cited in the *Cambridge Magazine* (November 16, 1918), p. 143.

BIBLIOGRAPHY

THIS BIBLIOGRAPHY includes only the most important primary and secondary sources consulted in the preparation of this study. Documents and papers, primarily of interest to the specialists, who are already familiar with them, are listed without comment. However, since nonspecialist scholars and readers might want to explore select secondary sources without or before consulting primary materials, critical comments about the scope and/or bias of nondocumentary materials may well prove useful.

Elie Halévy's three brief but brilliant Oxford lectures, *The World Crisis of 1914–1918* (London, 1930), continue to be an instructive starting point for the study of the relations of class, ideology, politics, and diplomacy both before and during World War I. Easily the most comprehensive and the best one-volume scholarly introduction to the politics, strategy, and diplomacy of the war is still Pierre Renouvin, *La Crise européenne et la première guerre mondiale,* 3d ed. Paris, 1948.

Renouvin's volume also provides basic and sound bibliographic guidance. In the area of wartime diplomacy C. Jay Smith, Jr., *The Russian Struggle for Power, 1914–1917* (New York, 1956), pp. 515–22, gives a careful listing of published and easily accessible documents pertaining to the secret treaties. Reliable bibliographies for the study of Russian-American and Allied-Russian relations for the 1917–18 period are in George F. Kennan, *Russia Leaves the War* (Princeton, 1956), pp. 525–32, and in Robert D. Warth, *The Allies and the Russian Revolution: From the Fall of the Monarchy to the Peace of Brest-Litovsk* (Durham, N.C., 1954), pp. 242–75.

Probably the most inclusive bibliography for the study of World War I, with particular emphasis on domestic developments within the major belligerent nations, was undertaken but not completed in Nazi Germany by the *Weltkriegsbücherei*, Institut für Weltpolitik, Stuttgart, Schloss Rosenstein. Successive topical volumes were published under the general title *Systematische Bibliographien mit Verfasserregister des deutschen und ausländischen Schrifttums zur Geschichte und Vorgeschichte des Weltkrieges mit seinen Folgen und zur historisch-politischen Auslandskunde*. Within this series the following volumes are here relevant: *Bibliographie zur englischen Propaganda im Weltkrieg*, October 1935; *Bibliographie zur Geschichte des britischen Reiches im Weltkrieg 1914–1918*, January–April, 1936; *Bibliographie zur politischen Geschichte Frankreichs in der Vorkriegszeit und im Weltkrieg*, January 1937; *Bibliographie zur Wirtschafts-, Sozial-, und Geistesgeschichte Frankreichs*, April 1937; and *Bibliographie zur Geschichte der Vereinigten Staaten im Weltkrieg*, July 1939. More readily available bibliographical guides to the literature dealing with the social, economic, and political aspects of the war are in select volumes of *The Economic and Social History of the World War*, published under the auspices of the Carnegie Endowment for International Peace.

In Carl E. Schorske, *German Social Democracy, 1905–1917: The Development of the Great Schism* (Cambridge, 1955), there is a superb, comprehensive bibliographical essay on works both by and about the leaders and factions of the German Left. A listing of the more important wartime pamphlets on war aims by Allied Socialists and Radicals is included in the bibliography of Austin Van Der Slice, *International Labor, Diplomacy and Peace, 1914–1919*, Philadelphia, 1941.

I. Unpublished Documents and Papers

A. *Official Documents in the National Archives of the United States Government*

> State Department Files, in the Foreign Affairs Section (Diplomatic correspondence pertaining to Russia in 1917 and 1918, especially file number 763.72)
>
> German Foreign Ministry: "Documents Concerning the 1914 War." (Microfilm files of captured documents):

"Peace Moves and Tendencies," February 24, 1917 to February 6, 1918. Microfilm Containers Nos. 2089–2103

"Peace Moves and Tendencies" (Secret), March 21, 1917, to December 25, 1917. Microfilm Containers Nos. 2116–28, 2160–70

"Materials Pertaining to Peace Negotiations" (Secret), July 1914 to July 1919. Microfilm Containers Nos. 1498–1500

B. *Private Papers*
In the Library of Congress:
Robert Lansing Papers
Woodrow Wilson Papers
In the Sterling Library of Yale University (Edward M. House Collection):
W. H. Buckler Papers
Edward M. House Papers
In the Library of Harvard University (Houghton Library):
W. H. Page Diary and Embassy Notebooks
In the Library of the London School of Economics:
E. D. Morel Papers

C. *Party and Society Archives*
Archives of the (British) Labour party, Transport House, London. Select files and papers
Archives of the Union of Democratic Control, London. The *Minutes of the Executive Committee* (1914–18)

II. PRINTED AND PUBLISHED GOVERNMENT PUBLICATIONS

A. *France*
Journal Officiel de la République Française, Chambre des Députés, *Débats Parlementaires*, Session Ordinaire, 1917–18
Journal Officiel de la République Française, Chambre des Députés, *Débats Parlementaires*, Session Ordinaire, 1919–20, 1922, 1925, 1933. The verbatim record of the eight wartime comités secrets of the French *Chambre* were published after the war, as follows:
Comité Secret of June 16–22, 1916, in *Débats Parlementaires*, October 24–30, 1919

Comité Secret of November 21, 1916, in *Débats Parlementaires,* November 21, 1919

Comité Secret of November 28, 1916, to December 7, 1916, in *Débats Parlementaires,* November 10–20, 1920

Comité Secret of March 14, 1917, in *Débats Parlementaires,* June 24, 1922

Comité Secret of May 25, 1917, in *Débats Parlementaires,* June 25, 1922

Comité Secret of June 1–4, 1917, in *Débats Parlementaires,* May 16–19, 1925

Comité Secret of June 29, 1917, to July 6, 1917, in *Débats Parlementaires,* June 26–30, 1922 and July 1–2, 1922

Comité Secret of October 16, 1917, in *Débats Parlementaires,* April 2, 1933

B. *Germany*

Verhandlungen des Reichstags: Stenographische Berichte, Legislaturperiode 13, Session 2. February 22, 1917, to April 17, 1918. Vols. *309–311*. Berlin, 1917–18

Das Werk des Untersuchungsausschusses der verfassungsgebenden deutschen Nationalversammlung und des deutschen Reichstages, 1919–28. *Die Ursachen des deutschen Zusammenbruches im Jahre 1918*, 4th ser., *Der Innere Zusammenbruch.* 12 vols. Berlin, 1925–29

Lutz, R. H., ed., *The Causes of the German Collapse in 1918.* (Sections of the official authorized report of the Commission of the German Constituent Assembly and of the German Reichstag, 1919–28.) Stanford, Stanford University Press, 1934

C. *Great Britain*

House of Commons, *Parliamentary Debates*, 5th ser. 1914–18, especially 1917 (Vols. *90–100*)

Woodward, E. L., and Butler, R., eds., *Documents on British Foreign Policy 1919–1939.* 1st ser. Vol. *4.* London, H. M. Stationery Office, 1952

D. *United States*

Complete Report of the Chairman of the Committee on Public Information. Washington, Government Printing Office, 1920

Department of State

Papers Relating to the Foreign Relations of the United States. Supplements. *The World War,* especially 1917, Supplement 2, Vol. *1,* and 1918, Supplement 1, Vol. *1.* Washington, Government Printing Office, 1932–33

Papers Relating to the Foreign Relations of the United States. Russia, 1918. 3 vols., especially Vols. *1* and *2.* Washington, Government Printing Office, 1931–32

Papers Relating to the Foreign Relations of the United States. The Lansing Papers, 1914–20. 2 vols. Washington, Government Printing Office, 1939–40

Papers Relating to the Foreign Relations of the United States. The Paris Peace Conference, 1919. Vol. *1.* Washington, Government Printing Office, 1942

U. S. Senate, Committee on the Judiciary. **Bolshevik Propaganda.** Sixty-fifth Congress, third session. **Washington,** Government Printing Office, 1919

War Labor Policies. *Report on Labor and Socialism in France.* Washington, Government Printing Office, 1919

III. PARTY AND SOCIETY DOCUMENTS AND PUBLICATIONS

A. *France*

Comité pour la Reprise des Relations Internationales (wartime pamphlets listed in approximate order of publication):

Les Socialistes et la guerre

Le Parti socialiste italien et la guerre

Conférence socialiste internationale de Zimmerwald

Lettre aux abonnés de la "Vie Ouvrière"

Seconde Conférence socialiste internationale de Zimmerwald

Les Socialistes de Zimmerwald et la guerre

Deuxième Lettre aux abonnés de la "Vie Ouvrière"

Un Désaccord: Lettre du groupe des "Temps Nouveaux"

Anarchistes de gouvernement

Le Crime de l'oligarchie roumaine

Projets d'avenir: Troisième Lettre du groupe des "Temps Nouveaux"

Aux Groupements socialistes; aux organisations syndicales
Troisième Lettre aux abonnés de la "Vie Ouvrière"
Quatrième Lettre aux abonnés de la "Vie Ouvrière"
Le Socialisme et la guerre
La Situation en Russie
Pour l'Action

Parti Socialiste (SFIO)

Congrès National de Bordeaux, 6, 7, 8, et 9 octobre 1917.
Paris, Editions de l'Humanité, n.d.

La Guerre et la paix: Toutes les résolutions et tous les docu-
ments du parti socialiste de juillet 1914 à fin 1917. Paris,
Librairie de l'Humanité, 1918

Réponse au questionnaire . . . en vue de la Conférence de
Stockholm. Paris, Librairie de l'Humanité, 1917

Rouger, Hubert, *L'Action socialiste au parlement, 1914–1919.*
Paris: Librairie du Parti Socialiste et de l'Humanité, 1919

Six Lettres du groupe socialiste aux Présidents du Conseil,
1915–1917. Paris: Editions de l'Humanité, n.d.

B. *Germany*

Sozialdemokratische Partei Deutschlands, *Protokoll über die Ver-*
handlungen des Parteitages, in Würzburg, October 14–20, 1917.
Berlin, 1917

Eichhorn, Emil, ed., *Protokoll über die Verhandlungen des Grün-*
dungsparteitages der U.S.P.D. vom 6. bis 8. April 1917 in Gotha.
Mit Anhang: Bericht über die gemeinsame Konferenz der Ar-
beitsgemeinschaft und der Spartakusgruppe vom 7. Januar 1917
in Berlin. Berlin, 1921

Drahn, Ernst, and Leonhard, Susanne, eds., *Unterirdische Literatur*
im revolutionären Deutschland während des Weltkrieges. Berlin,
1920

Meyer, Ernst, ed., *Spartakus im Weltkriege: Die illegalen Flug-*
blätter des Spartakusbundes im Kriege. Berlin, Vereinigung In-
ternationaler Verlagsanstalten, 1927

Spartakusbriefe. Herausgegeben von der Kommunistischen Partei
Deutschlands (Spartakusbund). Berlin, 1920

C. *Great Britain*

British Socialist party, *Statement on War Aims.* Submitted by the
British Socialist party to the Allied Socialist Conference, Lon-

don, August 28 and 29, 1917. London, Cooperative Printing Society (n.d.)

Fabian Society:
  Thirty-third Annual Report. London, 1916
  Thirty-fourth Annual Report. London, 1917
  Thirty-fifth Annual Report. London, 1918

Independent Labour party:
  Report of the Annual Conference Held at Norwich, April, 1915
  Report of the Annual Conference Held at Newcastle-on-Tyne, April, 1916
  Report of the Annual Conference Held at Leeds, April, 1917

Labour party:
  Report of the Fifteenth Annual Conference, Bristol, 1916
  Report of the Sixteenth Annual Conference, Manchester, 1917
  Report of the Seventeenth Annual Conference, Nottingham and London, 1918

The Labour party and the Trades Union Congress, *Memorandum on War Aims.* Approved by the Special Conference of the Labour Movement held at the Central Hall, Westminster, London, S.W., on December 28, 1917. London, Cooperative Printing Society, n.d.

Union of Democratic Control. A partial, chronological listing of the pamphlets issued by UDC during the war is contained in Austin Van Der Slice, *International Labor, Diplomacy and Peace, 1914–1919,* pp. 391–92

D. *The International Socialist Movement*
  Comité Organisateur de la Conférence Socialiste Internationale de Stockholm, *Stockholm.* Stockholm, Tidens, 1918 (introduction by Camille Huysmans)
  Inter-Allied Labour and Socialist Conference, *Memorandum on War Aims Agreed upon at the Central Hall, Westminster, London, S.W., on February 20 to 24, 1918.* London, Cooperative Printing Society, n.d.

IV. EDITED COLLECTIONS OF DOCUMENTS AND PAPERS

Baker, Ray Stannard, *Woodrow Wilson: Life and Letters.* 8 vols. New York, Doubleday, Doran, 1927–39

—— *Woodrow Wilson and World Settlement.* 3 vols. New York, Doubleday, Page, 1922

—— and Dodd, William Edward, eds., *The Public Papers of Woodrow Wilson.* 6 vols. New York, Harper, 1925–27

Bunyan, James, and Fisher, H. H., eds., *The Bolshevik Revolution, 1917–1918: Documents and Materials.* Stanford, Stanford University Press, 1934

Cocks, F. Seymour, ed., *The Secret Treaties and Understandings: Text of the Available Documents.* London, Union of Democratic Control, 1918

Cumming, C. K., and Pettit, Walter W., eds., *Russian-American Relations, March 1917–March 1920.* New York, Harcourt, Brace, and Howe, 1920

Degras, Jane, ed., *Soviet Documents on Foreign Policy.* Vol. *1*, 1917–24. Royal Institute of International Affairs. London, Oxford University Press, 1951

Dickinson, G. Lowes, ed., *Documents and Statements Relating to Peace Proposals and War Aims: December 1916 to November 1918.* London, Allen and Unwin, 1919

Golder, Frank Alfred, ed., *Documents of Russian History, 1914–1917.* New York, Century, 1927

Gankin, Olga Hess, and Fisher, H. H., eds., *The Bolsheviks and the World War: The Origin of the Third International.* Stanford, Stanford University Press, 1940

Hurewitz, J. C., ed., *Diplomacy in the Near and Middle East.* Vol. 2, 1914–56. New York, Van Nostrand, 1956

Laloy, Emile, ed., *Les Documents secrets des archives du Ministère des Affaires Etrangères de Russie publiés par les bolchéviks.* Paris, Bossard, 1920

Lenin, Vladimir Ilyich, *Collected Works.* Vols. *18–21.* New York, International Publishers, 1929–45:

    Vol. *18, The Imperialist War* (1914–16)

    Vol. *19, War and Revolution* (1916–17)

    Vol. *20, The Revolution of 1917: From the March Revolution to the July Days* (Books I and II)

    Vol. *21, Toward the Seizure of Power: From the July Days to the October Revolution* (Books I and II)

Lutz, R. H., ed., *Fall of the German Empire, 1914–1918,* 2 vols. Stanford, Stanford University Press, 1932

Magnes, Judah L., *Russia and Germany at Brest-Litovsk: A Documentary History of the Peace Negotiations*. New York, Rand School of Social Science, 1919

Scott, James Brown, ed., *Official Statements of War Aims and Peace Proposals: December 1916 to November 1918*. Washington, Carnegie Endowment for International Peace, 1921

Seymour, Charles, *The Intimate Papers of Colonel House*. 4 vols. Boston, Houghton Mifflin, 1926–28

Walling, English William, ed., *The Socialists and the War*. New York, Holt, 1915

V. NEWSPAPERS

A. *Daily Press*
   L'Action Française
   L'Humanité
   Le Temps

   Berliner Tageblatt
   Vorwärts

   Manchester Guardian
   The *Times*

B. *Special Collections*
   Review of the Foreign Press. Issued by the General Staff of the British War Office, and based on a systematic reading of the Allied, enemy, and neutral press. London, 1916–18:
       Daily Review of the Foreign Press
       Daily Review of the Foreign Press: Allied Press Supplement
       Daily Review of the Foreign Press: Enemy Press Supplement

VI. PERIODICALS

Demain: Pages et Documents (Geneva)
Labour Leader (Manchester)
Nation (New York)
Die Neue Zeit (Berlin)
New Europe (London)
New Republic (New York)
Revue des Deux Mondes (Paris)
Sozialistische Monatshefte (Berlin)

VII. Autobiographies, Biographies, Diaries, Letters, and Memoirs

The study of the crisis of 1917–18 would be impossible without an insight into the psychological and political reactions of leading government officials, party leaders, and intellectuals. These reactions can best be gathered from *contemporaneous* though not necessarily well-written diaries, letters, and speeches, or from *retrospective* memoirs, autobiographies, and biographies. For example, Romain Rolland's diligent and moving *Journal des années de guerre, 1914–1919* (Paris, 1952) gives an unequaled contemporaneous account of the changing thoughts and feelings of European pacifists and revolutionaries; *The War Memoirs of David Lloyd George* (2 vols. London, 1938) constitute the most inclusive and colorful, though repeatedly self-justifying, restrospective report by one of the war's foremost statesmen. As long as the French and British archives continue to be closed, personal testimony like Lloyd George's is particularly valuable because it contains extracts from primary materials and affords highly significant interpretations of official papers. For the same reasons the recollections of ambassadors often disclose crucial information about the politics and diplomacy of the countries to which they were accredited.

A. France

The materials by or about leading French personalities are not so numerous as those by or about their German, British, or American counterparts. In *Briand: Sa vie—son oeuvre* (Vol. *4,* Paris, 1940) Georges Suarez gives the reaction to the crisis of 1917 of the defeated Premier who never ceased to be one of the most influential Radical Socialist politicians. Briand's successor, Alexandre Ribot, recorded certain impressions and policies first as prime minister during the Stockholm imbroglio, and subsequently as foreign minister to Painlevé; hence, Ribot has left behind a limited self-portrait of his hesitant internal and external statesmanship in *Journal de Alexandre Ribot et correspondances inédites, 1914–1922,* Paris, 1936; and in *Lettres à un ami: Souvenirs de ma vie politique,* Paris, 1924. Paul Painlevé, *Comment j'ai nommé Foch et Pétain* (Paris, 1923) reveals little of interest to this study. However, henceforth students of the French mutinies in mid-1917 will benefit greatly from Lt. Colonel Henri Carré's adulatory but thoroughly documented *Les Grandes Heures du Général Pétain: 1917 et la crise du moral,* Paris, 1952.

Georges Clemenceau's confidently belligerent patriotism is most faithfully reflected in his wartime editorials in *l'Homme Enchaîné,* and in the first five chapters of his *Grandeurs et misères d'une victoire,* Paris, 1930. Before becoming premier, Clemenceau heatedly summarized his prejudiced criticism of the *défaitistes* in *L'Antipatriotisme devant le Sénat: Discours prononcé le 22 juillet 1917,* Paris, 1917. Three of the Tiger's colleagues have given strongly pro-Clemenceau testimony which is of only limited relevance to this study: L. L. Klotz, *De la Guerre à la paix: Souvenirs et documents,* Paris, 1924; Général Mordacq, *Le Ministère Clemenceau: Journal d'un témoin* (especially Vol. *1,* Paris, 1930); and André Tardieu, *La Paix,* Paris, 1921. But the ninth volume of President Raymond Poincaré's journal *Au Service de la France* (10 vols. Vol. *9: L'Année trouble, 1917,* Paris, 1932) easily remains the most compelling and authoritative right-wing commentary on France's nearly fatal domestic, military, and diplomatic crisis.

The near-hysteria with which the extreme Right questioned the loyalty of anyone who counseled either compromise with the SFIO and/or a negotiated peace with the Central Powers is evident from the columns of *l'Action Française.* The two guiding spirits of this paper conveniently collected most of their vitriolic articles about Stockholm, Russia, Malvy, and Caillaux in Maurice Barrès, *Chronique de la grande guerre* (especially Vols. *9–11,* Paris, 1923) and Charles Maurras, *Les Chefs socialistes pendant la guerre,* Paris, 1918. From the same royalist perspective the historian Jacques Bainville made a more sober record of his personal reactions in *Journal, 1901–1918,* Paris, 1948.

With the notable exception of B. W. Schaper's, *Albert Thomas: Dertig Jaar Sociaal Reformisme* (Leiden, 1953) there are neither journals nor biographies of French Socialists or syndicalists. However, fortunately there is the testimony of the two Radicals who were tried for treason partly because they fellow-traveled with the Socialists. In a relatively uninspiring style Joseph Caillaux gives his own version of his wartime odyssey in *Mes Mémoirs* (especially Vol. 3, Paris, 1947), and in *Mes Prisons,* Paris, 1921; with the support of important documents, L. J. Malvy pleads his personal cause in *Mon Crime,* Paris, 1921.

Incidental intelligence about French politics and policies in the second half of 1917 can be found in the memoirs of the American, and especially of the British, Ambassador in Paris: Warrington Dawson, ed., *The War Memoirs of William Graves Sharp* (London, 1931), and Lady Algernon Gordon Lennox, ed., *The Diary of Lord Bertie of Thame*, Vol. 2, London, 1924.

B. Germany

After the war, responsible civilian and military officials in France debated in their memoirs whether and by whom the peace was lost; in Germany, however, the debate centered on the causes and responsibilities for the military defeat. In the light of this still smoldering controversy, the following prominent non-Socialist political leaders wrote memoirs which are generally dull but which nevertheless remain essential sources for the study of the political struggle inside Germany 1917–18: T. von Bethmann-Hollweg, *Betrachtungen zum Weltkriege*, especially Vol. 2, Berlin, 1922; Matthias Erzberger, *Erlebnisse im Weltkrieg*, Stuttgart and Berlin, 1920; Maximilian Harden, *Krieg und Friede*, especially Vol. 2, Berlin, 1918; Karl Helfferich, *Der Weltkrieg*, 2 vols. Berlin, 1919; Richard von Kühlmann, *Erinnerungen*, Heidelberg, 1948; Prinz Max von Baden, *Erinnerungen und Dokumente*, Stuttgart, 1927; Georg Michaelis, *Für Staat und Volk*, Berlin, 1922; Friedrich von Payer, *Von Bethmann-Hollweg bis Ebert: Erinnerungen und Bilder*, Frankfurt a/M. 1923; and Gustav Stresemann, *Von der Revolution bis zum Frieden von Versailles*, Berlin, 1919.

Whereas this group of political leaders tends to put the blame for the debacle on the autocratic military leaders, the latter fix the responsibility on the former's compromising attitude toward the rebellious Left. In *Meine Kriegserinnerungen, 1914–1918* (Berlin, 1919) and in *Kriegsführung und Politik* (Berlin, 1922) Erich Ludendorff honestly records his immediate reaction to the Russian Revolution as well as to Lenin's trip through Germany, together with his violent polemic about the internal political causes for the military defeat. What Marshall von Hindenburg's *Aus meinem Leben* (Leipzig, 1920) lacks in objectivity and interest is more than compensated for in the magnificent biography of *Hindenburg, the Wooden Titan* (New York, 1936), by J. W. Wheeler-Bennett. That the extreme territorial and political ambitions of Ludendorff enjoyed considerable political support among the Right can be gathered from the detailed reminiscences of Graf Westarp in *Konservative Politik im letzten Jahrzehnt des Kaiserreiches,* Vol. 2, Berlin, 1935.

German intellectuals have left very few, if any, full-scale journals or autobiographies. There are Friedrich Meinecke's short memoir, *Strassburg, Freiburg, Berlin, 1901–1919: Erinnerungen* (Stuttgart, 1949), and his collected wartime writings, *Politische Schriften und Reden,* Darmstadt, 1958; both reveal this prominent historian's crisis-born conversion, in the conservative national interest, to domestic reforms and to moderate war aims. A less expediential espousal of liberal policies is apparent in Max Weber's *Gesammelte politische Schriften,* Munich, 1921.

The autobiographies, biographies, and other writings of German Socialists—Social Democrats, Indepedents, and Spartacists—are expertly commented upon by Carl Schorske in the bibliographical essay (pp. 334 ff.) in the above-cited *German Social Democracy, 1905–1917.*

C. Great Britain

In addition to the *War Memoirs of David Lloyd George* cited above, the following autobiographies and biographies by or of prominent Conservative and Liberal leaders are useful for the study of British wartime politics and diplomacy: Rt. Hon. Christopher Addison, *Four and a Half Years: A Personal Diary from June 1914 to January 1919* (2 vols. London, 1934), and his *Politics from Within, 1911–1918,* 2 vols. London, 1924; Herbert H. Asquith, *Memories and Reflections, 1852–1927,* Vol. 2, Boston, 1928; Robert Blake, ed., *The Private Papers of Douglas Haig, 1914–1918,* London, 1952; Blanche E. C. Dugdale, *Arthur James Balfour,* Vol. 2, New York, 1937; H. A. L. Fisher, *James Bryce,* Vol. 2, New York, 1927; P. C. Newton, *Lord Lansdowne: A Biography,* London, 1929; John A. Spender and Cyril Asquith, *Life of Herbert Henry Asquith, Lord Oxford and Asquith,* Vol. 2, London, 1932; and George M. Trevelyan, *Grey of Fallodon,* Boston, 1937.

Two Labourites who served Lloyd George as cabinet ministers in 1917–18 give the British Social Patriotic viewpoint in George N. Barnes, *From Workshop to War Cabinet* (London, 1924), and in J. R. Clynes, *Memoirs,* Vol. 1, London, 1937. Mary Agnes Hamilton's *Arthur Henderson* (London, 1938) is a sympathetic but generally balanced biography of the Labour leader who was chairman of the Parliamentary Labour party, cabinet member, and recent envoy to Russia at the time he resigned from the War Cabinet over the Stockholm issue. *Beatrice Webb's*

Diaries, 1912–1924 (London, 1952), superbly edited by Margaret I. Cole, is unquestionably a most beautifully written, a most candid autobiographic, and a most honest as well as informative reportorial journal by one of Europe's leading Socialist personalities. These *Diaries* are unequaled for their careful record of the changing personal attitudes of the Webbs, of the gradual crystallization of Labour's war and peace policies, and of the Left intelligentsia's nurtured relations with the establishment.

Biased but revealing insights into the opinions and policies of noted pacifists and/or Internationalists who worked through the dissident Independent Labour party can be gathered from Fenner Brockway, *Socialism over Sixty Years: The Life of Jowett of Bradford,* London, 1946; George Lansbury, *My Life,* London, 1928; Raymond Postgate, *The Life of George Lansbury,* London, 1951; Lord Elton, *Life of James Ramsay MacDonald, 1866–1919,* London, 1939; and above all from Viscount Philip Snowden, *An Autobiography,* Vol. *1,* London, 1934.

The dissent of the Radicals was originally formulated by John Viscount Morley in his *Memorandum on Resignation, August, 1914,* London, 1928. Norman Angell's autobiography *After All* (London, 1951) fails to do justice to the decisive imprint which his ideas on war and peace left on British Labour as well as on the Union of Democratic Control. The political and organizational contribution of the UDC's first secretary is reliably, even if devotedly, reported in F. Seymour Cocks, *E. D. Morel, the Man and His Work,* London, 1920; Hermann Lutz, *E. D. Morel, der Man und sein Werk* (Berlin, 1925), is a more sketchy biography. The Radicals' gradual disenchantment with the Liberal party, in addition to being evident from the aforementioned books, is manifest also in Charles Trevelyan, *From Liberalism to Labour,* London, 1921; Josiah C. Wedgwood, *Memoirs of a Fighting Life,* London, 1940; H. G. Wells, *Experiment in Autobiography,* New York, 1934; and Mosa Anderson, *Noel Buxton, a Life,* London, 1952.

In view of the great influence of the major daily newspapers and their editors in Britain's political life, their biographies prove to be very informative. Above all, no student of wartime Britain can afford to miss the thoroughly documented *The History of the Times: The 150th Anniversary and Beyond, 1912–1948,* Part I, London, 1952. This "biography" of the *Times* is reinforced by biographies of both its owner and its editor: Hamilton Fyfe, *Northcliffe: An Intimate Biography* (New York, 1930), and John Evelyn Wrench, *Geoffrey Dawson and Our Times,* London, 1955. Henry Wickham Steed's autobiography, *Through Thirty Years, 1892–1922* (2 vols. New York, 1924), is important because privately and as foreign editor of the *Times* Steed enthusiastically supported the cause of the Austrian nationalities. In *Lord Riddell's War Diary, 1914–1918* (London, 1933), George Allendice Riddell, a respected member of the British press who was on intimate terms with Lloyd George, carefully preserved many of his instructive conversations with the Prime Minister. The somewhat more critical but still loyal views of the widely respected editors of the *Nation* and the *Manchester Guardian,* the two most influential Liberal publications, are recorded in H. J. Massingham, ed., *A Selection of Writings of H. W. Massingham* (New York, 1925) and in J. L. Hammond, *C. P. Scott of the Manchester Guardian,* London, 1934.

Burton J. Hendrick, *The Life and Letters of Walter Hines Page* (3 vols. New York, 1926), is an uncritical and incomplete biography of the fervently anglophile American Ambassador to the Court of St. James which adds little to this study. On the other hand, Constantin Nabokoff, *The Ordeal of a Diplomat* (London, 1921) as a well-documented and well-informed memoir by Kerensky's chargé d'affaires in London; it comprises materials and recollections which are important for the clarification both of the Lloyd George – Henderson feud and of British policy toward revolutionary Russia.

D. *Russia*

All the major memoirs and biographies for the study of Russian developments in 1917–18 are listed or evaluated respectively in the above-cited George F. Kennan, *Russia Leaves the War* (pp. 526–32), and Robert D. Warth, *The Allies and the Russian Revolution* (pp. 247–59). Of particular importance for this study are the volumes by or about Sir George Buchanan, David R. Francis, Major-General Max von Hoffmann, Alexander F. Kerensky, Major-General Sir Alfred Knox, V. I. Lenin, R. H. Bruce Lockhart, General Niessel, Joseph Noulens, Maurice Paléologue, Bernard Pares, Raymond Robins, Jacques Sadoul, Edgar Sisson, N. N. Sukhanov, William Boyce Thompson, and Leon Trotsky.

E. *United States*

The pertinent American memoirs and biographies are expertly commented upon in the exhaustive "Essay on Sources" in Arthur S. Link,

Woodrow Wilson and the Progressive Era, 1910–1917 (New York, 1954), especially pp. 291–94.

F. Miscellaneous

Notwithstanding the unconcealed apologia in Ottokar Czernin's *Im Weltkriege* (Berlin, 1919), these recollections of the Austrian Foreign Minister shed important light on the Dual Monarchy's precarious political truce, her desperate search for a negotiated peace, and Czernin's role at Brest-Litovsk. Michael Graf Karolyi, *Gegen eine ganze Welt: Mein Kampf um den Frieden* (Munich, 1924), is a war memoir of the Hungarian Liberal leader who became increasingly skeptical of Czernin's professed conversion to internal reforms.

In the context of this study the memoirs of Eduard Beneš and Thomas G. Masaryk are of particular relevance because both establish an explicit connection among the revolt of the nationalities, the Russian Revolution, and the transformation of the war into an ideological crusade for total victory. Even the titles of the non-English editions of both memoirs point to this connection. Beneš' memoirs appeared in an emasculated English version under the neutral title *My War Memoirs* (London, 1928); however, the French translation, which is rigorously faithful to the Czech text, carries the significant title *Souvenirs de guerre et de révolution, 1914–1918: La Lutte pour l'indépendance des peuples*, 2 vols. Paris, 1928. Whereas Masaryk's *The Making of a State: Memories and Observations 1914–1918* (London, 1927) is a complete and accurate English translation of his memoirs, in Czech and in German his memoirs were published under the title *Die Weltrevolution: Erinnerungen und Betrachtungen 1914–1918*, Berlin, 1925. Because Masaryk's recollections are often vague and inaccurate, R. W. Seton-Watson's carefully documented and gracefully written profile, *Masaryk in England* (Cambridge, 1943), is of great value.

VIII. Histories, Treatises, and Special Studies

A. France

In *The Development of Modern France, 1870–1939* (London, 1940), D. W. Brogan has an incisive chapter about wartime France. The changing cabinet composition is closely examined in Marcel Laurent, *Nos Gouvernements de guerre* (Paris, 1920), and in Pierre Renouvin, *Les Formes du gouvernement de guerre*, Paris, 1925. Home-front politics and administration also are the focus of the following studies:

Armand Albert-Petit, *La France de la guerre*, 3 vols. Paris, 1918–19; A. Aulard, E. Bouvier, and A. Ganem, *Histoire politique de la grande guerre*, Paris, 1924; Georges Bonnefous, *Histoire politique de la Troisième République*, Vol. 2, *La Grande Guerre*, Paris, 1957; and L. Marcellin, *Politique et politiciens pendant la guerre*, 2 vols. Paris, 192?. Albert Pingaud's *Histoire diplomatique de la France pendant la guerre* (3 vols. Paris, 1938–39) is the only scholarly and comprehensive, though far from definitive, treatise on the diplomatic conduct of the war; especially the third volume is relevant to this study.

The civil–military relations, which were strained almost continuously are thoroughly analyzed in Jere Clemens King, *Generals and Politicians: Conflict between France's High Command, Parliament, and Government, 1914–1918*, Berkeley, 1951. Socioeconomic problems like production, wages, prices, and strikes, which were another major cause for political strife, are competently covered in Arthur Fontaine, *French Industry during the War*, New Haven, 1926; William Oualid and Charles Picquenard, *Salaires et tarifs*, Paris, 1929; and Roger Picard, *Le Mouvement syndical durant la guerre*, Paris, 1927. Some valuable information about behind-the-scenes politics in the cabinet, in Parliament, and in various administrations has been collected by Paul Allard in *Les Dessous de la guerre* (Paris, 1932), and *Les Enigmes de la guerre* (Paris, 1933), and by Marcel Berger and Paul Allard in *Les Secrets de la censure pendant la guerre*, Paris, 1932.

Conceptually the chapter on World War I in François Goguel's *La Politique des partis sous la IIIe République* (Paris, 1946) is unusually penetrating and represents a useful framework for the study of the wartime struggle between the parties of order and the parties of movement. For a reliable introduction to the institutional and ideological complexities of French political parties one must still turn to G. Bourgin, J. Carrère, and A. Guérin, *Manuel des partis politiques en France*, Paris, 1928; André Siegfried, *Tableau des partis en France*, Paris, 1930; and Albert Thibaudet, *Les Idées politiques de la France*, Paris, 1932.

There are no systematic, scholarly studies of the activities of right-wing parties, factions, and interest groups immediately preceding and during the war. René Rémond's *La Droite en France de 1815 à nos jours* (Paris, 1954) is a general survey in which there are only casual references to the war period. Though in his bibliography Rémond cites a number of works dealing with *Charles Maurras* and

l'Action Française, these works are concerned with personality, ideological, and programmatic factors rather than with interest politics.
What is needed is a systematic study which would clarify the expansionism and integral nationalism of the French Right; ideally such a
study should parallel Hans W. Gatzke's analysis of the political, social,
and economic roots of German westward imperialism in *Germany's
Drive to the West*, Baltimore, 1950. Likewise, there are no scholarly
monographs dealing with the right-Center, Center, and Center-left
parties.

Fortunately the French Socialist Left has been the subject of more
extensive, though often partisan, treatment. The best introduction to
developments within this Left during the war is to be found in *Histoire du socialisme en France* (5th ed. Paris, 1950) by the French
Socialist Paul Louis. A Center-left view of these same developments
in the SFIO is given in Alexandre Zévaès, *Le Parti socialiste de 1904
à 1923*, Paris, 1923. Hubert Bourgin's *Le Parti contre la patrie* (Paris,
1924) is a well-informed but crudely biased account of wartime politics within the SFIO by a leader of its extreme right wing. Edouard
Dolléans, in his elaborately documented *Histoire du mouvement
ouvrier* (4th ed. Vol. 2, Paris, 1953), has four sympathetic chapters
concerning the tensions between the Social Patriots and the Internationalists primarily within the CGT, but also within the SFIO.

The shortest and least partial introduction to the formation within
the SFIO of the Comité pour la Reprise des Relations Internationales
which eventually developed into the nucleus for the French Communist party is in the opening chapter of Gerard Walter, *Histoire du
Parti communiste français*, Paris, 1948. The following writings by
militant Communists about Left-radical wartime activities are vehemently critical of the nonrevolutionary policies of the Majoritarians
and Independents, and therefore must be consulted with great caution:
A. Ferrat, *Histoire du parti communiste français*, Paris, 1931; Henri
Guilbeaux, *Le Mouvement socialiste et syndicaliste français pendant
la guerre*, Petrograd, 1919; and J. Rocher, *Lénine et le mouvement
zimmerwaldien en France*, Paris, 1934. But unquestionably the most
detailed and authentically documented study of the nascent left opposition within the SFIO, and of the internecine struggles within that
opposition, is Alfred Rosmer's *Le Mouvement ouvrier pendant la
guerre: De l'Union sacrée à Zimmerwald*, Paris, 1936. Unfortunately
Rosmer, who as editor of *la Vie Ouvrière* was close to Trotsky during

the latter's exile in France, and who subsequently became a fervent Trotskyite, never carried his invaluable documentation and his judicious though excessively sectarian analysis beyond 1915.

Georges Demartial's *La Guerre de 1914: Comment on mobilisa les consciences* (Paris, 1922) is a study of internal war propaganda by a dissident Radical who was a leading member of the *Société d'études documentaires et critiques sur la guerre.* In *La Trahison des clercs* (Paris, 1927) Julien Benda denounces the uncritical state- and nation-worship of some of Europe's foremost intellectuals, and in particular of Barrès, Maurras, and Péguy. The following of Romain Rolland's writings are crucial for an insight not only into the ideology of his own dissent but also into the different degrees of loyalty within the French intelligentsia: *Journal des années de guerre, 1914–1919,* cited above; *Au-dessus de la mêlée,* Paris, 1915; and *Les Précurseurs,* Paris, 1920.

B. Germany

Arthur Rosenberg's *The Birth of the German Republic* (New York, 1931) unquestionably contains the soundest as well as the most suggestive analysis of wartime Germany. The essential secondary works about the politics and diplomacy of this period need not be listed or discussed primarily because the author fully accepts the evaluation given in the bibliographical notes of two recently published monographs. The bibliographical note in Hans W. Gatzke, *Germany's Drive to the West,* (especially pp. 298–300) critically reviews the key secondary sources dealing with the non-Socialist political forces and their activities which are relevant to this study. The pertinent secondary literature about the ideology, internal developments, and political activities of the major SPD factions is critically assessed in the bibliographical essay by Carl E. Schorske in *German Social Democracy, 1905–1917* (especially pp. 337–52). For the purpose of this study these two expert bibliographies need to be supplemented only slightly.

In addition to providing information and insight about German waraims politics, Professor Gatzke's monograph is a model analysis of the interaction of domestic and foreign policy. On this same subject, despite their right-wing bias, Richard Fester's *Die politischen Kämpfe um den Frieden, 1916–1918 und das Deutschtum* (Munich and Berlin, 1938), and *Die Politik Kaiser Karls und der Wendepunkt des Weltkrieges* (Munich, 1925) retain some informational value.

In *Mitteleuropa in German Thought and Action, 1815–1945* (the Hague, 1955) Henry Cord Meyer includes a first-rate discussion of the various formulations and the different political carriers of the idea of Central Europe during World War I.

Notwithstanding their pronounced Bolshevik bias, Klaus Mammach, *Der Einfluss der russischen Februarrevolution und der grossen Oktoberrevolution auf die deutsche Arbeiterklasse, Februar 1917– Oktober 1918* (Berlin, 1955) and Albert Schreiner, ed., *Revolutionäre Ereignisse und Probleme in Deutschland während der Periode der Grossen Sozialistischen Oktoberrevolution, 1917–1918* (Berlin, 1957) make a valuable contribution to the study of the weakening of the *Burgfrieden;* both studies are based on hitherto unexplored state and municipal records which disclose the quickening impact of Russian developments on domestic affairs in Germany. The catalytic effect of foreign propaganda on the political struggle inside Germany is discussed in the following studies: George G. Bruntz, *Allied Propaganda and the Collapse of the German Empire in 1918*, Stanford, 1938; Eugen Lahr, *Französische Kriegszielpropaganda am Ende des Weltkrieges*, Essen, 1941; Harold D. Lasswell, *Propaganda Technique in the World War*, New York, 1927; Joachim Seeberg, *Wilsons Botschaft der 14 Punkte vom 8. Januar 1918 im Urteil der grossen deutschen Tagespresse vom Januar bis zum Oktober 1918*, Berlin, 1936; John L. Snell, "Wilson's Peace Program and German Socialism, January–March, 1918," *Mississippi Valley Historical Review* (September 1951), pp. 187 ff., and "Wilsonian Rhetoric Goes to War," *The Historian* (spring 1952), pp. 191 ff.; and Hans Thimme, *Weltkrieg ohne Waffen: Die Propaganda der Westmächte gegen Deutschland, ihre Wirkung und ihre Abwehr*, Stuttgart and Berlin, 1932. In *German Social Democracy, 1905–1917*, Carl Schorske conclusively shows how during the war foreign and domestic pressures conspired to consummate the long-simmering schism between the forces of order and the forces of movement within the SPD; in 1917 and in early 1918 the struggle between these two forces centered heavily around the war-aims issue.

C. Great Britain

The wartime and especially the postwar polarization between the "Liberalized" Conservatives and the "Radicalized" Labourites was a natural outgrowth of prewar political developments which have been brilliantly analyzed in Elie Halévy, *A History of the English People in the Nineteenth Century* (Vol. 4, Bk. II: *The Rule of Democracy, 1905–1914;* 2d rev. ed. London, 1952), and in George Dangerfield, *The Strange Death of Liberal England,* New York, 1935. In *The Consequences of the War to Great Britain* (London, 1934) Francis W. Hirst, who shares Halévy's and Dangerfield's Radical-libertarian frame of reference, gives a remarkable summary of the unfolding of these prewar trends during both the war emergency and the immediate postwar period. This interpretive summary is based on the British series *Economic and Social History of the World War* (Carnegie), whose major volumes are reviewed in James T. Shotwell's preface to Hirst's study. Partly with the help of these same volumes in *State Intervention in Great Britain, 1914–1919* (New York, 1949), Samuel J. Hurwitz shows the emergency-motivated and ideologically undirected growth of government controls in Britain's economic and social affairs.

Frank P. Chambers' *The War behind the War, 1914–1918* (New York, 1939) deals with the "political and civilian fronts" of all the major belligerents; however, his discussion of cabinet as well as administrative politics and changes in England is particularly balanced. R. T. McKenzie, *British Political Parties* (New York, 1955) is a suggestive though excessively institutional-structural analysis of the 20th-century Conservative and Labour parties; in his bibliography McKenzie lists the essential histories of both parties and their affiliates.

The following historical-analytical surveys by prominent Labourites of the Labour party and the Trade Unions proved most useful for this study: Max Beer, *A History of British Socialism,* London, 1948; G. D. H. Cole, *A History of the Labour Party from 1914,* London, 1948; and his *A Short History of the British Working Class Movement, 1789–1947,* London, 1948; and Sidney and Beatrice Webb, *The History of Trade Unionism,* rev. ed. London, 1920. Carl F. Brand's *British Labour's Rise to Power* (Stanford, 1941) includes elaborately documented but analytically weak chapters on the evolution of Labour's war-aims platform and on Labour's response to Woodrow Wilson's peace program. The missing analytic dimension is partly provided in William P. Maddox, *Foreign Relations in British Labour Politics,* Cambridge, 1934; the discussion of the political and ideological impact of converted Radicals on Labour, especially on the ILP, is the most challenging part of Maddox's book. The Radical secession was accelerated by the radicalization of the Left during the last year of war; this radicalization is the subject of a journalistic account by two American Socialist news-papermen in Paul U. Kellogg and Arthur Gleason, *British Labor and the War*, New York, 1919. A scholarly report on Labour's reaction to the revolutionary developments in wartime Petrograd is part of Stephen R. Graubard's *British Labour and the Russian Revolution, 1917–1924*, Cambridge, 1957.

Thus far the Liberal party has not been well-served by historians or political scientists; except for Hamilton Fyfe's sketchy *The British Liberal Party* (London, 1928), there are no reliable comprehensive or monographic studies. Irene Cooper Willis, *England's Holy War* (New York, 1928) is an empathic Radical report on the ideology of Liberal idealism and its initial disregard but eventual expediential exploitation by the British Government. The most striking and best-remembered statement of this idealism is H. G. Well's *The War That Will End War*, London, 1914. Disillusioned by the Government's and the Liberal party's insensitivity to their utopian convictions, many prominent Radicals began to join the Labour party; according to G. T. Garratt, *The Mugwumps and the Labour Party* (London, 1932), they there became an essentially revisionist influence.

Many, though not all, of these prominent recruits to Labour first joined the Union of Democratic Control, whose wartime history is told by two of its active members in H. M. Swanwick, *Builders of Peace* (London, 1924) and in Charles Trevelyan, *The Union of Democratic Control: History of its Policy*, London, 1919. E. R. Pease, *History of the Fabian Society* (London, 1925) points to the UDC-type of cooperation of Radical and Labour intellectuals in the formulation and advocacy of the New Diplomacy in England's most respected brain trust. One of the memorable legacies of this cooperation is Leonard S. Woolf's programmatic *International Government: Two Reports Prepared for the Fabian Research Department*, New York, 1916. Henry R. Winkler, *The League of Nations Movement in Great Britain, 1914–1919* (New Brunswick, 1952) is a systematic but over-fastidious analysis of British wartime books and articles dealing with league-of-nations proposals and propaganda; Winkler only incidentally shows that the forces of movement initially were if not the only at any rate the most articulate advocates of international organization. The story of the Government's propaganda in enemy countries is told un-critically in Sir Campbell Stuart, *Secrets of Crewe House*, London, 1920.

D. Russia

The following studies have been particularly useful because of their special focus on the part which the military defeat played in the domestic as well as in the diplomatic unfolding of the Russian Revolution: E. H. Carr, *The Bolshevik Revolution, 1917–1923*, Vols. *1* and *3*, London, 1950–53; William Henry Chamberlin, *The Russian Revolution, 1917–1921*, 2 vols. New York, 1935; Louis Fischer, *The Soviets in World Affairs, 1917–1929*, 2d ed. 2 vols. Princeton, 1951; George F. Kennan, *Russia Leaves the War;* P. G. La Chesnais, *La Révolution russe et la paix*, Paris, 1917; Henri Rollin, *La Révolution russe*, 2 vols. Paris, 1931; Frederick L. Schumann, *American Policy toward Russia since 1917*, New York, 1928; Michael Smilg-Benario, *Von Kerenski zu Lenin: die Geschichte der zweiten Revolution*, Zurich, 1929; Leon Trotsky, *The History of the Russian Revolution*, 3 vols. London, 1932; Robert D. Warth, *The Allies and the Russian Revolution: From the Fall of the Monarchy to the Peace of Brest-Litovsk;* and William Appleman Williams, *American-Russian Relations, 1781–1947*, New York, 1952.

E. The International Socialist Movement

There still are no comprehensive historical and interpretive studies of the Second International before the war, or of International Socialism during the war. Such studies are needed in order to establish the extent to which the political carriers of International Socialism continued to represent an actual and potential force in spite of the usually overdramatized collapse of July–August 1914. James Joll, *The Second International, 1889–1914* (London, 1955) is an extremely competent but brief survey of the prewar International. G. D. H. Cole, *The History of Socialist Thought* (Vol. 3, Parts I and II, London, 1956) is an encyclopedic, analytically weak account of prewar doctrinal developments within the national constituencies of the Second International. A thorough case study of the debate of a key issue by Socialists on potentially enemy sides of national frontiers is Milorad M. Drachkovitch, *Les Socialismes français et allemand et le problème de la guerre, 1870–1914*, Geneva, 1953.

The only scholarly monograph on the Internationalist factions and congresses in wartime is Merle Fainsod, *International Socialism and the World War*, Cambridge, 1935. Austin Van Der Slice, *International Labor, Diplomacy, and Peace, 1914–1919*, emphasizes the evolution of the peace programs within the Allied Socialist parties and their affiliates. Less impartial but nevertheless suggestive insights into wartime internationalism can be gathered from the following Socialist writings: Karl Kautsky, *Sozialisten und Krieg*, Prague, 1937; Paul Louis, *La Crise du socialisme mondiale*, Paris, 1921; and R. W. Postgate, *The International during the War*, London, 1918.

Franz Borkenau's *The Communist International* (London, 1938) remains the best introduction to the nascent Third International during the war. As a result of their active participation in the Zimmerwald movement a few left-radical Socialists (i.e. Communists) have been able to write about this movement and its internal tensions with the support of authentic documents as well as of personal recollections. In the context of this study the following of their writings are most directly relevant: Angelica Balabanoff, *Die Zimmerwalder Bewegung, 1914–1919*, Leipzig, 1928; and her *My Life as a Rebel*, New York, 1938; Robert Grimm, *Zimmerwald und Kienthal*, Bern, 1917; V. I. Lenin, *Collected Works*, Vols. *18, 19,* New York, 1930, 1942; Alfred Rosmer, *Le Mouvement ouvrier pendant la guerre: De l'Union sacrée à Zimmerwald;* and Leon Trotsky, *My Life*, New York, 1930. On the basis of now available German Foreign Ministry documents, in "Lenins Reise durch Deutschland in April 1917," *Vierteljahreshefte für Zeitgeschichte* (October 1957), pp. 307 ff., Werner Hahlweg analyzes the preliminary negotiations for, as well as the actual course of, Lenin's momentous return to Russia.

F. Miscellaneous

As an introduction to the external and internal developments in the Dual Monarchy, it is safe to rely on the following excellent secondary sources: Bertrand Auerbach, *L'Autriche et la Hongrie pendant la guerre*, Paris, 1925; Otto Bauer, *Die Österreichische Revolution* (Vienna, 1923); Oscar Jaszi, *The Dissolution of the Habsburg Monarchy*, Chicago, 1929; Victor S. Mamatey, *The United States and East Central Europe, 1914–1918*, Princeton, 1957; Jan Opočenský, *Umsturz in Mitteleuropa*, Dresden, 1931; and A. J. P. Taylor, *The Habsburg Monarchy, 1809–1918*, London, 1948. The Pope's diplomatic initiative in 1917, which was considerably influenced by the mounting difficulties of Austria-Hungary, is viewed briefly but objectively in Humphrey Johnson, *Vatican Diplomacy in the World War*, Oxford, 1933. Friedrich Ritter von Lama, *Die Friedensvermittlung Papst Benedikts XV*

(Munich, 1932), is a much more detailed but also a decidedly pro-Vatican account of this unsuccessful mediation effort.

Because of the great depth of the psychological, social, economic, ideological, and political crisis which accompanied the taxing military effort and then continued into the postwar period, some of Europe's foremost intellectual and political personalities were driven to participate in the great debate about the meaning of that crisis. Much of this debate is preserved in articles, pamphlets, and speeches by European leaders of thought and of men. In the search for perspective, present-day students of World War I gratefully turn to representative meditations about the war and the Revolution by some of these leaders: Norman Angell, *The Great Illusion,* New York and London, 1910; and his *The British Revolution and the American Democracy,* New York, 1919; Henri Barbusse, *La Lueur dans l'abîme: Ce que veut le Groupe Clarté,* Paris, 1920; Matthias Erzberger, *Der Völkerbund, der Weg zum Weltfrieden,* Berlin, 1918; Guglielmo Ferrero, *Die Tragödie des Friedens von Versailles,* Jena, 1923; and his *Europe's Fateful Hour,* New York, 1918; Arthur Henderson, *The League of Nations and Labour,* London, 1918; Sigmund Freud, "Thoughts for the Times on War and Death" in *The Complete Psychological Works of Sigmund Freud,* Vol. *14,* London, 1957; John Maynard Keynes, *The Economic Consequences of the Peace,* New York, 1920; Rosa Luxemburg (Junius, pseud.), *Krise der Sozialdemokratie,* Berlin, 1916; Gilbert Murray, *The League of Nations and the Democratic Idea,* London, 1918; Karl Radek, *Die Entwicklung der Weltrevolution,* Berlin, 1919; Walter Rathenau, *Kritik der dreifachen Revolution,* Berlin, 1919; and his *Nach der Flut,* Berlin, 1919; Oswald Spengler, *Preussentum und Sozialismus,* Munich, 1922; and H. G. Wells, *In the Fourth Year: Anticipations of a World Peace,* London, 1918.

INDEX